The Extreme Right
in Europe and the USA

The Extreme Right in Europe and the USA

Edited by
Paul Hainsworth

St Martin's Press, New York

#25509748

All rights reserved. For information, write:
Scholarly and Reference Division,
St. Martin's Press, Inc., 175 Fifth Avenue, New York, NY 10010

First published in the United States of America in 1992

Printed in Great Britain

ISBN 0-312-08091-3

Library of Congress Cataloging-in-Publication Data
The Extreme right in Europe and the USA/edited by Paul Hainsworth.
    p.   cm.
  Includes index.
  ISBN 0-312-08091-3
  1. Conservatism—Europe.   2. Conservatism—United States.
3. Right and left (Political science) I. Hainsworth, Paul, 1950-

JA84,E9E97 1992
320.5′094—dc20   92-9314
                                       CIP

Contents

List of Contributors

Dr Jørgen Goul Andersen is Lecturer in Politics at the University of Aarhus, Denmark. He completed his PhD on the Danish Progress Party and his main fields of interest are comparative politics, electoral studies, welfarism and political culture. His recent publications include (joint author) *Taxes without Welfare: Public Expenditure in Denmark in a Comparative Perspective* (1991) and *Class Theory in Transition* (1991)

Michael Cox is Senior Lecturer in Politics at The Queen's University of Belfast where he lectures on the history of the Cold War and post-communist politics. He has been visiting professor at San Diego State University, The College of William and Mary, and the University of Wisconsin at Madison. His most recent book is *Beyond The Cold War: Superpowers at the Crossroads?* (1990)

Dr Panayote Elias Dimitras is Assistant Professor of Political Science at the Athens University of Economics and Business and Director of the Communication and Political Research Society. His fields of interest are modern Greek politics and the media, comparative public opinion and comparative representation and electoral systems. He is the author of *Politikos Perigyros, Kommata kai Ekloges stin Ellada* (Political Background, Parties and Elections in Greece) (1991)

Dr Roger Eatwell is Senior Lecturer in Politics at the University of Bath. His main fields of interest are the ideology and sociology of the right. He is editor of the series 'Themes in Right-Wing Ideology and Politics'. His publications on the right include articles in the *Political Quarterly*, and chapters in K. Lunn and T. Kushner (eds), *Traditions of Intolerance* (1989), L. Cheles et al. (eds), *Neo-Fascism in Europe* (1991)

Dr Tom Gallagher is Reader in Peace Studies at the University of Bradford. His main fields of interest include stateless nationalism in Europe and the transition to democracy in southern and eastern Europe. His publications include *Portugal: a Twentieth Century Interpretation* (1983), *Southern European Socialism* (1989), co-edited with Allan Williams, as well as a chapter in M. Blinkhorn (ed.), *Fascists and Conservatives* (1990)

Dr John Gilmour is Lecturer in Spanish at the University of Bristol. His main fields of interest are Spanish politics and society since the Civil War, especially the Francoist right in transition to democracy. His recent publications in this field include *From Francoism to Democracy: Fraga and the Spanish Right* (1988) and *Alianza Popular and Autonomias in Spain* (1989)

Dr Paul Hainsworth is Lecturer in Politics at the University of Ulster at Jordanstown. His main fields of interest are contemporary French politics, European integration and regional studies. He is (joint) editor of *Regional Politics and Policy: An International Journal* and author of several articles and chapters on French and European politics. Amongst his recent publications is (as editor) *Breaking and Preserving the Mould: The Third Direct Elections to the European Parliament (1989) the Irish Republic and Northern Ireland* (1992)

Dr Christopher T. Husbands is Reader in Sociology and Internal Academic Audit Officer at the London School of Economics and Political Science. He is the author of *Racial Exclusionism and the City: The Urban Support of the National Front* (1983) and is now working on studies of the extreme right and of immigration and asylum policies in contemporary Europe. He has also published numerous articles on both these themes

Eva Kolinsky Dr. Phil., FRSA is Professor of Modern German Studies and Director of the Centre for Modern German Studies at Keele University. She has published widely on aspects of contemporary German politics, political culture and the situation of women. Her books include: *Engagierter Expressionismus* (1970), *Parties, Opposition and Society in West Germany* (1984), *Opposition in Western Europe* (ed., 1987), *The Greens in West Germany* (ed., 1989), *Women in West Germany* (1989), *Women in Contemporary Germany* (2nd. ed., 1992), *Political Culture in France and Germany* (ed. with J. Gaffney 1991), *The Federal Republic of Germany – End of an Era* (ed., 1991). She is editor of the German Studies series of books (Berg) and co-editor of the journal *German Politics*

Dr Francesco Sidoti is Associate Professor of Sociology at the Faculty of Law of Bari University. He obtained a Doctorat de Troisième Cycle at the Ecole des Hautes Etudes en Sciences Sociales, Paris, and later studied at the Brookings Institute, Washington DC. He is a specialist in problems of deviance, and has various publications on the mafia, terrorism, crime and drugs trafficking. Among his most recent publications is *Povertà, devianza, criminalità nell 'Italia meridionale* (1989)

List of abbreviations

Belgium

CERSBER	Centre d'Étude et de Recherche Socio-biologiques et Raciales
CRISP	Centre de Recherche et d'Information Socio-Politiques
CVP	Christelijke Volkspartij
FJ	Front de la Jeunesse
FN-NF	Front National-Nationaal Front
JN	Jeune Nation
JNG	Jong-Nederlandse Gemeenschap
MAC	Mouvement d'Action Civique
MNW	Mouvement Nationaliste Wallon
NSJV	National-Socialistisch Jeugdverbond
PFN	Parti des Forces Nouvelles
PLC	Parti Libéral Chrétien (later the Parti de la Liberté du Citoyen)
PNB–BNP	Parti National Belge – Belgisch-Nationale Partij
PVV	Partij voor Vrijheid en Vooruitgang
RN	Rex National
SP	Socialistische Partij
UDRT	Union Démocratique pour le Respect du Travail
UND	Union Nationale et Démocratique
UNF	Union Nationale des Francophones
VB	Vlaams Blok
VBJ	Vlaams Blok Jongeren
VC	Vlaams Concentratie
VERDINASO	Verbond van Dietse Nationaal-Solidaristen
VMO	Vlaamse Militanten Orde
VNO	Vlaamse Nieuwe Orde
VNP	Vlaams-Nationale Partij
VNR	Vlaams-Nationale Raad
VNV	Vlaams Nationaal Verbond
VU	Volksunie
VVP	Vlaamse Volkspartij
WD, VNW	Were Di, Verbond van Nederlandse Werkgemeenschappen
WNP	Westland New Post

Britain

BNP	British National Party
BUF	British Union of Fascists
NF	National Front

France

ARLP	Alliance républicaine pour les libertés et progrés
FANE	Federation of National and European Action
FN	Front national
GRECE	Groupement de recherches et d'études pour la civilisation européenne
GUD	Groupe Union Droit
LCR	Ligue communiste révolutionnaire
LICRA	League against Racism and Anti-Semitism
MRAP	Movement against Racism and for Friendship amongst Peoples
OAS	Secret Army Organization
PCF	French Communist Party
PFN	Parti des Forces Nouvelles
PS	Socialist Party
RPR	Rassemblement pour la République
UDCA	Union de Défense des Commerçants et Artisans
UDF	Union for French Democracy

Germany

CDU/CSU	Christian Democratic Union/Christian Social Union
DRP	German Reichs Party
DVU	West German People's Union
FDP	Free Democrat Party
NPD	National Democratic Party
REP	Republikaner Partei
SPD	Social Democrat Party
SRP	Socialist Reichs Party

Greece

EDE	Ethniki Demokratiki Enosis (National Democratic Union)
EK	Ethniko Komma (National Party)
EP	Ethniki Parataxis (National Alignment)
EPEN	Ethniki Politiki Enosis (National Political Union)
KP	Komma Proodeftikon (Progressive Party)
KKE	Communist Party of Greece

ND	New Democracy
PASOK	Pantellinio Socialistiko Kinima (Panhellenic Socialist Movement)
KEME	Movement of Greek Reformers
ENEK	United Nationalist Movement
EOK	European Economic Movement
PAP	Politiki Anexartitos Parataxis
PASOK	Panhellenic Socialist Movement

Italy

DC	Christian Democrat Party
DN	Democrazia Nazionale
MSI	Italian Social Movement
MSI-DN	Italian Social Movement-National Right
PCI	Italian Communist Party
PSI	Italian Socialist Party

The Netherlands

ANS	Aktiefront Nationaal Socialisten
BP	Boerenpartij
BR	Binding Rechts
CDs	Centrumdemocraten
CDA	Christen Demokratisch Appel
CP	Centrum Partij
CP '86	Centrum Partij '86
ESB	Europese Sociale Beweging
KVP	Katholieke Volkspartij
NCP	Nationale Centrum Partij
NESB	Nationaal Europese Sociale Beweging
NOU	Nederlandse Oppositie Unie
NSB	Nationaal Socialistische Beweging
NVU	Nederlandse Volksunie
PvdA	Partij van de Arbeid
RVP	Rechtse Volkspartij
SOPD	Stichting Oud Politieke Delinquenten
STPD	Stichting Toezicht Politieke Delinquenten
VVD	Volkspartij voor Vrijheid en Democratie

Portugal

CAP	Confederation of Portuguese Farmers
CDS	Centre Social Democrats
CSD	Social Democrat Party

DA	Democratic Alliance
ELP	Portuguese Liberation Army
MDLP	Democratic Movement for the Liberation of Portugal
MIRN	Independent Movement of National Reconstruction
ON	New Order
PDC	Christian Democrat Party
PDP	Party of the Portuguese Right
PPD	Popular Democratic Party
PPM	Portuguese Monarchist Party
UN	National Union

Spain

AP	Alianza Popular
CC.OO.	Comisiones Obreras
CEDADE	Circulo Español de Amigos de Europa
DISPAR	Right-Wing University Group
FE de las JONS	Falange Española Tradicionalista y de las Juntas
FN	Fuerza Nueva (pre-1982)
FN	Frente Nacional (post-1986)
FNT	Fuerza Nueva del Trabajo
PSOE	Socialist Party
UCD	Unión de Centro Democrático
UGT	Unión General de Trabajadores

United States

CSA	The Covenant, the Sword and the Arm of the Lord
CPDL	Christian Patriots' Defense League
KKK	Ku Klux Klan
NSWPP	National Socialist White People's Party
UKA	United Klans of America
WAR	White Aryan Resistance

General

EC	European Community
EP	European Parliament
IMF	International Monetary Fund
MEP	Member of the European Parliament
MP	Member of Parliament
NATO	North Atlantic Treaty Organization
UN	United Nations

Preface and Acknowledgements

The origins of this book lay with the editor's interest in contemporary French political parties and the extreme right in France. A decade ago, I was pleased to contribute to a compendium on *Social Movements and Protest in France*, published appropriately by Frances Pinter in 1982. The contribution looked at the extreme right which at that time was a small electoral force in France. Shortly afterwards, however, the situation changed dramatically as the Front national made a watershed breakthrough which was confirmed repeatedly throughout the 1980s and early 1990s. Simultaneously, and in part inspired by the French example, a number of parallel movements achieved varied success throughout Western Europe campaigning upon similar issues and discourses. Furthermore, the breakdown of communism in Eastern Europe revealed that, albeit in different circumstances, the growth of movements and ideas - such as xenophobia, national-populism, anti-communism, anti-Semitism, immigration control and so on - associated with the extreme right's collective make-up was not confined to Western Europe. Moreover, in the United States, the same period was notable for the rise of the Duke phenomenon, which illustrated some of the same traits and reflexes on display on the other side of the Atlantic.

It follows from the above that much of the material presented in this volume has a certain immediacy and currency about it; in fact, contributors have taken care to up-date their chapters to take into consideration relevant developments in the 1990s. However, the emphasis of the book is reflected in the title and concentrates upon the post-World War II period as a whole. Respective authors have endeavoured to provide analyses of the extreme right from country to country within this context, and some pre-war data is provided to enable readers to be aware of the socio-political cultural background underpinning the extreme right's trajectory. The book, therefore, not only assesses the prevalence of the post-war extreme right but seeks to understand the latter in the context of what preceded it and, also, to explain why extreme right political movements and parties emerged significantly in some countries but not in others.

The focus of the volume is Western European (European Community) cum-Atlanticist with the inclusion of a chapter on Eastern European developments for reasons set out in Chapter 1. Chapter 1 discusses the problem of defining and identifying the extreme right, the issues and discourse which help us to do this, the evidence of and response to extreme right ascent in recent years and the scope and nature of the phenomenon. Consequently the chapter, by providing the parameters and overall assessment of the topic under discussion, serves as both an introduction and *de facto* conclusion. The subsequent chapters, with the exception of Chapter 13, deal specifically with individual countries; all are written by specialists in the field. However, a work of this nature inevitably and indispensably draws upon the advice, criticisms, comments and resources of several individuals and institutions.

In particular, I would like to thank all the individuals at Pinter Publishers for their encouragement, guidance, copy-editing skills, patience and expertise - notably Nicola Viinikka, Vanessa Harwood, Iain Stevenson - and Roger Eatwell, the series editor has provided invaluable support, advice, suggestions and criticisms. Glyn Ford, MEP and Proinsias de Rossa, MEP were most helpful and informative in interviews concerning the role of the European Parliament's Committee on Xenophobia and Racism. Various individuals read and refereed one or more chapters in the book or provided useful advice. These included David Archard, Arthur Aughey, Chris Bailey, Alain Bairner, John Brewer, Steve Bruce, Sheelagh Ellwood, Kevin Featherstone, John Fitzmaurice, Paul Furlong, Ken Gladdish, Gerry Grable, Adrian Guelke, Mike Kenny, Stephen Livingstone, John Loughlin, Paul Lucardie, Carolyn Mason, Hans Jørgen Nielsen, Willie Paterson, Geoffrey Pridham, Bill Riches, Jim Shields, Hans Speiet, Richard Stöss and Louis Vos. The editor owes a debt to sources that have supported his research in recent years, namely the British Council, the French Embassy (Cultural Services, London), the Faculty of Humanities and the McRea Fund, both of the University of Ulster. Terry O'Keeffe has been a supportive head of department and Troudi Laroussi a helpful adviser. Finally, a number of institutions, organisations and libraries provided information, facilities and services. These include the Center for Democratic Renewal, the Anti-Defamation League, the European Parliament, the Council of Europe, Searchlight, the Political Science Institute (Paris) and the University of Ulster library staff at Jordanstown.

While the above have greatly assisted in bringing the book to fruition none, of course, are responsible for the final outcome but all have helped to make the work a better offering than it would have been otherwise.

Paul Hainsworth
Belfast
April, 1992

1 Introduction. The Cutting Edge: The Extreme Right in Post-War Western Europe and the USA

Paul Hainsworth

Prior to 1945, twentieth-century Europe experienced the rise of diverse extremist, fascist, authoritarian and anti-Semitic movements. As a result, scholars have debated incessantly whether some generic interpretation might be applied to the range of varied socio-political forces then in existence. Others have contrasted totalitarianisms of the left and of the right to discern a form of mass or activist politics (De Felice, 1976; Larsen *et al.*, 1980; Payne, 1980; O'Sullivan, 1983). The starting-point of this volume is not to rehearse these arguments, rather to suggest that the realities and legacy of war, the Holocaust and fascism – in power or aspiring to it – have tended to delegitimize certain themes and movements associated (willingly or not) with the pre-1945 years. Moreover, with the triumph of liberal democracy and the dawning of a *de facto* US ideological and military hegemony over Western Europe, paralleled by the existence of the Soviet communist bloc in the East, 1945 served as a watershed after which forces and ideas located on or attributed to the extreme right failed to dictate the political agenda. For example, in reference to the Italian Social Movement (MSI), Peter Merkl (1980, p. 758) alludes to 'the loss of innocence after a decade or two of fascist dictatorship and war'. Nevertheless, with the passage of time, the growth of Cold War anti-communism, libertarianism and Third World immigration – and the recurrence of perennial economic problems – the extreme right began to assert itself perceptibly, illustrating Rémond's observation that each generation produces its own historic forms (Rémond, 1971). In post-war Western Europe and the United States, there have been numerous examples of extreme right-wing politics, many of them relatively minor and unsuccessful at the ballot box, others more noteworthy, significant and assessed below. Also addressed herein are examples of extreme right electoral failure, notably in the United States, Greece, Portugal and Spain, since this instructs us about the political culture of the country in question and helps provide an understanding of the circumstances conducive to extreme right-wing success. At the same time, we are reminded that electoral success is not the only yardstick of measurement for political ideas (cf. Falter and Schumann, 1988).

Basically, contributors to the book seek to examine the post-war emergence of the extreme right on a country by country basis with a view to assessing the nature and significance of certain contemporary socio-political phenomena. The focus is upon the European Community member states primarily – although, for reasons of space and scope, it has not been possible to include sections on Ireland or Luxembourg. Equally, for reasons of space and coherence, it has been impossible to incorporate analyses of Austria, Sweden, Switzerland or Norway, whose recent developments provide interesting parallels with much of the data presented below. For instance, in November 1991, the Austrian Freedom Party won 23 per cent in Vienna city elections on a platform of immigrant control and with opinion polls revealing disturbingly high levels of xenophobia and anti-Semitism in Austria. On the other hand, Michael Cox's study of the United States (Chapter 13) provides a useful Atlanticist perspective. As already intimated, the United States has influenced greatly the context of post-war politics through wartime victory, espousal of liberal democratic values and massive economic input. For example, Cold War politics has engaged Western Europe and anti-communism is a salient common characteristic of the cases discussed in this volume. However, with the demise of the former and developments in Eastern Europe, the context is changing rapidly. Of particular relevance here is the growth in Eastern Europe of extreme right-wing ideology and groups expounding anti-Semitism, racism and xenophobia, accelerated apparently by *inter alia* the sudden 'release' from Soviet-influenced communism, insecurity fears caused by rapid changes and, ironically, the resort to pluralism. These themes cannot be explored comprehensively, and in any case are changing day by day. Even so, in view of the European Community's developing *Ostpolitik*, the reunification of Germany in 1990, the aspiration of East European states to partake of Community membership and the widespread interest in these matters, an additional chapter was deemed appropriate to provide further material for comparison and comprehension. Indeed, as a recent study (Harris, 1990, p. xi) on the extreme right in Western Europe contends:

> The breakdown of communist regimes in Eastern Europe has seen the re-emergence of openly anti-Semitic groupings in East Germany and Poland, for example. In the Soviet Union itself anti-Semitism has been used to attack reformers and rekindle Russian nationalism

According to Mikhail Gorbachev, too, 'social expressions of anti-Semitism have not been surmounted and certain reactionary circles are exploiting the fact' (quoted in *The Guardian*, 11 October 1991). These issues are discussed in Chapter 12.

To some extent, of course, the study is a response to the resurgence of the extreme right over the past decade or so – in Western Europe and the USA and, in part, within the emerging states of contemporary Eastern Europe. Yet, as the individual case studies illustrate, post-war growth has been uneven and renaissance is not simply a new, still less a comprehensive, development. Also, in a comparative format such as this, it is not possible to include all candidates for assessment, even if indisputable agreement could be reached on what exactly constitutes the extreme right. Understandably, too, the contributors are somewhat subjective and selective in choice of subject-matter, albeit within editorial guidelines. Even so, the content of the chapters is conditioned obviously by the prevalence or otherwise of what respective authors perceive to be the most significant instances and lessons of post-war extreme right politics. For instance, the editor's contribution deals principally with Jean-Marie Le Pen's Front national (FN), given the success and influence of that movement. Similarly, Eva Kolinsky concentrates strongly on the Republican Party in Germany and Jørgen Goul Andersen solely on Mogens Glistrup's Danish Progress Party. In the same vein, though in a rather particular cultural-historical setting, the chapter on the United States is preoccupied with – although not exclusively – the Ku Klux Klan and one of its former leaders, David Duke. At this point, however, it will be useful to discuss the nature of the extreme right in order to identify our topic more closely.

The Nature of the Extreme Right: Some Observations

In approaching the extreme right, it may be noted that 'the dimensionality of extremism in general as well as of right-wing extremism in particular is unclear' (Westle and Niedermayer, 1990, p. 8). Still, it is worth recalling some of the parameters and provisos put down by an earlier contribution and masthead for the series incorporating this volume (Eatwell and O'Sullivan, 1989). Therein, Eatwell portrays the right as a variety of responses to the left, encompassing different styles of thought, namely the reactionary, moderate, radical, extreme and new rights. After discussing these, Eatwell (1989, pp. 74–5) provides a useful yardstick for analysis:

> It is especially difficult to understand the nature of right-wing thought if an essentialist answer is sought. . . . It is impossible to fit every single movement, thinker or ideology neatly. . . . There are blurred edges between the categories; and some individuals and movements seem to transcend the categories. . . . Brief description of each style tends to create a picture of thought which is relatively cut and dried. . . . However, as a whole, the right-wing tradition is multi-faceted, far from static, even imaginative.

The concept of the right, therefore, is elusive and, by extension, so is that of the extreme right. Of course, it would be wonderfully convenient – though academic wishful thinking – if leaders, parties and movements labelled themselves extreme right to make easier the task of comparison and analysis. Instead, organizations studiously avoid and reject extreme right labelling, preferring to operate under banners such as the National Front (United Kingdom), the Italian Social Movement, the Dutch Centre Party, the Danish Progress Party, and so on. Westle and Niedermayer (1990, p. 13) point to the West German Republican Party, for example, which in 1983 described itself as a 'conservative-liberal mass party' although 75 per cent of West Germans, and even 61 per cent of party supporters, saw it as the far right.

Problems of definition, then, are inevitable and are summed up usefully by Michael Billig (1989, p. 146) in his study of the extreme right:

> The term 'extreme right' is a particularly troubling one to use in political analysis. At first (it seems) to be an obvious label but it is one that can so easily cause a misleading impression. The term is obvious to the extent that there are a number of political parties, movements and individuals which it seems entirely appropriate to label as 'extreme right' to distinguish them from the traditional right or extreme left-wing. . . . [Also] in ordinary speech and in journalistic writing one could use the term . . . without being misunderstood and, intuitively, there seems to be a set of political parties, movements and tendencies which go together.

Klaus von Beyme (1988, p. 3) appears to support this approach with his observation that 'though formal definitions or derivations based on the history of ideas largely failed to provide a convincing concept for "right-wing extremism", research work on political parties of the right has not had serious problems in selecting appropriate cases'. However, von Beyme alludes clearly to definitional problems and Billig, too, adds that 'in an academic context' intuition is not sufficient: 'one would have to justify why such parties are being called both "extreme" and "right-wing". And it is here that the problems start' (Billig, 1989, p. 146).

Problems of definition are thus derived from the difficulty of providing watertight criteria to classify political movements. Various authorities (Adorno *et al.*, 1950; Lipset and Raab, 1971) have endeavoured to construct a comprehensive classification using such variables as social class, personality and economic policy, although exceptions have tended to defy the rule. According to Blinkhorn, 'the definitions, typologies and taxonomies beloved of social scientists tend to fit uncomfortably the intractable realities which are the raw material of the historian . . . Lines stubbornly refuse to be drawn . . . exceptions disprove more rules than they prove' (Blinkhorn, 1990, pp. 1–2). Concisely put, political philosophy does not always run in a straight line from left to right and back again (Green, 1987). Even the most sophisticated models, grids, circuits and typologies are not devoid of criticism. As intimated, Eatwell wonders whether it might be possible to find a common core of ideas to define the extreme right though he rejects this as too neat, albeit conceding that it 'might be possible to find a core which had significant heuristic value' (Eatwell, 1989, p. 19). Again however, it must be stressed that categories are not watertight: there is scope for overlap and overspill of ideas, personnel and electors as regards the extreme right and the traditional or moderate right and left or even the extreme left (e.g. on themes such as anti-capitalism, anti-statism and street politics). To take the case of the French Front national, for example, it tends to incorporate elements of the extreme, radical, reactionary and even moderate rights as categorized by Eatwell and O'Sullivan. Also, Paul Wilkinson sees many of the more recent historical occurrences of extreme rightism as examples of what he calls 'the new fascists': 'Many contemporary new fascisms have attempted to trick themselves out with new labels, styles and tactics in order to pass themselves off as respectable political parties, engaged in legitimate electoral competition' (Wilkinson, 1981, p. 5). Indeed, ex-MSI leader and mentor Giorgio Almirante referred tellingly to the politics of 'the cudgel and the double-breasted suit' (quoted in Caciagli, 1988, p. 24). Certainly, Hill's insider view of the British National Front (Hill and Bell, 1988, p. 297) would substantiate this line of analysis:

> Its ranks are full of fascists who sport with pride their convictions for racial or political violence. . . . Increasingly, the real bedrock views of the NF are revealed, not through the pronouncements of its leaders, but through the statements and activities of its members.

Notwithstanding this observation, the terms 'fascism' or 'new fascism' can be misleading and unhelpful labels if applied wholesale to the contemporary extreme right. For one thing, current phenomena are given a significance they manifestly do not possess (Genn and Lerman, 1986, p. 7), whereas blanket usage of terms such as fascism or neo-fascism imposes a coherence on post-war extreme right forces which misrepresents the diversity. Arguably, fascism in Europe is best seen as a historical product of specific circumstances, e.g. the effects of the First World War, the emergence of Soviet-inspired communism and the economic crisis of the late 1920s to 1930s. As Krejčí (1991, p. 1) contends, at 'present no such combination of factors exists in Europe', although rapid changes in *Eastern* Europe open up awesome possibilities and, according to one observer, 'Demoralised and broken, Eastern Europe is ripe for dictatorship' (Jonathan Eyal, *The Guardian*, 8 October 1991). Yet, as regards *Western* Europe, it would be erroneous and reductionist to stereotype the post-war extreme right as simply parodies of earlier fascist movements. The latter certainly exist and Husbands (1991, pp. 89–90), in fact, both explored this angle and made some useful distinctions between the extreme right and the neo-Nazi *groupuscules* in West Germany, based tentatively on factors such as electoralism, size, constitutional legality and attitudes towards violence. Moreover, the label 'neo-fascism' may be appropriate in some extreme right cases, for instance the Italian MSI, parts of the French Front national and some of the emergent forces in reunified Germany. Undoubtedly, then, neo-fascism and neo-Nazism play a role within the extreme right and beyond it. Also, the democratic pretensions of various forces on the extreme right are contested widely, and various contributors below indicate the capacity for violence on the extreme right. However, arguably, the flavour of much of the post-war West European extreme right as discussed herein is captured well by Westle and Niedermayer's view of the West German Republican Party as a force which 'represented extreme right topics in a harder style and more comprehensive way than the established parties, although in a modernised style of agitation that was not obviously linked to traditional National Socialism' (Westle and Niedermayer, 1990, p. 28). Furthermore, the extreme right's 'leaders seem to accept the institutions of liberal democracy, but reject the dominant liberal values with respect to ethnic minorities and cultural pluralism' (Lucardie and Voerman, 1990, p. 22). As such, the West European movements assessed below are often 'outsiders playing on the inside track'. Posing as the *vox populi* against 'the establishment', extreme right parties are defined too by their style as well as their discourse. In this respect, Malcolm Anderson's summing up is still pertinent (see Chapter 2 p. 30) as is the terminology of Chebel d'Appolonia (1988, pp. 12–14) i.e. *une droite de refus*.

Eatwell portrayed the extreme right strand as a nineteenth-century to early twentieth-century response to socialist and communist movements and doctrines. The former may be seen in the context of the growth of left-wing internationalism, class-based politics and the rise of mass politics. Allegedly, 'a defining characteristic of the extreme right is the paucity of its intellectual tradition' (Eatwell, 1989, p. 71). Nevertheless, we can attempt to sketch, without denying the specificity of national cultures, the broad philosophic-cum-programmatic make-up of a contemporar~ extreme right, bearing in mind the provisos above concerning the fuzzin ss of political boundaries, the osmotic qualities of political strands and the pitfalls of model-building. Indeed, Stanley Payne's commentary on fascism (Payne, 1980a, p. 21) could usefully be applied more widely:

> Much confusion has resulted from the assumption that if fascism is to be identifiable as a generic phenomenon it must somehow be regarded as a uniform type bearing essentially homogeneous traits, whereas in fact it was a broad species that included widely varying subtypes or subspecies.

Elsewhere, though, Payne cautions those who might shy away from comparative studies – of fascism, though again this can apply to other strands – on the grounds that like is not compared with like. According to Payne, (Payne, 1980b, p. 418):

> One could take the viewpoint . . . that we have no topic to study because of the difficulties of comparison. Against this extremely nominalistic position we are still left with the evident reality that new kinds of radical nationalism emerged in Europe in the interwar period.

Payne's approach, therefore, may be summed up as a 'unity in diversity' framework which is helpful in locating the parameters of our study. The intention is not to force square pegs into round holes, nor is it to forsake comparison and assessment in the absence of scientifically homogeneous units of analysis. Furthermore, Juan J. Linz, in discussing proto or pre-fascist movements prior to the First World War, pointed to a 'taxonomical and substantive uneasiness' in locating the boundaries from nation-state to nation-state. Ultimately, Linz placed these movements on the right, though not the establishment or conservative right (for discussions of conservatism, see O'Sullivan, 1976; Scruton, 1980 Aughey, 1989). Linz (1980, pp. 172–4) elaborates upon the problem of classification and is worth quoting at length:

> [S]ometimes the boundaries are fuzzy, but there can be little doubt that the leadership of these movements, their social basis, their style, their forms of action and their ideological themes are different from traditional conservatism while they share some of the same hostilities against the heirs of the French Revolution and the emerging, still internationalist labor movement as the conservatives. The problem becomes even more complicated because sectors of the Establishment have links with these forces, tolerate them, or attempt to manipulate them and sometimes go as far as incorporating into their own programmes some of their themes.

Indeed, whilst conscious of the dangers of extrapolation here, the thrust of Linz's analysis is none the less patently applicable – albeit in different historical circumstances and concerning different political phenomena – to the post-war extreme right as discussed below.

To sum up and re-emphasize, the quest for an essentialist core of extreme right values is fraught with difficulties and ideological dividing lines are not easily drawn. However, to understand, contrast and comment upon post-war political reality, it is appropriate to map out a working framework, identifying basic characteristics (such as national-populism, anti-communism and anti-Semitism) which contribute collectively, although unevenly, to the extreme right's make-up. As suggested, the task is made all the more difficult given the national specificities of respective countries. Eastern Europe, of course, is a special case owing to the long period of communist rule and quite sudden disintegration. The United States also is marked by a history and culture which has welcomed massive immigration, although it is still facing up to the legacy of slavery. Consequently, American blacks face similar problems to West European Third World immigrants with stereotyping over drugs and criminality particularly salient. Here, though, the situation is more complex with US blacks achieving significant positions notably in the armed forces, media and world of entertainment in contrast to the position of the large black underclass. Again (to pursue our theme), as Husbands points out in Chapter 5, Belgium is rather different because of the predominance of the linguistic question, and as Andersen explains in Chapter 8, the Danish Progress Party defies the extreme right label to some extent and is to the 'left' of traditional conservatism on some issues. Even so, by virtue of the style, populist overtones and (most of all) the priority given to anti-immigrant policy, the Belgian and Danish studies merit inclusion below.

Immigration: The Extreme Right's Issue *Par Excellence*

More than any other variable, the issue of immigration control has emerged as a key identifying factor of the extreme right in much of Western Europe to such an extent that one author (Mitra, 1988) could describe the most successful party on the extreme right, the French FN, as 'a single issue' movement. To some extent, notably in the United Kingdom, immigration politics helped to shape the political agenda prior to the 1980s. However, from the early 1980s onwards, immigration literally 'took off' as a prime mobilizing theme. As Martin Woollacott explained (*The Guardian*, 15 November 1991):

> Argument about immigration has been part of post-war politics since the 1950s and 1960s when governmentally encouraged labour migration began on a large scale in Britain, France and Germany. But it has this year taken on a new and sometimes monstrous life.

Impressed particularly by Jean-Marie Le Pen's success, (see Chapter 2 for details), extreme right parties have revalued the issue of immigration within their political discourses. Certainly, as authors below explain, this was very much the case in West Germany, Denmark, the Netherlands and, increasingly, Southern Europe.

As anti-immigrant policies attracted voters so this was reflected in opinion polls, testifying to the growing sentiment that there were too many immigrants and foreigners across Western Europe (*Eurobarometer*, 1989; Le Gall, 1989; Wallace 1991; *The European*, 27–29 September 1991). The debate has been given added impetus by the rapid international changes in process:, the movement towards a more open European Community after 1992, the effects of German reunification, demographic patterns, the growing assertiveness of Islamic fundamentalism war and unrest in the Middle East, the consequences of East European disintegration and the concomitant increasing demands for political asylum and refugee status in the West. The extreme right, in particular, has both exploited and exacerbated the situation, equating immigrants with unemployment, crime, urban degeneration, disease, falling standards, national decline, alien influences and so on. In language often suggestive of wartime or colonial experiences and calculated to rouse emotions, parties discussed below have accused immigrants of 'colonizing' and 'occupying' Western European nations. By the same token, those 'guilty' of protective legislation and positive discrimination measures are portrayed at best lax, at worst 'collaborators' and 'traitors'. A similar pattern emerged in the United States, as Cox illustrates, with the Ku Klux Klan's revival against civil rights legislation and punitive court decisions, followed by David Duke's campaigns in Louisiana against affirmative action programmes and for white 'equality'.

Broadly, the American extreme right's rhetoric against blacks mirrors the European extreme right's scapegoating of immigrants. David Duke's sloganizing against blacks ('having children faster than they can raise your taxes to pay for them' – see Chapter 13) finds an obvious parallel in the Front national's stereotypical polygamous North African immigrant 'milking' the French treasury for maximum support for his multitudinous offspring. Moreover, Jean-Marie Le Pen's movement condemns the (immigrant) 'invasion' of France with the party press carrying a regular column on 'the invaders', relating tales of delinquency, state-scrounging and so on.

Equally, the extreme right Centre Democrats in the Netherlands (see Chapter 4) have appealed to the government to 'protect its own population against foreign domination' and 'occupation' (Lucardie and Voerman, 1990, p. 9), and the campaign propaganda of the Belgian Vlaams Blok refers to areas 'plagued' by the foreign worker problem (see Chapter 5). In the opinion of the Flemish Belgian politician, Mark Eyskens, 'Enough is enough. We are the majority in this country' (quoted in *The Guardian*, 11 October 1991). In short, then, the immigrant, asylum-seeker and foreign worker are convenient scapegoats against which the West European extreme right has launched an increasingly successful campaign. According to one prominent spokesperson for the immigrant lobby, exclusion 'has become the social issue and it is in the urban environment that it has been revealed' (Harlem Désir, Exclusion Zone, interview in *The Guardian*, 21 June 1991). Combined with issues such as unemployment, insecurity, urban unrest and alienation, anti-immigrant policies, often straddling xenophobia and racism (European Parliament, 1990), have proved effective in enabling the extreme right to reshape the political agenda. The appeal of this approach to some strata is summed up first hand by Wallraff (1988) and, elsewhere, by Hill (Hill and Bell, 1988, p. 41):

We were being cheated of work, good housing, a decent education for our kids, things we believed were our birthright, while thousands of interlopers seemed to have little trouble in grabbing work, houses and every state benefit on offer, they got all this with help and encouragement from politicians of every political hue.

Anti-immigrant politics, therefore, has won sympathy amongst young unemployed sectors, the working and lower middle classes, with under resourced urban and suburban conglomerations particularly fertile reservoirs of support. However, as some authors explain (see, for instance, Hainsworth and Andersen in Chapters 2 and 8, Westle and Niedermayer (1990) and Mayer's (1987) study of the French Front national) and as the recent rise of the North Italian Leagues suggest (Mannheimer, 1991; Woods, 1992), votes for the extreme right cannot *simply* be correlated with either lower socio-economic status or even the number of immigrants in a given area. Other electoral variables come into play such as subjective feelings, integrative capacities *vis-à-vis* immigrants and the standing of existing élites and major political parties. Indeed, several authors point to the extreme right vote as an inter-class vote, a theme explored below in further detail (see also Mannheimer, 1991, pp. 85–8).

Nationalism, National-Populism

Central to the extreme right's discourse is the question of identity, national identity drawing upon language, religion, culture, history and other aspects.

Nation, national identity, ethnocentrism: these are at the core of the extreme right's value system. The rhetoric of the extreme right is based upon a vision of the nation supreme, heroic, pure and unsullied by alien forces such as Third World immigration and communist ideology. In some instances, extreme right nationalism is tied up with colonial experience, and reference points are times of national *grandeur* or some idealized 'golden age'. Immigrants, unless assimilable, and acceptable, therefore, are projected as dilutants of national (or local) culture, hence, the mobilizing slogans: 'France for the French', 'Germany for the Germans', 'Vienna for the Viennese' and so on. Although nationalism is a factor common to many contemporary political strands, it is the style of nationalist assertion – usually aggressive, exclusive, chauvinistic and historically selective – closely allied to anti-immigrant, anti-communist politics, which helps, to identify the nature of the extreme right. Contemporary extreme right movements offer their audience a messianic, crusading recipe of national redress and redemption often based upon simple slogans calculated to appeal populistically to the discontented and disillusioned. According to one view of Jean-Marie Le Pen, for instance, the FN's leader is 'the hero of the city dweller, the person who feels oppressed by bad housing, immigration, the threat of unemployment and a general sense that something has gone wrong with his country' (Harris, 1990, p. 89). This sense of malaise, then, enables the extreme right in several countries to tap a populist vein and pose as the voice of 'the silent majority', the 'small man' and those threatened by socio-economic change.

National-populism, although not simply a preserve of the extreme right (Canovan, 1950), helps largely to differentiate the extreme right from the moderate or traditional right, with the former often able to attract a significant number of voters – working-class, ex-left wing, unemployed, disaffected youth, former abstentionists and first-time voters – temporarily (or otherwise) denied to the latter. As authors below explain, although the extreme right may draw disproportionally from the traditional right, recent electoral gains in France, Germany, Belgium, the Netherlands, Denmark and Italy reflect the urban and 'popular' constituency of the extreme right. National-populist discourse enables the extreme right to function as a tribune and aggregate a protest vote, especially in the wake of the declining influence of former social support structures: community networks, churches, trade unions and so on. Mechanisms of direct, participatory democracy such as the referendum by popular initiative to decide upon major social and moral problems, including immigration and capital punishment, are therefore useful components of the extreme right's agenda. However, as suggested above, the protest element in the extreme right's electorate should not simply be equated with support from deprived, lower status and income strata. Voters are drawn from a wide reservoir of support. Woods (1992 p. 36), for instance, portrays the nascent Italian leagues in the prosperous north of the country as 'the sudden rise of political populism at the regional level' or (p. 50) 'a form of anti-system populism' and at the same time highlights extreme right success in this form in the wealthy, 'educated' towns of Brescia and Bergamo. Various studies, too, have revealed the extreme right voter to be no worse off objectively than the average voter and often better off (Mayer, 1987; Westle and Niedermayer, 1990; Orfali, 1990; Mannheimer, 1991). Nevertheless, a sense of pessimism, crisis and dissatis-faction is characteristic of the extreme right voter, who often exhibits an impatience to redress 'the situation' and a discontent with the established political parties' claims to represent the nation or people (Orfali, 1990). Disillusionment with traditional parties has contributed much to extreme right success. Weaker voter identification with existing mainstream parties and élites, partisan dealignment, electoral volatility, the rise of post-materialist (or non-materialist) issue politics, the obfuscation of class cleav-ages: these are all variables conducive to extreme right electoral progress. Conversely, though, strong right-wing leaders such as de Gaulle in the 1960s, Reagan and Thatcher in the 1980s (see below), have soaked up the potential for extreme right success via nationalism, populism, media skills and leadership style. Elsewhere too, authoritarian regimes in post-war Spain, Portugal and Greece (see Chapters 3, 10 and 11) have reduced the scope for mobilization and impeded electoral growth on the extreme right. More favourable terrain for the extreme right has often been situations where the ideological distance between the major parties was reduced, thereby creating a vacuum on the right conducive to extreme right success, e.g. 'the opening to the left' in Italy in the 1960s (see Chapter 6), the West German Grand Coalition of 1966–9 and the French 'power-sharing' (*cohabitation*) phase of the 1980s (see below). Progress on the extreme right has also been evident in instances of weak, discredited government (e.g. with Poujadist gains in France in the mid-1950s and with the MSI in Italy in the early 1970s) and/or where the establishment right out of office has radicalized its critique of an incumbent left in difficulty (e.g. in France in the 1980s, the United Kingdom in the mid-1970s and, to some extent, the United States under Carter's presidency). However, the most significant post-war pattern of extreme right gains has been across Europe in the past decade as immigration, unemployment, insecurity *and* disillusionment with mainstream parties emerged as key issues.

Despite conditions favourable to increased mobilization by the extreme right, however, this is not a foregone conclusion. Several factors militate against such a possibility. First, there is the ability of mainstream political parties to withstand the ascent of the extreme right, albeit by sometimes incorporating some of the latter's policies! Second, there is the collective weight of opposition groups, monitoring bodies, public opinion and liberal democratic values. Third, the extreme right is notoriously fratricidal, frag-mented and very prone to succession problems. Extreme right divisions within the European Parliament after 1989 testified to this as the Italian MSI distanced itself from the Front national/Republican Party Euro-right coali-tion. Fourth, the extreme right has to operate within the confines of existing electoral systems which even where proportional representation may be used, often tend to discriminate against small parties via quota stipulations. Fifth, the decline of communism has deprived the extreme right of a credible scapegoat, although instability through decline has, of course, provided favourable circumstances for the extreme right – a point already mentioned above and explored below (notably in Chapter 12). The recent developments within European communism, however, should not mask the fact that virulent anti-communism has been consistently a characteristic of much of the post-war extreme right.

Anti-Communism, Anti-Marxism

Reference has been made above to extreme right labelling as a product of nineteenth and twentieth-century history. In particular, the context has been the ascent of socialist, collectivist movements and the extension of the franchise. Consequently, although immigration has emerged (or resurfaced) recently as a vote-winning issue for several parties on the post-war extreme right in Europe, anti-communism remains a long-standing attribute. According to one view, the extreme right demonstrates 'a highly critical view of the left, especially its internationalist and class-based aspects. Communism in particular is attacked, both in its domestic and international form' (Eatwell, 1989, p. 71). Again, as with nationalism and populism *inter alia*, anti-communism is not the preserve of the extreme right and may be observed across various political strands. However, it is the nature of the anti-communism – strident, virulent, propagandist, uncompromising and consuming – that helps to identify the extreme right. For example, to take Jean-Marie Le Pen as a symbol (surely the most renowned) of the post-war extreme right, the Front national leader claims to be *un*extreme about anything except in his opposition to communism (Le Pen, 1984). On themes such as collective ownership of the means of production, class struggle, egalitarianism, the role and nature of the state, economic policy and socialist internationalism, the gulf between the extreme right and communism is appreciably wide. To be fair, some voices on the extreme right (e.g. within the Italian MSI) support corporatist or neo-corporatist ideas and some authors below allude to 'third way', anti-capitalist politics on the extreme right, although these are hardly typical or rarely substantial characteristics. On the contrary, parties such as the French Front national and Greek National Political Union (EPEN) (see Chapters 2 and 11) boast of having espoused free market liberalism, even before rivals on the moderate-cum-traditional right. In Denmark, too, neo-liberalism characterizes the extreme right Progress Party, although, as Andersen explains (in Chapter 8), this does not preclude progressive taxation and welfare measures amounting to a populist neo-liberalism and xenophobic 'welfare-state chauvinism'.

In some instances, anti-communism has served as a badge of legitimacy for the extreme right. Chiarini (1991, p. 28), for example, points to the MSI's early 'rehabilitation' in Italy via nascent Cold War politics. Similarly, in France in the 1980s, anti-communism and anti-socialism have been the alliance bridgeheads between the extreme and moderate rights. In the United States, too, McCarthyism and the Cold War were welcomed by organizations such as the Ku Klux Klan and the John Birch Society as a vindication of their world-views. Paradoxically, as Cox indicates (Chapter 13), capitalism created more problems – through modernization – for the Ku Klux Klan than did communism. Moreover, this body suffered the ultimate ignominy of being investigated by the (McCarthyite) House Committee on Un-American Activities. Of course, targeting the extreme right often provoked accusations of conspiracy, again revealing part of the former's make-up. As Eatwell (1989, p. 71) suggests:

> Extreme-right argument often centres on conspiracy theory. For example, a recurring extremist claim in America since the 1920s has been the charge that there is a communist conspiracy to undermine 'the American way of life', a key element in McCarthyism.

Furthermore, anti-communism and conspiracy theory overlap with anti-Semitism (Eatwell, 1989, p. 72; see also Billig, 1978; Billig, 1989; Cox, Chapter 13):

> A particularly virulent form of conspiracy theory involves anti-semitism. The Jews are alleged to be involved in a plot to dominate the world and undermine society's bonds. . . . Jews are also seen as the very heart of communism . . . were not Marx, and many of the Bolsheviks Jewish?

Clearly, these themes are not confined to the West; as already suggested, the retreat from communism in Eastern Europe provides a fertile terrain for the propagation of anti-communism, anti-Semitism and conspiracy theory.

A Suitable Case for Treatment?

That there is concern about the emergence of the extreme right is evident from the increasing plethora of reports, resolutions, addresses and writings devoted to this theme over the past decade or so and emanating from various sources. For instance, in 1979 following anti-Semitic incidents in France and elsewhere, Eric Hobsbawn asked, 'Are we now entering a new era of anti-semitism?' (*New Society*, 11 December 1980, pp. 503–5). The Chief Rabbi, Jacob Kaplan, summed up the mood in the French Jewish community in 1980: 'Since the last World War the doctrines of hatred – whether they be neo-Nazism, racism or anti-semitism – have never been propagated with so much evil intent and audacity than in our time' (quoted in Hainsworth, 1982, p. 153). Certainly there is some evidence to support a pattern of growing anti-Semitic and Holocaust revisionist sentiments on the West European extreme and 'new' rights at this time (Anne Frank Stichting, 1984; Billig, 1989; Eatwell, 1991;). Simultaneously, as Cox notes in Chapter 13, the period 1975–82, witnessed similar developments in the United States.

Nevertheless, as the contributors to this volume suggest, Third World immigrants – and blacks in the United States – emerged as more tangible and (electorally) rewarding scapegoats than Jews. Harris (1990, p. 69) explains: 'If anti-Semitism is not the main theme of contemporary extreme-right propaganda, it is primarily because the immigrant is a more visible, convenient and effective target, and the immigration issue produces a more

substantial opportunity for mobilisation'. Indeed, as argued earlier, immigration politics and the extreme right's cause became inextricably linked in
the 1980s in continental Europe. In 1980, for instance, the Krieps Report to
the Assembly of the Council of Europe led to a resolution 'on the need to
combat resurgent fascist propaganda and its racist appeals' (Council of
Europe, Resolution 743, 1980). This followed attacks on immigrants by the
extreme right throughout Europe, which, according to the resolution, 'bru-
tally underlined both the topicality and the gravity of the subject', and
'justify fears of a radicalisation of extremist groups at European level'. In
particular, the Krieps Report pointed to the following aspects (which are
recalled largely by contributors to this volume): the dangers of unemployment, weakness and division among mainstream political parties, reversion
to 'protective' naturalizations and 'a psychosis of fear and insecurity created,
maintained and exploited by conservative parties'. The Report warned, too,
that 'nationalism and chauvinism with their affirmation of superiority of
national virtues constitute psychological attitudes which pave the way for
discrimination based on race, language or national frontiers'. Alluding to
parties such as the Italian MSI, British National Front, West German
National Party (NPD) and People's Union (DVU) (see Chapter 3), Spanish
CEDADE (see Chapter 9) and other more extremist movements, the Krieps
Report (Council of Europe, 1980, pp. 18–19) concluded with an assessment
worth quoting in view of the subsequent course of the 1980s/1990s:

> It would be foolish, and premature, to say that a major revival of fascist
> or racist ideology was taking place in Europe today. . . . However,
> there have been enough examples of recent fascist and racialist out-
> bursts for us to say that, whilst they do not yet present a significant
> threat in themselves, they do warn us that the point where indifference
> and toleration could be the response has already passed.

Three years later in fact, following adoption of the Müller Report, the
Assembly of the Council of Europe passed a recommendation 'on xenophobic attitudes and movements in member countries with regard to migrant
workers' (Council of Europe, Recommendation 968, 1983). The text expressed concern that in part, the economic climate had resulted in the
scapegoating of migrant workers as job and social benefit 'takers', delin-
quents and threats to educational standards. As the 1980s unfolded – and as
suggested already – immigrants were under increasing attack and suspicion,
thereby providing the extreme right with a breakthrough issue.

More than any single development, the success of the French Front
national in the mid-1980s was a watershed for many on the European
extreme right: in short, it served as a beacon and model for counterparts
elsewhere. Glyn Ford, *rapporteur*, then chairman, of the European
Parliament's Committee on Xenophobia and Racism, pointed to the 'ripple
effect' of Jean-Marie Le Pen's success (Preface to Harris, 1990, p. ix), whilst
the Anne Frank Stichting (1984, p. 58) claimed that FN gains had exercised
'a great attraction for racists and fascist movements at home and abroad, and

bestowed upon them previously unthinkable self confidence'. Kolinsky (Chapter 3) and Husbands (Chapter 5), for instance, note the immediate impact of the FN's breakthrough upon West German and Belgian politics, respectively. Across Europe, too, the effect of the (June) 1984 direct elections to the European Parliament (EP) was to prompt greater vigilance and concern from watchdog bodies, including the setting up of the special European Parliament Committee on Xenophobia and Racism, an undisguised response to the organization of the extreme right within the European Parliament via a Euro-right group under Le Pen's presidency and incorporating the French Front national, the Italian Social Movement, the Greek EPEN and, after 1985, the Ulster Unionist MEP, John Taylor.

Following the 1984 European elections, the monitoring of the extreme right gathered a new momentum. At an international seminar in Amsterdam on this topic in November 1984, references were made to an 'alarming resurgence of fascist and racist propaganda', the 'increasing relevance' of the extreme right's international contacts, insufficient prosecutions and legal barriers and the incorporation of 'racist practices and discriminatory measures' by parties beyond the extreme right in response to the new agenda being set by the latter (Anne Frank Stichting, 1984, pp. i–iv). Of course, scrutiny of the extreme right varies from country to country, depending upon the particular growth of movements and the nature and preparedness of opposition groups which include political parties, churches, trade unions, rights organizations, diverse pressure groups and so on. Many of these, in fact, gave evidence to the aforementioned Committee on Xenophobia and Racism (see for details, European Parliament, 1985, pp. 143–55), to which we now turn.

According to a spokesperson for the Socialist Group in the European Parliament, the Committee was a reaction to the European extreme right and 'evidence of growing racist tendencies in many European countries' (A. Bell, 1986, p. 2). The Evrigenis Report – named after the Greek *rapporteur* to the Committee – was 'particularly concerned over any possibility of the re-emergence of fascist trends' and the climate of intolerance and xenophobia, seen as a by-product of ethnic mix and socio-economic crisis (European Parliament, 1985, p. 15). The Euro-right group within the European Community attempted to quash the Committee on the grounds of legal incompetence, also suggesting the aim was to discriminate simply against one specific Euro-group. However, European Community institutions validated the committee, which proceeded to make forty recommendations. One of these resulted in the 1986 'solemn declaration' and (EC institutional) Joint Declaration against Racism and Xenophobia, and another led to the special Eurobarometer study on racism and xenophobia in the EC, conducted in October/November 1988 and presented to the European Parliament in November 1989 (*Eurobarometer*, 1989). Other recommendations, too, were acted upon, at least in part, but the general response was deemed unsatisfactory by the Second European Parliament Committee on Xenophobia and Racism, launched after the renewed success of the extreme right in the 1989 European elections. Indeed, according to the ensuing Ford Report (again, named after the new *rapporteur*) (European Parliament, 1990, p. 99) of the 40 recommendations contained in the Evrigenis Report, only a few have been fully implemented so far and none has led to significant changes in anti-racism legislation, nor to action at the Community level to confront and tackle the root causes of racism and xenophobia.

Interviewed in June 1991, Glyn Ford argued *inter alia* for inclusion of issues of racism and xenophobia in the European Community's Social Action Programme and the creation of a Council of Ministers for Interior/Home Office ministers to ensure more effective and accountable 'reporting back' on the management of anti-racism, immigration and asylum matters. Overall, though, Ford felt that the EP Committee had succeeded in shaping the political agenda even if the European Community still had a long way to go in meeting the above problems (Hainsworth, 1991a). The latter opinion was certainly the viewpoint of another member of the Committee, the Workers' Party of Ireland MEP Proinsias de Rossa, who described the Committee as a 'damp squib' in terms of its real impact and thought the Community could do much more in this sphere (Hainsworth, 1991b).

As regards the Report of the second Committee on Xenophobia and Racism, this was presented formally to the European Parliament in October 1990. According to the *rapporteur*, extremist groups across Europe were creating a 'second class' population, i.e. immigrants. Anxiety and surprise were expressed at the 'huge increase' in racism and the growing threat of anti-Semitism since the first EP report (*The Times*, 24 July 1990).

Consequently, the Ford Report made seventy-seven recommendations to meet the problem. These are too many to discuss (or list) here, but among the most pertinent to our theme were the demands for a periodic report every eighteen to twenty-four months on racism, xenophobia, anti-Semitism and the extreme right; a European immigration officer; and a permanent European watchdog on the lines of the UK's Commission for Racial Equality; more significant accountability, anti-discrimination legislation, education, information, training and co-ordination at the Community and nation-state level; a European Residents Charter for 1992; and 1995 to be designated European Year of Racial Harmony. In October 1991 these demands were reiterated in a debate on the Ford Report before the European Parliament. During the latter, however, spokespersons for the Council of Ministers (Piet Dankert) and the European Commission (Vasso Papandreou) considered there was limited scope for action at the EC level with the main responsibility resting with member states and sub-national authorities. Nevertheless, simultaneous with almost daily reports of racist and anti-immigrant incidents throughout Europe, the issues raised in the Ford Report were taken up in December 1991 at the important Maastricht summit, when EC leaders passed a declaration condemning the growth of racism, anti-Semitism and neo-Nazism in Europe, East and West.

Elsewhere, the Council of Europe renewed its concern with the effects of immigration – via the Cuco Report (Council of Europe, 1990, Doc. 6211) – turning to the rise of xenophobia and racism in Southern European countries, previously suppliers of immigrants and now increasingly recipients. The Report strongly condemned 'the resurgence of xenophobia and racism' and called for 'a full scale European plan of action'. Although Third World immigration and, increasingly, political asylum-seekers dominate the above reports, anti-Semitism throughout Europe, particularly Eastern Europe, still remains a central concern. The desecration of Jewish tombs in Carpentras (France) in May 1990, for instance, drew widespread condemnation and declarations (see Council of Europe, 1990, Doc. 6245). Billig (1989, p. 162), in fact, emphasizes the persistence and non-substitutability of the anti-Semitic theme. Of course, the focus of this volume is not primarily the growth of racism, xenophobia and anti-Semitism, but specifically, the extreme right. Nevertheless, as Ford claims, these trends are 'linked with the rise of the far right and neo-fascist parties, and [are] perhaps a result of it' (*The Independent*, 12 April 1990).

What possibly has surprised some observers is the speed with which the extreme right has emerged and asserted itself over recent years in Europe. For instance, the sudden breakthrough of the French Front national (see Chapter 2 for details) came at a time when political scientists, historians and commentators were discounting the likelihood (even the possibility) of such an occurrence (Petifils, 1983). Writing in the mid-1970s David Bell (1976, p. 103) summed up accurately enough the standing of French extreme right parties:

> With . . . a narrow basis of support and with policies relatively indistinct from the moderate conservative 'majority', the extreme right seems to be no more than a fading echo. Despite a few noisy flashes in the storms of post-war French politics, the extreme right is no better off as an electoral force in the mid 1970s than it was at the Liberation of France thirty years earlier.

However, immigration as a mobilizing issue had not yet impacted significantly upon contemporary continental Europe to the advantage of the extreme right, although speeches by Enoch Powell and modest urban gains by the National Front in the United Kingdom testified to the potential of the issue (see Chapter 7). Therefore, Bell understated (excusably in view of the trends) the prospect for revival of the extreme right via immigration politics, which in France had not then emerged so prominently as in the 1980s: 'There is no issue on the horizon, such as Algerian independence, which will enable [it] to overcome this dilemma . . . there is very little to which [it] can look forward' (D. Bell, 1976, p. 92).

In West Germany, too, the success of the extreme right coincided with serious analyses of its demise. According to the Evrigenis Report (quoting from Dudek and Jaschke, 1984): 'In the middle term organized German right-wing extremism has no chances in electoral politics' (European Parliament, 1985, p. 33). Moreover, as late as 1988, one of the foremost scholars of the extreme right in West Germany maintained that; 'in face of the enormous integrative power of the two bourgeois parties, the CDU/CSU and SDP, and their virtually hegemonic position within the bourgeois camp, the prospects for right-wing extremism in West Germany were, and are very poor' (R. Stöss, quoted in Melvin, 1990, p. 17). However, as Childs (1991, p. 77) explains: 'The total electoral failure of the far right in West Germany between 1969 and 1988 disguised the fact that there is a constituency which is larger than membership of the various right-wing organisations would indicate'. Indeed, as Kolinsky points out in Chapter 3, 'right extremism has survived among the post-war generations and in the contemporary political culture as an acceptable way of articulating protest', with opinion surveys from the 1950s to the 1980s indicating the clear potential for extreme right revival. Wallraff's 'insider' view of West German anti-*gastarbeiter* attitudes would appear to substantiate these latter views (Wallraff, 1988).

The French and German patterns have direct parallels in, at least, Denmark, Belgium and the Netherlands. As regards the Netherlands, the extreme right's advances have been particularly noticeable in the 1990s with one authority depicting gains by extreme right forces in the March 1990 local elections as 'their biggest breakthrough since the Second World War' (European Parliament, 1990, p. 29). As a result, Lucardie and Voerman (1990, p. 22) claim that, in the Netherlands, 'opponents of right-wing extremism have not much ground for optimism'. Husbands, in Chapter 5, also notes the re-emergence of the extreme right in the Netherlands – after it seemed that it was in terminal decline – due to the increased salience on the political agenda of the foreigners issue . . . especially the concern about asylum seekers. Indeed, throughout Europe, governments have responded to increasing numbers of asylum seekers by tightening up entry procedures. This was the case in Germany, in October 1991, when the main political parties agreed upon measures to speed up asylum seekers' applications – and, if necessary, deport clandestines. Significantly, the measures followed several weeks of attacks by neo-Nazi groups upon immigrant hostels and an apparent and embarassing rise in xenophobia and racism. According to one analysis (Malik, 1991),

> the official clampdown has given licence to unofficial racists to go on the offensive too. From Berlin to Bari, there have been fire bombings of immigrant hostels and attacks on black communities. As the authorities try to buttress Fortress Europe, the Continent's black community is living in a stage of siege.

Arguably, the situation has as much to do with feelings of insecurity as the rising numbers of immigrants. In the view of Martin Woollacott (*The Guardian*, 15 November 1991), Western Europe is 'suffering from a kind of agorophobia following the end of the Cold War – a feeling that it is open to human movements from both East and South that it did not face before'.

Germany, of course, is a special case as far as the foreigner issue is concerned. Although recruitment of foreign labour and anti-immigrant sentiment (Wallraff, 1988) have been conspicuous features of the post-war economic boom, ever-changing circumstances on account of reunification and developments in Eastern Europe have made Germany far and away the main target place for migrants (Wallace, 1991, pp. 12–15). The position of economic migrants and 'genuine' asylum-seekers has allegedly been complicated by the growing number of clandestine and 'bogus' refugees. However, as Wallace (1991, p. 13) points out, it is not always possible to demarcate economic from political migrants:

> The crisis is exacerbated by the increasing difficulty of separating those who arrive into neat categories of 'political refugees' and 'economic migrants'. Motives for moving are almost always mixed: fear of starvation with fear of attack, desire for improvement with desire for freedom.

With the movement towards the Single European Market, too, there is greater vigilance over migratory movements, and civil liberties groups and immigrant/asylum lobbies are pessimistic about the post-1992 scenario. First, there is concern that sensitive issues such as immigration and asylum policy are being discussed in committees and councils outside the European Community's process of consultation and accountability, notably inside the Trevi Group, the Schengen Agreement and the EC's *Ad Hoc* Working Group on Immigration. Second, there are criticisms of the increasing tendencies of EC governments to put immigrants in the same basket as terrorists, drug-traffickers and criminals, thereby criminalizing immigrants as well. Third, there are anxieties that the movement towards a Single European Market is in danger of creating second class citizens (i.e. immigrants) in the future. These issues are too complicated to take up here. However, generally they have contributed to the revaluation and legitimation of the extreme right's key theme of immigrant control (for details on the above bodies and issues see Gordon, 1989; House of Lords Select Committee on the European Communities, 1989; Spencer, 1990; Ireland, 1991). This is not to say that there is an automatic link between extreme right success and the immigrant factor. As Cox and Kolinsky illustrate (Chapters 12 and 3), the German Republican Party enjoyed greater success prior to rather than after reunification, for the Christian Democrats garnered the immediate credits for reunification. Nevertheless, as the same authors again indicate, the new Germany has witnessed rising anti-Semitism, racism and anti-immigrant incidents capable of fuelling extreme right *and* neo-Nazi aspirations and contributing to a climate of insecurity.

Conclusion: The Extreme Right in Post-war Western Europe and the USA

In post-war Western Europe and the United States the extreme right has made an uneven impact, at times winning electoral success although nowhere securing major political office. As Harris (1990, p. 160) explains:

Democracy in Western Europe is not about to be overthrown by the extreme right any more than the prevailing order has been seriously imperilled by the terrorist revolutionaries of the extreme left. An electoral breakthrough by any overtly racist or fascist party is not about to occur.

However, as the same author contends, 'it is no more appropriate to deny or ignore the threat posed by right-wing extremists, than it is to over-react to their activities' (Harris, 1990, p. 160). Consequently, in approaching the topic, a measured perspective is imperative and, arguably, provided by the contributions below.

Of course, as already suggested, electoral returns and membership figures are not the only yardsticks of extreme right measurement. To some extent, the ideas, issues and values of the extreme right have straddled the social and political world of other actors. In Chapter 13, for instance, Cox suggests that the ideological world-view of the extreme right 'is shared in varying degrees by many white Americans'. Thus even though the extreme right may stand outside the political mainstream, it still articulates and promotes ideas held by a large number of people in the country. The rise of David Duke is instructive here. The thrust of this argument applies not only to Germany and France, for instance, but also to countries where although, as in the United States, the extreme right-wing parties are weak electorally, notably in Spain, Portugal and Greece (see Chapters 9, 10 and 11), the political culture has been receptive to prominent values (e.g. social conservatism, anti-communism, authoritarianism and religious traditionalism) cherished by the indigenous extreme right. For example, with reference to post-military dictatorship Greece in the late 1970s, Andricopoulos (1980, p. 582) noted the presence of latent authoritarianism and the consolidation of 'the most reactionary forces': 'authoritarianism is still present though in Sunday clothes'. Elsewhere, extreme right successes have forced the agenda by prompting mainstream political parties 'to steal their clothes', to revaluate particularly the issue of immigration control, or postpone certain policies, opposed by the extreme right such as the enfranchisement of immigrants in local elections. According to Andrew Bell, 'events have shown how even modest far right advances may frighten established conservative parties into shifting rightward to buy off what they perceive as a threat' (Bell, 1986, p. 8). In particular, he pointed to small gains by the British National Front in the mid-1970s (see Eatwell, Chapter 7; Hill and Bell, 1988) which contributed to a strong anti-immigrant manifesto from the Conservative Party in opposition and the following observation from the new party leader, Margaret Thatcher, in 1978: 'people are really rather afraid that this country might be rather swamped by people with a different culture' (quoted in Bell, 1986, p. 8). Subsequently, the then chairman of the National Front, John Tyndall, claimed: 'The Tories under Thatcher appeared to adopt a lot of our policies. She talked about Britain being swamped and a lot of people inferred she would do something about it' (*The Independent*, 17 March 1990). Hill and Bell, too, suggest that Margaret Thatcher's strong line on immigration swept the rug from under a rising National Front star (Hill and Bell, 1988, p. 85).

One outcome was the restrictive British Nationality Act of 1981, passed by the Conservative Party, and subsequent measures. A National Front-cum-extreme right revival was deemed unlikely by observers as long as the government remained strong on nationalism and immigration – and tough asylum measures taken in the late 1980s and the 1990s pointed in this direction (see Amnesty International, 1990), as well as key speeches during the October 1991 Conservative Party Conference and the new Conservative Government's programme in May 1992. Still, as Eatwell contends in Chapter 7, the former possibility could not be ruled out and as one authority pointed out, possibly prophetically, there would need to be 'a break down of Thatcherism, the return of Heathite Conservatism and more general break-down and increase of poverty and unemployment. And more immigration' (Tony Kushner in *The Independent*, 17 March 1990). After all, many of the factors favourable to the extreme right elsewhere exist in the United Kingdom too: urban unrest, high unemployment, racism, immigration, national decline, identity crises and so on. Prime Minister John Major, arguing in 1991 for tighter controls on asylum-seekers and immigrants across Europe, to emphasize his case, warned of the possibility of a 'right-wing backlash' similar to that in Britain in the mid-1970s (*The Independent*, 29 June 1991). According to one view, ('Huddled masses need not apply', *The Economist*, 26 October 1991):

immigration is a tricky issue for the Conservatives. Refugees pose a small threat to Britain by comparison with other countries . . . but there are a dozen marginal constituencies in which the ethnic vote may prove to be decisive . . . Most ministers reckon a heated debate about immigration will not harm the party's electoral prospects.

Significantly, faced with the prospect of tougher immigration controls, the opposition Labour Party's spokesperson, Roy Hattersley, accused the Conservatives of making 'a squalid appeal to racism' in the run-up to the 1992 general election. This accusation gathered momentum in November 1991 following a parliamentary election success by an Asian Labour candidate, Ashok Kumar in Langbaurgh, and during House of Commons debate on the Conservative Party's proposed asylum legislation. Eventually, though, with a general election imminent, pressures on the government time-table and considerable opposition, the asylum legislation was shelved but reintroduced by the new Conservative Government.

In the United Kingdom, of course, the electoral system of 'first past the post' majority voting and the country's political culture operate against parties outside the two-party system. In contrast, in continental Europe, even small advances by the extreme right have sometimes yielded elected representatives via proportional representation voting systems. European, regional and local elections, especially, have proved to be most fruitful for extreme right parties. At the same time, extreme right electoral success and opinion polls revealing sympathy for extreme right positions – on immigration, in particular – have served to force the moderate or traditional parties (not only on the right) further to the right. Particularly salient examples of this occurred in France throughout the summer of 1991 following urban disturbances in immigrant quarters and favourable opinion polls for the FN. Already, in 1990, President Mitterrand had spoken of France reaching 'the level of tolerance' as regards immigrant numbers. Now, the new Socialist Prime Minister, Edith Cresson, announced tougher immigration and asylum measures, and the two main opposition leaders spoke of an immigrant 'overdose' (Jacques Chirac) and 'invasion' (Valéry Giscard d'Estaing). Allegedly, therefore: 'Too many politicians are trying to exploit fears, prejudices and nationalist instincts in the search for a cheap vote' (Editorial, *The European*, 27–29 September 1991). Or, again: 'One by one, leaders of France's respectable parties are going public with views on immigration that seem borrowed straight from the virulently xenophobic Mr Le Pen' (*The Economist*, 28 September 1991). Consequently, the scene was set 'for a horrendous political auction on race' in the forthcoming regional (1992) and parliamentary (1993) elections in France (McShane, *New Socialist and Society*, 26 July 1991).

Similar patterns of appeasement and clothes-stealing were evident elsewhere, ranging from West German Chancellor Kohl's hesitations over Germany's borders (see Chapter 3) to US President George Bush's initial reluctance to support civil rights legislation in 1991 for fear of a right-wing backlash. Woollacott (*The Guardian*, 15 November 1991) moreover, accused the German Christian Democratic Union secretary-general, Volker Rühe, of even instructing party branches to utilize the immigration issue to gain votes. There are examples below of parallel practices. The result of these political manoeuvres is to legitimate the discourse of the extreme right and add to the climate of insecurity amongst immigrants, blacks, asylum-seekers and others. Further legitimation is provided where compromises, alliances and electoral arrangements have been made with the extreme right, usually for short-term political gain. For example, this is especially true within the new French regional assemblies since 1986, where proportional representation eased the FN into influential positions (see Schain 1987; Hainsworth and Loughlin, 1989; Chapter 2 below).

Clothes-stealing by rival parties reflects growing concern about the extreme right's ability to win votes and influence opinion. Of course, it is not simply a question of stealing clothes from the extreme right: immigrant control, anti-communism, nationalist fervour, and so on are also part of the agenda of other parties. If the extreme right did not exist, the themes would still preoccupy mainstream political forces. However, the effect of the extreme right has been to upgrade certain issues and present them in a more aggressive manner. Increasingly, this approach has begun to pay political dividends in several countries and impinged upon the struggle for votes. At this point, therefore, it will be useful to comment upon the extreme right's electorate. Although it is important not to stereotype the extreme right voter, undoubtedly a new set of values has gained relevance and prominence recently and new right-wing parties have emerged. Foremost here is immigration control. For the extreme right elector, immigration is not a secondary concern but often the main single issue determining political choice. Moreover, there is evidence to contend that support for the extreme right has not reached optimum levels of mobilization with opinion polls suggesting increasing numbers of voters are contemplating a vote for the extreme right (Oppenhuis, 1990). According to Westle and Niedermayer (1990, p. 18), 'there is a considerable potential for extreme right organisations, that is more or less latent and in part pre-political but may be mobilised under specific conditions.' Furthermore, opinion polls reveal that it is principally the immigration issue over which non-extreme right voters might switch their votes in the future to benefit the extreme right. Flashpoints, too, are capable of exploitation by the extreme right as the political temperature rises. Interestingly, some politicians, including Margaret Thatcher and the Conservative ex-Chancellor of the Exchequer, Nigel Lawson, pointed to accelerated European integration as a potential source of a right-wing nationalist backlash which could benefit the extreme right. Examples of typical mobilizing factors here, also, would be the dispute over Muslim girls wearing headscarfs in French schools (1989); urban unrest in France, Belgium and the United States (1990–2); sudden upsurges in requests for asylum (Albanians in Italy, East Europeans in Germany in the 1990s); possibly – as Eatwell suggests in Chapter 7 – the effects of considerable migration from Hong Kong to the United Kingdom (throughout the 1990s); the building of mosques from Antwerp to Amsterdam and Mulhouse to Marseille; and in the United States, the continuing success of David Duke in Louisiana since 1987, plus its consequences.

The above situations should not be viewed in isolation from one another since there is often a relationship based on influence or organization testifying to the internationalization of extreme right politics. This phenomenon may be observed across various countries at different times since 1945. For instance, developments in one country have a capacity to spark off similar movements elsewhere. As already argued, this is certainly the lesson of the French Front national's success in the mid-1980s, which inspired the extreme right across Europe, leading to a revival of immigration politics, the creation of the Euro-right group and even the birth of parties, in Belgium and Spain, drawing openly upon the FN's name and message. Significantly, too, the FN itself drew early inspiration from the Italian MSI in the 1970s (adopting the MSI's tricolour flame as a logo) before, in turn, influencing the Italian movement's revaluation of immigration politics. The Euro-right formation inside the European Parliament and Community represents, of course, the formal side of extreme right organization. Other links prevail, though of a less formal nature. For example, the Dutch Centre Party has enjoyed contacts with the MSI, Belgian VMO, West German NPD and the Ku Klux Klan *inter alia* (see Husbands, Chapter 4). In fact, missions from David Duke and other Klan leaders have even helped to set up Ku Klux Klan branches in Western Europe (*The European*, 25–27 October 1991). Again, there are links between the German Republican Party and the Danish extreme right (European Parliament, 1990), the MSI and the British National Front (Hill and Bell, 1988) and the British National Front and Ulster Loyalist extremists (Johnson 1986; Searchlight, 1989). Mention must be made also of the annual extreme right rallies at Diksmüide (Belgium). Although these occasions are dominated by neo-Nazis and neo-fascists, who tend to criticize parties like the Front national as being too 'soft', they nevertheless provide useful rendezvous for the wider extreme right political 'family'. Other fruitful venues for contact include the regular conferences, rallies and festivals of the extreme right, including, for example, the annual *Fête Bleu-Blanc-Rouge* of the French FN.

Although international contacts and cross-fertilization of ideas form an appreciable component of the post-war extreme right's make-up and are monitored by various anti-racist or rights organisations, they should neither be exaggerated nor used to substantiate theories of a 'black' international. Nevertheless, the prevalence and growth of extreme right forces and links do give opponents some grounds for concern. As authors below explain, the extreme right undoubtedly has made its presence felt in post-war politics, developed international contacts and helped to shape opinion, especially on certain issues.

Indeed, to return to what many observers see as the extreme right's most identifiable theme, Bernd Marin (quoted in *The Guardian*, 15 November 1991), who is Professor at Vienna's European Centre, suggests that 'there is something unhealthy about the way we are hanging our politics around [the] single issue [of immigration]. It's very sad that at the end of the 20th century we seem to have nothing else left to deal with'. Despite the apparent reductionism here, which underplays the complexity of extreme right politics, the immigration issue in particular has enabled the extreme right in Western Europe to claim nationalism and patriotism as its foremost values, whereas race in the United States and anti-Semitism in Eastern Europe have fuelled significantly the extreme right's cause. Indeed, it is not an exaggeration to claim that at no time since 1945 has the extreme right been so successful within and across nations as in the last decade or so. As such, the extreme right may be seen as the cutting-edge of contemporary politics – cutting into certain patterns and values which have formed part of the post-war consensus, siphoning off support from ex-abstentionists and mainstream political parties and, increasingly, forcing the agenda for the public at large.

References

Adorno, T. W., Frenkel-Brünswik E., Levinson D. J. and Sandford R. N., 1950. *The Authoritarian Personality*, The Norton Library, New York.

Amnesty International, British Section, 1990. *United Kingdom, Deficient Policy and Practice for the Protection of Asylum Seekers*, Amnesty International UK, London.

Anderson, M., 1974. *Conservative Politics in France*, Allen and Unwin, London.

Andricopoulos, A., 1980. The power base of Greek authoritarianism, in Larsen *et al.*

Anne Frank Stichting, 1984. *The Extreme Right in Europe and the United States*, Anne Frank Stichting, Amsterdam.

Aughey, A., 1989, The moderate right: the conservative tradition in America and

Britain, in R. Eatwell and N. O'Sullivan, *The Nature of the Right*, Pinter, London.

Bell, A., 1986. *Against Racism and Fascism in Europe*, Socialist Group of the European Parliament, Brussels.

Bell, D., 1976. The extreme right in France, in M. Kolinsky and W. E. Paterson (eds), *Social and Political Movements in Western Europe*, Croom Helm, London.

Beyme, K. von, 1988. Right-wing extremism in post-war Europe, in von Beyme (ed.), Right-Wing Extremism in Western Europe, *West European Politics* (special edition), Vol. 11, No. 2, pp. 2–18.

Billig, M., 1978. *Fascists: A Social Psychological View of the National Front*, Academic Press, London.

——, 1989. The extreme right: continuities in anti-Semitic conspiracy theory in post-war Europe, in R. Eatwell and N. O'Sullivan, *The Nature of the Right*, Pinter, London.

Blinkhorn, M., 1990. Introduction. Allies, rivals or antagonists? Fascists and Conservatives in modern Europe, in M. Blinkhorn (ed.), *Fascists and Conservatives*, Unwin Hyman, London.

Caciagli, M., 1988. The Movimento Sociale Italiano-Destra Nazionale and Neo-Fascism in Italy, in K. von Beyme (ed.), Right-Wing Extremism in Western Europe, *West European Politics*, Vol. 11, No. 2, pp. 19–33.

Canovan, M., 1950. *Populism*, Harcourt Brace Jovanovich, New York.

Chebel d'Appollonia, A., 1988. *L'Extrême Droite en France. De Maurras à Le Pen*, Editions Complexe, Brussels.

Cheles, L., Ferguson R. and Vaughan M., (eds), 1991. *Neo-Fascism in Europe*, Longman, Harlow.

Chiarini, R., 1991. The 'Movimento Sociale Italiano': a historical profile, in L. Cheles *et al.* (eds), *Neo-Fascism in Europe*, Longman, Harlow.

Childs, D., 1991. The far right in Germany since 1945, in Cheles *et al.*, *Neo-Fascism in Europe*, Longman, Harlow.

Commission of the European Communities, 1989. Racism and xenophobia, in *Eurobarometer* (Special), November, European Commission, Brussels.

Council of Europe, Parliamentary Assembly, 1980. Resolution on the need to combat resurgent fascist propaganda and its racist appeals, Resolution 743.

——, Parliamentary Assembly, 1983. Recommendation on xenophobic attitudes and movements in member countries with regard to migrant workers, Recommendation 968.

——, Parliamentary Assembly, 1989. Written Declaration No. 196 concerning the development of anti-Semitism and intolerance in Europe, DOC 6234, 8 May.

——, Parliamentary Assembly, 1990. Report on the new immigration countries, Document 6211, 26 April.

——, Parliamentary Assembly, 1990. Written Declaration No. 198 on the desecration of Jewish tombs in the Carpentras cemetery on 10 May 1990, DOC 6245, 11 May.

De Felice, R., 1976. *Fascism*, Transaction Books, New Brunswick, N. J.

Delvit, R., 1990. L'émergence de l'extrême droite en Belgique. Paper presented to a Workshop on *The Extreme Right in Europe* at the ECPR Joint Sessions, Bochum, April.

Eatwell, R., 1989. Right or rights? The rise of the 'new right', in R. Eatwell and N. O'Sullivan, *The Nature of the Right*, Pinter, London.

——, 1989. The rise of 'left–right' terminology: the confusions of social science, in R. Eatwell and N. O'Sullivan, *The Nature of the Right*, Pinter, London.

——, 1989. The nature of the right: is there an 'essentialist' philosophical core?, in R. Eatwell and N. O'Sullivan, *The Nature of the Right*, Pinter, London.

——, 1989; The nature of the right, 2: the right as a variety of 'styles of thought', in R. Eatwell and N. O'Sullivan, *The Nature of the Right*, Pinter, London.

——, 1991. The holocaust denial: a study in propaganda technique, in Cheles *et al.* (eds), *Neo-Fascism in Europe*, Longman, Harlow.

Eatwell, R. and O'Sullivan N., 1989. *The Nature of the Right*, Pinter, London.

European Parliament, 1985. Committee of Inquiry into the Rise of Fascism and Racism in Europe, *Report on the Findings of the Inquiry* (Evrigenis Report), European Parliament, Luxembourg, December.

——, Session Documents, 1990. *Report Drawn Up on Behalf of the Committee of Inquiry into Racism and Xenophobia* (Ford Report), 23 July, Document A3-195/90.

Falter, J. W. and Schumann S., 1988. Affinity towards right-wing extremism in Western Europe, *West European Politics*, Vol. 11, No. 2, pp. 96–110.

Genn, R. and Lerman A., 1986. Fascism and racism in Europe: the report of the European Parliament's Committee of Inquiry, *Patterns of Prejudice*, Vol. 20, No. 2, pp. 13–25.

Gordon, P., 1989. *Fortress Europe? The Meaning of 1992*, Runnymede Trust, London.

Green, D., 1987. *The New Right*, Wheatsheaf Books, Brighton.

Hainsworth, P., 1982. Anti-Semitism and neo-fascism on the contemporary right, in P. G. Cerny (ed.) *Social Movements and Protest in Modern France*, Pinter, London.

——, 1991a. *Interview with Proinsias de Rossa*, European Parliament, Strasbourg, June.

——, 1991b. *Interview with Glyn Ford*, European Parliament, Strasbourg, June.

Hainsworth, P. and Loughlin J., 1989. Coalitions in the new French regions, in C. Mellors and B. Pijnenburg, *Political Parties and Coalitions in European Local Government*, Routledge, London and New York.

Harris, G., 1990. *The Dark Side of Europe. The Extreme Right Today*, Edinburgh University Press, Edinburgh.

Hill, R. and Bell A., 1988. *The Other Side of Terror. Inside Europe's Neo-Nazi Network*, Grafton, London.

Hobsbawn. E., 1980. Are we entering a new era of anti-Semitism?, *New Society*, 11 December, pp. 503–5.

House of Lords Select Committee on the European Communities, 1989. *1992: Border Controls of People*, Session 1988–9, 22nd Report, HMSO, London.

Husbands, C., 1991. Militant neo-Nazism in the Federal Republic of Germany in the 1980s, in Cheles *et al.*, *Neo-Fascism in Europe*, Longman, Harlow.

Ireland, P. R., 1991. Facing the true 'Fortress Europe', immigrants and politics in the EC, *Journal of Common Market Studies*, Vol. 29, No. 5, September, pp. 457–80.

Johnson, K., 1986. The National Front and the Ulster connection, *Fortnight*, No. 242, July–September, pp. 7–9.

Krejčí, J., 1991. Introduction: concepts of right and left, in Cheles *et al.*, *Neo-Fascism in Europe*, Longman, Harlow.

Larsen. S, Hagtvet B. and Myklebust J., 1980. *Who Were the Fascists? Social Roots of European Fascism*, Universitetsforlaget, Bergen.

Le Gall, G., 1989. L'Effet Immigration, in SOFRES *L'Etat de l'Opinion, Clés pour 1989*, Flammarion, Paris, pp. 119–36.

Le Pen, J-M (1984), *Les Français d'Abord*, Carrère-Lafon, Paris.

Linz, J. J., 1980. Political space and fascism as a late-comer, in Larsen *et al.*, *Who Were the Fascists? Social Roots of European Fascism*, Universitetsforlaget, Bergen.

Lipset, S. M., 1960. *Political Man*, Heinemann, London.

Lipset, S. M. and Raab F., 1971. *The Politics of Unreason*, Heinemann, London.

Lucardie, P. and Voerman G., 1990. The extreme right in the Netherlands; the centrists and their radical rivals, Paper presented to a Workshop on *The Extreme Right in Europe* at the ECPR Joint Sessions, Bochum, April.

MacShane, D., 1991. France. Foul play, *New Statesman and Society*, 26 July, pp. 14–15.

Malik, K., 1991. Under siege in Fortress Europe, *Living Marxism*, October.

Mannheimer, R., 1991, *La Lega Lombarda*, Feltrinelli, Milan.

Mayer, N., 1987. De Passy à Barbes: deux visages du vote Le Pen à Paris, *Revue Française de Science Politique*, Vol. 37, No. 6, pp. 891–906.

Melvin, M., 1990. Right-wing extremist electorates in France and West Germany, Paper presented to a Workshop on *The Extreme Right in Europe* at the ECPR Joint Sessions, Bochum, April.

Merkl, P., 1980. Comparing fascist movements, in Larsen *et al.*, *Who Were the Fascists? Social Roots of European Fascism*, Universitetsforlaget, Bergen.

Mitra, S., 1988, The National Front in France: a single issue Movement?, *West European Politics*, Vol. 11, No. 2, pp. 47–64.

Oppenhuis, E., 1990. Extreme Right Voting in Germany, France and Italy, Paper presented to a Workshop on *The Extreme Right in Europe* at the ECPR Joint Sessions, Bochum, April.

Orfali, B., 1990. *L'Adhésion au Front National. De la minorité active au mouvement social*, Editions Kimé, Paris.

O'Sullivan, N., 1976. *Conservatism*, Dent, London.

——, 1983. *Fascism*, Dent, London.

Payne, S., 1980, Fascism: Comparison and Definition, University of Wisconsin Press, Madison.

Payne, S., 1980a. The concept of fascism, in Larsen *et al.*, *Who Were the Fascists? Social Roots of European Fascism*, Universitetsforlaget, Bergen.

——, 1980b. Introduction to 'The diffusion of fascism in Southern and Western Europe', in Larsen *et al.*, *Who Were the Fascists? Social Roots of European Fascism*, Universitetsforlaget, Bergen.

Petifils, J-C., 1983. *L'Extrême Droite en France*, Presses Universitaires de France, Paris.

Rémond, R., 1971. *The Right in France from 1814 to De Gaulle*, University of Pennsylvania Press, Philadelphia.

Schain, M., 1987. The National Front in France and the construction of political legitimacy, *West European Politics*, Vol. 10, No. 2, pp. 229–52.

Schepens, L., 1980. Fascists and Nationalists in Belgium 1919–1940, in Larsen *et al.*, *Who Were the Fascists? Social Roots of European Fascism*, Universitetsforlaget, Bergen.

Scruton, R., 1980. *The Meaning of Conservatism*, Penguin, Harmondsworth.

Searchlight, 1989. *From Ballots to Bombs. The Inside Story of the National Front's Political Soldiers*, Searchlight Publication, London.

Spencer, M., 1990. *1992 And All That: Civil Liberties in the Balance*, The Civil Liberties Trust, London.

Stöss, R., 1988. The problem of right-wing extremism in West Germany, *West European Politics*, Vol. 11, No. 2, pp. 34–46.

Usborne, D., 1991. Major calls for crackdown on immigration, *The Independent*, 29 June 1991.

Wallace, W., 1991. Migration. Tide of Crisis, *New Statesman and Society*, 17 May, pp. 12–15.

Wallraff, G., 1988. *The Lowest of the Low*, Methuen, London.

Westle, B. and Niedermayer O., 1990. Contemporary Right-Wing Extremism in West Germany: The 'Republicans' and Their Electorate, Paper Presented to a Workshop on *The Extreme Right in Europe* at the ECPR Joint Sessions, Bochum, April.

Wilkinson, P., 1981. *The New Fascists*, Grant McIntyre, London.

Woods, D., 1992, Les ligues régionales en Italie. L'émergence d'une réprésentation régionale indépendante des partis traditionnels, *Revue Française de Science Politique*, Vol. 42, No. 1, pp. 36–55.

2 The Extreme Right in Post-War France: The Emergence and Success of the Front National

Paul Hainsworth

Introduction

Prior to 1983, the extreme right in post-war France had experienced only fleeting and minor bouts of success, inflated notably – and subsequently deflated – by the Poujadist wave of the mid-1950s. Indeed, until quite recently, historians of the extreme right were at one in their perception of the French extreme right as a divided, disillusioned and spent force in French politics (Rémond, 1971; Duprat, 1972; Petifils, 1983). Writing in 1985, the Front national journalist-cum-philosopher, François Brigneau recalled 'thirty years of mistakes, setbacks, persistent efforts' (Bergeron and Vilgier, 1985, pp. 7–8). The emergence of the Front national (FN) since 1983 is without doubt, then, the most important development on the extreme right to date. Moreover, some observers (Rollat, 1985; Orfali, 1990) have interpreted the rise of the FN as the key political event of the first Mitterrand presidency (1981–88), and more recently, the movement has continued to maintain its high profile (Hainsworth, 1990; *Le Monde*, 27 March 1992). No political force on the extreme right across post-war Western Europe or the United States has equalled the Front national's impact and electoral success, illustrated vividly by the world press' coverage of Jean-Marie Le Pen's impressive performance in the 1988 presidential election. The movement has served increasingly as a beacon and example for like-minded parties campaigning upon themes such as immigration, security and fervent nationalism. As pointed out in Chapter 1 it was principally the success of the French FN and the creation of a French-dominated Euro-right group at Strasbourg in 1984 which prompted the creation of the European Parliament's Committee on Xenophobia and Racism.

In this chapter, in view of the pre-eminence of the FN, analysis will concentrate particularly upon this body: in brief, how might we measure, explain, assess and interpret the phenomenon? Initially, though, it will be useful to comment upon the French extreme right prior to the birth of the FN.

The Extreme Right in France

Historically, France has experienced various cycles of extreme right-wing activity over the past century or so, sparking off much debate about the nature and essence of this political family. As Chapter 1 in this volume contends, the frontiers of the extreme right are difficult to locate definitively and incontrovertibly. However, this has not deterred observers from attempting to define the French extreme right. Burrin, for instance, has likened it to a sea-snake which usually resides below the surface only to rise intermittently and unevenly (Burrin, 1983). We can agree with Chebel d'Appolonia's assessment of the French extreme right as a plurality of movements, a 'complex mosaic' with the emphasis upon constant adaptation and redefinition. For this author, the operating methods may vary but the horizon is a common one: 'the installation of a new order' – political, social, economic and sometimes cultural and religious (Chebel d'Appolonia, 1988 p. 13). Borella (1977) depicts the extreme right as basically groups outside the mainstream political system, dissatisfied with the latter though none the less prepared, at times, to adopt legal and parliamentary means (see also Bourseiller, 1991). Other authorities have pointed to the style of the extreme right as a distinguishing feature. Hoffmann's classic study of Poujadism (Hoffmann, 1957) fits into this category, and according to Anderson the aim of the French extreme right was to 'exacerbate political conflict, raise the temperature of debate by aggressive slogans and encourage the polarization of opinion to the benefit of those who proposed extreme solutions to the country's problems' (Anderson, 1974, p. 297). Certainly, before the turn of the century, writers such as Drumont and Barrès and political 'adventurers' such as Boulanger and Déroulède could be classified in this tradition. Significantly, contemporary assessors of the extreme right (Rémond, 1971; Taguieff, 1986; Buzzi, 1991) draw strong parallels between the Front national's president, Jean-Marie Le Pen, and the demagogic national-populism characteristic of the late nineteenth century.

Here is not the place to discuss in detail pre-1945 developments. However some observations are in order in view of Sternhell's portrayal of the right-wing nationalist revival of late nineteenth-century France as an incubator for ideas taken on board or reworked in twentieth-century France and elsewhere (Sternhell, 1978). Rémond, too, although subsequently rejecting Sternhell's concept of a pre-fascist or proto-fascist France, acknowledged an 'awakening of the authoritarian right' and the appearance of a 'new political temperament', 'more combative, more plebian than that of the traditional and right wing movements'. Moreover, Rémond saw this nationalism as imposing itself on other right-wing forces, 'even on those whose seniority and original tradition should have offered the best protection against such an infection' (Rémond, 1971, pp. 216–26).

Conscious again of the dangers of extrapolation, we can divine neverthe-less much of Jean-Marie Le Pen's style and substance in the above tradition. The political rationale of Barrès, Boulanger, Paul Déroulède's Ligue des Patriotes and Le Pen is premissed upon the perceived decadence and moral decline of France, attributable to political mismanagement and retreat from traditional values. Furthermore, Barrès evoked the will of a great country to rediscover its destiny, a theme echoed by Le Pen in his major speeches and writings.

According to Le Pen's predecessors, moral and national neglect spawned military defeat. Defeat in the Franco-Prussian War (1870–1) and loss of Alsace-Lorraine were bitter humiliations. Consequently, in Barrès' literature, Déroulède's demagogic speeches and Boulanger's posturing, *revanchiste* aspirations proliferated. Defeat and territorial loss were seen not only as military failures but also as symptoms of France's loss of moral direction. Similarly, various Vichyite apologists interpreted the defeat and occupation in 1940 as symptomatic of France's political misdirection and punishment for decades of waywardness and abandonment of traditional values. Le Pen and others confronted post-war decolonization and loss of empire in a similar vein. It matters little to the argument that Boulanger deemed empire to be a distraction (from recapturing Alsace-Lorraine) whereas Le Pen supported colonial acquisitions: the essential point is that national defeat and humiliation (Sedan, Dien Bien Phu, Algeria) provided the springboard for the propagation of national chauvinism and populist, demagogic ripostes based upon simplistic equations, scaremongering and open challenges to the 'political establishment'. Burrin, again, sums up the character of this particular family: 'obsession with decadence, call for national rallying behind an authoritarian leader, more or less explicit condemnation of democracy, elevation of xenophobia and racism as the panacea for the evils of modernity' (Burrin, 1987).

Nourished by defeatism and anxious for redress, the extreme right has found little difficulty in pinpointing scapegoats for France's failures: Jews, Freemasons, foreigners, communists and other allegedly alien influences. Part of Le Pen's success derives from his ability to offer the electorate something apparently new, whereas, in reality, neither the man nor the ideas are particularly novel. On immigration, for instance, the FN's most recognizable policy area, the pedigree is late nineteenth century. Paramount to the FN is the principle of 'national preference', that is, French nationals take precedence over immigrants in terms of jobs, housing and state benefits. Unemployment levels are correlated crudely with the number of resident immigrants. Déroulède, too, blamed foreign workers for unemployment, and Drumont's classic popular work, *La France juive* (1875), targeted the Jews as the main problem. Similarly, Barrès came to appreciate the electoral mileage from xenophobic, anti-immigrant platforms, at the same time regretting Boulanger's unwillingness to resort to anti-Semitism as a mobilizing theme. According to Barrès, 'the idea of the fatherland implies an inequality but to the detriment of outsiders' (quoted in Sternhell, 1978, p. 70). From Barrès, we have a demagogic and populist exploitation of the insecurity factor based opportunistically on economic difficulties and the scapegoating of foreign labour in a deliberately exclusionist manner. In particular, Barrès' national chauvinist press, *La Cocarde*, and his political platform for 1893 ('For the Protection of Workers') anticipate the key appeals of Jean-Marie Le Pen's movement. For example, in 1894, Barrès wrote in *La Cocarde* (quoted in Sternhell, 1978, p. 70), 'in France, the French must come first, the foreigner second', an attitude taken up enthusiastically in Le Pen's *Les Français d'Abord* (1984) and Front national theoretician Jean-Yves Le Gallou's *La Préférence Nationale* (1985). Moreover, the lexicography of Barresian propaganda *vis-à-vis* immigrants (invasion, hordes, parasites, etc.) is reproduced in the FN's press (*le National* and *National Hebdo*) and sources sympathetic to the movement (e.g. *Minute*). The so-called national preference is characteristic of various movements across the extreme right. For instance, it was adopted by Taittinger's Jeunesses patriotes and Bietry's Jaunes movement in the 1920s and the French 'new right''s *Club de l'Horloge* in the 1970s–80s. In this respect, there is a continuity of thought over a century of extreme right presence.

Above movements were also precursors of the panoply of leagues, movements and political groups which emerged on the extreme right in the interwar and collaborationist era. Again, this is not the place to discuss them in detail, merely to note their varying espousal of anti-Semitism, authoritarianism, anti-parliamentarianism, anti-communism and so on. Rémond, rejecting the label of fascism, defined the leagues as 'simply the latest incarnation of the old Bonapartist tradition – Caesarism, authoritarianism and plebiscitarianism – nationalism revised to fit current tastes' (Rémond, 1971, pp. 281). In turn, Pétain's Vichy regime was seen as 'conservatism triumphant, reaction in its pure state, a mixture of paternalism, clericalism, moralism, militarism and boy scoutism' (Rémond, 1971, pp. 316–17). Other writers, a minority, have tended to stress the fascist nature of this period in France contributing to a lively debate on the matter, (Soucy,1978–86; Sternhell, 1986). Whatever the interpretation, 1940–4 provided ample opportunities for fascist and extreme right forces to display their talents. More significantly for our purposes, the period served as a watershed for the extreme right. With the liberation of wartime France, the subsequent 'settling of accounts', the stigma of collaboration, the reality of the Holocaust and the Western embrace of liberal democratic values, post-war France provided a new socio-political environment. Nevertheless, despite these obvious restraints upon an extreme right-wing renaissance, events proved more propitious than might have been expected, notably as a result of political 'immobility' within the new Fourth Republic (1946–58), war and colonial defeat in Indochina and Algeria, reaction to Gaullism and the events of May 1968.

Gradually, forces on the extreme right began to emerge after 1945 (Duprat, 1972), with decolonization encouraging them to reclaim nationalism following the *de facto* forfeiture via the Vichy experience. Still, the Poujadist movement of the 1950s took France by surprise. Poujadism has been assessed elsewhere (Hoffmann, 1957; Borne, 1977; Eatwell, 1982), so we limit ourselves to a few comments. Essentially, under Pierre Poujade's leadership, the Union de Défense des Commerçants et Artisans (UDCA) and 'satellite' organizations were a rural and petty bourgeois revolt against *inter alia* the state, modernization and taxation. The high spot of Poujadist success was in 1956 when the movement won about 2.5 million votes, 11.6 per cent of the poll, and 52 *députés* (including a young Jean-Marie Le Pen) in the French National Assembly. Subsequently, Poujadism declined rapidly, unable to contend with internal divisions, resurgent Gaullism and the electoral reform of proportional representation in the direction of a majority system. Without doubt, the FN of Le Pen was to revive much of the substance and spirit of Poujadism: anti-intellectualism, anti-technocracy, demagogy, xenophobia, defence of 'the small man', authoritarianism, opposition to 'the political class', anti-statism, anti-bureaucracy, defence of the family, pro-French colonialism, strong law and order, *Jeanne d'Arc* reverence, rejection of perceived decadence, Vichyite nostalgia, populism, leadership cult, plebiscitarianism and so on. However, although both movements acted as tribunes, rallying the discontented and disillusioned sectors of society, there were also important variations between Poujadism and the Front national, notably the respective rural and urban bases.

The Poujadist phenomenon coincided with and was overtaken by the Algerian War (1954–62), and more specifically, de Gaulle's stewardship of France (1958–69). The Algerian War resulted in the formation and activity of various extreme right or terrorist groups, notably the violent Secret Army Organization (OAS) which attempted to impede Algerian independence with a scorched earth policy. However, as Duprat (1972) and Chiroux (1974) explain, Algerian decolonization was a missed opportunity for the extreme right, which failed to create a popular base to support ultimately the concept of French Algeria. Although certain groups such as Jeune Nation and Europe Action emerged on the extreme right during this period, their influence was limited. Chiroux contends that Algeria was for the extreme right 'a supplementary disillusion' (Chiroux, 1974, p. 88). De Gaulle was able to engineer Algerian independence without forfeiting nationalist pride as a distinguishing hallmark of Gaullism. Nevertheless, in the process, he created a reservoir of extreme right, *pied noir* and anti-Gaullist opinion unwilling to condone the 'abandonment' of French Algeria. Throughout the rest of the Fifth Republic, this opinion sustained various challenges to the Gaullist-inspired regime, notably that of Tixier-Vignancour in 1965, and contributed towards the FN's emergence in the 1980s.

Jean-Louis Tixier-Vignancour, Vichy minister and defending lawyer for condemned OAS leaders, stood against de Gaulle in the 1965 presidential election. With Le Pen as campaign manager and much support from the Algérie française lobby, he hoped to 'repay' de Gaulle for the Algerian settlement of 1962. In the event, Tixier managed to gain only 5.3 per cent of the vote, which was considered a failure since it did not even retain the 'No' vote of the referendum of 1962 (9.2 per cent) against de Gaulle's independence for Algeria option. Moreover, the 1965 election campaign ended in divisions and recriminations on the extreme right, with much questioning over Tixier's unilateral opting for François Mitterrand, the left-wing candidate, on the second ballot and criticisms of Le Pen's role as campaign manager. Le Pen had hoped that the campaign might serve as the basis for creating a new political party on the 'social and popular right', capable of uniting the extreme right political family. This was not to materialize and Le Pen withdrew temporarily from the political limelight. Nevertheless, events in the late 1960s and early 1970s were to lead to the formation of the FN.

Characteristically, the extreme right splintered after 1965. Tixier created the Alliance républicaine pour les libertés et progrès (ARLP), which was to the right of the traditional right though it shared many of its policies. Significantly, the ARLP provided a political home for several future leaders of the FN, including Jean-Pierre Stirbois. The ARLP made little impact in the 1967 legislative elections, although Tixier claimed that second ballot support for the left had helped defeat fifteen Gaullist candidates. However, increasing unity on the left to include the French Communist Party, the 'events' of May 1968, a Gaullist amnesty for OAS detainees and the emergence of Georges Pompidou on the right all helped to rally 'Tixierism' to the traditional right. Chiroux (1974, p. 207) refers to 'the strategic moderation of the extreme right' as Pompidou succeeded de Gaulle in 1969. Moreover, the ARLP even defined itself as part of the right wing majority (*Le Monde*, 12 November 1969). In contrast, the Occident movement (created in 1964) was critical of alleged Tixierist conservatism and the Gaullist regime. Occident came to prominence as a young, radical, confrontational movement and provided a base for two activists, Alain Madelin and Gérard Longuet, who later became government ministers under Chirac's premiership (1986–8) as well as leaders of the Giscardian Republican Party. Unlike the ARLP, Occident welcomed aspects of May 1968 and won support for confronting extreme left *groupuscules* in the faculties and in the streets. The events of May 1968, in fact, brought ambiguous fortunes for the extreme right. Gaullist embarrassment over domestic unrest and de Gaulle's defeat in the 1969 referendum was met with 'surprise, satisfaction and anxiety' on the extreme right (Chiroux, 1974, p. 213). On the one hand, solace could be drawn from seeing Gaullism in distress and the potential for change via the barricades; on the other hand, the left-wing, libertarian tone of May 1968 was the antithesis of extreme right values on the whole. For Occident, especially, May 1968 brought mixed rewards: initially new members and notoriety, followed by government proscription in October 1968. Proscription, though, resulted in the creation of New Order, in 1969, which quickly became the key group on the extreme right.

In effect, May 1968 triggered off some rethinking on the extreme right. For instance, the new right (see below), drawing upon neo-Gramscian themes of hegemony, counter-culture and the role of intellectuals, reasserted the case for a long cultural struggle of ideas to sow the seeds of right-wing themes in society and displace the alleged intellectual monopoly of the left (Brunn 1979; Vaughan 1987; Johnson, 1991). Similarly, forces on the extreme right looked to the creation of new political forms to counter the burgeoning flotilla of left-wing groups, parties, movements and ideas born out of May 1968. This purpose became even more expedient as, in the early 1970s, the revamped Socialist Party (PS) and French Communist Party (PCF) signed a Common Programme and formed an alliance capable of winning high political office from the right following de Gaulle's retirement and Pompidou's succession. New Order went some of the way to acting as an umbrella organization on the extreme right as recruits came from diverse sources such as Occident, Roger Holeindre's South Vietnam support network, the ARLP, the student-based Groupe Union Droit (GUD), the high schools and elsewhere. Abroad, too, links were established with the

German NPD (see Chapter 3) and Italian MSI (see Chapter 6), the latter actually serving as a model of success for the French extreme right in the early 1970s.

At its height, New Order was able to rely on some 4,000 or more militants (Duprat, 1972; Camus, 1985). Inspired by leftish ideas on the role of the revolutionary party, the movement's aim was to create a body of professional, organized activists structured around a precise political programme. Anti-communism, immigration control and the restoration of moral values figured prominently in New Order literature. Ideally, the party would become a mass party and break away from the nationalist past of 'salon plots', idle romanticism and the political ghetto. The key to real success was diagnosed as the creation of a larger political and electoral machine, à la MSI. Specifically excluded was the use of New Order as a trampoline for 'pseudo-*notables*' such as Tixier-Vignancour or the role of playing unofficial police for the establishment against the extreme left. Instead, New Order aspired to occupy the 'motor' role in the creation of a national front, a *rassemblement*. The aim was to realize a *parti unitaire des nationalistes et de l'opposition nationale* which would regroup 'our political family' (Rollat, 1985, pp. 53–5). In June 1972 the second national conference of New Order confirmed this strategy, and with the creation of the FN in October, New Order was easily the largest organized tendency therein.

The target of New Order strategists was clearly not only a mass party but also a revolutionary nationalist party, and not simply a nostalgic return to the leagues of the 1930s, Vichy or Algérie française. At the same time, national conference was critical of 'Nazi fossils', divided royalist sects and the obsolescence of the majority of nationalist *groupuscules* (Rollat, 1985, p. 52). Past experience showed that nothing less than a non-sectarian movement with 'a solid popular base' would suffice, with New Order constituting a 'nucleus of steel, a centre of united and effective leadership'. Despite the intention to abandon the past, however, New Order drew conveniently upon Jacques Doriot's slogan for his collaborationist, fascist-inspired, populist Parti populaire français: 'You owe everything to the party, the party owes you nothing' (Rollat, 1985).

The Front National and Extreme Right Divisions in the 1970s

New Order, therefore, should not be seen as synonymous with the FN, though without it the Front national would not have been created in 1972. Initially, New Order militants contemplated the title 'National Front for a New Order' but eventually settled for the shorter version. The goal of a mass supported national party was attractive to many on the extreme right, including Le Pen. As intimated, the 1965 campaign had led to Le Pen's semi-retirement from active politics following disagreements with Tixier-Vignancour. However, May 68 – 'nausea' according to Le Pen – had renewed Le Pen's interest in the formation and necessity of a new nationalist movement. Extraneous to Occident and New Order, though Le Pen was in no position to dictate the pattern of nationalist party formation.

Nevertheless, drawing upon his reputation, Le Pen was able to take advantage of the new development in 1972 and virtually inherit a structured apparatus to ease his political comeback. Unsurprisingly, many New Order militants were troubled from the outset by Le Pen's status as an ex-parliamentarian and *notable*. There were fears of 'Tixierism', i.e. that Le Pen might abuse the Front idea by manipulating it as a vehicle for his personal ambitions. Conversely, Le Pen could serve as a useful 'federator', a figure-head for different currents on the extreme right and testify to New Order's (tactical) conversion to electoral and *unitaire* politics. The latter argument won the day. In any case, New Order leaders (e.g. Alain Robert, François Brigneau and François Duprat) envisaged controlling Le Pen and reaping the benefits of New Order militants, the backbone of the FN.

The leadership of the new movement was shared between New Order (two seats), Le Pen (who became president), Pierre Durand (a close associate of Le Pen), Roger Holeindre (the ex-OAS and South Vietnam supporter) and Pierre Bousquet (leader of the small, 'third way', Mouvement Nationaliste de Progrès and a former Waffen SS participant). The rough balance within the leadership was clearly intended to rally different groups to the nationalist cause, and the nascent organization served as a meeting point for Pétainists, ex-OAS supporters, royalists, neo-fascists, revolutionary nationalists, ex-Occident, ex-ARLP, ex-Jeune Nation, ex-Europe-Action members, Tixierists, South Vietnamese supporters, etc. The movement was welcomed by the sympathetic extreme right press (e.g. *Minute, Rivarol* and the neo-fascist Bardèche's *Défense de l'Occident*) and the FN posed as *l'opposition nationale, la droite sociale, la droite populaire*. From the outset, the FN shunned the extremist label, preferring the more embracing term *mouvement* to *parti* and unashamedly claiming the term 'right', traditionally avoided by mainstream right-wing parties in France. With the birth and electoralism of the FN, Borella even alludes to the integration of the French extreme right into the political system (Borella, 1977, p. 47). *Vis-à-vis* Gaullists, Giscardians and their allies, however, the FN posed as the opposition and 'true' voice of French nationalism.

Both New Order and the FN turned to electoralism as a means of building up support. In 1971 in fact, New Order had demonstrated its small electoral base with 20,000 voters in fourteen Paris municipalities contested. In 1973 New Order provided two-thirds of FN militants and candidates for the legislative elections. Although there were some understandable reservations within the FN about contesting major elections whilst in political infancy, eagerness to make an early impression prevailed. Aspirations to field 400 candidates proved too ambitious and the movement settled for 104. Weakly organized and with unknown candidates, it fared badly, winning only 2.3 per cent of the vote in selected constituencies and obviously much less overall. Nevertheless, despite vociferous internal opposition (notably from GUD), the third annual conference of New Order in May 1973 reaffirmed the line of a national front and electoralist strategy, at the same time launching a campaign against *l'immigration sauvage*, i.e. uncontrolled immigration. Paradoxically in view of Le Pen's later rise to prominence on an anti-immigration discourse – New Order strategy resulted in strengthening

Le Pen's hand inside the Front national. In June 1973, following violent clashes between New Order militants, the police and the extreme left on the occasion of a meeting against immigration, the Council of Ministers dissolved New Order and the Trotskyist Ligue communiste révolutionnaire (LCR). Subsequently, New Order leaders such as Alain Robert were to explain how unexpected the decision was: it caught the organization unawares.

The reaction of New Order militants to proscription was protracted. As president of the FN, Le Pen was unwilling to concede any new leadership positions to New Order colleagues to compensate for proscription. In turn, these colleagues protested against Le Pen's 'methods' and dictatorship. Robert recalled the principle of collegial leadership against the *führerprinzip*, and criticisms, in part, echoed Le Pen's own critique of Tixier-Vignancour's leadership in 1965. In November 1973 Brigneau resigned from the FN, and Robert accused Le Pen of manipulating the organization for his French presidential aspirations. Rebuffed by Le Pen and on the defensive, ex-New Order militants created the movement Faire Front (in December 1973) which claimed 70 per cent of FN local delegates. By the end of 1973, therefore, Le Pen had strengthened his leadership over a somewhat depleted party with ex-New Order elements protesting strongly against his 'political piracy'.

In the spring of 1974, after President Pompidou's death, Le Pen duly emerged as the FN's presidential candidate. Although Le Pen's leadership depended upon his brokerage between different factions inside the FN, his status as a presidential candidate, with media access, served to enhance his leadership credentials. In the 1974 presidential election, Le Pen proposed 'to create around the national opposition a wide popular current in favour of a true French renaissance'. Standing as the spokesman of 'the silent majority', Le Pen purported to display an image of moderation via his television performances. The FN's 'programme of public safety' included such measures as immigration control, a French natalist policy, a professional army and protection of the environment. Interestingly, at this stage, Le Pen offered a 'third way', between right and left if necessary, though this did not necessarily preclude a vote for Giscard d'Estaing on the second ballot. On the first ballot, Le Pen collected a modest 0.74 per cent (190,000) of the votes cast (Rollat, 1985, p. 63). In compensation, Giscard's victory at least barred the path of the Socialist-Communist common candidate, François Mitterrand, and inflicted a defeat upon the despised Gaullism, represented by Jacques Chaban-Delmas.

Unsurprisingly, Faire Front attacked Le Pen's meagre electoral returns as detrimental to 'the national right' since they underplayed the 'real' strength of this political family. Atlanticism and liberal capitalism were criticized, too, in Le Pen's programme. Faire Front dissidents had actually contributed to Le Pen's low poll by voting and working for Giscard *ab initio*. Mitterrand alluded to this scathingly and given a very close second ballot, extreme right wing support undoubtedly played its part in Giscard's success. Accused by Le Pen of treachery, Faire Front leaders explained their voting tactics in 1974 as a blow against Gaullism and a means of reinserting 'the national right' into the political mainstream. Moreover, the active support for Giscard yielded important financial rewards which the ex-FN dissidents used to launch a new extreme right-wing force, the Parti des forces nouvelles (PFN). Launched at Bagnolet in November 1974, the PFN's arrival signalled a decade of intra-extreme right rivalry which would be resolved conclusively only by the sudden, decisive breakthrough of the FN in 1984.

The birth of the PFN represented another watershed on the extreme right in that the FN's claim to lead *la droite populaire et sociale* was put to the test. At this point, therefore, it will be useful to recap on the status of the FN in the movement's early years:

1. The 1972–4 phase established Le Pen's leadership of an organization initiated mainly by New Order militants, and adoption as a candidate in the 1974 French presidential election enhanced Le Pen's leadership claims.
2. Differences between Le Pen's supporters and ex-New Order elements led to the creation of a serious rival to the FN's attempted hegemony of the extreme right political family.
3. Key themes of the mid-1980s which assisted in the Front national's ascension (notably anti-immigrant policies) were already present in the early 1970s though their day had not yet arrived.

The struggle between the FN and PFN dominated extreme right wing politics in the Giscardian presidency (1974–81). Anxious to play the electoral game, the FN (unlike the PFN) would have no truck with the traditional right. Not until the 1980s did Le Pen seek a role *within* (on the right of) the classic right. In contrast, ex-New Order (Faire Front) militants who had supported Giscard in 1974 transferred to Jacques Chirac in 1976–7, and in the 1977 municipal elections, the PFN worked with Chirac's neo-Gaullist Rassemblement pour la République (RPR). Consequently, Le Pen castigated the PFN as 'a government war machine against the national opposition'. According to Marc Frédériksen – leader of the neo-fascist Federation of National and European Action (FANE) and an electoral candidate for the FN in 1977 – the PFN was simply the hard wing of the Giscardo-Gaullist majority: 'They are notables. They are always ready to please the government. For example, they don't hesitate to stick up Chirac's posters' (Hainsworth, 1982, p. 150). The PFN leader, Pascal Gauchon, summed up his party's attitude to the RPR as 'oui, mais', though the FN interpreted the PFN as a tool or design of the traditional right to ruin the Front National. The PFN justified its collaboration with the RPR as an attempt to tilt the traditional right further to the right. However, again the FN attacked the PFN militants as 'mercenaries' or (ironically, in view of past accusations against Le Pen) 'would-be Tixierists'.

Apart from electoral and personal rivalries, the PFN and FN differed from each other in various ways. For instance, the PFN constantly posed as the newer, progressive, modern face of the right against the FN 'dinosaur'. However, this did not preclude laudations for Brasillach, Drieu La Rochelle, Bardèche, Maurras, Algérie française and other historic symbols cherished on the extreme right. At times, anti-capitalism was also part of the PFN's repertoire despite attempts to come to terms with the traditional right. Furthermore, the PFN, programme overlapped consciously with the anti-egalitarian, elitist, bio-political themes of the new right, some of whose ideas were frowned upon officially by Le Pen (see below) for their anti-Christian, paganistic values. Although in part the PFN echoed the philosophy and tactics of former prominent extreme right-wing groups such as Jeune Nation, Occident and New Order, its willingness to work with the traditional right was novel.

Faced with PFN competition and unable to build up support in any significant proportions, the FN spent a decade in the political wilderness on the periphery of French politics. In May 1975, at the third FN annual conference, survival of the movement emerged as the main concern. Moreover, in November 1977, at the fifth national conference, the movement resolved to continue without any deals or alliances with the traditional right. At the same time, the FN aspired to surpass the image of a mere *groupuscule*. However, the organization hardly prospered, and observers and supporters described the 1970s as a phase of crossing the desert for Le Pen.

Crisis followed crisis as the FN failed to escape from the political ghetto. In 1976 Le Pen escaped an assassination attempt, when a bomb destroyed his Paris apartment. In 1978 leading FN theoretician François Duprat was not so fortunate when a car bomb claimed his life. In elections, too, the FN continued to perform badly: in the 1977 municipal elections the movement could muster only 15,800 votes in Paris, and in the 1978 legislative election 137 FN candidates polled 1.6 per cent. In 1978 the PFN's 89 candidates, too, polled only 0.9 per cent, and the isolation of the FN was particularly revealed in 1979 when the PFN engineered a European alliance.

The 1979 Euro-elections temporarily gave the PFN a psychological advance over the FN. In June 1978 the PFN had organized a meeting with the Italian MSI and the Spanish New Forces movement, (see Chapter 9) with the participation of Tixier-Vignancour. This resulted in the formation of the Euro-right alliance for June 1979. Well-attended rallies took place in Rome, Naples, Madrid and Paris, and the new alliance looked to the Christian Social Union's leader, Franz Josef Strauss, as a potential West German ally. Prior to January 1979, the FN had demonstrated little interest in contesting the Euro-elections, with anti-democratic Maurrassians in the movement particularly disinterested. However, mildly encouraging results in the 1979 cantonal (departmental) elections, the increasing publicity surrounding the Euro-right alliance and the utilization of proportional representation persuaded the FN to rethink strategy. Consequently, in April 1979 negotiations between the PFN and FN realized a new Union pour l'Euro-droite des patries. Further discussions, press conferences and encouragement from media sources such as *Rivarol* and *Minute* transferred the running label into the Union française pour l'Euro-droite des patries with Michel de Saint-Pierre, the Catholic *intégrist* author, placed first on the list of candidates, Tixier-Vignancour second and Le Pen third. Ultimately, programmatic and financial problems dogged the hastily struck alliance, which collapsed several days before the closing date for nominations. This was not the end of the episode, for at the eleventh hour the PFN (and Tixier-Vignancour) registered the Union française pour l'Euro-droite as a contestant for June 1979.

Amidst FN accusations of deception and treachery, the Euro-right polled 1.3 per cent in France, well below the 5 per cent quota necessary to ensure representation in the European Parliament. The case of the extreme right was complicated not only, by PFN/FN divisions but also by the participation of rival candidates likely to benefit from extreme right-wing votes. Furthermore, Chirac and Michel Debré conducted an extremely nationalistic, xenophobic, Gaullist campaign which shared common themes with extreme right candidates (Hollick, 1979).

The 1979 election was yet another watershed for the FN. Despite a commitment to electoralism, the movement played no electoral role in June 1979. Indeed, the FN's militants were more conspicuous for their disruptive behaviour at Simone Veil's (UDF/Giscardian) meetings. As Giscard's Minister for Health, Veil had pioneered the controversial 1974 Abortion Act, thereby earning the wrath of the FN. Le Pen's natalist politics and the presence of traditional Catholics inside the FN made anti-abortion an important component of the movement's policies. Accordingly, Veil was attacked as 'the immaculate contraception' and subject to rowdy behaviour at meetings. Anti-Semitism (against Veil) played some part in the 1979 European election, too, and the FN's role was somewhat akin to *groupuscule* behaviour.

The Euro-election had altered appreciably the complexion of extreme right-wing politics in France, depriving the FN of any valid leadership claims. After the election, the PFN followed a path close to the RPR *and* new right thinking. This culminated in support for Chirac on the *first* ballot of the 1981 presidential election, as Pascal Gauchon shared Le Pen's inability to collect the statutory 500 signatures (of elected representatives) necessary to contest the election. Le Pen's failure in this respect testified to the weakness and isolation of the FN movement in 1981, underlined by the derisory 0.35 per cent in the 1981 (June) legislative elections. The FN was unquestionably at a low ebb. Almost a decade of existence had yielded little electoral support and much extreme right-wing division. The reality of a Socialist–Communist government coalition in 1981 was a further source of despondency within the FN. The crossing of the desert was proving arduous for the FN with no oases in sight. Few observers could have predicted the resurgence of the FN in the immediate future, yet paradoxically, the success of long-standing opponents proved to be the trampoline of extreme right-wing revival at a time of virtual Front national demise.

The Ascent of the Front National

Writing in the 1970s, Duprat argued that no formation on the extreme right looked capable of emulating Poujade's 1956 success (Duprat, 1972). Rémond's classic work on the French right, too, concluded: 'The extreme right no longer figures as a political force . . . it involves only minorities incapable of acting effectively or of changing the development of political society' (Rémond, 1971, p. 338). Moreover, Petifils could agree with this assessment, virtually on the eve of the FN's breakthrough: 'Even the Socialist victory in 1981 and the coming to power of the socialist–communist coalition have not been able to wake up the sleeping demons of the extreme right' (Petifils, 1983, p. 123). Consequently, as Shields (1990, p. 186) points out, 'the tendency among commentators at large was to consign the far right in France to an opprobious past from which escape was deemed impossible'. Yet, as Mayer and Perrineau (1989b, p. 343) rightly point out, it was the alternation of power, the Socialist–Communist displacement of the Giscardo-Gaullist coalition in 1981, which served as the catalyst for the emergence of the FN.

No single factor will suffice to explain the rise and success of the FN. Rather, the elevation of the movement as a force in contemporary French politics rests upon a complex alchemy and conjuncture of variables. Initially, mere survival enabled the movement to benefit from the 'quasi-disappearance' (Bergeron and Vilgier, 1985, p. 83) of the PFN after 1981. At last, with some credence, the FN could pose as the vanguard of 'the national and popular right'. Le Pen, too, must take some credit for steering the organization through the political wilderness. In 1981 and after, the FN began to take advantage of a divided and demoralized right-wing opposition, and especially the presence of Communist Party (PCF) ministers inside the government, itself concerned initially to pursue markedly left-wing policies. Simultaneously, after twenty-three unbroken years of office, the right had lost, even squandered, political power in 1981 in a fratricidal manner, exposing fatal divisions and thereby opening up the arena to 'new' forces on the right. In opposition, the Gaullist–Giscardian (RPR–UDF) right adopted an aggressive, radicalized discourse which narrowed the ideological ground between the right and the extreme right and in effect, played into the hands of and legitimated the FN as the radical wing of opposition to the incumbent left. Moreover, by anchoring much opposition criticism around themes such as immigration, anti-communism and law and order, the traditional right further legitimated the FN's programme. The process of legitimation continued, notably at Dreux in 1983, when a second ballot agreement between the extreme right (Stirbois) and the right won the local election against the left, though at the price of seats on the council for the FN and a massive revaluation of immigration as a key electoral theme.

By 1984, the FN was very much the right party in the right place at the right time. Benefiting greatly from impressive electoral returns in 1983 and much media attention (particularly Le Pen's interview on the popular *L'Heure de Vérité* television programme in February 1984), the FN took advantage of the nature of the June Euro-election. Proportional representation, the secondary status of the election and right-wing tactics all worked to the FN's advantage. Although the RPR and Union for French Democracy (UDF) patched together an electoral alliance under Simone Veil's leadership, right-wing voters were insufficiently convinced about unity after several years of fratricide and doubtful about the compatibility of RPR and UDF perspectives on Europe. Veil, too, was a controversial choice, for despite her undoubted popularity and status, some potential right-wing voters might be uncomfortable with her Europhilism, liberalism and Jewish origins. Furthermore, voters from all major parties and beyond welcomed the opportunity of voting against previous choices without immediately altering the national balance of power, though in practice, voting for the FN created a precedent. With 11 per cent of the vote and ten MEPs, the FN created the shock of the 1984 Euro-election (Charlot, 1984), enabling the movement to lead the Euro-right group inside the European Parliament and establish links across the European extreme right. Equally significant, the FN had polled the same proportion of votes as the hitherto strong PCF and now entered the mainstream of French politics.

Euro-success brought funds and supporters into the FN, and the movement set about organizing on a comprehensive, national basis. By 1985 the FN had created structures throughout the French regions, departments and localities with thirty or so permanent offices, a revamped press, political education channels, an active youth movement (the FNJ), various socio-professional work and policy groups, propaganda and press sections and so on. Much of the organizational work was done initially by the FN's Secretary-General Jean-Pierre Stirbois, and continued in the late 1980s and the 1990s by his successor, Carl Lang. Membership, too, increased, with party spokesman Michel Collinot claiming 60,000 members in 1985. More realistically, the figure had jumped from a few hundred in 1982 to about 30,000 with also an active nucleus of about 5,000 to 6,000. New recruits – about 6,000 to 7,000 according to some estimates – came especially from the RPR and served as useful, experienced, influential individuals within the movement (Lorien *et al.*, 1985, pp. 323–41; Milza, 1987). More recent data, in fact, based upon FN responses at the 1990 annual conference in Nice, indicates that 40 per cent of post-1981 delegates emanated from Gaullism (Ysmal, 1991, p. 186). The Nice Conference was interesting for introducing an element of democracy into a hierarchical and centralized movement. For the first time, regional and departmental preparatory sessions elected some one thousand delegates to national conference, whereas a hierarchised selection procedure had previously sufficed. Certain delegates (about 6000) however still earned their conference place of right: members of the political bureau and central committee and national, regional and departmental elected representatives (Mayer, 1991, p. 114).

An early test of the FN's new-found status after the Euro-election was the 1985 cantonal elections. These were held only in parts of France and heavily dependent upon parties and movements exploiting well-established local roots and support structures. As a relative newcomer the FN could not expect to secure massive returns or even put up sufficient candidates to contest all seats. Nevertheless, even in these circumstances, the FN polled extremely well, fielding candidates in three-quarters of the 2,000 constituencies, therein securing 10.4 per cent therein (8.8 per cent overall) and performing impressively in the south-east of France. This left the movement in a strong position to contest the 1986 legislative and regional elections, where the Socialists had opted for proportional representation instead of the customary two-ballot majority voting system (*scrutin d'arrondissement*).

The 1986 elections represented another very successful watershed and consolidation of the FN vote as the party entered the French National Assembly for the first time, with 9.9 per cent of the votes (thirty-five seats), and comparable success, 9.6 per cent of the votes (135 seats), left the FN arbiter between right and left in several regions (Hainsworth and Loughlin, 1989). Once inside the National Assembly, the FN *députés* took up the role of constructive opposition to premier Jacques Chirac's new right-wing government, albeit generally voting with the latter against the left. On the whole, despite one controversial occasion in October 1987 when they created a fracas inside the National Assembly, the FN *députés* played the parliamentary game, enhanced the movement's legitimacy and were deprived of representation only by the premature 1988 legislative elections held, following Chirac's electoral reform, and Mitterrand's successful presidential re-election, by returning to *scrutin d'arrondissement*, which discriminates against smaller and/or friendless parties. Despite losing all but one *député* – Yann Piat, who subsequently parted with the FN over tactics and presentation in 1988 – the FN regional councillors were in place until 1992, and here too the role of constructive opposition was pursued.

Five consecutive years of national prominence, largely favourable opinion polls and Le Pen's apparent ability to surmount crises within the movement – often caused by his own occasional utterances of an anti-Semitic nature – left the party in a favourable position to contest the 1988 presidential elections. Moreover, again right-wing divisions were evident and likely to benefit rivals. The 1988 presidential election was the pinnacle of FN success: 14.4 per cent and 4.4 million votes for Le Pen (Hainsworth, 1988b; Shields, 1989). The organization had progressed from an active minority into a social movement (Orfali, 1990). In the legislative elections which immediately followed the presidential election, the FN share of the poll reverted to customary levels (9.8 per cent of the votes) as anticipated widely. However, cantonal elections in the autumn of 1988 yielded particularly bad results for the FN (5.3 per cent of the votes), thereby prompting talk of decline in the media and among some political analysts. Nevertheless, in the 1989 municipal elections the FN bounced back impressively refusing to compromise with the right and withdraw candidates on the second ballot. Although, the party was unable to field candidates in many of France's 36,000 plus communes, the FN won 10 per cent of the votes in towns with over 20,000 inhabitants, emphasizing the urban nature of its support. Also, in the 1989 Euro-elections, the movement polled its second highest share of any national election (11.73 per cent of the votes), comfortably retaining its contingent of ten MEPs and recreating the Euro-right political grouping – with the West German Republican Party, without the Italian MSI – inside the European Parliament (Hainsworth, 1990).

Furthermore, in November 1989 Marie-France Stirbois (widow of the FN's ex-secretary-general) became the FN's sole *député* after winning 42.5 per cent of the votes on the first ballot and outright victory on the second at the Dreux by-election, and in a Marseille by-election the FN's candidate achieved a creditable 33 per cent. Dreux, or more precisely the encompassing department of Eure-et-Loir, was the setting for the FN's greatest progress in the 1992 regional elections as Marie-France Stirbois pushed support for the movement up 10.65 points to 20.61 per cent (*Le Monde*, 27 March 1992). Overall the FN won 13.9 per cent, (3.4m voters) up 4.2 points since the 1986 regional elections, and returned 239 regional councillors, against a peak of 137 councillors in 1986–92. In cantonal (i.e. departmental) elections held simultaneously, the FN won 11.48 per cent, an improvement on previous such elections. Mayer's pen portrait of the FN in 1990–91, in fact, revealed a party which also boasted 35 mayers, 4 general councillors (reduced to one in 1992) and over 1600 municipal councillors (Mayer, 1991). Over a period of nine years, then, the FN had retained a strong presence through a variety of elections. In the next section, therefore, we examine the nature of the party's electorate.

The Front National Voter

The heterogeneous nature of the FN's electorate defies any stereotyping of the party's voter. Certainly, the movement draws upon long-standing extreme right voters who sustained the party through the 1970s. However, throughout the 1980s the FN was able to poll significant levels of support from all social classes, regions and age groups. Also, the FN electorate is a volatile phenomenon: the voters of 1984 (11.2 per cent) were not simply the voters of 1986 (9.9 per cent), and in 1988, within a few weeks Le Pen polled the FN's highest ever share (14.4 per cent) of the poll, only to see the loss of half his presidential election aggregate in the subsequent legislative election (9.8 per cent).

As we have noted, the movement first began to poll well in 1983 in various local and parliamentary by-elections, achieving good results in urban areas of high immigration such as Dreux and Paris (Le Pen in the twentieth *arrondissement*). The 1984 elections provided an opportunity to assess the nature of the FN's electoral base. Plenel and Rollat (1984) indicated the main features of the FN constituency:

1. a masculine and urban vote;
2. support from predominantly right-wing voters: three in five FN voters had backed a right-wing candidate in April 1981, one in five voted left.
3. the party successfully mobilized abstentionists and first-time voters: one in five voted FN;
4. compared with the right, the extreme right voter was younger, more working-class, less feminine and less inclined to practise religion regularly.

The FN did particularly well in the south-east of France (Alpes-Maritîmes, Bouches-du-Rhône, Var, etc.) and the Paris region, benefiting from anti-immigrant voters and Tixier-Vignancour's areas of strength in 1965. At first, rural and central France proved resistant to the FN, thereby ruling out crude parallels with the Poujadist success of 1956. However, like Poujade and

Tixier-Vignancour, the FN won good support from the *pieds noirs*, lower middle classes, shopkeepers, artisans and small business people.

Analysis of the 1986 FN vote revealed some changes since 1984: the right recuperated about one-third of the FN's electorate although this loss was more than compensated by the increase of working-class (popular), first-time and hitherto abstentionist voters. The 1984 and, especially, the 1986 elections illustrated the FN's ability to attract more working-class voters than the traditional right (Jaffré, 1987). The 1988 presidential election further testified to the increasing 'popularization' of the FN vote as the 'motley ranks of far-rightists who make up the *noyau dur* of the National Front were swollen beyond all proportion by a popular constituency which the party found itself denied in the first decade of its existence' (Shields, 1990, p. 191). The main right-wing candidates in 1988, Jacques Chirac and Raymond Barre, drew support particularly from farmers, executives, liberal professionals, salaried middle classes, and higher social classes, whereas Le Pen's vote was younger, more masculine, 'small man' orientated with an overrepresentation of the self-employed and more working class (Grünberg *et al.*, 1988). In 1988 Le Pen won 20 per cent of the 'popular' vote against the combined 16 per cent of Barre and Chirac. Clearly then, the FN is an impediment to the right's conquest of more working-class voters, as in de Gaulle's day. Like other examples discussed in this volume, the contemporary French extreme right attracts a certain working-class protest vote, a factor that has given rise to comparisons with Paisleyism (Goldring, 1987) and Powellism (Charlot, 1986) in the United Kingdom.

To some extent, the FN has replaced the French Communist Party as a tribune and protest pole. However to what extent has the former movement drawn support away from the latter, the traditional recipient of working-class support? To take one example, in the 1981 presidential election, PCF leader Georges Marchais topped the poll in Marseille; in 1988 Le Pen came in first, with the PCF relegated to fifth position. Again, the FN has made good progress in the Paris red belt, a PCF bastion. Nevertheless, simple correlations between PCF decline and FN ascent are not substantiated on the whole. In fact, the PCF has lost more to the PS than to the FN, and in turn the PS has lost more to the NF than has the PCF. Platone and Rey (1989) assess the 1988 presidential results in Seine-Saint Denis, an area of FN and PCF strength, concluding that no more than 8 per cent and probably only 3 to 5 per cent of the PCF's voters switched to the FN. Other studies tend to confirm this trend (Mayer and Perrineau, 1989; Husbands, 1991). However, the FN's ability to recruit young, first-time and working-class support suggests the movement is able to attract *potential* PCF reservoirs of electors in cohorts previously favourable to the PCF. Undoubtedly, both parties have benefited in turn from a 'popular' reaction to the establishment and status quo.

Whilst the PCF's electorate declined in the 1980s, with PCF presidential candidate André Lajoinie securing only 6.8 per cent in 1988 (Marchais, 15.3 per cent in 1981), Le Pen managed to retain most of the FN's 1986 voters as well as greatly adding to these, doubling the vote and achieving a comprehensive enough 'nationalization' of the FN's support. With good support from all regions, belatedly the Poujadist circle was squared as the FN president polled well in rural France as well as in urban bastions. In eight *départements*, Le Pen polled more than 20 per cent, outdistancing all rivals in key towns such as Marseille and Nice, and beating Chirac and Barre in others such as Strasbourg and Dreux. In traditional strongholds in southern/south-east France, roughly one in four voters elected for Le Pen, e.g. 26 per cent in Bouches-du-Rhône, 24 per cent in Alpes-Maritîmes and 23 per cent in Var. Equally spectacular were the results in Eastern France: 22 per cent in Bas-Rhin, 22 per cent in Haut-Rhin and 20 per cent in Moselle. Here, although immigrant and unemployment levels were lower than elsewhere, success could be attributed to other factors (Hainsworth, 1988b, p. 167):

> The decline of Gaullist and Christian Democratic structures, reaction to the *notables* and political class, discontent with socio-economic restructuring, the effects of religious decline, envious glances across the border to more prosperous countries, nostalgia for traditional values (for instance, the family) championed by the FN and increasing receptivity to the movement's themes.

Also, the restructuring of the steel industry, rising unemployment and dispute over the construction of a local mosque (in Mulhouse) no doubt swelled the FN's share of the poll.

Of course, where immigration was high and could be linked with themes such as urban blight, insecurity and declining standards, Le Pen polled well, notably in high-rise public housing areas as existed in northern Marseille and elsewhere. According to Shields (1990, p. 192), when 'competition for scarce social and economic resources is compounded by the tensions of coexisting cultures, Le Pen is assured a ready audience.' However, in the 1980s there was no simple correlation between immigration and votes for Le Pen in that often districts of relatively low immigrant penetration (though high fears of rising levels of immigrants) supported the extreme right (Mayer, 1989). Further, where immigrants had been integrated successfully, this was reflected in lower votes for the FN (Mayer and Perrineau, 1989a). Nevertheless, there is little doubt about the potency of immigration control as a successful mobilizing factor for the FN, and as noted in Chapter 1, one author has referred pointedly to the movement as a single-issue party (Mitra, 1988). Compared with other voters, the FN voter prioritizes immigration as a factor for voting behaviour, with insecurity and unemployment as the other top themes (Perrineau, 1989). Collectively, these themes enabled Le Pen to attract votes from all quarters, including about 17 per cent of UDF–RPR 1986 voters, 15 per cent of young and hitherto abstentionist voters and 6 per cent of PCF/PS voters (Duhamel and Jaffré, 1989). The FN voter certainly tends to be more pessimistic and dissatisfied about life and politics than the average voter. However, various observers warn against portraying the FN voter as simply a discontented and deprived being. Indeed, although the party attracts votes in poorer and troubled areas, where immigration and security are key issues, the FN voter is not necessarily at the bottom of the social ladder. In a paper based on a recent survey, Mayer and Perrineau (1990) point to the FN electorate as an 'interclassist' phenomenon, not an underprivileged corpus, and if anything more upwardly mobile and better off than the average (and certainly the left-wing) voter.

In many respects, FN voters and members share the same characteristics. For instance, opting for the FN is a defiant choice, against the grain. This, of course, is particularly so for those members who profess openly their political affiliation, whereas some FN voters prefer anonymity, a fact reflected in the opinion polls which often tend to underestimate FN support through unwillingness to tell the truth about likely voting intentions. Members, especially activists, are imbued with a much greater sense of mission and crusade. Interviews with FN members reveal their main concern to be the establishment of a new moral order to surmount the alleged decadence and decline of France. Voters, on the other hand, are more specifically associated with the triptych: unemployment, immigration and insecurity (Ivaldi, 1990, p. 11). Belonging to the movement helps to remove a sense of isolation and alienation felt by individuals even though membership also stigmatizes adherents in the eyes of 'the outside world'. Through the FN, activists and members are able to (re)construct their identity and are provided with a discourse to decode socio-political matters (Orfali, 1988, pp. 122–31). Orfali talks of a psychological release experienced, 'a psycho-social prometheism' in belonging to the FN (Orfali, 1990, p. 132). Many are attracted by the FN's patriotic, nationalistic stance against the decline or decadence of contemporary France, accentuated by the retreat from traditional values such as the family, religion and authority symbols. Again, as Orfali explains, using a sample survey of FN members, there is 'a feeling of urgency' in belonging to the movement, an impatience with other parties (cf. Bachelot, 1986; Ysmal, 1991) and a desire for redress.

Drawing upon and adapting the works of Adorno, Moscovici, Billig and Cantril *inter alia*, Orfali produces a typology of FN members: the man of order, the man of violence and the subjugated man. The characteristics of the former include respect for order, authority, property, leadership and the social role of the family; opposition to traditional parties, social democracy, egalitarianism, sexual liberation and 'working' wives. These individuals, predominantly male (80 per cent), are the backbone of the party. The second category incorporates the following features: a belief in violence, though only if necessary; a penchant for conflict, struggle, antagonistic and uncompromising attitudes; a reassurance and identity satisfaction in belonging to the FN; a tendency to be young atheists *or* old diehard (*intégriste*) Catholics. Those in the third category tend to join the movement through family or friends and are impressed particularly with Le Pen's charisma as well as his ability to talk to 'the people'. The last cohort is predominantly female (77 per cent) and practising Catholic. For all recruits, membership of the FN is a badge of Frenchness summed up by one interviewee's response: 'In the Front one feels French and proud to be so' (Orfali, 1990, p. 272).

For FN members and voters then, Frenchness, identity, nationalism and patriotism are motivating factors which benefit the movement, and these themes are explored further in the next section which examines FN policy make-up.

Policies and Perspectives

In part, the vote-winning issues of the FN have been noted: immigration, security and unemployment. Here we concentrate in more detail upon major policy areas, without professing to be comprehensive though attempting to understand the nature and self-image of the main force on the contemporary French and European extreme right.

As regards self-definition, we have already pointed to the FN's willingness – unlike right-wing rivals in France – to accept the term 'right' for political location. Since inception, we recall, the FN has posed as *la droite sociale et populaire*, the 'true' right against the 'soft' right. According to Le Pen, the established political parties are 'the gang of four' (RPR, UDF, PS, PCF). A choice between right and left, i.e. PS or RPR–UDF, is tantamount to choosing between 'galloping' or 'creeping' socialism in the eyes of the FN. Of course, Le Pen rejects the label 'extreme right', admitting to only extreme anti-communism as a virtue (Le Pen, 1984a). Instead, he describes himself as a Churchillian democrat, i.e. not a great supporter of democracy, although knowing no better system. For the majority of FN voters, too, self-placement is not on the extreme right but elsewhere (the right, centre and so on). According to Ranger (1989), only one-third classify themselves as extreme right, and we have observed above how the movement has been able to draw support from all main parties and beyond. Moreover, in the 1960s a classic study by Deutsch, Lindon and Weil (1966) revealed a close attitudinal affinity in general between right and extreme right cohorts. Two decades later, parallels were apparent across the spectrum of the French right.

On economic policy, the FN claimed to be a free-market liberal even before the established right moved away from post-war, *dirigiste*, Gaullist ideas. By courtesy of the 1978 economic programme (reprinted in the 1980s), *Droite et Démocratie Economique*, the FN purported to be Reaganite before Reagan, vaunting the role of the free market against the power of the state. The 1985 FN programme, *Pour la France* (Le Pen, 1985a, pp. 66–9), praises Margaret Thatcher's economics, popular capitalism and privatization of the public sector. Throughout FN programmes and propaganda there are constant attacks on state bureaucratization coupled with appeals for less company and personal taxation, including the gradual abolition of income tax. In 1986–8, too, the FN representatives campaigned strongly inside the French National Assembly, pressurizing the right-wing government of Chirac to honour free market pledges. Certainly, there appears to be less in the FN's policy make-up of the old corporatist reflexes characteristic of parts of the French extreme right and more in evidence within the early FN. Indeed, adoption of the above (1978) programme sparked off resignations from the FN by so-called revolutionary nationalists or third way (anti-communist and anti-capitalist) elements centred on François Duprat and Pierre Bousquet's Militant faction. Furthermore, incoming *solidariste* forces under Jean-Pierre Stirbois' leadership increasingly distanced themselves from third way-cum-corporatist ideology to support free-market liberalism inside the FN. These trends, apparent in the late 1970s to early 1980s, were accentuated after the breakthrough of the movement in the mid-1980s as new recruits of *laissez-faire* persuasion swelled the party's rank and file.

However, immigration policy rather than economic policy has been the movement's most distinguishing mark (Mitra, 1988), although both themes overlap considerably, as in the infamous FN campaign slogan: 'two million unemployed = two million immigrants too many'. On immigration, the FN oscillated from a draconian expulsion policy to a slightly more tempered one of repatriation, financed, in theory, by the social security contributions of immigrants (Le Pen, 1984a; Le Pen, 1985a; Stirbois and Jalkh, 1985; Le Gallou, 1985). In December 1991, however, much outcry and opposition greeted the FN's latest policy document on immigration setting out fifty proposals for its restriction. Among these were measures to enable retroactive deprivation of naturalized status, to abrogate 1972 and 1990 legislation against racism and anti-Semitism, to repatriate long-term unemployed immigrants, to enforce the 'national preference' and restrict the building of mosques and Islamic institutions inside France. Some critics pointed to a return to Vichy; others spoke of apartheid (*Le Nouvel Observateur*, 28 November–4 December, 1991). In addition, the FN would like to see tighter restrictions on accession to French nationality, family grouping through immigration, 'convenience' marriages, rights of asylum-seekers and clandestine immigrants. As suggested above, central to the FN's programme is the concept of a national (and European) preference, i.e. preferential treatment for French citizens in matters of employment, housing, state benefits, educational provision and so on. Immigration, particularly from North Africa, is correlated negatively with crime, unemployment, health risks, cultural dilution and loss of French identity. The last is a key concern of the FN, as Orfali (1990) illustrates, and much output from the party centres on the theme, including a series of pamphlets from the *Institut de Formation Nationale*, the FN's think-tank (launched in 1989). Usually, the crusade for recapturing French identity – cultural, religious, ethnic, linguistic, etc. – is accompanied by the critique of alleged decadence, decline and immorality. The remedy is summed up in Le Pen's most celebrated slogan: *Les Français d'abord* (Le Pen, 1984a).

For immigrants, the FN's policy of 'French first' connotes a climate of uncertainty, racial exclusion, a selective interpretation of French colonialism and a concomitant tendency to scapegoat immigrants (Désir, 1985). Moreover, if empowered, the FN would submit major questions of society, such as immigration, abortion and capital punishment, to a Swiss-inspired referendum by popular initiative (RIP), enabling the movement to pose as the expression of the *vox populi*. Essentially, FN perspectives on immigration and plebiscitary democracy place the party in the national-populist tradition (Taguieff, 1986; Buzzi, 1991), although some critics suggest other labels such as populist conservatism (Camus, 1985), fascist (Chatain, 1987) or neo-fascist (Wilkinson, 1981). Jean-Pierre Stirbois, ex number two in the

FN, accepted the first interpretation. According to Stirbois, 'we want . . . above all, the reconciliation and unity of the French, of the popular community' (Stirbois, 1988, pp. 215–22). Drawing from Rénan, Barrès and Le Pen, Stirbois defined the nation approvingly as the political expression of the people and castigated immigrants from Muslim countries as 'a foreign invasion' (Stirbois, 1988, pp. 204–22). Parallel with this is the FN's adoption of Joan of Arc as a symbol of French purity and heroism against alien invaders (i.e. immigrants).

Besides immigrants, the FN conjures up a motley collection of scapegoats: communists, socialists, liberals, the media, Freemasons, homosexuals, progressive clergy, technocrats, bureaucrats, *grands écoliers*, AIDS carriers, intellectuals, and so on. Wherever possible, these too are portrayed as alien or malevolent forces. More often than not, a linkage is alleged between these categories and immigrants, for instance by portraying immigrants as AIDS carriers or accusing left-wing politicians, intellectuals or clergymen of indulgence towards immigrants. Undoubtedly, the movement's policy on immigration has had considerable impact, mobilizing public opinion, forcing the right to re-examine the question of French nationality and revalue immigration as a policy priority, and at the same time, retarding President Mitterrand's long-standing aspiration to grant local election voting rights to immigrants.

Particularly associating immigrants with rising crime rates, the FN stands for tougher law and order, sentencing and security measures, including the return of the death penalty for criminals, drug-pushers and terrorists. In these matters, the FN reaches a wider audience than its electoral appeal, according to opinion polls. On law and order, Le Pen supports a strong, authoritarian state with a stronger presidency elected for seven years, nonrenewable. According to the 1988 pocket-book programme, *Passeport pour la Victoire*, used to supplement Le Pen's impressive presidential campaign: 'We are not anarchists. We know that the state is necessary and we want it strong and respected in its regalian functions: defence, policing, justice, diplomacy.' On defence, the FN has quite distinctive policies: not only support for France in NATO but also creation of a European defence umbrella, civil defence measures and a professional – as opposed to conscript – army. Opting for European defence, however, should not be taken as a sign of enthusiasm for European integration. In the 1989 Euro-elections, the movement campaigned upon the old Gaullist theme of a Europe of nation-states (Hainsworth, 1990), and the European Commission, in particular, is singled out for 'bureaucratic socialism' and the European Parliament for Marxist and Third World oversensitivity (Le Pen, 1985b, pp. 188–9). At the time of the Maastricht summit, too, Le Pen attacked the abandonment of national sovereignty and poured scorn upon 'l'Europe des fédérastes'. (*Le Figaro*, 11 December, 1991).

In social affairs, the FN is rather conservative, even reactionary, reflecting the influence of Catholic traditionalists upon and within the movement. The family is supported as an institution of merit with preference for generous family allowance and a maternal wage to enable mothers to stay at home with young children. Abortion is fiercely opposed by the party – though not, it seems, by FN voters (Rollat, 1984; Mayer and Perrineau, 1990) – in line with the movement's fears about denatality and subsequent loss of French identity as a result of a declining birth rate in contrast to higher immigrant birth rates. Divorce, single-parent families, mixed marriages (French/immigrant) and homosexual/lesbian relationships are all frowned upon by the FN – notwithstanding Le Pen's own marital status as a divorcee. To promote the specifically French traditional family, the FN has proposed a rather convoluted, impractical, paternal, popular capital, owner-ship policy (Le Pen, 1985a). Again, the theme of a 'national preference' runs strongly through FN social policy.

Other FN policies are less prominent: they include support for edu-cational vouchers, private schools, separation of state and school, and reform of the disliked (by the FN) *grandes écoles* at the top of the educational apex. In educational matters, the emphasis is primarily upon choice and freedom, with equality, multiculturalism or even the rights of man seen as erroneous concepts. In addition, trade unions in the educational sector (and elsewhere) are criticized as too bureaucratic and class-orientated.

Regarding class, the FN attacks all doctrines and institutions based upon themes of class struggle. As indicated in Chapter 1 and here above, Marxism, communism and socialism are top of this agenda and, arguably, as much attention in FN propaganda has been devoted to anti-communism as to immigration matters. Also, despite the prevalence of such forces as de-Sovietization and *pereströika* in recent years, the FN's rank and file remained resolutely opposed to and conscious of a perceived Soviet menace. At the 1990 annual FN conference, for instance, 82 per cent of delegates listed the Soviet Union as the country posing the biggest threat to France, followed by Iran, Libya and Algeria (Ysmal, 1991, p. 195). Nationalism, moral revival and cultural identity are proferred as the bulwarks, in FN eyes, against the respective alien influences represented by these countries. Consequently, according to Shields (1991, p. 189), 'nationalism, the moral order, socio-economic decline and the conjoined threat of communism and Islamic Arab immigration have from the outset constituted the rudiments of the party's message.' At the same time, social Darwinism, bio-politics and elitism have made some (albeit patchy) contribution to the FN's make-up, thereby connecting the party to some extent to the French new right.

Above, reference was made to espousal of new right thinking as a dis-tinguishing feature of the PFN *vis-à-vis* the FN. This was certainly the case in the 1970s. Subsequently, however, new right influences upon the FN became more noticeable although they conflicted with the Catholic *inté-griste* tradition, influential within the party since 1977 and associated par-ticularly with the MEP and ex-FN *député*, Bernard Antony (alias Roman Marie), and the pro-FN daily newspaper, *Présent*. Partially in view of the latter influences, the FN was less comfortable with the GRECE (the Groupement de recherche et d'études pour la civilisation européenne) com-ponent of the new right – with its criticism of Christianity's heritage and economic neo-liberalism – than with the *Club de l'Horloge*, which provided several notable recruits to the party, including Bruno Mégret and Jean-Yves Le Gallou. On many issues, though, the FN shared a common empathy with the whole of the new right, e.g. reform of the French nationality code, immigration, anti-bureaucracy, hierarchization, critique of the state, cultural identity and anti-egalitarianism (Buzzi, 1991).

According to Vaughan (1987, pp. 302–4), the 'Nouvelle Droite, by clothing widespread prejudices in unemotional language and endowing them with the prestige of scientific corroboration, had prepared the ground. Themes which it brought back into intellectual arguments served the purposes of parliamentary politics.' Furthermore, the attraction of the FN's propaganda was 'enchanced by the veneer of sophistication derived to a great extent from the literature of the New Right' as similar themes were taken up by Le Pen and colleagues 'in a more direct and populist style'. Consequently, the writings of Le Pen incorporated 'rather loose' concepts of natural selection , i.e. *de facto* racial criteria in the guise of establishing French cultural identity. As Taguieff (*Le Nouvel Observateur*, 28 November–4 December 1991) explains, direct racist language and crude biological references are usually avoided, though as a result of socio-biological ideas, indirect racist discourse is apparent in the quest for national ethnic identity, tantamount to 'a cultural and differentialist neo-racism'. Again, 'biological considerations are not very far from the core of the NF's propaganda, but they remain linked to assertions of cultural superiority' (Vaughan, 1987, p. 306; see also Le Pen, 1984a; Goldring 1987). Certainly, anti-Semitism is part of the FN's make-up and particularly associated with the ultra-Catholic wing of the party under Romain Marie's ideological leadership. However, Le Pen himself is noted for his anti-Semitic remarks. According to Buzzi (1991, p. 43), these utterances are of an 'episodic' nature but other observers suggest Le Pen's anti-Semitism is more deep-rooted. In the view of one critic (D. MacShane, *New Statesman and Society*, 6 March 1992): '. . . to attend Le Pen's meetings is to confront an anti-semitism unheard in mainstream public discourse in Europe since the 1930s . . . Le Pen does not explicitly denounce someone as Jewish . . . But he finds it difficult to keep the beast under control. In 1990, he dismissed the holocaust as a minor detail and last year his wordplay linking a Jewish minister's name to gas ovens popped out spontaneously . . .'

From this brief excursion into the FN's policy agenda, it can be seen that the movement cannot simply be reduced to a single issue. This viewpoint is well articulated by Shields (1989, pp. 143–4), whose summing up is worth quoting at length:

Le Pen has crystallised support around a complex of issues and sub-issues which relate loosely to one another and which are easily, if at times spuriously, linked in the popular imagination. Immigration, law and order, and unemployment are no doubt the principal themes of Le Pen's political populism. Yet other 'issues', too, feature large. Conservatism in religion, the defence of traditional education, concern other moral standards and family values, the backlash against the perceived excesses of state *dirigisme*, opposition to prevailing tax structures, questions of national identity and of France's world role, apprehension over the implication for national character and individual well-being of the single European market of 1992, fear of AIDS and drug abuse, all are grist to the mill of a demagogue who promotes himself as a champion of the small man against an indifferent political establishment.

Shields' comments are useful for alluding to Le Pen's leadership role for clearly the movement depends much upon his charismatic, oratorical and populist attributes. Not only has the electorate responded to Le Pen's leadership – either very supportively or very antagonistically, but rarely with indifference – but his success has consisted of uniting or rallying a previously divided political family. According to Borella (quoted in *Le Point*, 25 January 1992), Le Pen has brought together a multitude of *groupuscules* and two basic currents of thought: one is elitist and ideological and turned towards the past; the other is populist, anti-intellectual and wants to construct the future through the alliance of a leader and a people. In part, this sums up the FN although throughout this chapter we have pointed to the complexity of the movement. Unquestionably, though, the leader, the policies and the party's impact upon French politics and society, combined with the ability to draw support from many quarters, have necessitated a response from other forces and this aspect is dealt with in the penultimate section.

Confronting the Front National

The emergence of the FN has posed all kinds of problems for political rivals, unsure of how to interpret and respond to the newcomer to the fore of French politics. On the right, for instance, forces have oscillated from outright condemnation and ostracism (Noir, Veil, Stasi, etc.) to condemnation of national alliances with the movement (Chirac), to willingness to strike up local (Dreux, Marseille) or regional (Bouches-du-Rhône, Languedoc) agreements to keep out the left (Schain, 1987; Hainsworth and Loughlin, 1989). Some right-wing politicians prefer defeat to victory with the FN's connivance. Others tend to view the FN as basically the right of the right and warn against ghettoization. Some of the smaller political forces sandwiched between the extreme right and right favour a 'no enemies on the right' approach. On one level, the ex-Gaullist Interior Minister (1986–8), Charles Pasqua, could point to the extreme right and traditional right as sharing essentially the same values, whereas Simone Veil and Jacques Chirac could condemn the Dreux and other alliances as 'against nature'. During and following the 1992 regional elections, notably, the right pursued a basically intransigent policy, refusing to do 'deals' with the FN. Nevertheless, the results of these elections left many 'hung' regional councils making it not out of the question that some bargaining would follow to ensure viable majorities. Hitherto, where the right had needed FN votes to secure a regional presidency or budget, concessions often were made, realizing short-term gain for continuing legitimation of the FN. As Schain (1987) has pointed out, legitimation here has complemented legitimation through electoral success and policy acceptance.

Opinion polls, we recall, indicate a wider support for FN policy – notably on immigration – than for the movement itself, prompting from rivals a degree of clothes-stealing or genuflections in Le Pen's direction. In late 1991, one third of French opinion agreed with the ideas defended by Le Pen whereas the figure has been one in four or five in preceding years (SOFRES/ RTL poll in *Le Monde*, 25 October 1991) For the right, facing up to the FN is tantamount to walking through a political minefield: too much adoption of FN policies both legitimizes the movement and frightens away the centre ground essential to winning major elections; insufficient cognisance of FN themes means loss of votes to the extreme right. This dilemma is particularly acute for the Gaullist RPR, squeezed between a renaissant extreme right and a persistent centre, and for politicians in FN strongholds such as the south-east of France. Moreover, in the 1980s the FN (as already noted) was able to recruit leaders, activists and members from the traditional right (Bachelot, 1986; Mégret, 1990; Ysmal, 1991). Under these circumstances, it is unsurprising if the right criticizes the Socialist Party (PS) for nourishing the Le Pen 'factor' in order to keep the right divided and out of office. Political developments after June 1988, too, indicated the utility of the FN as a lever to prise the centre-right away from the right towards the PS's centrist overtures. A further dilemma for the right has been how to attack the FN without patronizing or insulting its voters. Simultaneously, the right has its own agenda on immigration, security, law and order, and so on. At times, this is not unlike that of the FN. As pointed out in Chapter 1, it is not simply a question of clothes-stealing, but often a process of articulating policy which, for better or worse, may approximate aspects of rival political programmes, e.g. that of the FN.

On the left, also, confronting the FN has been problematical. Here, political parties have oscillated between ostracism and participation in televised debates with Le Pen in order to 'unmask' him. Like the right, the left faces a strategic dilemma: too much attention to Le Pen tends to martyr him or provide useful publicity; insufficient criticism opens up the left to charges of complacency and inaction. Certainly, prior to the 1992 regional and departmental elections, the PS made the struggle against the FN one of the main pillars of its campaign. Similarly, a wave of opposition, demonstrations, disruptions and debates against the FN characterized the 1992 campaign. For example, PS *député* Jean-Christophe Cambadélis organized a 'Manifesto against the Front national' followed up by an 'états généraux contre le national-populisme'. In the eyes of the right, though, the left stands accused of promoting the FN with the reintroduction of proportional representation in 1986 and the failure of PS economic and social policies, including immigration, security and employment matters. In turn, some left-wing critics have accused forces on the traditional right and left of approaching the FN on tactical rather than moral grounds. Similarly, the PCF has encountered criticism for its cavalier treatment of immigrants in overcrowded, underfunded communist-controlled municipalities (Hainsworth, 1981; Schain, 1988), again serving to legitimate FN themes. Basically, though, the PCF condemns the FN, interpreting it as the extremist wing of the whole right at a time of the movement of the political agenda to the right (Calderon, 1985, Chatain, 1987). For the PS, PCF and others on the left, the right stands accused of playing the role of sorcerer's apprentice on account of radicalized opposition after 1981, collusion and extreme right clothes-stealing. Indeed, interviews with PCF regional representatives in Bouches-du-Rhône (Hainsworth, 1987) revealed that the PCF saw no real difference between the right and extreme right as regards alliances, policies, perspectives and voting record in the national and regional assemblies. Calderon (1985) points to a difference in tone between extreme right and right though not in content. This view is shared by organizations on the extreme left such as the Trotskyist Lutte Ouvrière and Ligue Communiste. These parties participate actively in anti-racist demonstrations against the FN. Also in the vanguard of anti-FN protest are pro-immigrant and rights groups such as SOS Racisme, France Plus, Fraternité Marseille, the League against Racism and Anti-Semitism (LICRA), the Movement against Racism and for Friendship amongst Peoples (MRAP), the Young Catholic Workers (JOC), the Amicale des Algériens and Jewish lobbies. The churches and main trade unions, too, have been conspicuous in their opposition to the FN. A reflection of this was Le Pen's statement after the 1992 regional elections which denounced political interference from 'religious or philosophic, Jewish and Masonic organisations' (*Libération*, 27 March 1992; see also 'L'Eglise et le Front National', *National Hebdo*, 20–26 February 1992).

Conclusion

The extreme right in post-war France has enjoyed mixed fortunes. Largely swimming against the current, it experienced limited waves of success until, in the 1980s, the Front national emerged as a movement capable of sustaining a high profile over a number of years. Besides electoral success, the FN has made a considerable impact upon French and European society provoking *inter alia* the growth of watchdog and opposition bodies such as the aforementioned European Parliament Committee on Xenophobia and Racism. We can, in fact, agree with Harris that the rise of Jean-Marie Le Pen represents 'the most dramatic illustration of the strength and potential of the extreme right' throughout contemporary Europe (Harris, 1990, p. 34).

As argued above, no single reason explains the success of the FN as Shields (1990, p. 195) explains:

> To ascribe the success of the National Front to economic recession, immigration or the problems of law and order is to provide a quite inadequate account of the factors underlying the rise of this party. For it is to take cognisance neither of the situation prevailing in the period prior to Le Pen's success, nor of the very specific context within which this success was achieved.

Undoubtedly, though, disillusionment with mainstream political parties is an important factor (Charlot, 1986; SOFRES, 1989). The RPR–UDF right, in particular, has faced a major challenge from the FN as Gaullist hegemony of the 1960s and Giscardo-Gaullist rule of the 1970s have given way to a basically tripartite right-wing situation including the FN, and with the RPR and UDF also subject to splinter movements conditioned by the question of facing up to the FN. In fact, developments since the early 1980s have left a space which the extreme right has been able to occupy. Trading upon post-materialist issue politics (immigration, security), the FN has exploited reservoirs of support, prevailing electoral volatility and French extreme right-wing traditions. However, the party is essentially a modern phenomenon, a by-product of contemporary urbanized capitalism in crisis, even if Le Pen's view of society and the FN's discourse may be seen as authoritarian and reactionary (see comments by Jean-Christophe Cambadélis in *Le Monde*, 3 March 1992). Shields (1990) rightly views the FN as a new chapter or departure in French right-wing extremism. Le Pen's success rests largely upon his ability to disengage from the stereotypical images of the extreme right 'to put a lot of water in his wine' (K. Muir, *The Independent*, 6 December 1991) and renounce, not always consistently, 'the cruder trappings of right-extremism in favour of a more acceptable guise' (Shields, 1989, pp. 147–8). Again, according to Harris, Le Pen is the 'hero of the city dweller, the person who feels oppressed by bad housing, immigration, the threat of unemployment, and a general sense that something has gone wrong with his country' (Harris, 1990, p. 89). For Mayer and Perrineau, too, the FN is the 'political echo of urban anomie', a consequence of social disintegration and the decline of traditional intermediaries such as the churches, the local community, the extended family and the PCF (Mayer and Perrineau, 1989b, pp. 346–7; see also Le Bras, 1986; Todd, 1988). Elsewhere, Anne Tristan's analysis of the FN in Marseille reveals well how the movement has occupied a solidarity vacuum to serve as a tribune for local malcontents (Tristan, 1987). In this respect, we have made guarded comparisons with the PCF.

As with the PCF, the FN is not widely perceived as 'a party like the others'. Public opinion continues to see the movement as a danger for democracy despite the FN's professed democratic pretensions (see, for instance, the SOFRES/RTL poll in *Le Monde*, 25 October 1991). Nor is it possible to dissociate the party – in view of statements made and policies adopted – from the rising levels of racial intolerance in recent years, as evidenced in a report to Premier Michel Rocard in 1989, which aroused much comment. Nevertheless, legitimation by agreements with other parties has strengthened the FN's status, and with 30,000 (Milza) to more realistically 50,000 (Mayer, 1991) or 60,000 (Collinot) to 75,000 (*Science et Vie Economie*, February, 1992) members and up to at least 4.4 million voters (1988), the FN has evolved into an important movement. Leadership of the Euro-right group inside the European Parliament has further enhanced the FN's standing and made it a sort of model for other extreme right groups.

Prospects for the future are uncertain though not unpromising on some levels. According to one view, 'the party of J-M Le Pen can still draw voters, among the underdogs, the least politically and socially integrated, as well as among the well integrated conservative right' (Mayer and Perrineau, 1990, p. 10). Moreover, success in attracting young voters, abstainers and disillusioned right-wing voters are positive omens for the FN. Fragmentation on the right and failure on the incumbent left would enhance this process. Le

Pen's 1988 presidential trawl benefited, too, from a certain disillusionment on the part of some voters with the power-sharing experience of 1986–8, which appeared to validate Le Pen's jibes about 'the gang of four' (albeit three, minus the declining PCF). In the 1990s, as the left pursues an opening to the centre, a *de facto* diluted form of *cohabitation*, and the right fragments, there remains scope and space for the FN.

The onset of '1993' and the accelerated pace of European integration and change provide further opportunity for the extreme right across Europe to fulfil the tribune function. Significantly, in the 1989 Euro-elections, the FN was successfully campaigning under the old Gaullist banner of a *Europe des patries*, whereas the RPR allied with the more Europhile UDF (Hainsworth, 1990). With PR in operation for Euro-elections the FN easily gained more than the 5 per cent electoral quota to ensure representation, and on current strengths the quota looks attainable in the future. Indeed, the target set at the 1990 annual conference – held significantly under the banner of 'the conquest of power' – is 30 per cent of the poll. More immediately, the FN aspired to 15 to 20 per cent in the 1992 regional elections. In the event, therefore, 13.9 per cent was perceived – within and without the party – as something of a set-back. Even so, it constituted the FN's second highest share of the poll nationally, after Le Pen's 14.4 per cent in 1988, and left the movement with a hundred more regional councillors than in 1986. At the same time, the PS plummeted to below 20 per cent and the right lost ground too.

Proposals to dilute PR for French regional elections would certainly reduce the FN presence in future regional councils. (Alternatively, the reintroduction of PR for general elections would be a huge bonus to the FN!) Moreover, although electoral volatility has so far largely benefited the party, opinion surveys reveal that the majority of FN voters identify primarily with other parties. For instance, only 57 per cent of Le Pen's 1988 presidential voters promised to stick with the FN (Perrineau, 1990). Again, it is at the European level where the movement can anticipate sustenance, notably by opposing proposals to extend immigrant voting and circulation rights and questioning the status of migrants and refugees in the new Europe of the 1990s. Historic French fears of a resurgent united Germany, albeit within a European Community framework, are also there to be exploited, even though this may complicate the FN's Euro-alliance with the equally national-chauvinist German Republican Party. At the national level, too, factors contributing to FN success – immigration, unemployment, insecurity, economic and social crisis – are unlikely to disappear. Provided divisions and political gaffes do not overtake the party, the FN – with or possibly without Le Pen, since the ideas attract as well as the person and personality – appears to have secured a niche on the French and European extreme right.

References

Anderson, M., 1974. *Conservative Politics in France*, Allen and Unwin, London.
Bachelot, F., 1986. *Ne dites pas à ma mére que je suis chez Le Pen, elle me croit au RPR*, Albatros, Paris.

58 *Paul Hainsworth*

Bell, D., 1976. The extreme right in France, in M. Kolinsky and W. E. Paterson, *Social and Political Movements in Western Europe*, Croom Helm, London.
Bergeron, F. and Vilgier, P., 1985. *De Le Pen à Le Pen. Une histoire des nationaux et nationalistes sous la Ve République*, Dominique Martin Morin, Paris.
Borella, F., 1977. *Les partis politiques*, Seuil, Paris.
Borne, D., 1977. *Petits Bourgeois en révolte. Le Mouvement Poujade*, Flammarion, Paris.
Bourseiller, C., 1991. *Extrême Droite*, François Bourin, Paris.
Brunn, P., 1979. *La Nouvelle Droite*, Nouvelles Editions Oswald, Paris.
Burrin, P., 1983. La France dans le champ magnétique des fascismes, *L'Histoire*, No. 61, November.
Burrin, P., 1987. Les racines du mal, *Nouvel Observateur*, 5–11 June.
Buzzi, P., 1991. Le Front national entre national-populisme et extrêmisme de droit, in *Regards sur l'actualité*, No. 169, March, pp. 31–43.
Calderon, D., 1985. *La Droite française*, Editions Sociales, Paris.
Camus, J-Y., 1985. Les familles de l'extrême droite, *Projet* (193), June, pp. 30–8.
Cerny, P., 1982. *Social Movements and Protest in France*, Frances Pinter, London.
Charlot, J., 1984. France, in *Electoral Studies*, 3:3 (1984). 274–7.
Charlot, M., 1986. L'émergence du Front national, *Revue Française de Science Politique*, Vol. 36, No. 1 pp. 30–45.
Chatain, J., 1987. *Les Affaires de M Le Pen*, Editions Messidor, Paris.
Chebel d'Appollonia, A., 1988. *L'Extrême-Droite en France. De Maurras à Le Pen*, Editions Complexe, Brussels.
Chiroux, R., 1974. *L'Extrême-Droite sous la Ve République*, Librairie Générale de Droit et de Jurisprudence, Paris.
Cole, A., 1990. *French Political Parties in Transition*, Dartmouth, Aldershot.
Désir, H., 1985. *Touche pas à mon pote*, Grasset, Paris.
Deutsch, E., Lindon, D., and Weill, P., 1966. *Les Familles Politiques*, Editions du Minuit, Paris.
Duhamel, O., Jaffré, J. (eds), 1989. *L'Etat de l'opinion. Clés pour 1989*, SOFRES/ Seuil, Paris.
Duprat, F., 1972. *Les mouvements d'extrême droite en France depuis 1944*, Albatros, Paris.
Eatwell, R., 1982. Poujadism and neo-Poujadism: from revolt to reconciliation, in P. Cerny, *Social Movements and Protest in France*, Frances Pinter, London.
Goldring, M., 1987. *Comparative Study of Protestant Populism and the Ideology of the French National Front*, Paper presented to Political Studies Association of Ireland Annual Conference, Newcastle, County Down.
Grünberg, G. *et al.*, 1988. Trois candidats, trois droites, trois électorats, l'élection présidentielle, *Le Monde: dossiers et documents*, May.
Hainsworth, P., 1981. A majority for the president: the French left and the 1981 presidential election, *Parliamentary Affairs*, Vol. 32, No. 4, Autumn.
——, 1982. Anti-Semitism and Neo-fascism on the contemporary right, in P. Cerny, *Social Movements and Protest in France*, Frances Pinter, London.
——, 1987. Interviews with French Communist Party representatives/regional councillors, Marseilles, 1987.
——, 1988a. The Re-election of Francois Mitterrand: the 1988 French Presidential Election, *Parliamentary Affairs*, Vol. 41, No. 4, October 1988.
——, 1988b. The triumph of the outsider: Jean-Marie Le Pen and the 1988 presidential election in J. Howorth, and G. Ross, *Contemporary France*, Frances Pinter, London.
——, 1990. France, in J. Lodge (ed), *The 1989 Election of the European Parliament*,

Macmillan, London.

Hainsworth. P. and Loughlin, J., 1989. Coalitions in the new French regions, in C. Mellors and B. Pijnenburg, *Political Parties and Coalitions in European Local Government*, Routledge, London.

Harris, G., 1990. *The Dark Side of Europe. The Extreme Right Today*, Edinburgh University Press, Edinburgh.

Hoffmann, S., 1956. *Le Mouvement Poujade*, A. Colin, Paris.

Hollick, C., 1979. The European Election of 1979 in France: A Masked Ball for 1981, *Parliamentary Affairs*, Vol. 32, No. 4, Autumn.

Husbands, C., 1991. The Support for the *Front National*: analyses and findings, *Ethnic and Racial Studies*, Vol. 14, No. 3, July, pp. 382–416.

Ivaldi, G., 1990. The world as they see it. A study of the ideological adherence to the French National Front, Paper presented to a Workshop on the Extreme Right in Europe at the ECPR Joint Sessions, Bochum, April.

Jaffré, J., 1987. Trois postulats sur l'électorate d'extrême droite. Ne pas se tromper sur M. Le Pen, *Le Monde*, 26 May.

Johnson, D., 1991. The new right in France, in L. Cheles *et al.*, *Neo-Fascism in Europe*, Longman, Harlow.

Le Bras, H., 1986. *Les Trois Frances*, Editions Odile Jacob, Paris.

Le Gallou, J-Y., 1985. *La Préférence Nationale: Réponse à l'Immigration*, Albin Michel, Paris.

Le Pen, J-M., 1984a. *Les Français d'abord*, Carrère-Michel Lafon, Paris.

——, 1984b. Preface, Droite et démocratie économique. Doctrine économique et sociale du Front National, Supplement to *National Hebdo* 10.

——, 1985a. Foreward *Pour la France. Programme du Front National*, Albatros, Paris.

——, 1985b. *La France est de retour*, Carrère-Michel Lafon, Paris.

Lorien, J., Criton, K. and Dumont, S., 1985. *Le système Le Pen*, EPO, Anvers.

Mayer, N., 1989. Le vote FN de Passy à Barbès (1984–1988), in N. Mayer and P. Perrineau, *Le Front national a découvert*, FNSP, Paris.

——, 1991. Le Front National, in D. Chagnollaud (ed), *Bilan Politique de la France*, Hachette, Paris.

Mayer, N. and Perrineau, P., 1989a. *Le Front national a découvert*, FNSP, Paris.

Mayer, N. and Perrineau, P., 1989b. Conclusion. L'introuvable équation Le Pen, in N. Mayer and P. Perrineau, *Le Front National a découvert*, FNSP, Paris.

——, 1990. Why do they vote for the National Front? Paper presented to a Workshop on the Extreme Right in Europe, at the ECPR Joint Sessions April.

Mégret, B., 1990. *La Flamme. Les Voies de la Renaissance*, Robert Laffont, Paris.

Milza, P,, 1987. *Les Fascismes français*, Flammarion, Paris.

Mitra, S., 1988. The National Front in France – a single-issue movement?, in K. von Beyne, Right-wing extremism in Western Europe, Special issue of *West European Politics*, Vol. 11, No. 2.

Orfali, B., 1989. Le droit chemin ou les mécanismes de l'adhésion politique, in N. Mayer and P. Perrineau, *Le Front national a découvert*, FNSP, Paris.

——, 1990. *L'Adhésion au Front National. De la minorité active au mouvement social*, Editions Kimé, Paris.

Petifils, J-C., 1983. *L'Extrême Droite en France*, Presses Universitaires de France, Paris.

Perrineau, P., 1989. Les étapes d'une implantation électorale, in N. Mayer and P. Perrineau, *Le Front national a découvert*, FNSP, Paris.

——, 1990. Le Front national, d'une élection l'autre *Regards sur l'actualité*, No. 161, May.

Platone, F., and Rey, H., 1989. Le FN en terre communiste, in N. Mayer and P. Perrineau, *Le Front national a découvert*, FNSP, Paris.

Plenel, E. and Rollat, A., 1984. L'effet Le Pen, La Découverte/Le Monde, Paris.

Ranger, J., 1989. Le cercle des sympathisants, in N. Mayer and P. Perrineau, *Le Front national a découvert*, FNSP, Paris.

Rémond, R., 1971. *The Right in France from 1814 to De Gaulle*, University of Pennslyvania Press, Philadelphia.

Rollat, A., 1985. *Les hommes de l'extrême droite. Le Pen, Ortiz et les autres*, Calmann-Lévy, Paris.

Schain, M., 1987. The National Front in France and the construction of political legitimacy, *West European Politics*, Vol. 10, No. 2.

——, 1988. Immigration and changes in the French party system, in *European Journal of Political Research*, 16, pp. 597–621.

Shields, J. G., 1989. Campaigning from the fringe: Jean-Marie Le Pen, in J. Gaffney (ed.), *The French Presidential Elections of 1988*, Dartmouth, Aldershot.

Shields, J. G., 1990. A new chapter in the history of the French extreme right: the National Front, in A. Cole (ed.), *French Political Parties in Transition*, Dartmouth, Aldershot.

Soucy, R., 1986. *French Fascism: the First Wave, 1924–1933*, Yale University Press, New Haven.

Sternhell, Z., 1978. *La Droite révolutionnaire 1885–1914, les origines françaises du fascisme*, Seuil, Paris.

——, 1986. *Neither Right Nor Left*, University of California Press, Berkeley.

Stirbois, J.-P. and Jalkh, J.-F., 1985. Dossier immigration, Supplement to *National Hebdo*, No. 61, 19 September.

Stirbois, J.-P., 1988. *Tonnerre de Dreux. L'avenir nous appartient*, Editions National-Hebdo, Paris.

Taguieff, P.-A., 1984. La rhétorique du national-populisme (11), *Mots*, 9, pp. 113–19.

——, 1986. La doctrine du national-populisme en France, *Etudes*, January, 27–46.

Todd, E., 1988. *La nouvelle France*, Seuil, Paris.

Tristan, A., 1987. *Au Front*, Gallimard, Paris.

Vaughan, M., 1987. The wrong right in France, in E. Kolinsky, *Opposition in Western Europe*, Croom Helm, London, pp. 289–317.

Wilkinson, P., 1981. *The New Fascists*, Grant McIntyre, London.

Ysmal, C., 1991. Les cadres du Front national: les habits neufs de l'extrême droite, in O. Duhamel and J. Jaffré, *L'Etat de l'Opinion 1991*, SOFRES/Seuil, Paris, 1991, pp. 181–97.

3 A Future for Right Extremism in Germany?

Eva Kolinsky

Until 1945, nationalist and anti-democratic parties were the dominant political forces in Germany. In Imperial Germany, they constituted the so-called 'national camp' and were aligned with the autocratic and militarist government of the day. In the Weimar Republic, such parties proved strong enough to destroy democracy. National Socialism abolished democratic government and elevated nationalism to the rank of official state ideology. After 1945 the dominant political forces of yesteryear were banned in the East and in the West relegated to the extreme right; and the Catholic and the social democratic opposition to the former 'national camp' shaped post-war politics and relocated its political centre. Although right extremist parties have been represented in West German parliaments only intermittently, they have retained enough electoral potential to be relevant, not least as channels for social and political discontent. Since right extremist parties have once again entered parliamentary politics in the 1980s, it is necessary to examine the political focus and the socio-economic environment which helped mobilize voters and contributed to the success of the extreme right.

The Development of Right Extremism

Broadly speaking, right extremism in the Federal Republic developed in three separate phases and around three different parties or groups of parties: the German Reichs Party (DRP) and the Socialist Reichs Party (SRP) in the late 1940s and early 1950s, the National Democratic Party (NPD) in the 1960s and 1970s, and the Republicans in the 1980s. Each phase has been marked by some parliamentary representation, and a distinctive momentum of extra-parliamentary political activity on the extreme right.

During the first phase of West German right extremism in the 1940s and 1950s, former National Socialists tried to regroup and overcome the ban on National Socialist organizations and aims, which the wartime allies had instituted and which had cushioned the fledgling democracy from anti-democratic ideologies and practices.

Table 3.1   Right extremist votes in the 1949 federal elections

Votes for	Total	Bundestag seats
Independent candidates	893.342	2
Organizations for refugees/war/ denazification damaged	242.305	–
Legalized parties of the extreme right: DReP/DKP; WAV	1.353.830	16
Votes overall	2.495.477 = 10.5%	18

Source: Calculations after Stöss, Parteien Handbuch and Statistische Jahrbücher der Bundesrepublik Deutschland.

In the first Bundestag, 10.5 per cent of the elected delegates represented parties of the extreme right (Table 3.1). Subsequently, no right extremist party won seats in the Bundestag, and early representation in regional parliaments soon disappeared (Table 3.2). The right extremists of the immediate post-war years assumed that a silent majority in the German population was only waiting to speak out again. They misjudged the capacity of the Christian Democrats to incorporate former National Socialists and to absorb the right-wing electorate of the past. Furthermore, the banning in 1952 of the only success story of right extremism in these years, the Socialist Reichs Party, sufficed to cut short its resurgence as a significant force in parliamentary politics.

Two aspects need to be highlighted for this period since they carried over into subsequent decades: the aggressively anti-democratic position adopted by the SRP between 1950 and 1952 captured up to 11 per cent of the vote in regional elections and twenty-two parliamentary seats for a party which made no secret of its complete rejection of parliamentary government and of the Federal Republic as a legitimate German state (Table 3.3). The second aspect concerns the network of associations, newspapers, groups and book clubs which emerged after the parliamentary voice of the extreme right had evaporated (Tauber, 1967). Originally organized by former National Socialists, the network of extra-parliamentary right extremism has since become the political training-ground for neo-Nazis, the post-war newcomers to right extremism.

The second phase of West German right extremism stretched from the mid-1960s to the mid-1980s. At its core were the success and subsequent decline of the National Democratic Party (NPD) as a parliamentary force. More important, however, was the transition within this period of right extremism from a replica ideology of National Socialism or similar vintage to a selective focus on contemporary issues. When the NPD entered seven *Land* parliaments and won sixty-one seats between 1966 and 1968 (Table 3.3), the party had a dual appeal. On the one hand, it was perceived as the party political mouthpiece of the extreme right, the successor organization of the right extremist parties which had declined during the 1950s.

Table 3.2 Results of right extremist political parties in Federal and European elections, 1953–89

Party		Federal Elections		European Elections	
		%	Seats		%	Seats
AUD	1965	0.2	–		
	1976	0.1	–		
DG	1953	0.3	–		
	1957	0.1	–		
	1961	0.1	–		
DRP	1953	1.1	–		
	1957	1.0	–		
	1961	0.8	–		
DVU	1987	0.6	–	1989	1.6	–
FAP	1987	0.0	–	1989	0.1	–
NPD	1965	2.0	–		
	1969	4.3	–		
	1972	0.6	–		
	1976	0.3	–		
	1980	0.2	–		
	1983	0.2	–		
	1987	0.6	–	1984	0.8	–
Republicans	none			1989	7.1	6

Notes:
AUD: Aktion unabhängiger Deutscher; since 1980 part of the Greens, especially in Bavaria.
DG: Deutsche Gemeinschaft, some of it participated in founding the NPD.
DVU: Deutsche Volksunion (Liste D) founded as a political party in 1987 by Dr Gerhard Frey (chairman). The DVU is based on the association of the same name which Frey founded in 1971, affiliated to his mass circulation weekly (120,000 copies) *Deutsche Nationalzeitung*. In the spectrum of the extreme right, the DVU and DNZ are the most important voices of the old right.
DRP: Deutsche Reichspartei; successor organization of the Deutsche Rechts Partei/Deutsch Konservative Partei, DReP/DKP which had won 5 seats in the Bundestag and split into DRP and the SRP.
FAP: Freiheitliche Deutsche Arbeiterpartei, an extreme right party founded in 1984.
NPD: founded in 1964, based on the DRP, the conservative Deutsche Partei, a section of the DG and others to provide a new party political focal point on the extreme right.
Republicans: founded in 1983.
Sources: Richard Stöss, Parteien Handbuch, Vol. 1, 1983, 242–3; and own calculations.

Analyses of the party élite and of the party programme indicated that this perception was accurate, with a high degree of continuity between the right extremism of the 1950s and that of the mid-1960s (Stöss, 1983). On the other hand, the NPD had only been founded at the end of 1964 by merging right extremist and conservative groupings. To the electorate, therefore, it could appear as a new political force. Studies of the electoral support for the NPD in the 1960s have revealed two distinct sources: about half of the voters were ideological voters, adherents of right extremist views and former voters of

Table 3.3   Right extremists in *Land* parliaments since 1946

Party	In existence	Total no. of seats *Land* Parl.	Bundestag
DG	1949–65	22	0
DReP/DKP	1946–50	0	5
DRP	1950–65	10	0
NPD	1964 to date	61	0
SRP	1949–52	24	0
WAV*	1946–53	13	12
Republicans	1983 to date	11	0
		(Euro 6)	

Note: WAV: Wiederaufbau Vereinigung, a right extremist party which existed only in Bavaria. For other acronyms see notes to Table 3.2.

Sources: as for table 3.2.

similar parties; the other half were voters who feared unemployment or economic uncertainties during the first economic recession since post-war reconstruction. Most of these voters perceived the NPD as a protest force, a party against the system. They had neither read its programme nor defined their own political position as right extremist (Nagle, 1970, pp. 124f). Once the economy stabilized, the NPD vote regressed to its extremist core. In 1969, the party nearly entered the Bundestag with 4.3 per cent – just short of the 5 per cent quota necessary for representation. After that, its support dropped to about 0.2 per cent with only pockets of representation remaining at a local level (Kolinsky, 1984, p. 266).

In its social composition, the NPD vote pointed to one important change: although right extremism had in the past been supported by the middle or lower middle class, working-class voters were now more strongly represented. To be more specific, the NPD attracted electoral support from trained craftsmen in blue-collar occupations, notably non-unionized and predominantly from small towns or rural areas. The majority of NPD voters, however, were at least middle-aged; the post-war generations had not been reached. Within the NPD radical and even terrorist groupings emerged – the Aktion Widerstand, the Young National Democrats – to agitate against the *Ostpolitik* of the early 1970s (Stöss, 1989). Where the NPD failed, the radical and extra-parliamentary successor organizations succeeded in winning support among the post-war generations.

Throughout the 1970s neo-Nazi groups attracted young people, predominantly from the working class. At the end of the decade, although right extremism had lost its parliamentary representation, it developed a two-pronged organizational structure which bridged the generations and combined conventional right extremism with a radicalized protest culture of the extreme right. The 'old right' was represented by the NPD, by the *Deutsche Nationalzeitung*, which, having a circulation of 120,000 weekly copies, was the largest paper on the extreme right; by a network of groups such as the

German Peace Union or the Freedom Council under the control of the editor of the *Deutsche Nationalzeitung*, Gerhard Frey: and by a host of other groups, book clubs and publishing-houses, many of them dating back to the 1950s. Although these groups continued to aim at rehabilitating National Socialism, the neo-Nazi groups of the period adopted a more radical approach and frequently used political violence. Criminal offences with right extremist motives soared and changed in nature: in the 1950s and early 1960s, anti-Semitic daubing was the most common type of offence; now it was more generally directed against foreigners, and physical attacks, arson and murder increased sharply. Between 1969 and 1989, criminal offences with right extremist motives rose by 150 per cent (Betrifft, 1969 and following years).

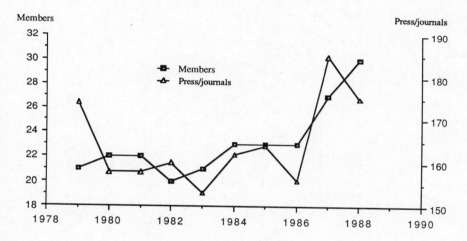

Figure 3.1 Membership and journal or newspaper publications of right extremist organizations, 1979–88 (in 1,000.)

Note: the membership data include all groups and parties surveyed by the Office for the Protection of the Constitution, including the NPD and the DVU. Publication figures for newspapers and journals are calculated for regular weekly editions. In fact, many appear only three or four times a year. In 1988 seventy-three publications in this category were printed with a total of 8,882,200 copies.

The third phase of West German right extremism commenced in the mid-1980s. At the extra-parliamentary level the associations, action groups, book clubs and publishing ventures of the extreme right enjoyed rising member-ships or circulation figures (see Figure 3.1 and below), a trend which has been exacerbated since unification. More significantly, the extreme right made some headway in the 1980s at electoral level. In January 1989 the Republikaner (Republicans) won 6 per cent of the vote and eleven seats in the *Land* parliament in Berlin (West) and in June 1989 entered the European Parliament with six MEPs and 7.1 per cent of the vote (Table 3.4). Local

Table 3.4 Voting in the federal elections 1987 and the European elections 1989 by parties and regions (in %)

Region	Election/ Year	Election Turnout	Greens	Rep.	NPD/ DVU	SPD	CDU/ CSU	FDP
FRG	E89	62.9	37.3	37.8	5.6	8.4	7.1	1.6
	BT87[1]	84.3	37.0	44.3	9.1	8.3	–	0.6
Schleswig-Holstein	E89	58.5	44.4	36.4	5.3	6.7	4.6	1.3
	BT87	84.4	39.8	41.9	9.4	8.0	–	0.5
Hamburg	E89	56.6	41.9	31.5	6.2	11.5	6.0	1.5
	BT87	83.0	41.2	37.4	9.2	11.0	–	0.4
Lower Saxony	E89	63.3	42.0	35.9	5.8	8.4	4.8	1.6
	BT87	85.0	41.4	41.5	8.8	7.4	–	0.5
Bremen	E89	58.7	46.4	23.3	7.0	13.8	4.4	3.2
	BT87	82.7	46.5	28.9	8.8	14.5	–	0.5
North Rh.-Westfalia	E89	62.4	43.6	35.2	5.7	7.9	4.1	1.3
	BT87	85.4	43.2	40.1	8.4	7.5	–	0.4
Hesse	E89	60.2	40.5	33.2	5.5	9.9	6.5	2.3
	BT87	85.7	38.7	41.3	9.1	9.4	–	0.8
Rhineld.-Palat.	E89	78.0	40.2	38.8	5.7	7.3	4.6	1.5
	BT87	86.7	37.1	45.1	9.1	7.5	–	0.7
Baden-Württbg	E89	58.4	29.1	39.3	7.2	10.0	8.7	2.4
	BT87	83.1	29.3	46.7	12.0	10.0	–	1.0
Bavaria	E89[2]	61.1	24.2	45.4	4.0	7.8	14.6	1.0
	BT87	81.7	27.0	55.1	8.1	7.7	–	0.6
Saar	E89	78.8	45.3	34.5	4.8	6.2	5.8	1.3
	BT87	87.3	43.5	41.2	6.9	7.1	–	0.8
Berlin[3]	LT89	78.3	37.3	37.7	3.9	11.8	7.5	–[4]
	LT85	82.6	32.4	46.4	8.5	10.6	–	–

Differences E89/BT87

	Election Turnout	SPD	CDU/ CSU	FDP	Greens	Rep.	NPD/ DVU
in %	-25.98	0.81	-14.67	-38.46	1.20	100	166.67
in 1,000	-9,713	-3,502	-6,103	-1,865	-745	2,005	218

Notes:
1. BT= Federal Elections (*Bundestagswahl*) 25 January 1987.
2. In the Bavarian *Land* elections on 14 October 1990, the Republican Party gained its best result since 1989 (4.9%).
3. In 1989 the Berlin Agreement was still in force, and the *Land* did not vote in federal or European elections; according to size of party representation, elected members of the *Land* parliament were delegated to serve in the national or European parliaments. Since unification, Berlin is a bona fide *Bundesland*.
4. The Western Allies refused permission to the NPD (and its current partner, DVU) to compete in elections in Berlin.

Sources: data compiled from Eike Hennig and Manfried Kieserling, Aktuelle Wahlerfolge kleiner Rechtsparteien in der Bundesrepublik, in *Gewerkschaftliche Monatshefte*, No.9, 1989, 524, 526; and Horst Schmollinger, Die Wahl zum Berliner Abgeordnetenhaus, in *Zeitschrift für Parlamentsfragen*, No.3, 1989, 313, 316.

elections in March and June 1989 resulted in similar gains for the extreme right – for the NPD in Frankfurt, where the Republicans had few candidates, and the Republicans in Rhineland Palatinate and in the Saar region. After a surge in 1989, the Republican vote collapsed when unification redrafted the German political agenda. As a potential electoral and political force, however, the extreme right holds a place in the institutional setting of unified Germany.

Right Extremism: the Contemporary Setting

The Republicans made their political gains at a time when party systems in many Western European democracies became more diversified with small parties challenging established electoral hegemonies (von Beyme, 1985, pp. 276ff). Two special developments in the German party system of the 1980s suggest that a parliamentary party on the extreme right could play a more visible role than in the 1950s or 1960s. First, both main political parties, the Christian Democratic Union/Christian Social Union (CDU/CSU) and Social Democratic Party (SPD), have lost electoral support and increasingly depend on coalition governments at national and regional level to command parliamentary majorities. Translated to the national level, the outcome of the 1989 European elections suggested that neither of the two main parties would have been able to secure a parliamentary majority in a coalition with just one small party.

Coalition governments have, of course, been established practice in German democracy. They tended to include one small party, normally the Free Democratic Party (FDP) and to be orientated towards the centre (Schmidt, 1983; Smith, 1986). Since the mid-1980s the composition of coalitions has become less predictable as small parties take a larger share of the vote (Padgett and Burkett, 1986). Coalitions between SPD and Greens suggest that a position off-centre cannot be ruled out: to the left in the case of SPD and Greens; to the right if the Republicans or a similar party were to be included. Before unification, the West German electorate had shown itself more willing to support new parties or change established preferences; therefore, established majorities were no longer certain and coalition opportunities were prone to arise quickly for newcomer parties (Smith and Paterson 1989). The first taste of free elections in the former German Democratic Republic (GDR) served to strengthen the centre and consolidate the established parties, notably the party of government at the national level, the Christian Democratic Union. On the left, successor parties of the citizens' opposition against state socialism secured some parliamentary representation, and the extreme right remained well below the parliamentary threshold of 5 per cent (Table 3.5). In electoral terms, therefore, German unification has reinforced the predominance of the major parties and reversed the recent trends in West German politics.

The second special development can be summed up as a trend towards issue politics. Since the early 1970s the broad church approach to policy

Table 3.5   Electoral performance of the extreme right in the new *Länder* (former GDR)

Election	Party	%
A. *Land* elections, 14.10.1990		
Brandenburg	Rep.	1.1
Mecklemburg-Vorpommern	Rep.	0.9
Sachsen-Anhalt	Rep.	0.6
Saxony	NPD	0.7
Thuringia	Rep.	0.8
B. *Land* election 2.12.1990		
Berlin (East+West)	Rep.	3.1
C. Federal Election, 2.12.1990		
Former West Germany	Rep.	2.3
Former East Germany	Rep.	1.3
FRG overall	Rep.	2.4

Sources: Summary of results in *Zeitschrift für Parlamentsfragen*, No.1, 1991, 16–20; Irving and Paterson, in *Parliamentary Affairs*, Vol.44, No.3 1991, 366; Wahlen '90 in Berlin, Amtliches Endergebnis.

articulation, which has been the hallmark of the West German catch-all parties (*Volksparteien*) no longer satisfied expectations of specific policy changes. Citizens' initiatives, new social movements and the Green Party built their political role on specific issues which seemed to be bypassed by mainstream parties and parliaments (Hülsberg, 1988). With parties no longer able to ignore public sentiments at the risk of losing voters, the articulation of issues inside and outside parliaments by Greens and social movements has been an effective lever of policy change (Raschke 1985, Roth and Rucht, 1988). Provided that a party of the extreme right – be it the Republicans, the NPD or a similar group – can establish itself as a political force which might win enough votes to matter, they can expect to influence the political agenda even if they do not achieve parliamentary representation. Since a small change in party fortunes can unseat a government and elevate an opposition, a party need not score 5 or more per cent to influence German politics: a 2 per cent shift could already be decisive, and render such an electoral potential a political trump card. To this extent, the starting-position of any party of the extreme right today is stronger than that of the NPD in the 1960s. Then, the integrative capacity of the two main parties was still on the increase; now it is on the decline, notwithstanding that unification has reduced the speed of this decline. In the early 1970s CDU/CSU and SPD together won well over 90 per cent of the vote and issue politics or the new viability of small parties had yet to emerge. At the threshold of the 1990s, CDU/CSU and SPD together command 75–80 per cent of the vote, leaving more potential scope for others, including parties of the extreme right. (Irving and Paterson, 1991, p. 370).

The Republicans: the Party and its Voters

The Republican Party (Die Republikaner) was founded in 1983 as a break-away group from the CSU and as a protest against the leading role played by Franz Josef Strauß in negotiating special credits to the GDR. During the first years of its organizational existence it seemed fully preoccupied with infight-ing and court proceedings between the three founders – a battle finally won in 1985 by Franz Schönhuber, the present party chairman. Schönhuber had a varied political history. In the 1940s he had been a member of the Waffen SS, in the late 1960s he joined the SPD, and in the 1970s he changed to the CSU. Having made his name as a journalist and producer for Bavarian television, he was tipped as a future producer-in-chief. In 1982, though, he was dismissed from his post. After glorifying the Waffen SS in his memoirs – *Ich war dabei* [I was there] – , Schönhuber had become a liability (*Der Spiegel*, 22, 1989; Leggewie, 1989). He did, however, receive DM 300,000 in com-pensation which allowed him to live in comfort and engage in his political activities. By November 1989 his book had been published in its twelfth edition and in paperback.

National Socialist leanings like those of Schönhuber have been common-place among the leading circles of right extremist parties in West Germany. What sets him apart is his flair for the media and an ease of communication not commonly found among the heavy ideologues of the extreme right. Schönhuber was able to create the impression that the political aims of his party were altogether more contemporary and less stagnant than those of the 'old right', a variant of conservatism rather than of right extremism (Die REP, 1989, pp. 6ff).

After a modest start in Bavaria, the party established *Land* organizations throughout the Federal Republic by November 1989, increasing its member-ship from 9,000 to 14,000 within a year (Lepszy, 1989, p. 3). However, the Republicans proved unable to consolidate their electoral position. In the Berlin elections held in December 1990 after unification, the Republicans lost their seats; in the Bavarian *Land* elections (October 1990), they nar-rowly missed representation with 4.9 per cent of the vote; and despite a groundswell of right extremism in the political culture of the former GDR, the Republicans did not enter a single one of the new *Land* parliaments or, indeed, the new German Bundestag (Table 3.5).

Similar to the NPD in the 1960s, the Republicans recruited two sets of members. On the one hand, they attracted what I like to call the consoli-dated right, i.e. former NPD functionaries, often with their own National Socialist or SS past and neo-Nazi activities. Many of these again held party posts in the Republican Party. On the other hand, many of the new members had no right extremist history or previous party commitment, joining the Republicans simply to change the style or direction of contem-porary politics. In the NPD, the duality of traditional right extremists in the membership and especially in leadership positions and the new members with new motivations to effect changes led to a detachment of the leadership from the rank and file, and a radicalization towards neo-Nazism, above all among younger NPD members (Kolinsky, 1984, p. 268f). Among the

Republicans, a similar pattern has been apparent. The organizational and electoral decline of the party has been complemented by an increase in neo-Nazism from around 2,000 to at least twice that number of organized members and an estimated 15,000 followers in the new German *Länder* alone (Betrifft, 1990).

The Social Basis of Right Extremism

Despite their short-lived electoral successes, the social composition of the party's electorate can help us to understand the social base of right extremism and its electoral potential in the Germany of the 1990s. Like the NPD, the Republicans obtained their best results in the south and among men (see Tables 3.4 and 3.12) Whereas the NPD fared best in rural areas and medium-sized towns, the Republicans have been stronger in large cities. In Berlin, gains were largest in working-class districts where people had shifted from the SPD towards the CDU since the mid-1970s and now began to look towards the Republicans. The inner-city area; with sizeable immigrant populations or high unemployment were not th: main areas of Republican support, but rather the established, modest, residential districts or suburbs, the *Viertel der kleinen Leute* (Schmollinger, 1989, p. 319). These are the people with no more than basic education, the blue-collar workers or low-status employees. Members of the police force – allegedly disappointed with the government's leniency towards former terrorists and their perceived indecision in matters of law and order – figure strongly among Republican voters and members.

Traditional cleavage lines of electoral behaviour do not fully apply to the Republicans: trade union membership, which has been linked to a preference for the SPD, does not appear to prevent a preference for the Republicans (Henning and Kieserling, 1989, pp. 524ff). A second cleavage line, religious observance, does apply. Although Catholics outnumber Protestants in the Republican electorate, it would be wrong to conclude that Catholics are more inclined towards the Republicans. In the 1989 European elections, for instance, the party won more than half of its votes in Bavaria and Baden-Württemberg. Both are predominantly Catholic regions, which explains the numerical strength of Catholic Republican voters. Denomination itself seems less significant than intensity: among active church-goers, Republicans have won below-average support (Niedermayer, 1990, p. 580). In other words, those Catholics who have opted for the Republicans have lost their close affinity to the church amidst a broader trend towards a secular society in West Germany. Secularization, it has been argued, detaches the individual from established institutions and customs whose integrative function may not be replaced (Alber, 1989). As we shall see later, the changes in the social environment had a similar effect of disrupting traditional expectations and spreading uncertainties about status and personal prospects among the so-called *kleine Leute*, who constitute the core of the Republican vote.

The electoral potential of the Republican Party rests on a sense of disappointment with established parties, the focus on national and especially xenophobic issues and the fear of modernization among the bottom third in Germany's affluent and educated society. The party has been perceived as a new venture close to but not part of the extreme right with a leader who has been more articulate and effective through the media than other would-be leaders of the extreme right. This has helped the Republicans to turn electoral potential into actual votes. Republican support cuts across party lines with sizeable gains from CDU, CSU, SPD and also from the silent clientele of non-voters. The political background of Republican voters varies between regions and localities. In Bavaria or Berlin, for instance, losses were heaviest for the Christian Democrats; in North Rhine – Westphalia, the Republicans won support from the Social Democrats. Two examples from the European elections illustrate the diversity of Republican support. In the Bavarian town of Rosenheim, where CSU lists had in the past pushed towards the 70 per cent mark, the Republicans gained 22 per cent. In a northern suburb of Dortmund, an SPD stronghold, the Republicans gained nearly 10 per cent, although in the region as a whole, they failed to clear the 5 per cent hurdle. Rosenheim is one of the most affluent localities in the Federal Republic with, so it is said, the highest concentration of Porsche cars per inhabitant. As a coal and steel town, Dortmund, by contrast, has been badly hit by the crisis in the industry and mass redundancies at Hoesch, the major employer in the area. Although the personal circumstances of the Republican voters in Rosenheim and Dortmund were as different as their previous party orientations had been, their personal perceptions of economic and social uncertainties were similar. Both adopted the perspective of *die Betroffenen* [the personally affected]. Voting Republican followed from a subjective sense of losing out. Where political milieux and social networks may have offered personal reference points and shaped party preferences in the past, issues have gained the upper hand and made party preferences more volatile. More than ever, they reflect personalized perceptions. Programmatic or ideological details, therefore, are less relevant to explaining the aims and success of right extremism than its place in the political culture and its proximity to popular attitudes.

Right Extremism and Political Culture

When the Federal Republic was created in the late 1940s, one of the lessons learnt from the destruction of the Weimar Republic and the dictatorship of National Socialism was the need to safeguard democratic institutions against anti-democratic forces of any political persuasion. Allied prerogatives to license political parties, electoral hurdles to reduce political splintering and the democracy clause in the Basic Law together underlined the resolve to prevent a repetition of National Socialism and nip any successor movements in the bud. The allegiance of the élites to the new democratic polity and neo-corporatist decision-making generated a framework for stable government and facilitated a change of political culture (Edinger, 1988; Merkl, 1989).

Right extremism with its core themes of nationalism, racism and authoritarian leadership had been official government policy under National Socialism (Eatwell and O'Sullivan, 1989). Recasting the political system into a democracy meant recasting the policies and reshaping popular value orientations at a time when they could not have been modified substantively by new social or political experiences.

In Germany, the dividing-line between right extremist and democratic political orientations consists, above all, of the endorsement of or detachment from National Socialism. As we shall see later, detachment itself has not been unequivocal. However, the extreme right in all its variations – from old to new right, from post-fascist to neo-fascist – has been unified by its nationalism and racism, its refusal to accept the political, social or personal consequences of the Second World War, including the existence of the Federal Republic as a state *sui generis* and, not least, its refusal to recognize the criminal, terrorist nature and actions of National Socialism (Dudek, 1984; Feit, 1987). The denial that the Holocaust happened or allegations that the Allies constructed the death camps to slander Germany are just two examples which set the discourse of the extreme right apart from the official political culture of the recast democracy of the post-war era (Paul, 1989). Studies of right extremism have tended to focus on the organized and self-confessed extreme right to determine its scope and significance (overview in Backes and Jesse, 1989), and they have centred on the potential for right extremism in Western Germany. That orientations towards the extreme right and a fervent neo-Nazi potential should have survived the prescribed anti-fascism of East German state socialism has been one of the shock discoveries of German unification. The spread of a neo-Nazi and skinhead protest culture in the new federal states still bears the hallmarks of defiance against the system of yesteryear, a system whose security machine is said to have financed right extremism in the West in an attempt to discredit capitalism as intrinsically fascist. More important, however, is the question of the extent to which right extremism relates to the socio-economic and political situation of Germans since unification and whether its themes find echoes in the mainstream political culture.

Attitudes in Transition

In East Germany, the rapid installation of a socialist system created a dual political culture of public subservience and a persistence of views and attitudes of a pre-socialist type. Since *Ostpolitik* improved East–West communication, Western lifestyles modelled East German expectations, though the emphasis was, above all, on affluence and consumerism, not on patterns of political participation. As mentioned earlier, anti-system protest in the East seized on aspects which the socialist state culture was eager to ban and neo-Nazi activity featured here.

Only in the West did political detachment and containment of post-war right extremism occur. Uncertain about the depth of democratic commitment among West Germans, the Americans in particular conducted regular surveys of public opinion in the 1940s and 1950s which suggested that one in three adults at the time held anti-democratic attitudes and showed little interest in the political changes that took place (Merritt and Merritt, 1980). Ten years later, Almond and Verba's study of the civic culture revealed that West Germans had come to accept democracy in a pragmatic fashion as a set of rules to be followed. They also highlighted the integrative power of economic success which played a major role in persuading a disillusioned, politically disorientated population to throw their lot in with democracy (Almond and Verba, 1963). When Conradt 'revisited' the German civic culture in the early 1980s, he found that pragmatic conformity had given way to an endorsement of democratic values and a preference for democratic practices (Conradt, 1980). Generally speaking, Germans today declare themselves satisfied with their political system and the number of people who still look towards a one-party state, or a leader in times of crisis, has declined sharply, in particular among the post-war generations (Kaase, 1989). Even among former citizens of the GDR, who are keenly aware of being the poorer cousins and feel under threat of unemployment and the socio-economic uncertainties of competitive capitalism, support for the new political system in which they find themselves is stronger than its rejection.

The democratic political culture has been based on the implication that post-war Germany commenced at zero hour in 1945. The task which in German has been called *Aufarbeitung der Vergangenheit* [destroying the trappings of anti-democratic politics by facing up to their inhumanity and by finding the culprits] has not been embraced as an aspect of turning towards democracy in the West or the self-styled socialist democracy of the East. In the systems of both Germanys, normalization proceeded apace. In the West, denazification as an organized programme to cleanse the élites of former National Socialists was resented from the start as a bureaucratic witch-hunt, which collapsed in mountains of paperwork and special hearings once the administration was passed on to the German authorities. Similarly, the early resolve to bring the Nazi criminals to justice stagnated after the Nuremberg trials and German courts were put in charge (Götz, 1986). Given that more than 10 million people fell victim to National Socialist persecutions and mass murder, the number of sentences seems pitiful (see Table 3.6). In the East, early purges generated their own myth that the National Socialist past belonged to the West, and the East Germans had no legacy to bear from it.

Generally, Germans believe widely that other countries committed equally horrendous crimes. In 1989 a majority from all political persuasions – with the exception of Green supporters – declared themselves in favour of 'closing the books on [their] past since equally bad things happened elsewhere' (Emnid, 1989, p. 154). Earlier, the late ex-chairman of the CSU, Franz Josef Strauß, had already called for an 'amnesty' and 'an end to the time for repentance' [Ende der Büßerzeit] (*The Times*, 16 August 1978). This kind of rehabilitation of the past is one of the set pieces of public opinion and of contemporary right extremism. In a similar vein, recent dispute among West German historians discounts the severity of National Socialist crimes and tends to excuse them by reference to the misdeeds of other nations or regimes.

Table 3.6   Nazi criminals before West German courts, 1945–85

	Total	%	
Prosecution files opened against individuals	90 921	100	
Sentences passed	6,479	7.1	
Cases not (yet) tried in court	84,442	92.9	
Types of sentences	*Total*	*% of all cases*	*% of sentences*
Death penalty*	12	0.01	0.1
Life sentence	160	0.2	2.5
Other imprisonment	6 192	6.8	95.7
Fine	114	0.1	1.7
Warning according to juvenile law	1	*	*

Note: *Figures are too small to calculate percentages.
Source: adapted from Richard Stöss, Politics against Democracy. *Right-Wing Extremism in West Germany*, German Studies Series Berg, Oxford, 1991.

In public education, the task of critically examining National Socialism has also been largely ignored (Renn, 1987). Young people's views about the past have mostly been shaped in the home: parents rather than schools, personal recollections rather than scholarly studies have played a formative role in creating a dual political culture of general democratic orientations and a selective emphasis on presumably good aspects of National Socialism. In 1977 Dieter Boßmann asked West German secondary school students to write an essay on 'What I have heard about Hitler'. He found astounding gaps in students' knowledge alongside persistent beliefs that the war interrupted what had essentially been positive government under Hitler (Boßmann, 1977). These sentiments were echoed during the official commemoration of the fiftieth anniversary of the 1938 November pogroms, which was held in the Bundestag in 1988. The then Speaker of the House, Philip Jenninger, drew a vivid picture of improved living conditions, reduced unemployment and the 'amazing successes of Hitler' (*Die Welt*, 12 November 1988, p. 6):

Of course, some cantankerous characters kept on nagging and were prosecuted by the Security Police and the Gestapo but most Germans – from all social classes, the bourgeoisie as much as the working class – would have believed in 1938 that Hitler could be regarded as the greatest statesman of our history.

Delivered from the lectern of the Bundestag, Jenninger's empathy with National Socialism caused acute political embarrassment and led to his resignation. In substance, however, Jenninger's approach was close to popular perceptions of National Socialism in West Germany, although élite opinion has tended to be more critical (Hoffmann-Lange, 1987). When Jenninger used Nazi terms like *Rassenschande* [racial offence] or quoted from Himmler's infamous Posen speech to explain the sentiments of the SS at work in the concentration camps and ghettos, he did what scores of school textbooks and other educational tools have done for decades: he referred to National Socialism as a separate, cohesive world in National Socialism's own language and in its own terms of reference – i.e. West German pupils learn how National Socialism justified itself and its actions, not how detached criticism should be defined and formulated (Kolinsky, 1989).

In German political culture, a positive evaluation of certain aspects of National Socialism has existed side by side with democratic orientations.[1] This duality is an important precondition for right extremism. For example, popular beliefs that Hitler could be ranked among the greatest statesmen weakened in the 1950s though they have hardly changed since the 1960s (see Table 3.7). In 1989, 38 per cent of West Germans thought Hitler might be counted among the top statesmen. Table 3.8 shows that those with lower levels of education and with party preferences right of centre tend to hold more favourable views about Hitler than the better educated, or SPD, *Free Democrat Party* (FDP) and Green voters. Answers to the question of whether National Socialism should be regarded as mostly good or mostly bad match party divides, and can cast some light on the spread of opinions about the past: the left–right divide is also a divide about evaluating National Socialism (see Table 3.9) In 1989 just over half of the West German population regarded National Socialism as mainly negative; those right of centre tended to emphasize 'good sides', those left of centre 'bad sides'. Greens and Republicans are clearly juxtaposed in their views of the past: 81 per cent of Green voters rejected National Socialism as bad, 79 per cent of Republican voters accepted it as partly or wholly good. In 1981 the Sinus study found that some 5 million West Germans hoped for the return of a politician like Hitler, 13 per cent could be classified as ardent right extremists according to their views about political and social matters at the time, and a further 37 per cent were just as firmly positioned on the political right (Sinus, 1981). The older generations who received their personal socialization in traditional family environments and their political socialization during the period of National Socialism or earlier were more prone to hold right extremist views than post-war generations. Anti-Semitic incidents in 1959/60 first drew attention to the fact that some right extremists were young West Germans without personal memories or formative experiences beyond the Federal Republic. For these new recruits, right extremism has been a vehicle of political protest and their affinity to National Socialism a deliberate detachment from the democratic organizations and processes of the environment in which they grew up (Stöss, 1986). In 1987, a survey of 16–17 year olds concluded that 16 per cent held right extremist views: certainly right extremism has been widespread among young football fans and skinheads (Heitmeyer, 1987; Heitmeyer and Peter, 1988). On a more casual level, Dudek observed a proliferation of racialist jokes in West German schools and the skilful adjustment of right extremist media to environmentalist concerns and informal communication styles of the young (Dudek and Jaschke, 1981). At the very least, right extremism has survived among post-war generations and in contemporary political culture as an acceptable way of articulating protest.

Table 3.7   Hitler – without the war, one of the greatest German statesmen (1955–89*)?

Question: Everything which had been built up between 1933 and 1939 and much more has been destroyed through the war. Would you say that but for the war Hitler would have been one of the greatest German statesmen?

*Question in 1989: Would you say that but for the war and the persecution of the Jews, Hitler would have been one of the greatest German statesmen

	1955	1960	1964	1967	1972	1975	1978	1989
Yes	48	34	29	32	35	38	31	38
No	36	43	44	52	49	44	44	60
No answer	16	23	27	16	16	18	25	2

Source: Institut für Demoskopie, *Demokratieverankerung in der Bundesrepublik. Ein empirische Untersuchung zum 30 jährigen Bestehen der Bundesrepublik*, Allensbach, 1979, 96; *Der Spiegel*, No.15, 1989, 151.

Table 3.8   Hitler – without the war and the persecution of the Jews, one of the greatest statesmen?

By party preference*	
CDU/CSU voters	47
SPD voters	32
FDP voters	29
Green voters	18
Republican voters	67
By educational background *	
Basic Education (Haupt/Volksschule)	45
Intermediate Education (Mittlere Reife)	34
Advanced Education (Abitur or higher)	22

Note: *Only 'yes' options reported.
Source: Institut für Demoskopie, published in *Der Spiegel*, No.15, 1989, 151.

Right Extremism in a Changing Society

In the 1950s the decline of right extremism into a subculture of extra-parliamentary activity occurred against the national backcloth of social integration and economic success. West Germans of all social strata experi-

Table 3.9 National Socialism: good or bad?

	Bad	More bad than good	Mostly good	Good
West Germans overall	16	38	43	3
By party preference:				
CDU/CSU voters	9	36	51	4
SPD voters	19	41	39	1
FDP voters	16	51	31	1
Green voters	50	31	18	1
Republican voters	2	19	64	15

Source: Emnid Institut, Die Einstellungen der Bundesbürger zum Nationalsozialismus, quoted in *Der Spiegel*, No.15, 1989, 151.

enced marked improvements in their standard of living. Former National Socialists who had been demoted regained their positions and benefited from a climate in which the past tended to be ignored. For the older generations, circumstances had prescribed lifestyles, educational opportunities and employment. By contrast, the post-war generations began to enjoy choices and fashioned their lives according to their interests and abilities.

The social and economic conditions of right extremist political parties have not been analysed thoroughly since the brief successes of the NPD. As a new party with parliamentary representation, however, the Greens have attracted a significant body of research, which provides some information on the social basis of small parties in general in contemporary politics. The Greens made the transition from extra-parliamentary movement to party when they mobilized a specific clientele: a milieu of educated, urban, middle-class voters of the post-war generations who appear to share specific values and critical views of contemporary society (Veen, 1989a). Protest voters who cast their vote for a small party in order to register their negative views of the main party choices, have played a part in the Green success although do not constitute the core of their support (Feist and Krieger, 1987; Bürklin, 1988).

For the emergence of the Green 'milieu' two aspects of social change have been of central importance: educational and professional qualifications improved markledly, and unemployment re-emerged as an endemic problem of West German society [after the oil crisis of 1973]. The mismatch of occupational motivation or expectations, on the one hand, and employment opportunities, on the other, has been a breeding-ground for the disaffection among the well-educated which has characterized the Green 'milieu'.

Modernisierungsverlierer

At the other end of the educational range, problems are different but no less severe. The influx of highly educated people into the labour market has raised employers' expectations about qualifications and made it more diffi-cult for the less well-educated to secure training or employment. Those who obtain qualifications are often confined to the craft sector (*Handwerk*) where employment opportunities have been diminishing. Moreover, many young people with only basic education have been unable to obtain vocatio-nal training. In an economic culture which requires vocational qualifications for any type of skilled work, young people at the bottom of the educational ladder have been confined to unskilled or semi-skilled jobs. In this sector of the labour market, unemployment has always been a threat. Now, new technologies and the shift towards managerial tasks and advanced technical skills have threatened whole occupational sectors with a relative loss of qualifications and occupational status. A new polarization has begun to emerge between hi-tech specialists who are irreplaceable and the semi-skilled whose jobs may disappear as a result of new technology or whose tasks could easily be carried out by somebody else (Kern and Schumann, 1984). Technological modernization has been particularly rapid during the period of the CDU/CSU government since 1982, not least in anticipation of the intensified competition in a Single European Market after 1992 (Alber, 1989). Moreover, unification has rendered most of the former East German population *Modernisierungsverlierer* for whom the collapse of political institutions entailed an unexpected collapse of economic and social prospects (Habich *et al* 1991, pp. 27–32).

The *Modernisierungsverlierer*, those who feel threatened by technological innovation and the erosion of traditional qualifications, occupational recog-nition and work processes, are the potential clientele of the extreme right today (Table 3.10). Losing out through modernization is, above all, a subjective view. In comparison with other sectors or groups in society, those at the bottom of the educational ladder and at risk of de-skilling may regard themselves as disadvantaged in their income, lifestyle and opportunities even though their situation would count as advantageous in other countries. Although Germany has emerged as one of the wealthiest societies in Western Europe, internal divisions between 'Wessies and Ossies', i.e. people living in the West and those living in the East and more generally, divisions between rich and poor, have largely persisted. Today's poor are richer than yesterday's poor; however, the gap between them and their wealthier neigh-bours has not diminished (Hradil, 1987; Glatzer, 1984, pp. 45ff). An esti-mated one in three West Germans has been excluded from the affluence which has become the hallmark of the country (Beck, 1986). Unemploy-ment, whose material impact should be cushioned by the welfare state, has in fact created a new kind of poverty among those who lost their entitlement to benefit, whose benefits were reduced or who, as unemployed school-leavers, failed to qualify for benefit (*Die neue Armut*, 1983). In the former GDR, the worst effects of unemployment have been lessened by transitional welfare measures, though they will be felt in full force as special programmes are phased out. For West Germany, the social and economic successes of more education, qualifications, income levels, productivity or general economic performance generated a two-thirds society where one-third have been bypassed or feel they have been bypassed (Feist, 1989). The accession of the former GDR extended this two-thirds society into the new *Länder*. This is the milieu for contemporary right extremism.

The Social Detachment of the *Volksparteien*

The established parties themselves contributed to the emergence of 'alternative' milieus at both ends of the political spectrum. For the left, it has been shown that issues, styles of participation and expectations of democratic accountability did not appear to be met by a party culture based on hierarchies and well-entrenched party élites, fearful of anything except the broad church approach of a catch-all party, and competing on similar policies and in similar ways for the electoral middle ground.

Since the mid-1970s, views and attitudes have changed in two directions: among the educated and qualified they shifted towards the left; at the opposite end of the social and educational spectrum, they shifted towards the right. Studies of adolescents and young adults found that right extremist or authoritarian views, which had almost disappeared in the student population, were commonplace among semi-skilled or unskilled young workers and apprentices (Castner and Castner, 1989). Many of these young people tended to abstain in elections; some turned to the Greens to voice their discontent (Hofmann-Göttig, 1989a, pp. 13ff).

For the right extremist electoral potential, the disaffection from mainstream political parties has largely been overlooked. The number of neo-Nazi activists seemed too small to have political repercussions, and terrorist actions on the extreme right were too lightly written off as merely mimicking the extra-parliamentary movements on the left (Kolinsky, 1988, pp. 71ff). It is true that none of the extra-parliamentary activities which emanated from the extreme right could match the public impact and political stir caused by the new social movements of the 1970s and 1980s. Since the extreme right seemed to appeal only to a circumscribed number of fellow travellers, none of their activities elicited any special interest from the major parties. The established parties and their political leaders overlooked the fact that the clientele of the *Modernisierungsverlierer* were losing confidence in their ability, to cater for the interests of the person in the street. This scepticism made the *Modernisierungsverlierer* a potential clientele of the extreme right.

Surveys in the wake of the Republican gains in 1989 have shown that right extremism draws on a distinct clientele whose views of contemporary politics are more negative than those of other groups (see Table 3.11). Also, the themes which have dominated the party culture of the 1970s and 1980s held no attraction for the extreme right or disaffected West Germans with right-wing inclinations. Issues such as equal opportunities and women's quotas, ecology, abortion or disarmament were taken up by the new social movements to the left of the main parties. In trying to secure the electoral support of key groups such as women, young people, adherents of new values or new politics, parties could not afford to ignore new issue politics and therefore adjusted their policies accordingly. The political discourse of

Table 3.10   The Social Basis of Right Extremist Political Parties in the Federal Republic of Germany (1989, in %)

Question: Would you personally vote for a party to the right of the CDU/CSU, or have you voted for such a party already?

Listed below are positive replies: people who would vote for such a party or have already done so:

Social Group	%	Gender	%
Overall (Jan. 1989)	5	Men	14
Overall (May/June 89)	12	Women	9
Age		*Education*	
18–24 years	15	Basic education (Volksschule)	
25–34 years	10	without vocational training	11
35–49 years	9	Basic education with	13
		vocational training	
50–64 years	13		
65 years and over	12	Intermediate education	11
		A levels/University	9
In Employment:	13		
of these:			
– self-employed	10		
– managerial/civil service	9		
– other white-collar	10		
– blue-collar workers	18		
of these:			
– trade union members	14		
– not trade union members	20		

	%
Personal experience of unemployment	21
Fears of experiencing unemployment	14
Social class: self-identification	
upper class/upper middle class	7
middle class	9
working class	17

Source: Infas representative survey in the FRG and Berlin (West) January 1989 and May/June 1989; quoted in Ursula Feist, 'Rechtsparteien im Vormarsch' in *Gegenwartskunde*, No.3, 1989, 324.

the main parties and their public image were conditioned by the attempt to prove themselves capable of offering and implementing policies in line with issues which had been raised in protest by the new social movements. In fact, political parties responded to the demands of an articulate and potentially volatile electorate, whilst the dissatisfactions and concerns of less articulate sections of the population who feared change rather than demanded transformations found no such echo. In the 1970s and 1980s the agenda of contemporary politics has been set largely by the educated and articulate at the expense of the less well-educated and less articulate. Some of the *kleinen Leute* (the 'ordinary people') have now opted for an extremist stance on the right and their own agenda of issues.

Table 3.11 Party preferences and policy competence in 1989 (per cent)

Evaluation of EC membership for the FRG:

Party preference	Mainly good	Good and bad	Mainly bad
CDU/CSU	15	46	29
SPD	27	43	30
FDP	23	52	24
Greens	36	45	19
Republicans	13	25	64
Average	24	44	31

Payments by the FRG into EC funds are:

Party preference	Too high	Just right	Too low
CDU/CSU	64	34	1
SPD	62	34	2
FDP	60	30	0
Greens	49	46	4
Republicans	88	10	2
Average	63	33	2

Feeling that politics failed to tackle key issues:

Party preference	Always	Often	sometimes	never
CDU/CSU	5	38	48	9
SPD	11	50	35	4
FDP	11	40	46	4
Greens	17	55	25	2
Republicans	26	55	20	0
Average	12	46	37	5

Sources: Trends in der öffentlichen Meinung im Vorfeld der Europawahl. Konrad Adenauer interne Studien 12, 1989 p. 4;6. Hans-Joachim Veen, Viel Verdruß und wenig Ideologie, in *Rheinischer Merkur*, No.40, 6 October 1989.

Table 3.12   The Republican vote* by age and gender (European elections, 1989) (per cent)

	Age groups					
	18–24	25–34	35–44	45–59	60 and over	Average
M+F	7.9	7.0	7.0	7.4	6.8	7.1
Men	10.4	9.0	9.0	9.6	10.2	9.6
Women	5.1	4.8	4.9	5.2	4.6	4.9
Diff. F/M	−5.3	−4.2	−4.1	−4.4	−5.6	−4.7

Note: *Data for the electoral performance of the German People's Union in the regions show much the same pattern that has been familiar from the NPD with the best results among the older age groups, and a women's deficit much as that for the Republicans; see Hofmann-Göttig, pp. 28–9.

Source: Joachim Hofmann-Göttig, Die Neue Rechte: Die Männerparteien, in *Aus Politik und Zeitgeschichte*, B41–42, 1989, 26.

Issues and Events

Political support for parties of the extreme right springs from two sources: ideology and protest (*Die REP*, 1989). The ideological component is most evident in the organizational networks and circles of the extreme right, although it feeds on anti-democratic attitudes and orientations which have remained unchanged or have re-emerged in a contemporary setting (Stöss, 1989). The protest component, on the other hand, is more closely related to the present, and responds to the issues and events of the day. Ideological components alone are not sufficient to launch or sustain a political party at the parliamentary level. For established political parties, it has been shown that issues have increased in importance, as potential voters are less bound by traditional party preferences and more inclined to opt for the political party which they perceive to be capable of addressing itself to the priority issues in question. For small or new parties which cannot build on an electoral clientele, the balance between party issues and popular concerns holds the key to electoral success.

For the electoral and organizational successes of the extreme right since the late 1980s, the single most important issue has been that of hostility towards foreigners [*Ausländerfeindlichkeit*] (Ely, 1989, pp. 12ff; Roth, 1989, 16). There is no substantive difference between the positions adopted by the various parties of the extreme right, nor do their programmes mince words. For the 1989 European elections, the Republicans decreed: 'As one of the most densely populated countries in Europe, the Federal Republic of Germany is not a country of immigration. It has to remain the land of the Germans [*das Land der Deutschen*]' (Programm 1989, 9). The German People's Union, which forged an electoral alliance with the NPD, announced in the European campaign (Programm 1989, p. 1):

Germany shall remain the land of the Germans. The German people must enjoy the same rights as other peoples. This includes the right to the land of their heritage [*das angestammte Land*], national identity and self-determination. From this follows: limitations on the number of foreigners, stopping the ever increasing stream of foreigners, speeding up procedures to screen asylum seekers, expelling criminal foreigners.

The party press of the Republican Party conjured up the spectre of national decline on a massive scale (*Der Republikaner* 4, 1988, p. 1):

The number of West Germans is dwindling, the numbers of unemployed are soaring, the forests are dying, the farmlands are dying, the defence capacity is declining, families are increasingly falling apart. But the number of foreigners is growing all the time, criminality is rising, AIDS is spreading as fast as ever, nobody even mentions drug addiction any more and the young are left to search in vain for clear models of how to lead their lives.

Much the same kind of message is typical for the largest circulation weekly paper on the extreme right, the *Deutsche Nationalzeitung*.

According to the reports on political extremism, which are published annually by the Ministry of the Interior to monitor potentially anti-constitutional activities, the extreme right has reversed earlier membership trends and begun to grow since it chose hostility towards foreigners as its key theme (see Figure 3.1). In 1986, about the same number of groups had a total of 23,000 members, an increase of one-third within two years (Verfassungsschutzbericht, 1988, pp. 114–17). In 1988, the report listed over seventy such extra-parliamentary groups and parties with collective membership of 30,000. Thus even before unification, neo-Nazism had gained ground. However, these figures exclude the Republican Party which is not officially regarded as right extremist, and is not discussed in the annual report on political extremism. In 1988 the Republicans had 8,000 members; at the end of 1989 (November) the party claimed to have 24,000 members, although various reports published in the press suggest that the true figure was closer to 12,000 (Stöss, 1990).

A further indicator that the extreme right has grown since it concentrated upon hostility against foreigners is the election record of recent years: in the early 1980s a group calling itself Liste Ausländerstopp won 3 per cent of the vote at regional level; the National Democratic Party, which had hovered around 0.2 per cent throughout the 1970s, can now win more than 0.5 per cent in regional elections. In 1987 too, an electoral alliance of NPD and the German People's Union (DVU) fought a vituperative campaign against foreigners and won one seat in the *Land* Parliament in Bremen. Moreover, the Republicans grew from around 3 per cent in the early 1980s to over 7 per cent at the close of the decade. After apparently stabilising at around 2 per cent in 1990, the Republicans and the German People's Union in 1992 entered the *Land* parliaments of Bäden-Württtenberg and Schleswig-

Holstein. Their electoral focus had been hostility against foreigners. Although the percentage figures are generally small, political parties qualify for state funding as reimbursement of campaign costs if they poll at least 0.5 per cent of the vote. The policy of hostility towards foreigners has helped lift the NPD, its DVU ally and the Republicans comfortably over the percentage threshold for funding, and promoted them from the relegation zone of insignificance to the status of contestant in the electoral stakes.

Germans and Others: Recent Developments

German right extremism has always been anti-Semitic (Billig, 1989). As mentioned above, exonerating National Socialism and its leaders, defending or denying the existence of death camps and the policy of persecution have been strong themes of German right extremism. Negative references to Jews in contemporary society belong to the same anti-Semitic discourse and draw on similar attitudes in the population. Thus, in calling Jews 'the fifth occupying power of Germany', REP leader Franz Schönhuber, articulated widespread resentment against the Jewish community and its leaders in post-war Germany, restitution payment and the commemorations to the Holocaust (Stöss, 1990). Anti-Semitism has certainly not disappeared. Studies have revealed that virtually since the 1950s, some 20 per cent of West Germans held clearly anti-Semitic and a further 50 per cent somewhat anti-Semitic views (Silbermann, 1982; Rosen, 1986). Within the extreme right, 52 per cent have been identified as anti-Semitic, with anti-Semitism more common among the older age groups, whose views have been influenced directly by National Socialism, (*Der Spiegel*, 15, 1989, p. 15; *Der Stern*, 18 May 1989). However, there is no evidence that anti-Semitism broadened the electoral appeal of the extreme right, although there is proof that it boosted neo-Nazism (Kolinsky, 1984).

Hostility towards foreigners rather than Jews, however, has emerged as a salient electoral issue (see Chapter 1). Pitched against recent arrivals of *Gastarbeiter*, asylum-seekers, resettlers from Eastern European countries and a persistent stream of East Germans (*Übersiedler*), xenophobia has become a political and electoral issue. In a society where immigration is high, although only one in three of the population approves of it, right extremist hostility towards foreigners encourages reservation and resentment. Moreover, Germans appear to be shedding former inhibitions to expressing xenophobia openly (*Infas*, 1989). In 1978, for instance, 39 per cent favoured the return of foreigners to their country of origin; in 1989, 60 per cent expressed this opinion (*Der Spiegel*, 18, 1982, 37; Veen, 1989b). At the same time, Germans today are more inclined to engage in unconventional political actions including the use of violence, with East Germans particularly assertive that civil disobedience against the perceived 'system' is justified (Fuchs *et al.*, 1991, p. 44). Coupled with an East German legacy of excluding foreigners from social integration, this disposition has rendered East German right extremists particularly aggressive towards non-Germans or German nationals from Eastern Europe who seek refuge or residency in their regions. Among self-confessed Republican voters notably over 90 per cent objected to foreigners living in Germany. As a priority issue across the extreme right, xenophobia has a political function similar to the issue of environmentalism for the Greens: it is a common battle-cry across the factions and ideological subsections.

At this point, it will be instructive to briefly identify these 'foreigners', the reasons why they came to West Germany and the official and informal responses they have elicited.

Gastarbeiter

The first group consists of the *Gastarbeiter*. Originally, they were recruited in the mid-1950s at a time of economic boom and acute labour shortage. In 1973 the federal government decreed a halt to recruitment. The oil crisis had apparently ended the post-war era of economic growth and full employ-ment, and, since then, mass unemployment has not been below the million mark. The *Anwerbestopp*, therefore, was intended to reduce unemployment, as guest workers would return to their country of origin. The opposite happened for they made use of the right to bring their families into the Federal Republic, thereby altering the composition of the *Gastarbeiter* population. The challenge of social integration arose only after employment had become scarce. By the end of 1989, 4.5 million *Gastarbeiter* lived in West Germany, about half of them were active in the labour force, the others were children, housewives, pensioners or unemployed. Families tended to be large and whereas deaths outnumber births among West Germans, the *Gastarbeiter* population is still growing. The demographic change generated fears, in particular on the political right, that the country could face a shortage of Germans to run the country's economy and institutions in the next century. These concerns found expression in the 'Germany for the Germans' rallying cry of the extreme right.

Asylum-Seekers

The second group to have aroused hostility has been asylum-seekers and political refugees, notably from Third World countries. In deliberate con-trast to the racism of the National Socialist era, the Basic Law welcomes people who seek political asylum, and the government undertakes to house and financially support them until their individual cases have been investi-gated. Normally, proceedings take about one year to complete; applicants may appeal, and cases may take as long as four years until asylum is granted or an expulsion ordered. In the 1980s about 700,000 asylum-seekers entered the Federal Republic, more than half arriving after 1986 (see Figure 3.2); in 1988, about 15 per cent gained recognition as bona fide refugees. In 1989, this proportion dropped to 5 per cent; in January 1990, to just 3 per cent (*Das Parlament*, 9–10, 1990, p. 11). In practice, West Germans have not been as welcoming as their Basic Law would imply. In 1989, 57 per cent of West

Germans and over 90 per cent of Republican followers believed that asylum-seekers were treated too generously (*Infas*, 1989). Just one in five West Germans was prepared to accept asylum-seekers; the remainder were not (*Der Spiegel*, 9, 1990, p. 36). Attitudes in the new *Länder* seem to be tilted even more strongly against tolerance and integration.

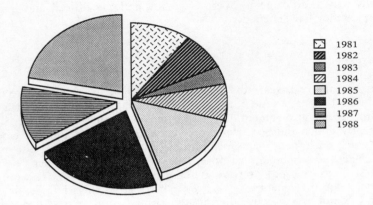

▨	1981
▨	1982
▦	1983
▨	1984
☐	1985
■	1986
▤	1987
▨	1988

Figure 3.2   Asylum-seekers in the Federal Republic of Germany, 1981–8

Source: Statistisches Jahrbuch der Bundesrepublik Deutschland, 1981 and subsequent years.

Government legislation in 1990 restricted access for asylum-seekers and other immigrants, curtailed their rights of appeal and facilitated expulsion, the last being a measure both demanded and welcomed by the opposition Social Democrats. In response to negative public sentiments against asylum-seekers and in an attempt to deflate a potential election issue of the extreme right, the government has moved in its direction and tried to implement enough of the extreme right's demands to blunt its cutting-edge. Indeed, with hostility against asylum-seekers persisting and the extreme right able to capitalize on this, the policy debate has shifted towards further curtailing rights of entry through European Community action and especially through an amendment of the Basic Law and its liberal approach to the issue of political asylum.

Germans or Foreigners?

The biggest group to enter the Federal Republic in recent years with intent to settle were, in fact, German nationals from Eastern Europe and, prior to unification in October 1990, from the German Democratic Republic. Since the division of Germany and Europe, a steady stream of people slipped through the Iron Curtain, illegally or after obtaining exit visas. Between 1950 and 1988, 3.3 million Germans left the GDR and 1.6 million so-called resettlers came to the Federal Republic (Figure 3.3) from a variety of Eastern bloc countries. Since then, the number of resettlers has increased to 200,000 or more per annum as Eastern Europe has become more tolerant of emigration. In 1989, the major wave of newcomers to West Germany originated in the East. Since August 1989, tens of thousands have crossed into West Germany via Hungary, Poland, Czechoslovakia and directly from East Germany. After the Berlin Wall had been breached in November 1989, the Federal Republic received over half a million people. Even following the collapse of the Communist (GDR) government in December 1989, between 2,000 and 3,000 East Germans per day continued to arrive in the West; since unification, an estimated 2,000 people a month are moving west. In 1989, 750,000 people of German nationality sought refuge in West Germany; for 1990, the influx has been estimated at 3 million (*Das Parlament*, 9–10, 1990, p. 12).

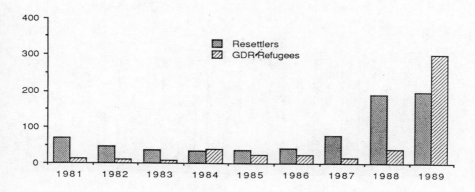

Figure 3.3 Immigration of German resettlers and East Germans into the Federal Republic 1981–9 (thousands)

Sources: Statistisches Jahrbuch, 1981–8; *Wirtschaft und Statistik*, No.9, 1989.

Although the German constitution extends full citizens' rights to German nationals behind the Iron Curtain and migration from East to West has continued for decades, the population movements have gathered momentum since the conservative-led government of Helmut Kohl, which came into office in 1982, regarded it as a key feature of its *Ostpolitik*. On arrival, resettlers were to be provided with housing and employment, and were entitled to state benefits during the initial integration period for at least one year. What had been intended as a national gesture and a mere facet of the *Wende*, i.e the complete turn-round the government had promised to set in motion, became a social liability. First, the number of people in Eastern Europe who claimed to be German by culture or origin turned out to be more than double the original estimate of 1.5 to 2 million. Second, the majority of resettlers had no command of the German language and were not readily accepted by the West German population as bona fide Germans. Press reports about false documents and bogus certificates underpinned a

88   *Eva Kolinsky*

general reluctance to regard the new arrivals from Eastern Europe as fellow Germans. Third, the policy of preferential treatment for resettlers in allocating housing coincided with a housing shortfall of at least 100,000 dwellings in 1988, rising to 250,000 in 1989 (see Figure 3.4). Furthermore, resettlers were engaged in looking for work in occupations which had been hit by unemployment or which seemed threatened by modernization and new technologies. In 1988, 49 per cent were skilled craftsmen working in small businesses or in industry, and 40 per cent carried out non-managerial tasks in the service sector (*Wirtschaft und Statistik*, 9, 1989, p. 588).

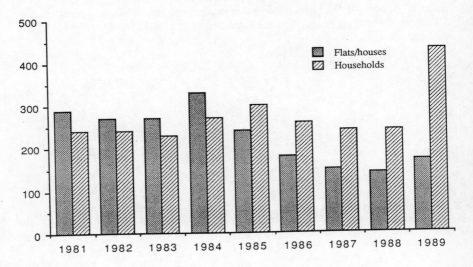

Figure 3.4   The new housing shortage, 1981–9 (thousands)
Source: Deutsches Institut für Wirtschaftsforschung (DIW), data quoted in *Staatsbürgerkundliche Arbeitsmappe*, No. 6, Schmidt, Berlin, January 1990.

Germans in the old and the new *Länder* perceived the resettlers as unwelcome competitors for jobs and services at a time of scarcity. In June 1988, 29 per cent welcomed their presence; one year later, only about 20 per cent did so (*Deutschlandarchiv*, 9, 1989, p. 920). The remaining 70–80 per cent were doubtful or opposed. In 1989, 83 per cent of right extremist voters refused to accept resettlers as German nationals (Roth, 1989, p. 17). Under the impact of popular misgivings, the Kohl government has extended preferential treatment of German nationals in the countries where they now live in order to persuade them to stay there. Given the divisive effect of such a policy, and the turmoil in a collapsing Eastern Europe, resettlers have continued to arrive. In April 1990, new regulations were passed compelling resettlers to prove their German origins before being allowed entry into the Federal Republic. Previously, this recognition constituted part of the absorption and integration process.

Despite their claim to German nationality, the resettlers have not been recognized as German nationals by most Germans, especially on the right of the political spectrum. The whole process has reopened questions of nation, national identity and the status of former German territories. In the founding years of the Federal Republic, a reunification of the two parts of Germany was widely expected to take place (e.g. by 66 per cent in 1956). As Schweigler explained, many first-generation refugees and expellees even advocated the use of violence to regain their former homelands (Schweigler 1975). Thirty years later, 80 per cent of West Germans saw reunification in general terms as a good thing, though only 3 per cent expected it to happen (Jansen, 1989, p. 1140). When it did happen, the groundswell of opinion surfaced in the East, with nation as prominent as living standards to flavour the demand.

The parties of the extreme right which had achieved electoral successes since the 1980s supported the familiar nationalist line and demanded a return to pre-war German borders. Mere unification with East Germany never matched up to the extreme right's concept of the nation. However, the national mood which surfaced in 1990 could not be utilized by an extreme right wrapped up in its clamouring for the greater Germany of yesteryear. The issue which has mobilized additional support for the extreme right since the mid-1980s has not been the national question but that of hostility towards foreigners. Despite their official status as German nationals – after the first hours of enthusiasm and welcome – resettlers and even refugees from East Germany, were perceived – and resented – as foreigners and unwelcome competitors for employment, housing and welfare support (*Der Spiegel*, 8, 1990, p. 37; *Der Spiegel*, 9, 1990, pp. 36f)

'The Extreme Right Co-Governs Already'[2]

Several attempts have been made to dilute the extreme right's electoral potential by incorporating its key issue. On the eve of regional elections in the Saarland, the SPD responded to popular disquiet and adopted a policy of benefit cuts and restricted access for East Germans (*Frankfurter Rundschau*, 26 October 1989). The SPD won an absolute majority in the Saar and the Republicans failed to enter the regional parliament. In North Rhine–Westphalia, a region with similar problems of economic restructuring, high unemployment and blue-collar *Modernisierungsverlierer*, the SPD proposed that East Germans should be allowed to settle only if they had a home and employment to go to. Similar measures have been introduced in Berlin, Bremen and also Bavaria and Baden-Württemberg where *Modernisierungs-verlierer*, opting for the Republicans in the 1989 European elections, had deprived both CSU and CDU of their customary absolute majorities (see Table 3.4). Futhermore, two days after the alliance of conservative parties won the East German elections on 18 March 1990, Chancellor Kohl announced that all benefits to East German newcomers would be discontinued from July 1990. Again, in August 1991 Oskar Lafontaine, failed candidate for the chancellorship and a vice-chairman of the SPD argued that the Basic Law should be amended to keep asylum-seekers and others out of Germany.

The expansive nationalism of the extreme right has left its mark on the process leading up to unification. The refusal of the extreme right to accept any of the post-1945 German borders influenced the government's handling of the territorial dimension of German unification. When Chancellor Kohl presented his ten-point plan for a German–German confederation to the Bundestag in November 1989, he chose not to mention the western border of Poland. His strategy was to pursue unification and side-step the border issue – not to challenge the Polish territory but to assure the extreme right that their visions of national unity might become political reality. To win support from the extreme right, Kohl tried to defer a decision on the German–Polish border to an all-German parliament, and warned Poland not to demand reparation payments from a united Germany. Under pressure from his own Foreign Minister, Hans-Dietrich Genscher, and in the face of international indignation, Kohl backed down. In March 1990, the Bundestag undertook what seemed unconstitutional just a few weeks earlier: the confirmation of Polish borders. The very fact, however, that Kohl raised the border issue implied that Germany's political frontier to the East remained contentious. This position has been at the heart of right extremism and the nationalism of refugee organizations in Germany since the demise of National Socialism. Kohl's position turned out to be more attuned to their vision of Germany than to European or international orientations.

The unification of the two Germanys does not match up with the extreme right's goal of restoring the German nation. On the question of nation, though, the extremists have some vociferous allies. The associations for refugees and expellees from the East, which have functioned as pressure groups on the right since the early 1950s also demanded that the Sudetenland, Silesia, Pomerania, West and East Prussia should be included in the reunification process. The calls for reunification which dominated GDR politics in 1989 and 1990 precipitated and assisted the collapse of state socialism. For most East Germans, reunification meant little more than access to the lifestyles and opportunities of West Germany; within weeks, however, right extremists emerged in East Germany and gave a different twist to the theme. *Vaterland* for this extreme right also implied the borders and the political status of pre-1945 Germany and a sharp polarization between Germans and Poles or other Eastern Europeans. Although the Republikaner as a political party was banned when the 1990 East German Parliament was elected, and has made little headway since, right extremism has a visible clientele in the East (see Chapter 12). Support for neo-Nazism had been estimated at 10 per cent in Berlin and at between 3 per cent and 6 per cent in former GDR regions.[3]

Outlook

For the electoral potential of the extreme right, the socio-economic effects of German unification are likely to be more significant than the issue of nation.

For a transition period at least, West Germans and especially East Germans are experiencing a reduction in their standards of living, increased inflation, and social instability. In the former GDR, unemployment and a blend of massive economic restructuring and total collapse confront a population used to state-allocated work, planning, and an institutionalized grid of opportunities and social roles. The syndrome of *Modernisierungsverlierer*, of people who see themselves threatened or bypassed by the affluence and the opportunities they expect in contemporary society, is gaining ground in a society which had underestimated the personal dislocations in the wake of unification, and only discovered its cost after the event (see Chapter 12). German political culture mirrors in its contemporary divisions the gravity of the change. In the political culture of the former GDR, confidence in democracy has yet to emerge as citizens look towards the state to conjure up improvements; in West German political culture the answers of the extreme right have been uncomfortably close to public sentiment on some issues and in both parts of Germany socio-economic anxieties still translate into anti-democratic attitudes, and into a future for right extremism.

Notes

1. The relevant surveys centre on West Germany (East Germany is dealt with specifically in Chapter 12). Since West German institutions and political culture have emerged as the dominant influence in unification, and since side-stepping the issue in the East failed to generate political views of democracy which also incorporate an evaluation and informed refutation of the National Socialist past, the findings reported here also pertain to German political culture since unification.
2. Erika Trenz of the Greens in the Bundestag, March 1990.
3. The data for East Berlin are based on preliminary findings of a survey on right extremism in Berlin (West and East) conducted jointly by the Free University and the Akademie der Wissenschaften; the data for the GDR are based on findings of a youth survey conducted by the Institut für Jugendforschung in Leipzig. At the time of writing, the survey had not been published in full since many of its findings did not match the SED's expectations of young people's behaviour. The figure on right extremism had 'leaked out' and was given to the author by several GDR researchers; it is also mentioned in Stöss, 1990.

References

Alber, J., 1989. Social Structure and politics in the Federal Republic of Germany. Paper delivered at the Havens Centre, University of Wisconsin at Madison, 3 April (mimeo).

Almond, G. and Verba, S., 1963. *The Civic Culture*, Little Brown, Boston.

Backes, U. and Jesse, E., 1989. *Politischer Extremismus in der Bundesrepublik Deutschland*. Vol. 1, Wissenschaft und Politik, Cologne.

Beck, U., 1986. *Die Risikogesellschaft*, Suhrkamp, Frankfurt-on-Main.

Betrifft: Verfassungsschutz, 1969 and following years, Ministry of the Interior, Bonn.

Beyme, K. von, 1985. *Political Parties in Western Democracies*, Gower, Aldershot.
——, 1988. Right-wing extremism in post-war Europe, *West European Politics*, Vol. 11, No. 2, 1–19.
Billig, M., 1989. The Extreme Right in R. Eatwell, and N. O'Sullivan, *The Nature of the Right*, Pinter, London.
Boßmann, D. (ed.), 1977. *Was ich über Adolf Hitler gehört habe*, Fischer, Frankfurt-on-Main.
Bürklin, W., 1988. *Wählerbewegungen*, Westdeutscher Verlag, Opladen.
Castner, H. and Castner, T., 1989. Rechtsextremismus und Jugend, *Aus Politik und Zeitgeschichte*, B41, 32–9.
Conradt, D., 1980. Changing German Political Culture, in G. Almond and S. Verba (eds), *The Civic Culture Revisited*, Little Brown, Boston, 212–72.
Die neue Armut, 1983, Hans Böckler Foundation, Düsseldorf (mimeo).
Die REP, 1989. Analyse und politische Bewertung einer rechtsradikalen Partei, ed. CDU Bundesgeschäftsstelle, Bonn.
Dudek, P. and Jaschke H.-G., 1981. *Revolte von rechts. Anatomie einer neuen Jugendpresse*, Campus, Frankfurt-on-Main.
—— and ——, 1984. *Entstehung und Entwicklung des Rechtsextremismus in der Bundesrepublik Deutschland*, 2, vols, Westdeutscher Verlag, Opladen.
Eatwell, R, and O'Sullivan, N., 1989. *The Nature of the Right*, Pinter, London.
Edinger, L.J., 1988. *Germany*, 2nd edn, Little Brown, Boston.
Ely, J., 1989. Republicans: neo-Nazis or the black–brown hazelnut? Recent successes of the radical right in West Germany, *German Politics and Society*, No. 18, 1–17.
Emnid, 1989. Die Einstellungen der Bundesbürger zum Nationalsozialismus, *Der Spiegel*, No. 15.
Falter J. and Schumann, S., 1988. Affinity towards right-wing extremism in Western Europe, *West European Politics*, Vol. 11, No. 2, 96–110.
Feist, U., 1989. Rechtsparteien im Vormarsch, *Gegenwartskunde*, No. 3, 321–30.
Feist, U. and Krieger, H., 1987. Alte und neue Scheidelinien des politischen Verhaltens, *Aus Politik und Zeitgeschichte*, B12, 33–47.
Feit, Margret, 1987. *Die 'Neue Rechte' in der Bundesrepublik*, Campus, Frankfurt-on-Main.
Fuchs, D., Klingemann, H.-D. and Schröbel, D., 1991. Perspektiven der politischen Kultur in vereinigten Deutschland, in *Aus Politik und Zeitgeschichte* Vol. 32, 1991, 35–46.
Geiss, I., 1988. *Geschichte des Rassismus*, Suhrkamp, Frankfurt-on-Main.
Glatzer, W., 1984. Einkommensverteilung und Einkommenszufriedenheit, in W. Glatzer and W. Zapf, *Lebensqualität in der Bundesrepublik*, Campus, Frankfurt-on-Main, 45–73.
Götz, A., 1986. *Bilanz der Verfolgung von NS-Straftaten*, Pahl-Rugenstein, Cologne.
Heitmeyer, W., 1987. *Rechtsextremistische Orientierungen bei Jugendlichen*, Beltz, Weinheim.
Heitmeyer, W. and Peter, J.I., 1988. *Jugendliche Fußballfans – soziale und politische Orientierungen, Gesellungsformen, Gewalt*, Beltz, Weinheim.
Hennig E. and Kieserling, M., 1989. Aktuelle Wahlerfolge kleinerer Rechtsparteien in der Bundesrepublik, *Gewerkschaftliche Monatshefte*, No. 9, 524–37
Herdegen, G., 1989. Aussiedler in der Bundesrepublik, in *Deutschlandarchiv*, No. 8, 912–24.
Hilmer, R. and Köhler, A., 1989. Übersiedler- und Flüchtlingswelle im Sommer 1989, in *Deutschlandarchiv*, No. 11, 1382–93

Hoffmann-Lange, U., Eliten als Hüter der Demokratie, in D. Berg-Schlosser and J. Schissler, *Politische Kultur in Deutschland*, Politische Vierteljahresschrift Sonderheft 18, 1987, 378–91.

Hofmann-Göttig, J., 1989a. *Die Mehrheit steht links*, Materialien, ed. SPD Bundesvorstand, Bonn.

—, 1989b. Die Neue Rechte: Die Männerparteien, *Aus Politik und Zeitgeschichte* B41, 21–31.

Hradil, S., 1987. *Sozialstrukturanalyse in einer fortgeschrittenen Gesellschaft*, Leske & Budrich, Opladen.

Hülsberg, W., 1988. *The German Greens*, Verso, London.

Infas Report, 1989. Politogramm Berlin 1989, Bonn.

Irving, R.E.M. and Paterson W. E., 1991. The 1990 German General Election, in *Parliamentary Affairs*, Vol. 44, No. 3, 353–72.

Jansen, S., 1989. Meinungsbilder zur deutschen Frage, in *Deutschlandarchiv*, No. 10, 1132–43.

Kaase, M., 1989. Bewußtseinslagen und Leitbilder in der Bundesrepublik Deutschland, in W. Weidenfeld and H. Zimmermann (eds), *Deutschland Handbuch*, Hanser, Munich, 203–20.

Kern, H. and Schumann, M., 1984. *Das Ende der Arbeitsteilung?* Frankfurt/Main: Campus.

Kolinsky, E., 1984. *Parties, Opposition and Society in West Germany*, Croom Helm, London.

—, 1988. Terrorism in West Germany, in J. Lodge, *The Threat of Terrorism*, Wheatsheaf Books, Brighton, 57–87.

—, 1989. Sachlichkeit statt Menschlichkeit. *Sozialwissenschaftliche Informationen – Deutsche Juden. Jüdische Deutsche*, 197–203.

Leggewie, C., 1989. *Die Republikaner*, Rotbuch, Berlin.

Lepszy, R., 1989, Die Republikaner, *Aus Politik und Zeitgeschichte*, B41, 3–9.

Merkl, P. (ed.), 1989. *Germany at Forty*, New York University Press.

Merritt, A.J. and Merritt R. L., 1980. *Public Opinion in Semisovereign Germany*. The HICOG surveys 1949–55, University of Illinois Press, Urbana.

Nagle, J. D., 1970. *The National Democratic Party. Right Radicalism in the Federal Republic of Germany*, University of California Press, Berkeley.

Niedermayer, O., 1990. Sozialstruktur, politische Orientierungen und die Unterstützung extrem rechter Parteien in Westeuropa, in *Zeitschrift für Parlamentsfragen*, No. 4, 564–82.

Padgett, S. and Burkett A., 1986. *Political Parties and Elections in West Germany* Hurst, London.

Paul, G. (ed.), 1989. *Hitlers Schatten verblaßt. Die Normalisierung des Rechtsextremismus*, Neue Gesellschaft, Berlin/Bonn.

Raschke, J., 1985. *Soziale Bewegungen*, Campus, Frankfurt-on-Main.

Renn, W. F., 1987. Federal Republic of Germany: Germans, Jews and genocide, in R.L. Braham (ed.), *The Treatment of the Holocaust in Textbooks* Columbia University Press, New York, 1–75.

Rohe, K., 1989. *Elections, Parties and Political Traditions in Germany 1867–1987* Berg, Oxford.

Rosen, K.-H., 1984. Vorurteile im Verborgenen. Zum Antisemitismus in der Bundesrepublik in Strauss H. A. and Kampfe N. (eds), *Antisemitismus. Von der Judenfeindschaft zum Holocaust*. Bundeszentrale für politische Bildung, Bonn 256–297.

Roth, D., 1989. Sind die Republikaner die fünfte Partei, *Aus Politik und Zeitgeschichte*, B41, 10–20.

94   *Eva Kolinsky*

Roth, R. and Rucht, D. (eds) 1988. *Neue soziale Bewegungen in der Bundesrepublik Deutschland*, Bundeszentrale für politische Bildung, Bonn.
Schmidt, Manfred, 1983. Two logics of coalition policy: the West German case, in V. Bogdanor, *Coalition Government in Western Europe*, Heinemann, London, 38–58.
Schmollinger, H., 1989. Die Wahl zum Abgeordneten haus von Berlin, *Zeitschrift für Parlamentsfragen*, No. 3, 309–22.
Schönhuber, F., 1981. *Ich war dabei* Hanser Munich.
Schweigler, G.L., 1975. *National Consciousness in Divided Germany*, Sage, London.
Silbermann, A., 1982. *Sind wir Antisemiten?*, Wissenschaft und Politik, Cologne.
Silbermann, A. and J.H. Schoeps (eds), *Antisemitismus nach dem Holocaust*, Wissenschaft und Politik, Cologne, 163–92.
Sinus Institute, 1981. *Fünf Millionen Deutsche – Wir wollen wieder einen Führer haben*, Rowohlt, Hamburg.
Smith, G., 1986. *Democracy in Western Germany*, 3rd edn, Gower, Aldershot.
Smith, G. and Paterson, W.E. (eds), 1989. *Developments in Western Germany* Macmillan, London.
Stöss, R. (ed.), 1983. Parteien Handbuch, 2 Vols, Westdeutscher Verlag, Opladen.
——, 1986. Pronazistisches Protestverhalten unter Jugendlichen, in *Extremismus und Schure*, Schriftenreihe de Bundeszentrale für politische Bildung vol. 212, Bonn, 171–94.
——, 1989. *Die Extreme Rechte in der Bundesrepublik. Entwicklung, Ursachen, Gegenmaßnahmen* Westdeutscher Verlag, Opladen.
——, 1990. *Die 'Republikaner'. Woher sie kommen, was sie wollen, wer sie wählt, was sie tun*. Bund, Cologne.
Tauber, K., 1967. *Beyond Eagle and Swastika*, 2 vols, Middletown, Wesleyan University Press.
Veen, H.-J., 1989a. The Greens as a milieu party, in E. Kolinsky (ed.), *The Greens in West Germany*, Berg, Oxford. 31–62.
——, 1989b, Trends in der öffentlichen Meinung im Vorfeld der Europawahl, *Interne Studien* 12, Konrad Adenauer Foundation, St Augustin.
Verfassungschutzbericht, see *Betrifft*.

4 The Netherlands: Irritants on the Body Politic[1]

Christopher T. Husbands

Introduction

In *Bleak House* Dickens chided Mrs Jellyby for her 'telescopic philanth-ropy', for being more concerned about the natives of Borrioboola-Gha than about those unfortunates nearer home; her eyes 'seemed to look a long way off, as if . . . they could see nothing nearer than Africa'. British political science has not been quite as telescopic, although it is ironic that less is known and taught about the politics of The Netherlands than about those of many more distant countries, despite the fact that in some aspects of social structure and historical experience it is a country which closely resembles Great Britain.[2]

Political racism, a crucial factor in understanding the contemporary ex-treme right in The Netherlands, developed there rather similarly – if later – to the pattern of its growth in Great Britain. In character and content, it has many affinities to the British National Front (NF) when the latter was most active during the 1970s. Thus, although The Netherlands, unlike Britain, had a truly significant national-socialist movement during the 1930s, much post-war extreme-right activity, certainly in the 1980s, has had only ambiguous links to the pre-war phenomenon. During the Second World War, The Netherlands experienced full occupation after a short attempt at resistance against difficult odds, described succinctly by, for example, Shirer (1960, pp. 721–3). Alone of cities in The Netherlands, Rotterdam was heavily bombed on 14 May 1940, leaving a symbolic memory of what the Dutch suffered. Occupation was often particularly brutal and it left an understandable legacy of bitter feelings in Dutch politics about Nazism and the War that has lasted to the present. During late 1988 and early 1989 there was a major contro-versy (including a debate in the country's nationally elected legislature, the Second Chamber) about the pensions being paid by the state to the widows of Meinoud Marinus Rost van Tonningen and Graaf De Marchant et d'Ansembourg, two leading figures in the pre-war Dutch national-socialist movement, the Nationaal Socialistische Beweging (NSB), and subsequently condemned to death and fifteen years' imprisonment respectively for collaboration. However, the former died in mysterious circumstances just before his execution although he is usually reckoned to have committed suicide). The widows' entitlements to their pensions were based upon their husbands' election to the Second Chamber in the May 1937 general election. Also, the question of whether the last two German war criminals imprisoned in The Netherlands, Ferdinand aus der Fünten and Franz Fischer (popularly called 'The Two of Breda', after the location of the gaol where German war criminals had been kept), should be released out of compassion for their age and health caused a spirited debate in January 1989, splitting the major political parties on a free vote in the Second Chamber before their release was finally granted and they were thereupon deported to the Federal Republic of Germany as 'undesirable aliens' (*NRC Handelsblad*, 28 January 1989, p. 1). The authorities are still attempting to pursue Dutch war criminals who collaborated with the German occupation and managed to escape arrest at the end of the Second World War, mostly by flight to South American countries.

The Dutch war-time experience discredited the extreme right more comprehensively than was the case in France, for example, where the presence of an albeit short-lived puppet regime in a part of the country left a mixed legacy. Moreover, the Dutch history of decolonization was relatively painless, unlike that of France. True, between 1945 and 1949 there was intermittent conflict between Dutch and nationalist forces in the Netherlands East Indies, subsequently Indonesia, although negotiated sovereignty was given to the nationalists in December 1949; this was nothing like the costly and bloody wars of liberation faced by the French in Indo-China and Algeria.

Post-war Demography and Immigration in The Netherlands[3]

Even so, the fact that The Netherlands was once a significant colonial power in the Caribbean as well as the Far East has had important consequences for its demography. It now contains a sizeable population originally from one-time Dutch colonies. Initially entitled to Dutch nationality on criteria which, though containing an element of patriality, were none the less quite generous, many such settlers were assimilated into Dutch society without demur, and unless in some way distinctive like the South Moluccans, were difficult to isolate in any demographic attempt to count the 'non-indigenous' population of the country. However, there are now reasonably good estimates of the size of the two most important groups of colonial origin, those from Surinam and the Dutch Antilles. Surinam was granted independence in 1975 largely to be able more easily to stem the flow of its residents to The Netherlands itself. During the early 1970s immigration from this source increased sharply in reaction to economic difficulties in the colony and the great need for labour in the Dutch economy. At the beginning of 1971 there were about 31,700 Surinam-born residents in The Netherlands. Four years later the figure was 68,500 and there was a precipitate entry during 1975 to beat the barrier whose imposition after independence was feared. The figure for the beginning of 1976 was 103,500. During 1979 and 1980 there was a further minor wave of new arrivals and by 1983 the Surinam-born population was assessed at 141,000, from which it has been estimated that the 'Surinamese population' (including those born to a Surinamese parent) was around 180,000 to 190,000 (van Amersfoort, 1986, p. 18;1987); this is about 1.3 per cent of the resident population of the country at that time. The Dutch Antilles produced a smaller but still important population. The Central Bureau of Statistics' estimate at the beginning of 1983 of the number of Antilles-born residents of The Netherlands was 34,900, about 0.2 per cent of the national resident population. The Surinamese were especially seen as a 'problem' group' in Dutch society, though they were in truth an internally heterogeneous population.

However, the reputation of the Surinamese in The Netherlands has undoubtedly been overtaken by that of other and more recent arrivals for, like France and the ex-Federal Republic of Germany, The Netherlands now contains groups that are typical of labour migrations to northern Europe from the European periphery and North Africa. In the case of The Netherlands, Turkey and Morocco have been the most important sending countries. These were recruited during the 1960s when there were shortages of labour in certain older industries that could not be accommodated by the indigenous labour force or by colonial migration. These nationalities came to dominate the foreign population of The Netherlands from the 1960s, to the detriment of the Spanish, Portuguese and Italians who had composed the bulk of the foreign population in the early period of importation of migrant labour from the European periphery. On 1 January 1984 according to the estimate of the Central Bureau of Statistics, there were 155,280 Turks and 106,435 Moroccans in the country, respectively 1.1 and 0.7 per cent of the resident population. These figures greatly exceed the numbers of registered foreign workers from these countries who were active in the labour force, which on 31 March 1987 were 33,600 Turks (0.2 per cent) and 23,200 Moroccans (0.2 per cent) (Netherlands Central Bureau of Statistics, 1989, p. 141).

These two groups have become especially important for understanding the geographical distribution of political racism in The Netherlands. Support for racist political parties has been most pronounced in certain parts of the major cities, especially Amsterdam, Rotterdam, The Hague and, to a lesser extent, Utrecht (all of them by coincidence or association having football teams with supporters holding some notoriety for their hooliganism) in the provinces of North Holland and South Holland (i.e., in the so-called Randstad). It is particularly in these cities where the foreign groups were concentrated. At the beginning of 1985 2.4 per cent of the population of Amsterdam were Turkish nationals, 3.7 per cent were Moroccan nationals and the total non-Dutch population of the municipality was 12.3 per cent. The respective figures for the other mentioned municipalities were: Rotterdam: 3.8, 2.0 and 10.1 per cent; The Hague: 2.3, 1.7 and 8.2 per cent; and Utrecht: 2.7, 4.0 and 9.3 per cent.[4]

Some of the circumstances of these foreign populations resemble those of similar groups in other Western European capitalist economies, although the more ordered system of labour recruitment of the Federal Republic of

Germany is closer to the Dutch model than is the chaotic pattern seen in France during the heyday of labour migration to that country in the 1960s and early 1970s. Nevertheless, the disadvantage that has been the invariant and amply documented lot of immigrant workers in Western Europe in such spheres as housing, education and the labour market is repeated in The Netherlands. On the other hand, there have been important differences in how Dutch policy towards immigrant workers was conceived and executed (Entzinger, 1984, pp. 67–158). The Dutch government has long been officially committed to multiculturalism, and in many respects the Dutch system has been closer to the Scandinavian model – or at least the one-time Scandinavian model until the restrictions on asylum-seekers and immigrants introduced in all the Scandinavian countries during the past few years – than to those of the ex-Federal Republic of Germany or France. This is especially true where civic rights and civic integration have been concerned, though in any case immigration and immigrant workers have not been an issue exploited by mainstream politicians, especially those of the right, in the flagrant manner to be seen in the ex-Federal Republic of Germany, France or (going back to the 1950s) Great Britain. One indication of this difference is the provision of the franchise, which continues to be a contentious and unpopular matter in contemporary French politics and is equally a cause for trauma in German politics. Dutch non-citizens have had the right to vote in all municipal council elections since March 1986, and the first experiment of extending the franchise in this way occurred in six voting districts of Rotterdam on 28 May 1980 (Rath, 1983), although these had been preceded by so-called immigrant councils in a number of Dutch cities during the 1970s, to which each ethnic group could elect only its own ethnic peers.

Prejudice against the country's ethnic minorities has been thoroughly researched in The Netherlands since the 1970s. For example, van Praag (1983) performed secondary analyses on a number of studies conducted between 1975 and 1983, both those concerned explicitly with prejudice and those also dealing with other subjects. The principal finding from these nation-wide samples was the difficulty of explaining prejudiced attitudes using as independent variables the social characteristics of respondents (1983, p. 73). There have recently been other studies that have examined the attitudes of the Dutch to ethnic minorities. For example, van Leusden and Moors (1988) reported on a survey done in late 1986/early 1987, being a follow-up of a similar one in 1983, in which 1,451 respondents were asked their views on foreigners. Although only basic results were published, they revealed considerable indifference or hostility: thus, over 50 per cent favoured financial incentives to foreigners to encourage them to return to their country of origin; nearly 60 per cent saw no benefit from their presence. In a more sophisticated manner, the social psychologists, Hagendoorn and Hraba have extensively developed an ethnic hierarchy concept, successfully isolating the criteria of differentiation by which the native Dutch locate themselves cognitively closest to the English and most distant from Moluccans and Turks (e.g., Hagendoorn and Hraba, 1989). For reasons discussed by several writers elsewhere (e.g., Husbands, 1988), the question of whether one country's population is more or less inherently

racist or ethnically intolerant than that of another, although not an impossible research task, is none the less fraught with contextual and methodologi-
cal problems that make an absolute answer rather difficult. However,
consistent with the already mentioned fact that this issue has been less
emotively used in Dutch politics than in those of certain other countries, it is
worth noting the findings of a Eurobarometer study conducted in March–
April 1984. Levels of agreement with a statement, 'We have too many
immigrant workers', were, for The Netherlands, 40 per cent broadly or
completely agreeing and 23 per cent completely agreeing. The respective
results for the Federal Republic of Germany (old regions), France and the
United Kingdom were: 59 and 30 per cent; 58 and 34 per cent; and 51 and 29
per cent (BASS, 1984). Thus, the Dutch population certainly contains a
strain of ethnic intolerance; even so, this may not be an issue of major
relevance to the theme of this chapter, since the penetration of general
attitudinal racism is not necessarily correlated with the contemporary occurrence of political racism and extreme right-wing support with its specific
metropolitan and regional concentration.

Along with other Western European countries, The Netherlands has been
attempting in recent years to deal with the increased numbers seeking
political asylum, which have grown from fewer than 1,000 in 1981 to around
14,000 in 1989. The pressure began particularly in 1987 when the Second
Chamber was urged to deal with the large number of Tamil refugees from Sri
Lanka (*NRC Handelsblad* (Zaterdags Bijvoegsel), 12 May 1990, p. 5). The
increase in asylum-seekers is widely seen as a major factor in the re-
emergence of the European extreme right in the late 1980s, especially since
the issue has been problematized by certain politicians and sections of the
mass media in many countries (see Chapter 1). The Netherlands too has
been caught in a hypocrisy trap, attempting to retain the purported genero-
sity of its reputation on asylum issues, and at the same time wanting
increased restriction. It has therefore participated enthusiastically in the
general move to restrict asylum. It has been proposed by the Minister of
Justice, Ernst Hirsch Ballin, that asylum applicants should be physically
segregated into two types of camp during the processing of their applications, one for those with a reasonable chance of success and one for those
without, the latter available for ready deportation. However, this plan was
originally opposed by the Second Chamber, especially when the security
problems in concentrating large numbers of desperate no-hope cases within
individual enclosures were pointed out (*NRC Handelsblad*, 10 June 1991,
p. 3). With its new asylum law that came into force on 1 October 1991, The
Netherlands has accelerated the process with which asylum cases are pro-
cessed and, as necessary, deported if rejected. A number of stratagems have
been adopted to keep out as many asylum-seekers as possible, especially by
labelling claimants as economic refugees: 'For this group the right of asylum
does not apply. They are not wanted. Even The Netherlands is not a land of
milk and honey', said Aad Kosto, Secretary of State in the Ministry of
Justice (*Süddeutsche Zeitung* (Munich), 17/18 August 1991, p. 9).

Having reviewed the contemporary ethnic dimensions to Dutch society
and discussed the country's difficulties in reconciling its purported liberal

credentials with its desire to restrict the arrival of asylum-seekers, this chapter now considers the extreme right in The Netherlands since 1945 under the following principal organizational headings:

1. the legacy of the pre-war extreme right and post-war developments, specifically concerning the small groups that sought clandestinely and semi-clandestinely to perpetuate the pre-war ideologies of the extreme right;
2. the new extremism from the 1960s onwards, which is measured (in Table 4.1) by the election results for the extreme right from 1959 to the present, making clear the timing of peaks and troughs during the past thirty years for the several parties concerned and periodizing their respective importance in the light of the consequential sections;
3. the emergence of a form of populist right-wing *ressentiment* in the 1960s in the shape of the Boerenpartij (BP), representing the first major post-war electoral resurgence of a recognizably extreme-right phenomenon;
4. the emergence of anti-foreigner and anti-immigrant politics in The Netherlands in the 1970s in the shape of the Nederlandse Volksunie (NVU);
5. the continuation of these politics from the early 1980s to the present with the Centrum Partij (CP) (to metamorphose into the Centrum Partij '86 (CP '86)) and later also the Centrumdemocraten (CDs); and
6. in brief conclusion, the future of the contemporary extreme right in The Netherlands in comparison with that in other Western European countries, especially Great Britain, France and Belgium.

The sections on the immediate post-war groups, the period dominated by the BP and that in which the NVU was a temporary force, each give some indications of these parties' origins, ideologies and programmes, their leadership characteristics and, for the BP and NVU, their mass support, as well as general historical details. However, because of the greater and continuing significance of the CP and the CDs and the growing analytical literature about them, and considering the contemporary role of the politics of ethnic exclusionism in The Netherlands, section 5 not only gives a general account of the history of the CP and CDs and some information about their leaderships but also contains two further specific subsections:

(a) these parties' ideologies and programmes; and
(b) the debates about the character of their mass support, based upon available individual-level data from nation-wide surveys and from local and city-wide studies, and upon aggregate data, both at the national level and within the major cities where they have attracted particular support (notably Amsterdam, Rotterdam and The Hague).

The Legacy of the Pre-War Extreme Right

Van der Wusten, in discussing the extreme right in The Netherlands during the 1930s, wrote that: 'no fascist movement, with the exception of the

Nationaal Socialistische Beweging, ever had more than a little over one thousand members in the entire inter-war period' (van der Wusten, 1987, p. 213). The NSB had been formed by Anton Adriaan Mussert in December 1931 (Meyers, 1984, pp. 55–67), and its major membership surge occurred from 1933 till 1935, when it achieved its maximum of 47,000 members; this declined to 28,000 by the occupation of the country in May 1940, after which unsurprisingly there was a rapid influx, assisted in 1941 by the consolidation of all Dutch fascist groups into the NSB.

The NSB's most successful electoral performance was in the provincial council elections of April 1935, when it won 7.9 per cent of votes cast. In the elections to the Second Chamber in May 1937 it won only 4.2 per cent of the national vote, although it did secure four seats in the legislature. There has been some discussion and controversy about the support for the NSB. De Jong, in the first volume of his monumental multi-volume history of The Netherlands in the Second World War (1969, p. 302), summarized this as follows:

> considered overall, it seems that the NSB electorate consisted, in regional terms, of dissatisfied farmers and sometimes also of agricultural workers and, in national terms, of dissatisfied members of the middle class – with considerable support among the best-off in society (the results in the wealthiest municipalities and in the richest neighbourhoods of Amsterdam, The Hague and Rotterdam point in this direction).

The rural focus of this encapsulation does, however, need some modification. The Netherlands is divided into eighteen constituencies, and in 1935 the NSB won 12.0, 10.8 and 9.0 per cent of the votes in The Hague, Amsterdam and Rotterdam constituencies, in comparison with its 7.9 per cent overall (*de Volkskrant*, 27 May 1937, p. 1). Kooy (1964, p. 290) has shown that there was no direct correlation in the 1935 results between NSB support and levels of urbanization and his general, if to be disputed, conclusion is that the party's success was to be explained by the effect of Mussert's charismatic appeal upon the awakening class-consciousness of the *petit bourgeoisie* of both city and country (p. 292).

Passchier and van der Wusten (1979) were among the first to seek to modify the earlier work of Kooy. They emphasized the importance of urbanization after controls upon levels of affluence. In general, those municipalities that they defined as urbanized supported the NSB disproportionately, especially if well-off and having lower levels of unemployment. However, in poorer rural municipalities, greater unemployment predicted higher levels of NSB support. Van der Wusten and Smit (1980) also mention the wealthier, better-educated component of the NSB vote, along with more marginal, unintegrated groups. In the case of the city of Amsterdam itself, Schmidt's (1979) study with ecological data demonstrates the strong dependence of the NSB vote on the affluence of individual neighbourhoods, although structural factors were less important after 1935. Passchier (1987) has recently reasserted this basis to NSB support in Amsterdam in 1935, to be contrasted (as will be seen) with support there for the CP in the June 1984 Euro-election and with the generally more marginalized support for the contemporary extreme right in The Netherlands.

Thus, despite the debate about the nature of NSB support, the contribution to this of sections of the more affluent, most indisputably in certain urban populations, is now widely accepted. This is a characteristic to be found in 1930s fascism in a number of countries; Husbands (forthcoming, ch. 7) demonstrates it for Switzerland in the case of Zürich and it is well established for several, though not all, German cities (Hamilton, 1982, e.g., pp. 64–128), despite recent arguments against such class distinctiveness overall in Nationalsozialistische Deutsche Arbeiterpartei (NSDAP) support (Falter, 1991, pp. 285–9).

The NSB collapsed in 1945, of course, amid suicides and trials for collaboration of its leaders and members. The level of collaboration in The Netherlands may have been higher than in most other occupied countries, at least in Western Europe, or perhaps it was more purposefully prosecuted after the war, although some, especially non-Dutch, historians of the German occupation have rather moved from a polarization between the 'evil' who collaborated and the 'good' who resisted (e.g., Warmbrunn, 1963, pp. 272–5; Hirschfeld, 1988, p. 7). In the summer of 1945 more than 100,000 people were being held pending judgments about their collaboration with the occupying Germans (van Donselaar, 1991, p. 28), including those who fought in the Westland regiment of the Waffen-SS, which was composed of Dutch and Flemings. Although by 1950 most had been freed, often conditionally, and had had their civil rights restored, the issue of war-time collaboration remained a sensitive one in The Netherlands and, as described in the introduction to this chapter, does so to this day.

The first attempted revival of the Dutch extreme right in the post-war era was the so-called Stichting Oud Politieke Delinquenten (SOPD), which claimed to be non-political in character. Various small groups of those with NSB and collaborationist backgrounds had been formed in the late 1940s and the consolidating organization was founded in April 1951. The deliberately mischievous title of the new group was intended as a facetious variation on Stichting Toezicht Politieke Delinquenten (STPD), the body originally responsible for supervising the parole of those charged with collaboration after they had been conditionally released. The SOPD survived without proscription, which encouraged its activists to consider the founding of a formal political party in the mould of the pre-war NSB. The name chosen for the new group, formally founded in June 1953, was the Nationaal Europese Sociale Beweging (NESB), whose initials were a deliberate resonance of NSB and which became the Dutch component of the internationally based Europese Sociale Beweging (ESB), founded in 1951. The push for the Dutch branch of this latter movement came from Paul van Tienen, onetime Waffen-SS Untersturmführer, who, although having been sentenced to eight years' imprisonment in 1948, benefited from an amnesty in 1949. However, unlike the preceding SOPD, the NESB was eventually in effect proscribed by April 1955 after a complexity of legal machinations involving two of its principal leaders. As van Donselaar says (1991, p. 79): 'ten years after the war the limit of what was permissible was established; a coterie of national socialists was tolerated but a political party of national socialists definitely was not.'

The New Extremism: The *Boerenpartij* and Beyond

As van Donselaar's comprehensive account describes, there were a number of clandestine neo-Nazi initiatives after the proscription of the NESB. The only non-clandestine extreme-right body that sought electoral support was the ineffective Nederlandse Oppositie Unie (NOU). More interesting and relevant to the mainstream development of the Dutch extreme right is, however, the emergence in the early 1960s of an example of right-wing populism in the BP and later, in the 1970s, of an ethnically exclusionist extreme right.

Because of the continuing significance of the electoral dimension in development from the early 1960s, it is helpful to present details of the levels of success of all the relevant parties as a single table. The four parties considered in this summary coverage are the BP, the NVU, the CP (later renamed CP '86), and the CDs. This presentation is defensible as a means of giving an indication of the oscillations in support for the extreme right, even if the BP is ideologically rather different from the other parties.

Table 4.1 presents data on levels of support for the country as a whole and then separately for the three largest cities, Amsterdam, Rotterdam and The Hague; the latter are considered individually because of their importance in providing electoral support to the parties concerned and because there exist a number of studies using aggregate and individual level data on the characteristics of this support within them. Table 4.1 covers all elections from 1959 to the present in which one or more of these parties was standing and where it is possible to provide nation-wide and/or city-wide calculations of the results. Thus, it features elections to the European Parliament, the Second Chamber, the provincial councils, and the municipal councils.[5] It may be seen from Table 4.1 that electoral support for the Dutch extreme right has varied noticeably over time. Slightly arbitrarily, an election or series of elections where the cumulated extreme-right support among all the above parties competing exceeds 2.0 per cent nation-wide and/or 4.0 per cent in one or more of the three cities considered, is to be seen as indicating a period of heightened support. Since 1959 there have been four such episodes, which are italicized in Table 4.1.

1. from before the May 1963 Second Chamber elections to after the February 1967 Second Chamber elections;
2. around the provincial council elections of March 1974;
3. from before the September 1982 Second Chamber elections to after the June 1984 European Parliament election; and
4. from before the March 1990 municipal council elections until the present (late 1991), as seen in the March 1991 provincial council elections (although this latest upsurge was partly anticipated in the September

Table 4.1 Percentages voting for Dutch extreme-right parties in various elections between 1959 and 1991 in The Netherlands as a whole and in the cities of Amsterdam, Rotterdam and The Hague

	The Netherlands					Amsterdam				
	BP	NVU	CP/ CP'86	CD	Total	BP	NVU	CP/ CP'86	CD	Total
12 March 1959 (Second Chamber)	0.7	–	–	–	0.7	1.2	–	–	–	1.2
15 May 1963 (Second Chamber)	*2.1*	–	–	–	*2.1*	*1.9*	–	–	–	*1.9*
23 March 1966 (Provincial Councils)	*6.7*	–	–	–	*6.7*	*9.0*	–	–	–	*9.0*
1 June 1966 (Municipal Councils)	*5.7[1]*	–	–	–	*5.7*	*9.5*	–	–	–	*9.5*
15 February 1967 (Second Chamber)	*4.7*	–	–	–	*4.7*	*4.6*	–	–	–	*4.6*
18 March 1970 (Provincial Councils)	1.7	–	–	–	1.7	1.5	–	–	–	1.5
3 June 1970 (Municipal Councils)	0.6[1]	–	–	–	0.6	0.7	–	–	–	0.7
28 April 1971 (Second Chamber)	1.1	–	–	–	1.1	0.5	–	–	–	0.5
29 November 1972 (Second Chamber)	1.9	–	–	–	1.9	1.0	–	–	–	1.0
27 March 1974 (Provincial Councils)	*3.1*	–	–	–	*3.1*	*2.1*	–	–	–	*2.1*
29 May 1974 (Municipal Councils)	0.7[1]	–	–	–	0.7	0.9	–	–	–	0.9
25 May 1977 (Second Chamber)	0.8	0.4	–	–	1.2	0.6	1.2	–	–	1.8
29 March 1978 (Provincial Councils)	0.5[2]	–	–	–	0.5	0.5	–	–	–	0.5
31 May 1978 (Municipal Councils)	0.1[1]	–	–	–	0.1	0.2	–	–	–	0.2
26 May 1981 (Second Chamber)	–	0.1[3]	0.1[3]	–	0.2	–	–	1.0	–	1.0
2 June 1982 (Municipal Councils)	*	–	0.2	–	0.2	–	–	1.5	–	1.5
8 September 1982 (Second Chamber)	0.3[4]	–[5]	0.8	–	1.1	0.2	0.3	2.8	–	3.3
14 June 1984 (European Parliament)	–	–	*2.5*	–	*2.5*	–	–	*6.9*	–	*6.9*

Table 4.1   Continued

	The Netherlands					Amsterdam				
	BP	NVU	CP/CP'86	CD	Total	BP	NVU	CP/CP'86	CD	Total
19 March 1986 (Municipal Councils)	–	–	*	*	*	–	–	2.6	0.9	3.5
21 May 1986 (Second Chamber)	–	–	0.4[6]	0.1[6]	0.5	–	–	1.5	0.6	2.1
18 March 1987 (Provincial Councils)	–	–	–[7]	0.3[7]	0.3	–	–	–	1.4	1.4
15 June 1989 (European Parliament)	–	–	–	0.8	0.8	–	–	–	2.3	2.3
6 September 1989 (Second Chamber)	–	–	–	0.9	0.9	–	–	–	3.1	3.1
21 March 1990 (Municipal Councils)	–	–	*	0.5	0.5	–	–	2.4	4.4	6.8
6 March 1991 (Provincial Councils)	–	–	0.3[8]	1.0[8]	1.3	–	–	1.4	4.1	5.5

	Rotterdam					The Hague				
	BP	NVU	CP/CP'86	CD	Total	BP	NVU	CP/CP'86	CD	Total
12 March 1959 (Second Chamber)	0.6	–	–	–	0.6	0.8	–	–	–	0.8
15 May 1963 (Second Chamber)	0.9	–	–	–	0.9	1.1	–	–	–	1.1
23 March 1966 (Provincial Councils)	4.2	–	–	–	4.2	6.9	–	–	–	6.9
1 June 1966 (Municipal Councils)	7.2	–	–	–	7.2	10.9	–	–	–	10.9
15 February 1967 (Second Chamber)	2.4	–	–	–	2.4	3.4	–	–	–	3.4
18 March 1970 (Provincial Councils)	0.9	–	–	–	0.9	1.1	–	–	–	1.1
3 June 1970 (Municipal Councils)	0.7	–	–	–	0.7	0.6	–	–	–	0.6
28 April 1971 (Second Chamber)	0.4	–	–	–	0.4	0.4	–	–	–	0.4
29 November 1972 (Second Chamber)	0.9	–	–	–	0.9	1.0	–	–	–	1.0

Table 4.1   Continued

	Rotterdam					The Hague			
	BP	NVU	CP/ CP'86	CD	Total	BP	NVU	CP/ CP'86	CD	Total
27 March 1974 *(Provincial Councils)*	1.8	–	–	–	1.8	1.9	–	–	–	1.9
29 May 1974 (Municipal Councils)	0.7	–	–	–	0.7	–	1.8	–	–	1.8
25 May 1977 (Second Chamber)	0.3	1.1	–	–	1.4	0.4	1.3	–	–	1.7
29 March 1978 (Provincial Councils)	0.3	–	–	–	0.3	0.5	–	–	–	0.5
31 May 1978 (Municipal Councils)	–	–	–	–	–	0.2	–	–	–	0.2
26 May 1981 (Second Chamber)	–	–	–	–	–	–	–	1.0	–	1.0
2 June 1982 (Municipal Councils)	*	–	1.7	–	1.7	*	–	1.3	–	1.3
8 September 1982 (Second Chamber)	0.2	–	4.0	–	4.2	0.2	0.3	2.2	–	2.7
14 June 1984 *(European Parliament)*	–	–	8.1	–	8.1	–	–	6.4	–	6.4
19 March 1986 (Municipal Councils)	–	–	3.4	0.6	4.0	–	–	2.0	1.1	3.1
21 May 1986 (Second Chamber)	–	–	1.5	0.4	1.9	–	–	1.0	0.4	1.4
18 March 1987 (Provincial Councils)	–	–	–	1.6	1.6	–	–	–	1.3	1.3
15 June 1989 (European Parliament)	–	–	–	2.7	2.7	–	–	–	2.3	2.3
6 September 1989 (Second Chamber)	–	–	–	3.4	3.4	–	–	–	3.2	3.2
21 March 1990 *(Municipal Councils)*	–	–	3.3	3.8	7.1	–	–	2.1	4.3	6.4
6 March 1991 *(Provincial Councils)*	–	–	1.7	4.1	5.8	–	–	1.5	4.5	6.0

1989 Second Chamber elections, which saw the success of the leader of the CDs in securing renewed membership of the legislature).

In the first two episodes the beneficiary was the BP and in the latter two it was the CP/CP '86 and/or the CDs. However, although it is important to appreciate that support for the extreme right has come in waves and troughs, it is now sensible to restructure the following presentation in decades since, albeit rather loosely, the 1960s were the decade of the BP, the 1970s of the NVU, and the 1980s of the CP/CP '86 and the CDs. This compartmentalization is defensible in terms of profile even if, during the early 1970s, the BP (though declining) still attracted some votes, outpolling the NVU in the country as a whole in the May 1977 Second Chamber elections; in fact, the NVU's few electoral appearances were not marked by conspicuous success.

The era of the Boerenpartij

The BP is still considered to have been an enigma in Dutch politics; even its name belies the fact that, at its peak, it had disproportionate electoral appeal in the country's largest cities, and as is later mentioned, within certain cities such as Amsterdam and Rotterdam the subdistrict-based distribution of its vote in some elections anticipated that for the extreme right parties of the 1970s and 1980s.

Symbols:
– No candidature standing
* Party concerned not listed separately in the official statistics of election results published by the Netherlands Central Bureau of Statistics

Notes:
1. In the various municipal council elections between 1966 and 1978 the BP did not offer lists in many municipalities. The percentages given are of votes received where the party stood, calculated upon votes for all parties cast in the country as a whole. In 1966 the BP covered fewer than a third of municipalities, being particularly sparse in the south of the country. In 1970, 1974 and 1978 there were also very many municipalities without a BP candidature.
2. In the 1978 provincial council elections the BP had no candidatures in the provinces of Drenthe, Friesland and Limburg.
3. In the 1981 Second Chamber elections the NVU had no candidatures in the provinces of Drenthe, North Holland and South Holland, and the CP had none in South Holland (except in The Hague).
4. By the 1982 Second Chamber elections the BP had altered its name to the Rechtse Volkspartij.
5. In the 1982 Second Chamber elections the NVU stood only in Amsterdam and The Hague.
6. In the 1986 Second Chamber elections the CP had no candidatures in the province of Drenthe, and the CDs had none in Limburg.
7. In the 1987 provincial council elections the CP '86 stood only in the province of Flevoland (where it won 1.2 per cent of votes cast); the CDs stood only in the provinces of South Holland, Utrecht and parts of North Holland.
8. In the 1991 provincial council elections the CP '86 stood only in the provinces of North Holland, South Holland and North Brabant; the CDs stood in the provinces of Flevoland, Friesland, Gelderland, North Brabant, North Holland, South Holland and Utrecht.

The BP particularly flourished in the period when Dutch politics were being generally restructured; the telescopic style of political science with which this chapter was introduced did condescend to mention in the Dutch case the concept of *verzuiling* ('pillarization' is the usual ungainly translation), by which the religious and class divisions of Dutch society were mirrored in its political system. By the 1960s the politics of *verzuiling* were in some disarray and the BP was undoubtedly able to profit from the disruption of political partisanships. Also, the albeit short-lived Poujadist movement in France in the later 1950s had provided a model for such a style of political movement and in recent decades the Scandinavian Progress Parties have been later examples.

Interestingly enough, Denmark had supposedly provided the initial inspiration to Henrik Koekoek, who founded the BP in 1958 after the example of a Danish agrarian party (van Donselaar, 1991, p. 122).[6] In his research on the support of the BP, Nooij (1969), author of a standard work on the party, adopted a social-psychological approach, employing concepts such as authoritarianism and disaffection. The party's urban successes show that it was able to transcend its agrarian origins, though one must emphasize its extreme-right nature. Its expansion between 1963 and 1967 was greeted with universal surprise, though this meant that it suffered a not uncommon fate among right-wing parties achieving sudden and unexpected electoral success in countries with voting systems incorporating some form of proportional representation: it faced a dearth of suitable people to cover the election seats that it won. In the BP's case there emerged a number of individuals with unpalatable war-time pasts. Partly as a result of one such scandal, the BP's support fell from 6.7 per cent in the March 1966 provincial council elections to 4.7 per cent in the Second Chamber elections less than a year later. None the less, the BP managed to increase its parliamentary representation to seven seats from the three won in May 1963. In June 1968 the parliamentary group split into two, four members forming a party called Binding Rechts (BR) later in the year. It was hoped that this would prove more successful than the BP; however, it quickly disappeared. As the result of its performance in the April 1971 Second Chamber elections, the BP held only one seat. There was a modest recovery in the Second Chamber elections of November 1972 (two seats) and the party achieved 3.1 per cent of the national vote in the March 1974 provincial council elections, partly as a consequence of the economic crisis of the period. However, Dutch politics were more settled by the 1970s and the BP was by then politically functionless. In the May 1977 Second Chamber elections, it managed just one seat with less than 1 per cent of the national vote. This was lost in 1981 after an inopportune attempt to revive the party with a change of name to Rechtse Volkspartij (RVP).

What is left, from the perspective of the political analyst, is a debate about whether or not the BP is to be regarded as a neo-fascist and/or extreme-right party. Certainly, it sought strenuously to distance itself from such an attribution. However, Nooij (1969, p. 217) had no hesitation in regarding it, if not as fascist, then as an extreme-right party on the basis of the oppositional character of its programmes and the strenuousness of this opposition. Van Donselaar (1991, p. 125) is more measured: 'The question of how far the description "extreme-right protest party" offers sufficient leverage in order also to label it as fascist can in no sense be simply answered and lends itself to a great degree of subjectivity.'

The degree of territorial continuity in support for the BP and between support for it and other or later examples of the Dutch extreme right depends very much on the period and the context. Within Amsterdam, for example, there is a correlation of 0.879 between percentaged BP support in the Second Chamber elections of May 1963 and February 1967 across sixty-eight subdistricts [*buurtcombinaties*], though one of only 0.145 between the latter occasion and the Second Chamber results in May 1977 across sixty-six subdistricts. There are small variations in the correlations between BP support in 1963, 1967 and 1977, and that for the NVU in May 1977: 0.384, 0.447, and 0.441. There are larger variations with that for the CP in September 1982: 0.001, 0.148, and 0.616. Across Rotterdam's twenty-five subdistricts [*wijken*] the BP's percentaged support in the April 1971 and November 1972 Second Chamber elections correlated respectively 0.769 and 0.753 with NVU support in May 1977, and 0.752 and 0.685 with CP support in September 1982. However, across the 129 economic-geographical areas covering the whole country, BP support in May 1977 correlated negatively at −0.335 with NVU support on the same occasion, and −0.413 with CP support in September 1982. At the BP's peak its greatest strength was in the east of the country: in the February 1967 elections it won 6.5 per cent of the votes in the province of Drenthe, 5.7 per cent in Overijssel, 7.0 per cent in Gelderland, and 6.7 per cent in North Brabant, compared with 4.7 per cent in the country as a whole.

The era of the Nederlandse Volksunie

The NVU dominated the Dutch extreme right in the later 1970s, despite the fact that it never won a single parliamentary seat, and even if partly because of legal harassment, never managed to elect members to municipal councils. It achieved its short period of attention largely through its aggressive anti-foreigner policies, whose outspokenness was very much a novelty in Dutch politics in the 1970s (in contrast to Great Britain, of course), even though the BP was also on record as being opposed to the presence in The Netherlands of immigrant workers.

The NVU was formed in 1971 with, according to van Donselaar (1991, p. 143), a persistent presence of former NSB members among its leadership. Although the early years were uneventful, the party was pushed into the headlines by Joop Glimmerveen when he stood for the municipal council in The Hague in May 1974 on an unabashedly racist platform opposing ethnic minorities. Glimmerveen came to be the figure most associated with the party, though he had not originally been in its national leadership. The party's leader, Bernard Postma, had in fact taken a decision that the NVU should 'sit out' the municipal council elections of May 1974 rather than risk an embarrassing performance (Bouw, van Donselaar and Nelissen, 1981, p. 81). However, opinions were divided, and Glimmerveen was able to win an endorsement of his wish to press ahead and stand in The Hague. His election pamphlet was pointedly direct:

> The Hague must stay white and safe!
> Away with the Surinamese and Antillianese who parasite on our energy and welfare.
> Help me free our city from the plague of Surinamese and Antillianese.

Glimmerveen won 3,977 votes, 1.8 per cent of those cast and just a few hundred short of the 2.2 per cent that would have secured one seat in The Hague municipal council. Postma's hesitation in supporting Glimmerveen cost him his leadership position; he resigned in October 1974 and eventually left the party in 1976. Glimmerveen became the new leader, buttressed by the fact that the media were already recognizing him as such because of the personal publicity arising from the campaign in The Hague.

The party became even more prominent as the 1970s progressed: by 1976 anti-fascist and anti-racist committees of action were being formed to oppose it in numerous cities (Bouw, van Donselaar and Nelissen, 1981, pp. 94–5). The NVU itself was not slow to seize opportunities to pass on its message. In August 1976 there was a minor riot in the city of Schiedam, west of Rotterdam, when Dutch youths attacked Turkish residents after a Dutch person had been murdered by a Turk. The NVU was quick to distribute pamphlets whose contents were subsequently held to be inciting to riot and racial hatred and those distributing them were arrested and charged; in March 1977 Glimmerveen himself was sentenced to fourteen days in gaol as a result. The NVU indulged in other attempts to stir up animosities between Dutch and non-Dutch, for example in Lelystad (a new town east of Amsterdam on reclaimed land that is now the Province of Flevoland) and Utrecht.

Despite the poor performance of the NVU in the May 1977 Second Chamber elections (0.4 per cent nationally, well under the 0.67 per cent needed to secure one seat), there was a continuing fear about the NVU that in 1978 produced attempts to impose a *de facto* proscription. The process was a complicated one, initiated and carried through not (at least directly) by the national ministries concerned but by local officials. The law officer in Amsterdam moved to proscribe the party, basing his case on the party's programme and pamphlets, what its leaders had said, and the convictions against Glimmerveen. This meant that the party was prevented from participation in the May 1978 municipal council elections. In April 1978 Glimmerveen attempted to circumvent this by handing in lists without the party designation though with himself as first candidate. This was done in Amsterdam, Rotterdam and The Hague and election officials ruled these lists invalid in all three cases. Also, by an interesting coincidence, Glimmerveen was called to serve his two-week gaol term during the time of these elections. Later, in 1979, the Dutch Supreme Court confirmed the decision of the lower court *de facto* to proscribe the NVU but did not impose any consequences of this confirmation; thus, electoral participation remained theoretically possible, albeit rather difficult.

Still, these frustrations at the hands of the state's authorities, although in the end not conclusive, were sufficient to harass the NVU into inconsequentiality. By late 1979, with the electoral road effectively blocked, the party and its publications had lapsed overtly into neo-Nazi sympathy, bemoaning the continued imprisonment of Rudolf Hess and openly adopting revisionist positions about the Holocaust. In 1981 Glimmerveen was deposed as leader by the rump of the party, though he returned to lead a minuscule group in 1983. In the May 1981 Second Chamber elections the NVU managed 0.1 per cent of votes cast; it had no lists in Amsterdam, Rotterdam or The Hague. Still, although the NVU lapsed into insignificance, its role and that of Glimmerveen in putting racist politics on to the Dutch political agenda must be recognized.

Despite the limited electoral support of the NVU, there has been one study of its voters, using aggregate data. Bovenkerk *et al.* (1978) point out that the two provinces of North Holland and South Holland gave it disproportionate support in the May 1977 Second Chamber elections; support was higher in cities rather than the countryside, especially older industrial areas. Only in Amsterdam, Rotterdam and The Hague did it exceed 1 per cent, and then only barely. In The Hague it was higher in impoverished, older neighbourhoods containing many Surinamese and foreign workers. A similar, if less clear, pattern was found in Rotterdam, although in Amsterdam support for the NVU seemed a more dispersed phenomenon.

The NVU largely anticipated the geographical distribution of later support for the CP in the 1980s, both nationally and locally. The correlation coefficient between NVU support in 1977 and CP support in 1982 was 0.854 across the 129 Dutch economic-geographical areas; it was as high as 0.929 across thirty-one subdistricts [*wijken*] in The Hague and 0.835 across twenty-five Rotterdam subdistricts. However, as to be expected from its more dispersed character, it correlated rather less, at 0.549, with the CP's support in 1982 across sixty-five Amsterdam subdistricts.

Into the 1980s: the Centrumpartij and the Centrumdemocraten

As the NVU collapsed into semi-clandestinity and became a political sect rather than a party, moves were afoot on the Dutch extreme right to found a party with a clear ethnically exclusionist appeal though without the connotations of outright extremism and neo-Nazism attached to the former party. The CP was the outcome of this process. In December 1979 the immediate forerunner of the CP was founded, called the Nationale Centrum Partij (NCP). Four young men (according to Brants and Hogendoorn, 1983, p. 18) or three (according to van Donselaar, 1991, p. 173), disappointed in the NVU and finding that Glimmerveen's politics were going rather too far, decided to set up a new party. The man who was to become almost synonymous with the Dutch extreme right during the 1980s, Hans Janmaat, holder of a degree in political science, was an early member, though not one of the founders. Brants and Hogendoorn (1983, p. 20) say that his background was in the Katholieke Volkspartij (KVP) – to become a component of the centre-right Christen Democratisch Appel (CDA) (Gladdish, 1991, pp. 54–6) – although van Donselaar emphasizes Janmaat's varied political past in support of several of the mainstream parties. Janmaat joined this venture under fortuitous circumstances. At the first congress of the NCP in February 1980, two of the founders had left the event with some cronies, intending to attack a group of illegal immigrants seeking refuge in a nearby church. The attackers were repulsed and the two were arrested. The principal of the founding leaders, Henry Brookman, thereupon expelled them and dissolved the NCP, establishing instead the CP. Janmaat, allegedly attracted by the publicity and harbouring a growing resentment about foreigners, contacted Brookman to express his interest. The latter himself was facing a dilemma: his political activities had attracted some dubious publicity for his employers and he was forced to choose between his career and his party. He decided to choose his career and Janmaat was able to emerge as the new party leader. The latter had some attractive features, as far as Brookman had been concerned. He was well educated and respectably employed as a teacher. He was untainted by a past on the extreme right, not having been a member of the NVU. During 1980 Janmaat moved into the leadership.

The CP and NVU sparred with each other in the early days of the former though it was not long before the NVU was finally eclipsed. However, the CP's very modest result in the May 1981 Second Chamber elections (0.1 per cent of the national vote) scarcely augured well for racist politics in The Netherlands. There was some slight increase in the June 1982 municipal council elections, although even in the three principal cities, the CP failed to win any council seats. Then, the extreme proportionality principle of the Dutch electoral system permitted Janmaat to win a seat in the Second Chamber in the September 1982 general election when, amid jubilation from its supporters, the CP won 0.8 per cent of the national vote.

Still, its major successes occurred in 1983 and 1984. In September 1983 the CP became the third-largest party by winning 9.1 per cent of the vote and two seats in a municipal election in newly incorporated Almere, an Amsterdam overspill town in the reclaimed province of Flevoland. Van Donselaar and van Praag (1983, pp. 89–95) have considered the Almere result in some detail, arguing that it was in part due to political alienation rather than contact racism against ethnic minority members, since, in contrast in particular to Rotterdam and The Hague, the CP vote correlated poorly with ethnic-minority presence. In December 1983 one survey, based upon telephone interviews with 21,000 people, even calculated the CP's national support as 2.5 per cent (de Hond, 1983, p. 1), which turned out to be the CP's percentage of the national vote in the Euro-poll of June 1984 – not enough for a seat but still a significant performance in Dutch terms.

However, in the late summer and autumn of 1984, all this success began to fall apart as the party split badly, expelling its parliamentary representative in a bitter internal row in which malfeasance, misappropriation of funds and sexual impropriety were alleged (*Leidse Courant*, 3 August 1984; *Het Vrije Volk*, 11 October 1984).[7] Janmaat refused to surrender his Second Chamber seat and in mid-November 1984 he riposted rather feebly by setting up his own new party, the Centrumdemocraten. For a while, they both competed in elections, certainly in the municipal council and Second Chamber elections of March and May 1986, when the CP performed noticeably better than the CDs. However, as Table 4.1 shows neither party was especially successful, although the CP did elect single members to the Amsterdam, Rotterdam, Utrecht, Almere and Lelystad (in Flevoland) municipal councils in March. The period in the council chamber of the Amsterdam representative was marked more by taciturnity than intervention.

Later in 1986 the CP went bankrupt, to be refounded subsequently as the Centrum Partij '86. By 1987 it was apparently finished, and in the March 1987 provincial council elections, except for its presence in Flevoland, the CDs fought a lone and rather futile contest. However, by 1989 the principal parties were nervous on the issue of political asylum, which was clearly a vote-loser if too generously granted. In the September 1989 general election Janmaat returned to the Second Chamber, the CDs winning 0.9 per cent of the vote. However, the CP '86 did not manage to present any lists on that occasion. In the municipal council elections six months later, the CDs and the resuscitated CP '86, having survived a legal challenge from Janmaat claiming that it was not the original party, made a significant breakthrough, especially in the larger cities. Their electoral performances were even more impressive than the raw percentages suggest, since they are based on an electorate that includes non-Dutch voters; excluding these from the base (since few are likely to have chosen these parties) the percentage-level of support for the combined CP '86 and CDs often rises markedly – for example, reaching nearly 15 per cent in such inner-city localities as Schildersbuurt and Transvaalkwartier in The Hague (a third of the former's population and over a quarter of the latter's were Turkish or Moroccan at the end of 1989). These successes produced eleven council members for the CDs and four (later three) for the CP '86. The CDs are represented now in Amsterdam (two seats), Dordrecht (one), The Hague (two), Haarlem (one), Purmerend (one), Rotterdam (one), Schiedam (two) and Utrecht (one); the CP '86 has councillors in Amsterdam (one), The Hague (one) and Rotterdam (one). In Almere, the CP '86 also won a seat though there was no one available to take it up. There were protests by several hundred people in Amsterdam, The Hague, Dordrecht, Purmerend and elsewhere against the installation of the extreme-right councillors (*Trouw*, 2 May 1990).

In October 1990 the CDs' councillor in Purmerend (north of Amsterdam) was acquitted on a technicality after being summoned for being a member of the forbidden neo-Nazi organization, Aktiefront Nationaal Socialisten (ANS), and for illegal possession of firearms (*NRC Handelsblad*, 24 October 1990, p. 7). More generally, of the fourteen municipal councillors elected, three had been found guilty in the past of racist behaviour, one of these on two occasions, and the case of a fourth was being investigated (*Algemeen Dagblad*, 1 May 1990). The general reaction of the other parties to the extreme-right councillors was ostracism and exclusion. Amsterdam officials intended to keep their servicing of these councillors to an absolute minimum and in numerous cities, including Amsterdam, Rotterdam and The Hague, other parties deliberately excluded CD and or CP '86 councillors from committees (*Het Parool*, 2 April 1990; *Algemeen Dagblad*,

25 April 1990), although in the context of national politics a mainstream right-wing member of the liberal-right Volkspartij voor Vrijheid en Democratie (VVD) called in May 1990 for a discontinuation of the Second Chamber's ostracism policy against Janmaat (*Algmeen Dagblad*, 8 May 1990).

In the provincial council elections in March 1991 the two parties slipped back very slightly although the CDs still performed well enough to take single seats in the North Holland, South Holland and Utrecht provincial councils, with 2.1, 2.1 and 1.6 per cent of votes cast respectively. Janmaat was elected to both the first two councils, as head of both of the party's lists, but he withdrew from each in favour of an alternate in view of his parliamentary commitments (*Trouw*, 21 March 1991, p. 4). As in the past, both the North and South Holland councillors were the targets of anti-racist protests when they later took up their seats for the first time (*NRC Handelsblad*, 17 April 1991, p. 7).

The ideologies and programmes of the CP/CP '86 and the CDs[8] Political racism by extreme right parties is seldom expressed with any concessions to subtlety and in this respect the Dutch parties are fairly typical. Perhaps the only major distinctiveness is their self-conscious use of the word *Centrum* in their titles. This, of course, was a legacy from the short-lived NCP, although the CP came to display the slogan 'Neither right nor left' prominently on much of its literature. Still, its political pamphlets necessarily had to demand other policies than the exclusion of foreigners. One produced in 1983 listed these as the introduction of the referendum; full employment for all Dutch people; an attack on the 'scandalous housing shortage'; multilateral disarmament; an out-and-out attack on the drugs trade; the reduction of government expenditures and activities; no cutback on social payments, though an attack on their abuse; an attack on the evasion of social security contributions and on tax fraud; no aid to undemocratic countries; a purposeful attack on the mistreatment of animals, environmental pollution and despoiling of the countryside; and (finally) 'The Netherlands is not an immigration country; therefore stop the flood of foreigners'. In short, there was a potpourri of measures apparently intended to cultivate a populist cross-class audience.

Unsurprisingly, the contemporary CDs have a similar appeal, having also continued using the 'Neither right nor left' slogan. Of course, some of the issues have been updated. Asylum-seekers are mentioned more explicitly; yet the 'Stop the flood of foreigners' has persisted too. The 'deliberate infection with AIDS' should be a punishable offence. Although the CDs do not aspire to great intellectual sophistication in defence of their position, their quarterly publication, *CD-actueel*, a rather cheaply produced effort, does include odd articles with pretensions to scholarship.

The CP '86 is perhaps somewhat more interesting. Now much smaller than the CDs, it has been faced with a problem of self-definition *vis-à-vis* the latter. It has apparently resolved this by a self-conscious resort to aggressive nationalism, combined paradoxically with a form of Europeanism. It has developed links with the German Nationaldemokratische Partei Deutschlands (NPD) (see Chapter 3); it now calls itself 'the national-democratic party in The Netherlands' and attempts to mobilize around slogans such as 'A new fatherland; a new Europe'. As Chapter 5 on Belgium elaborates in more detail, it has also developed links with the Belgian Vlaams Blok (VB). Of course, it too has latched on to the asylum issue, as well as calling for enforced emigration of certain groups of foreigners.

Mass support for the CP/CP '86 and the CDs There have been a number of studies on support for these two parties, during the CP's first phase of success and also the post-1989 surge for both parties. Some of these studies are based on individual-level data, either nationally or locally collected; others are based on urban subdistrict data, usually in the three largest cities. Before introducing and discussing some of these studies, certain primary data for the three principal cities are presented. It has already been seen that there are geographical continuities between support for some of the earlier extreme-right candidacies and those of the CP, though the pattern is less clear in Amsterdam than in Rotterdam and The Hague.

Tables 4.2 to 4.4 now give correlational analyses for Amsterdam, Rotterdam and The Hague between subdistrict distributions of support in elections from 1982 to 1991 and various aggregate social characteristics that reflect ethnic minority presence and general social and economic status. [9] These data show both similarities and differences, Amsterdam being significantly aberrant from the other two.

Table 4.2 shows that, inferring from the values of the coefficients of variation, [10] support for the CP/CP '86 and the CDs has generally displayed throughout this period a similar spread across the subdistricts of Amsterdam, except for the more concentrated character of the CP's performance in the 1984 Euro-election and the suggestion of slightly more dispersed distributions in the 1990 and 1991 elections. These vote distributions generally correlate only mildly with the local presence of foreigners, but the reason for this is not so much the exceptionalism of Amsterdam in comparison with the other two cities but rather that this variable is a particularly poor operationalization of the presence of ethnic outgroups in the former case. However, the correlation coefficients with the number of Turks and Moroccans considered separately, these being among the most distantly regarded outgroups in The Netherlands' ethnic hierarchy (Hagendoorn and Hraba, 1989), are higher and compare better with the respective results for the other two cities; even so, there are indications of a decline in this relationship in the 1991 results. Loef (1990), using data on the larger subdistricts of Amsterdam (the seventeen *stadsdelen*), reported a correlation coefficient of 0.89 between CD support in September 1989 and the percentage point change in the presence of Turks and Moroccans between 1982 and 1988. He also observed that CD support was higher in the western, twentieth-century part of the city than in the nineteenth-century zone. In Amsterdam the localities with numerous Turks and Moroccans are not particularly those with the highest levels of unemployment or the lowest

Table 4.2 Selected univariate statistics of percentaged support for the Centrumpartij/Centrumpartij '86 and Centrumdemocraten and Pearson product-moment correlation coefficients between these distributions and some aggregate characteristics in seventy-eight subdistricts [buurtcombinaties] of Amsterdam, 1982–91

Date and type of election	Party	Unweighted mean	Coefficient of variation	% foreigners[1]	% Turks and Moroccans[1]	% unemployed[1]	Status score[1]
8 September 1982[2] (Second Chamber)	CP	2.8	0.44	0.385	0.717	0.259	0.289
14 June 1984[2] (European Parliament)	CP	6.8	0.32	0.232	0.695	0.025	0.117
21 May 1986 (Second Chamber)	CP	1.4	0.42	0.404	0.672	0.029	0.119
	CD	0.6	0.44	0.317	0.523	0.117	0.228
	Total	2.0	0.39	0.410	0.681	0.060	0.164
18 March 1987 (Provincial Councils)	CD	1.4	0.42	0.421	0.683	0.043	0.166
15 June 1989 (European Parliament)	CD	2.3	0.49	0.357	0.526	−0.020	−0.049
6 September 1989 (Second Chamber)	CD	3.1	0.50	0.389	0.566	−0.008	0.044
21 March 1990 (Municipal Councils)[3]	CP '86	2.9	0.55	0.505	0.593	0.125	0.068
	CD	5.4	0.60	0.512	0.623	0.104	0.101
	Total	8.3	0.55	0.541	0.650	0.118	0.095
6 March 1991 (Provincial Councils)	CP '86	1.5	0.64	0.318	0.489	−0.063	−0.013
	CD	4.1	0.57	0.353	0.556	−0.052	0.007
	Total	5.6	0.56	0.362	0.565	−0.058	0.001

Notes:
1. The respective data for 1 January 1984 are those correlated with the 1982 and 1984 candidatures; data for 1 January 1987 are correlated with the 1986 and 1987 candidatures; and data for 1 January 1990 are correlated with the candidatures from 1989.
2. Because the city of Amsterdam redesigned the boundaries of its buurtcombinaties before 1986 and because aggregate data were published only upon certain combinations of the pre-1986 subdistricts the correlation coefficients in these rows have been calculated upon thirty-seven consolidated subdistricts.
3. For the March 1990 municipal council elections the levels of percentaged support for the extreme-right parties have been adjusted by an estimate of the presence of foreigners in order to exclude them from the numerical base on which the percentaged support has been calculated.

status scores,[11] unlike Rotterdam and The Hague. Therefore the relationships seen in Table 4.2 between extreme-right support and these latter indices are effectively negligible, especially after 1982. Van Amersfoort (1984, p. 224) has mapped the distribution of the Turkish population in Amsterdam in 1982, showing two concentrations: one in the west and the other in the south-east, both outside the canal-interspersed inner city.

Table 4.3 shows a rather different pattern in the case of Rotterdam. These parties have consistently – from 1982 to 1991 – performed noticeably better in impoverished, low-status neighbourhoods, in which in this case there are also higher proportions of Turks and Moroccans; variations from this characterization have over the past decade been minimal. Moreover, in Rotterdam, the presence of foreigners better operationalizes ethnic outgroups than in Amsterdam and the coefficients are not greatly different from those for the presence of Turks and Moroccans. These findings do not imply a single epicentre for such voting. An early geographical analysis, looking at CP support in September 1982, noted that it was concentrated in central and older neighbourhoods, but there were pockets of support elsewhere (Mik and Stikkelbroek, 1985, p. 107). There have been slight changes in character over the decade; one feature of support for the extreme right in Rotterdam that is worthy of comment and has not been noted by Dutch researchers is its tendency to somewhat greater spatial variation in the post-1989 results, suggesting that it is becoming rather less an entrenched characteristic of certain areas at the expense of others, as shown by the trend in the values of the coefficient of variation.

Table 4.4 shows a median pattern for The Hague, although the similarities are greater with Rotterdam. There is the same picture of continuity and concentration in poorer, low-status neighbourhoods with higher numbers of outgroup members, especially Turks and Moroccans (though the presence of foreigners is a good surrogate for the latter in this case). However, there is no clear pattern or trend in the data on spatial variation from which a substantive interpretation could be drawn.

It is worth observing that The Netherlands offers one specific model of what can happen to the electoral support of the extreme right when there is a party fission. In some cases, one new party attracts a reactionary bourgeois support, whereas the other collects the votes of working-class racists, as happened in Switzerland's split in the 1970s between the Schweizerische Republikanische Bewegung (SRB) and the formerly named Nationale Aktion für Volk und Heimat (NA). However, in The Netherlands the two parties which emerged from the split apparently have types of support that in social and motivational terms have been rather similar, in both cases generally working-class voters opposed to the local presence of particular ethnic outgroups.

In the light of the CDs' success in the September 1989 Second Chamber elections, there was a renewed debate about whether the surge was xenophobic in origin, either a reaction to the presence of non-indigenous people or to a local increase in their numbers, or merely a consequence of, say, political alienation. A study by Hoogendoorn *et al.* (1990) sought to answer this – highly unsatisfactorily – by correlating CP results in the September 1982

Table 4.3 Selected univariate statistics of percentaged support for the Centrumpartij/Centrumpartij '86 and Centrumdemocraten and Pearson product-moment correlation coefficients between these distributions and some aggregate characteristics in twenty-five subdistricts [wijken] of Rotterdam (excluding Hook of Holland), 1982–91

Date and type of election	Party	Unweighted mean	Coefficient of variation	% foreigners[1]	% Turks and Moroccans[2]	Annual income per earner 1982	Status score 1986
8 September 1982 (Second Chamber)	CP	4.4	0.37	0.826	0.765	−0.796	0.834
14 June 1984 (European Parliament)	CP	9.2	0.32	0.828	0.800	−0.843	0.858
21 May 1986 (Second Chamber)	CP	1.8	0.35	0.764	0.732	−0.841	0.824
	CD	0.5	0.44	0.657	0.655	−0.711	0.707
	Total	2.3	0.35	0.770	0.745	−0.845	0.830
18 March 1987 (Provincial Councils)	CD	1.8	0.31	0.820	0.758	−0.841	0.830
15 June 1989 (European Parliament)	CD	3.1	0.32	0.733	0.758	−0.811	0.756
6 September 1989 (Second Chamber)	CD	4.0	0.38	0.734	0.765	−0.808	0.765
21 March 1990 (Municipal Councils)[3]	CP '86	4.9	0.46	0.826	0.841	−0.840	0.846
	CD	5.6	0.47	0.754	0.790	−0.814	0.775
	Total	10.5	0.45	0.810	0.838	−0.850	0.832
6 March 1991 (Provincial Councils)	CP '86	2.1	0.45	0.666	0.686	−0.769	0.721
	CD	4.9	0.44	0.613	0.668	−0.700	0.628
	Total	7.0	0.43	0.647	0.692	−0.741	0.675

Notes:
1. The respective data for 1 January 1986 are those correlated with the candidatures up to 1987; those for 1 January 1988 are correlated with the later candidatures.
2. The respective data for 1 January 1984 are those correlated with the 1982 and 1984 candidatures; those for 1 January 1988 are correlated with the later candidatures.
3. For the March 1990 municipal council elections the levels of percentaged support for the extreme-right parties have been adjusted by an estimate of the presence of foreigners in order to exclude them from the numerical base on which the percentaged support has been calculated.

Table 4.4 Selected univariate statistics of percentaged support for the Centrumpartij/Centrumpartij '86 and Centrumdemocraten and Pearson product-moment correlation coefficients between these distributions and some aggregate characteristics in thirty-three subdistricts [wijken] of The Hague, 1982–91

Date and type of election	Party	Unweighted mean	Coefficient of variation	% foreigners[1]	% Turks and Moroccans[1]	% under Fl. 8,000 per annum 1971	Status position
8 September 1982 (Second Chamber)	CP	2.1	0.67	0.614	0.736	0.739	0.788
21 May 1986 (Second Chamber)	CP	1.0	0.64	0.494	0.636	0.694	0.765
	CD	0.4	0.61	0.674	0.762	0.653	0.686
	Total	1.4	0.62	0.561	0.692	0.704	0.766
18 March 1987 (Provincial Councils)	CD	1.3	0.47	0.601	0.721	0.779	0.857
15 June 1989 (European Parliament)	CD	2.3	0.52	0.517	0.696	0.616	0.751
6 September 1989 (Second Chamber)	CD	2.8	0.67	0.533	0.678	0.570	0.682
21 March 1990 (Municipal Councils)[2]	CP '86	2.2	0.57	0.551	0.715	0.640	0.791
	CD	4.6	0.55	0.466	0.663	0.549	0.718
	Total	6.8	0.54	0.506	0.696	0.593	0.760
6 March 1991 (Provincial Councils)	CP '86	1.5	0.73	0.520	0.670	0.377	0.583
	CD	4.6	0.60	0.531	0.709	0.669	0.790
	Total	6.1	0.60	0.553	0.732	0.615	0.768

Notes:
1. The respective data for 31 December 1980 are those correlated with the 1982 candidature; those for 31 December 1989 are correlated with the later candidatures.
2. For the March 1990 municipal council elections the levels of percentaged support for the extreme-right parties have been adjusted by an estimate of the presence of foreigners in order to exclude them from the numerical base on which the percentaged support has been calculated.

Second Chamber elections at the subdistrict level merely with the proportion of non-indigenous residents in the three principal Dutch cities, and then repeating the same analysis with the CD results in the election seven years later. The outcome, concentrating only on a single independent variable (and one that is a crude operationalization of its research intention), was unconvincing and the exercise has even less sophistication than those in Tables 4.2 to 4.4. As Tanja (1990) says, the research hardly deserved the media attention that it received.

However, there have been a number of studies of individual-level support, most of them dating from the early 1980s phase of CP success. These are drawn upon generously by van Donselaar and van Praag (1983, pp. 62–74) in their round-up of relevant research, which also included the aggregate data research then available. De Hond's (1983) large-sample analysis derived from 21,000 telephone interviews showed some particular, often predictable, distinctivenesses in CP supporters. They tended to be male and to have lower educational attainment, lower-than-average incomes and no religious affiliation, in comparison with the general Dutch population. As we know, they were more urban-based, stronger in the west of the country and (unsurprisingly) had little trust in government. Daudt (1983) showed that over a fifth of CP voters in the September 1982 Second Chamber elections came from the May 1981 supporters of the Partij van de Arbeid (PvdA), the country's conventional social-democratic party, and about the same number were from the previous year's CP voters. Rath's study of voting for the local councils in Rotterdam in 1984 showed the usual pro-male disposition among CP voters; there were even occasional CP supporters in his sample of non-Dutch and Surinamese/Antillianese voters (Rath, 1985, pp. 187–9). Rather interestingly, Buijs and Rath's (1986, p. 48) research on the Rotterdam municipal council elections in March 1986, which sampled in two predominantly working-class areas of the city, found no extra disposition among the unemployed to favour the CP. Rath's (1990, p. 31) study of the same elections four years later presents little data on CP '86 and CD support, except that it is clear the pro-male disposition persists.

Conclusion: What does the Future hold for the Dutch Extreme Right?

Although Dutch radicals and anti-fascists are prone to see dangers in the resurgence of the extreme right there since 1989, it has to be said that in contemporary Europe The Netherlands presents an interesting, though minor, example of the phenomenon: merely an irritant on the body politic. Very differently from countries such as Belgium and France, Ó Maoláin's (1987, pp. 198–202) compendium reports relatively few extreme right groups. The European Parliament's report drawn up on behalf of the Committee of Inquiry into Racism and Xenophobia (see Chapter 1) mentions the CDs and CP '86, plus only three small neo-Nazi groups, none of them particularly important in profile (European Parliament, 1990, pp. 29–30). Looking at the wider public, Dutch opinion polls by NIPO, the Dutch affiliate of Gallup International, were reporting support for the CDs at less than 0.5 per cent nationally in its 1990s omnibus polls – hardly *une situation française*!

Thus, the Dutch extreme right, despite the assistance that it has received from the country's voting system in local and national elections and despite its street presence in the major cities of the country, is really rather comparable to that in Great Britain. The CDs had about 1,000 members in 1990, only about a hundred of them active; the CP '86's national membership was put at a mere seventy-five (European Parliament, 1990, p. 29). Certainly, there is no sense in which the Dutch example has the importance of that in France or even Belgium (see Chapters 2 and 5), where Flemish nationalism has so stimulated the VB's support. Of course, the Dutch extreme right parties have to an extent set the agenda, as elsewhere in Western Europe, though the recent restrictive initiatives on immigration and asylum are likely to have been adopted in any case.

Notes

1. In the preparation of this chapter I have benefited from being able to consult material made available to me by the Anne Frank Foundation and the Steinmetzarchief in Amsterdam, by the Central Public Libraries, the Elections Offices and the Statistical Offices of the cities of Amsterdam, Rotterdam and The Hague, and by a number of Dutch academic colleagues. Research visits to The Netherlands to collect material were supported financially by the British Academy's Small Personal Research Grants scheme and the Nuffield Foundation's Small Grants scheme. My thanks are extended to the British Academy and to the Nuffield Foundation.
2. A very recent textbook addition to the literature on Dutch politics is Gladdish (1991); unfortunately, what he says on the extreme right parties is minimal and, in any case, not fully accurate. For a summary (in Dutch) of electoral research about The Netherlands, concentrating on electoral geography and including a section on the extreme right, see van der Wusten (1991).
3. Summaries of patterns of colonial and labour migration to The Netherlands are given in a number of sources. An early account is Schumacher (1981). Several of van Amersfoort's authored or co-authored articles contain information on the history of the phenomenon (e.g., van Amersfoort, 1984, 1986; van Amersfoort and Surie, 1987). His book (van Amersfoort, 1982) provides a fuller treatment, but only up to 1975. More recent is Entzinger's (1984) comparative account and one of the latest summaries is Cornelis (1990).
4. There has been no Dutch census in the conventional sense since 1971 and it has been adjudged that equally or more accurate demographic data may be compiled using both large-scale sample surveys, such as the labour-force survey required of member countries of the European Community (in the technical processing of which the Netherlands Central Bureau of Statistics has been a pioneer, developing computer hardware and software subsequently adopted in other countries), and also the registration of the population, which enables the ready preparation of up-to-date data on essential demographic characteristics for a complex hierarchy of subdistricts.
5. The Netherlands' national Parliament in The Hague has two chambers, the Second Chamber being directly elected. Second Chamber elections normally occur every four years, unless called early, the most recent being in 1989. The

country has twelve provinces: Drenthe, Friesland and Groningen form the North; Flevoland, Gelderland and Overijssel form the East; North Holland, South Holland, Utrecht and Zeeland form the West; and Limburg and North Brabant form the South. The most recent addition, Flevoland, has existed separately since 1 January 1986. Elections to the provincial councils are held every four years (most recently in 1991), except that those originally scheduled for 1986 were held in 1987. The Netherlands has 677 municipalities [*gemeenten*], ranging in population from the very largest, Amsterdam (695,162), Rotterdam (579,179) and The Hague (441,506) (1 January 1990) to rural municipalities with a few thousand residents, the mean population being about 22,000. Municipality boundaries are not infrequently altered, usually by amalgamations. Municipal council elections are held every four years, the most recent being in 1990.

6. This was Ventre, the Liberal Party, which won over 25 per cent of the vote in the May 1957 Danish general election, a high point in its level of support.

7. Newspaper citations without page numbers have been taken from the unpaginated clippings of the Anne Frank Foundation.

8. Of course, there is by now a quite sizeable *exposé* literature about the history and the ideology of the CP and, to a lesser extent, the CP '86 and the CDs. Much of it has been prepared by self-consciously anti-fascist groups. See, for example, FOK (1986), Kniesmeijer and Anne Frank Foundation (n.d.), SUA (1983) and, on extreme-right support among the young, VKPG (1985). A slightly more extended discussion of the ideology of the contemporary extreme right parties in The Netherlands is given by Lucardie and Voerman (1990).

9. There are certain clarifications about Tables 4.2 to 4.4 which should be given. First, it is considerably easier to acquire historical data on subdistrict voting for Amsterdam than for the other two cities. Full results for each *buurtcombinatie* (the basic urban subdistrict in Amsterdam) have long been published in the Amsterdam press, especially by *Het Parool*. The Rotterdam and The Hague press have not done this service and it is not possible readily to acquire historical data from the relevant electoral office, since records of these results have been inaccessibly archived. Thus, an analysis of The Hague's European Parliament results of June 1984 could not be included. Rotterdam collects subdistrict social and economic data on a variable basis but does not publish a regular compilation. Whereas Amsterdam annually publishes a comprehensive data book, *Amsterdam in cijfers*, that for The Hague has not been published since 1980, thus accounting for the ancient status of some of the data cited.

10. The coefficient of variation is a dimensionless measure of dispersion, independent of the absolute values of the distribution concerned, which is calculated by dividing the standard deviation of the distribution by its mean.

11. 'Status scores' are derived directly or indirectly from subdistrict factor scores of the socio-economic dimension of a factor analysis of standard socio-economic variables. They have been taken from relevant official sources in the cases of Rotterdam and The Hague and have been calculated by the author from his own data-compilation in the case of Amsterdam. In order to maintain scoring consistency among the socio-economic variables, numerically lower factor scores indicate higher status.

References

BASS, 1984. *Eurobarometer 21 (BASS 8420)*, Belgian Archives for the Social Sciences, Brussels.

Bouw, C., van Donselaar, J., Nelissen, C., 1981. *De Nederlandse Volks-unie: portret van een racistische splinterpartij*, Het Wereldvenster, Bussum.

Bovenkerk, F. *et al.*, 1978. 'De verkiezingsaanhang van de Nederlandse Volksunie', in F. Bovenkerk (ed.), *Omdat zij anders zijn: patronen van rasdiscriminatie in Nederland*, Boom, Meppel, pp. 103–18.

Brants, K. and Hogendoorn, W., 1983. *Van vreemde smetten vrij: opkomst van de Centrumpartij*, De Haan/Unieboek, Bussum.

Buijs, F. and Rath, J., 1986. *De stem van migranten en werklozen: de gemeenteraadsverkiezingen van 19 maart te Rotterdam*, Publication No. 25, Centrum voor Onderzoek van Maatschappelijke Tegenstellingen (COMT), University of Leiden.

Cornelis, B., 1990. 'Migratie naar Nederland', in H. B. Entzinger and P. J. J. Stijnen (eds), *Etnische minderheden in Nederland*, Boom, Meppel, pp. 13–30.

Daudt, H., 1983. 'Wisselende kiezers', *Acta Politica*, Vol. 18, No. 2, 274–86.

de Hond, M., 1983. *De opkomst van de Centrumpartij: een onderzoek onder de aanhang van de Centrumpartij in het najaar van 1983*, Inter/View B.V., Amsterdam.

de Jong, L., 1969. *Het Koninkrijk der Nederlanden in de Tweede Wereldoorlog: Deel I, Voorspel*, Martinus Nijhoff, The Hague.

Entzinger, H. B., 1984. *Het minderhedenbeleid: dilemma's voor de overheid in Nederland en zes andere immigratielanden in Europa*, Boom, Meppel.

European Parliament, 1990. *Report drawn up on behalf of the Committee of Inquiry into Racism and Xenophobia on the findings of the Committee of Inquiry*, European Parliament Document A3-195/90.

Falter, J. W., 1991. *Hitlers Wähler*, Verlag C. H. Beck, Munich.

FOK, 1986. *Opkomst en afgang van Centrumpartij en Centrumdemocraten*, Fascisme Onderzoek Kollektief, Amsterdam.

Gladdish, K., 1991. *Governing from the Centre: Politics and Policy-Making in The Netherlands*, Hurst, London.

Hagendoorn, L. and Hraba, J., 1989. 'Foreign, different, deviant, seclusive and working class: anchors to an ethnic hierarchy in The Netherlands', *Ethnic and Racial Studies*, Vol. 12, No. 4, 441–68.

Hamilton, R. F., 1982. *Who voted for Hitler?*, Princeton University Press, Princeton, NJ.

Hirschfeld, G., 1988. *Nazi Rule and Dutch Collaboration: The Netherlands under German Occupation, 1940–1945*, Berg Publishers, Oxford (first published in German in 1984).

Hoogendoorn, J. *et al.*, 1990. *Extreem-rechts en allochtonen in de vier grote steden: een problematische relatie*, Working Paper No. 122 Planologisch Demografisch Instituut, University of Amsterdam.

Husbands, C. T., 1988. 'The dynamics of racial exclusion and expulsion: racist politics in western Europe', *European Journal of Political Research*, Vol. 16, No. 6, 701–20.

——forthcoming. *Racist Political Movements in Western Europe*, Routledge, London.

Kniesmeijer, J., Anne Frank Foundation, n.d. *De crisis en de nieuwe zondebok: de racistische politiek van de Centrumpartij*, Anne Frank Foundation, Amsterdam.

Kooy, G.A., 1964. *Het echec van een 'volkse' beweging: nazificatie en denazificatie in Nederland, 1931–1945*, Van Gorcum & Comp., Assen.

Loef, K., 1990. *Centrumdemocraten in Amsterdam: een cijfermatige analyse in opdracht van Het College van B en W*, Amsterdamse Bureau voor Onderzoek en Statistiek, Amsterdam.

Lucardie, A. P. M. and Voerman, G., 1990. 'Extreem-rechts in Nederland: de

124   *Christopher T. Husbands*

Centrumdemocraten en hun radicale rivalen–II', *Namens*, Vol. 5, No. 7, 4–8.

Meyers, J., 1984. *Mussert: een politiek leven*, Uitgeverij De Arbeiderspers, Amsterdam.

Mik, G. and Stikkelbroek, J. H., 1985. *Verkiezingen in Rotterdam: een geografische verkenning van de verkiezingsuitslagen 1970–1982 en een nadere analyse van de ruimtelijke structuur der tweede kamerverkiezingen van 1982*, Koninklijk Nederlands Aardrijkskundig Genootschap, Amsterdam/Economisch Geografisch Institut, Erasmus University, Rotterdam.

Netherlands Central Bureau of Statistics, 1989, *Statistical Yearbook for The Netherlands, 1988*, SDU/Publishers, The Hague.

Nooij, A. T. J., 1969. *De Boerenpartij: desoriëntatie en radicalisme onder de boeren*, J. A. Boom en Zoon, Meppel.

Ó Maoláin, C. (comp.), 1987. *The Radical Right: A World Directory*, Longman, Harlow.

Passchier, N. P., 1987. 'Centrumpartij en N.S.B.: een vergelijking vanuit het sociaal-ecologisch gezichtspunt', *Koninklijk Nederlands Aardrijkskundig Genootschap Geografisch Tijdschrift*, Vol. 13, No. 1, 39–50.

Passchier, N. P. and van der Wusten, H. H., 1979. 'Het electoraal succes van de NSB in 1935; enige achtergronden van verschillen tussen de gemeenten', in P. W. Klein and G. J. Borger (eds), *De jaren dertig: aspecten van crisis en werkloosheid*, Meulenhoff Educatief, Amsterdam, pp. 262–72.

Rath, J., 1983. 'The enfranchisement of immigrants in practice: Turkish and Moroccan islands in the fairway of Dutch politics', *Netherlands Journal of Sociology*, Vol. 19, No. 2, 150–79.

——, 1985. *Migranten, de Centrumpartij en de deelraadsverkiezingen van 16 mai 1984 te Rotterdam*, Publication No. 20. Centrum voor Onderzoek van Maatschappelijke Tegenstellingen (COMT), University of Leiden.

——, 1990. *Kenterend tij: migranten en de gemeenteraadsverkiezingen van 21 maart 1990 te Rotterdam*, Vakgroep Culturele Antropologie, University of Utrecht.

Schmidt, O., 1979. 'A quantitative analysis of support for the National-Socialist Movement (NSB) from 1935 to 1940 in the City of Amsterdam', *Acta Politica* Vol. 14, No. 4, 479–508.

Schumacher, P., 1981. *De minderheden: 600,000 vreemdelingen in Nederland*, Van Gennep, Amsterdam.

Shirer, W. L., 1960. *The Rise and Fall of the Third Reich: A History of Nazi Germany*, Simon and Schuster, New York.

SUA, 1983, *De rechterkant van Nederland: een overzicht van conservatieve, extreem-rechtse en fascistische verschijnselen in Nederland en hun onderlinge contacten*, SUA, Amsterdam.

Tanja, J., 1990. Wetenschappelijk gebroddel: rapport over extreemrechts en allochtonen', *Afdruk*, 12–13.

van Amersfoort, H., 1982. *Immigration and the Formation of Minority Groups: The Dutch Experience, 1945–1975*, Cambridge University Press, Cambridge (first published in Dutch in 1974, with 1945–1973 in the subtitle).

——, 1984. 'Immigration and settlement in the Netherlands', *New Community*, Vol. 11, No. 3, 214–24.

——, 1986. 'Nederland als immigratieland', in L. van den Berg-Eldering (ed.), *Van gastarbeider tot immigrant: Marokkanen en Turken in Nederland, 1965–1985*, Samson Uitgeverij, Alphen aan den Rijn, pp. 15–46.

——, 1987. 'Van William Kegge tot Ruud Gullit: de Surinaamse migratie naar Nederland: realiteit, beeldvorming en beleid', *Tijdschrift voor Geschiedenis*, No. 100, 475–90.

van Amersfoort, H. and Surie, B., 1987. 'Reluctant hosts: immigration into Dutch society, 1970–1985', *Ethnic and Racial Studies*, Vol. 10, No. 2, 169–85.

van der Wusten, H., 1987. 'The Low Countries', in D. Mühlberger (ed.), *The Social Basis of European Fascist Movements*, Croom Helm, London, pp. 213–41.

——, 1991. 'Onderzoek van verkiezingsuitslagen', in *Compendium politiek en samenleving*, April, pp. 1–35.

van der Wusten, H. and Smit, R. E., 1980. 'Dynamics of the Dutch National Socialist Movement (the NSB): 1931–35', in S. U. Larsen, B. Hagtvet and J. P. Myklebust (eds), *Who were the Fascists: Social Roots of European Fascism*, Universitetsforlaget, Bergen, pp. 524–41.

van Donselaar, J., 1991. *Fout na de oorlog: fascistische en racistische organisaties in Nederland, 1950–1990*, Uitgeverij Bert Bakker, Amsterdam.

van Donselaar, J. and van Praag, C., 1983. *Stemmen op de Centrumpartij: de opkomst van antivreemdelingen partijen in Nederland*, Publication No. 13, Centrum voor Onderzoek van Maatschappelijke Tegenstellingen (COMT), University of Leiden.

van Leusden, H. and Moors, H., 1988. 'Mede-landers?: meningen en opvattingen over buitenlanders in Nederland', *Demos: Bulletin over Bevolking en Samenleving*, Vol. 4, No. 5, 33–6.

van Praag, C. S., 1983. *Vooroordeel tegenover etnische minderheden: resultaten van Nederlands opinieonderzoek*, Sociaal en Cultureel Planbureau, SCP Publication No. 37, Rijswijk.

VKPG, 1985. *Rechts-extreme jongeren*, Vakgroep Kollektief Polititiek Gedrag, University of Amsterdam.

Warmbrunn, W., 1963. *The Dutch under German Occupation, 1940–1945*, Stanford University Press, Stanford, Calif.

5 Belgium: Flemish Legions on the March[1]

Christopher T. Husbands

Tolstoy began *Anna Karenin* by saying that all happy families resemble each other but each unhappy family is unhappy in its own way. Contemporary extreme-right phenomena in the various countries of Western Europe are similar in many elements of their political extremism though they possess features that make each case idiosyncratic. Common to all of them – the only traditional exception being perhaps the Movimento Sociale Italiano (MSI) – is their use of racist mobilization based on hostility to one or more of a common collection of outgroups (immigrant workers, particular ethnic groups, asylum-seekers, foreigners in general). However, transcending this similarity are country-level specificities that derive from different political or historical circumstances.

Until recently, the extreme right in Belgium has received little international attention,[2] except perhaps from The Netherlands. Belgium does offer an interesting crucible of extreme-right activity, in some ways mirroring what one sees elsewhere (if not universally) in Western Europe. However, partly because of the distinctive political situation within the country, it has its own model of the right-wing extremist phenomenon. Although one might dispute the implicit emphases, this chapter is organized on the premise that there are three particular themes for the analysis of the contemporary Belgian extreme right:

1. Suggestions have been made about the infiltration of certain higher levels of the state, particularly the security service, the police and parts of the Army, by a well-organized extreme-right conspiracy. A comparable instance might perhaps be Italy during, say, the early 1970s but such organized infiltration is rare elsewhere. True, in the early days of the Federal Republic of Germany there were holdovers from the Nazi era in some offices. More recently there, as also in France, plenty of evidence has emerged that lower and middle-ranking elements in the police have been drawn disproportionately to supporting the extreme right. However, since the decline of suspicion in the early and mid-1960s about the disposition of the Army, this type of infiltration has not

been a major factor in analysing the French extreme right. Although it is difficult to be definitive, the infiltration aspect is a phenomenon more of the French than the Dutch-speaking section of the Belgian extreme right.

2. There is the proliferation of numerous small extreme-right groupings (charmingly known in French as *groupuscules*), in both the French and Dutch-speaking parts of the country, none of which has attracted much electoral support (at least until recently) and several of which do not even seriously contest elections. However, they do exist to a disproportionate degree in Belgium, often co-operating on the international level with similarly oriented groups elsewhere (e.g., in France and the ex-Federal Republic of Germany, in particular, and The Netherlands). Some of the older activists in these groups have experienced political extremism back to the immediate post-war era and even before.

3. Finally, there is the self-defined electoral (and now increasingly successful) extreme right, which in the present situation in Belgium means the Vlaams Blok (VB), based particularly in the Antwerp area but also active in parts of the provinces of East Flanders and Brabant. Inevitably, a substantial section of this chapter is devoted to an analysis of the characteristics and support of the VB.

These three themes form the basis for the major sections of this chapter. Although there is necessarily some substantive overlap (especially between the second and third themes), the three are none the less autonomous because the significant linkages between them, such as personnel, are not always known.

In the first section of the chapter are summarized some of the accusations and themes of the literature on élite infiltration by the extreme right. In the second section is provided a brief historical overview of the history of extreme right groupings since 1945. The third section is devoted exclusively to VB, given its significance in the contemporary situation. A concluding section then examines the likely future prospects of the extreme right in Belgium and discusses contemporary reactions in the mainstream of the country's politics to the rise of the VB and certain other groups, especially intended changes in policies on citizenship, immigration and political asylum.

The Infiltration of Institutions of State

Among certain circles in Belgium there has for some time been quite serious talk of an 'Italian situation' in the country (see Chapter 6).[3] Some left-wing commentators have drawn an explicit analogy between the political instability of Italy during the 1970s, when there was endemic violence from both political extremes and attested accounts of extreme-right sympathy among some agencies of state security, and Belgium's so-called 'black years' of the 1980s, when there were comparable outbursts of violence from left and right, including a wave of bloody supermarket hold-ups (Gijsels, 1990, esp. pp. 203–4). The latter came to be known as 'the Brabant massacres'.

There have been persistent suspicions about the reliability of the police and state security services in defending the country against dangers from the extreme right. This is not a new phenomenon. One episode in the 1930s was an attempted *coup d'état* by the police, according to De Bock (1984a), although others have dismissed such a Manichean interpretation. Whatever the truth about that particular incident and despite questions about the political disposition of the Belgian king, Léopold III (e.g., De Bock, 1984b), it seems during the 1930s – more so than in some other countries with fascist movements – to have been especially in the coercive state apparatuses where such sympathies and activities were concentrated.

This particular tendency emerged in the 1970s and 1980s in a number of incidents that showed extreme-right activity not only in the same institutions of state, but also within some of the conventional political parties. Certain of these incidents have indicated extreme-right sympathies among full-time and often quite senior functionaries of the institutions concerned. Others indicate easy penetration by individuals or small groups of extreme-right activists anxious to obtain secret information from the penetrated organization. Indeed, such affairs have become the material of periodic scandals in Belgian public life. There is a significant *exposé* literature concerning them and there have been parliamentary inquiries into these matters, the most recent of which reported at the beginning of May 1990 (Mottard and Haquin, 1990).

Extreme-right sympathies among senior officials were exemplified in a series of incidents that happened at the beginning of the 1980s. Around that time there was a clear expansion of extreme right racist activity, associated particularly with the Vlaamse Militanten Orde (VMO) in Dutch-speaking Flanders and the Front de la Jeunesse (FJ) in French-speaking Wallonia, the history of both of which is summarized later in this chapter. The FJ was disbanded in May 1981 as a paramilitary organization, its members having participated in numerous well-attested outrages, including arson attacks on buildings and facilities used by immigrants and an attack on the office of the left-wing weekly publication, *Pour* (Maesschalk, 1984, esp. pp. 159–60). Members of the VMO also attracted the increasing attentions of the authorities and it too was subsequently condemned in May 1983 as a private militia. Public disquiet about the developments on the extreme right had been instrumental in the establishment by Parliament of a special Senate inquiry, called the Wijninckx Commission, although certain Senate members were responsible for leaking details of its supposedly secret deliberations to some of those being investigated (De Bock, 1984c).

An example of penetration is seen in the case of the shadowy neo-Nazi organization calling itself Westland New Post (WNP). In February 1982 two gruesome professional murders were discovered by the police in Anderlecht, a suburb outside Brussels. The crime was solved only later, in August 1983, after the police elsewhere arrested a drunken right-wing extremist called Marcel Barbier in the street, after he was threatening passers-by with a revolver. In a subsequent search of his residence, which was shared with a like-minded friend called Michel Libert, the police found

secret NATO documents and blank passes to an army barracks. Both
Barbier and Libert were former members of the proscribed FJ and had been
instrumental in the emergence of the WNP organization between 1978 and
1981. Between 1980 and 1983 the WNP succeeded in penetrating the Belgian
military security services with a spy-cell of seven hardened militants, who
provided a substantial amount of secret military information concerning
both NATO and the Belgian Army (Haquin, 1984; Haquin, 1985; Gijsels,
1990, pp. 103–18). The same incident aroused suspicions about police sympathy for the extreme right, since it has also been alleged that many of the
documents of WNP confiscated in police raids were then retrieved with the
active connivance of the police (Gijsels, 1990, pp. 117–18). When Barbier
was eventually tried for the double murder and condemned to life imprisonment in May 1987, he attempted to retract a confession made when arrested
in August 1983. His trial excited some interest in Belgium because of the
questions it necessarily raised about the relationship between the extreme
right and certain law enforcement functionaries, specifically who was infil-
trating whom (*Le Monde*, 27 May 1987, p. 13).

In fact, it is difficult to offer a summary judgement about the precise
significance of these various shady activities; unsurprisingly, many of the
questions that they provoke necessarily remain unanswered. The extent of
their linkage, if any, with many of the more publicly visible extreme-right
phenomena has not been adequately established and there is a tendency by
more sanguine commentators to dismiss their importance, even if not their
actual occurrence. Even so, the more *engagé* assessments do worry about the
health of a polity where such events seem to happen with disturbing
frequency.

Extreme-Right Groups in Flanders and Wallonia

Overlying much of the extreme-right scene in Belgium is the Flemish–
Walloon linguistic, cultural and nationalist division of the country which has
also intruded into mainstream politics, especially since the rise of the
linguistic issue in the early 1970s.[4] This has affected the organization of the
extreme right in its numbers of groups and geographical coverage, for
example, the nature of its appeal, and its ideological orientations, which do
tend to distinguish the Belgian extreme right from that in other countries.

Ó Maoláin (1987, pp. 23–34), in discussing the position between 1985 and
1987, listed twenty-nine active extreme-right groups of one or another sort
in Belgium, eighteen based in the Dutch-speaking part, eight in the French-
speaking part, and three with bilingual names. In November 1987 a confi-
dential list of subversive groupings in Belgium (of both left and right)
produced by the Ministry of the Interior and reprinted by Gijsels (1990, pp.
192–3) gave a somewhat different collection of thirty-three apparently right-
wing groups, ranging from extreme-right study groups e.g., a Centre
d'Étude et de Recherche Socio-biologiques et Raciales (CERSBER), through
terrorist groups like the former VMO and the WNP, to diffuse collections of
skinheads. Of these, fourteen had clearly Dutch names, nine had obviously

French ones, five were French–Dutch, one Dutch–French, two German and two were linguistically ambiguous (including WNP, though this is to be considered French). In fact, both lists excluded a number of the smaller and more marginal electoral groupings that we shall mention; even so, the variety among those actually listed – in size, level of activity, degree of extremism, propensity to violence, ideological orientation and level of interest in electoral participation – is of course considerable. Any summary can discuss only the principal groups, although an attempt will be made to describe the historical continuities and traditions to be seen on the contemporary extreme right in Belgium.

As elsewhere, there have long been extreme-right or explicitly authoritarian movements in Belgian politics. Before the war there was the Rex National movement of Léon Degrelle, which was active and popular in Wallonia, and the Vlaams Nationaal Verbond (VNV) and the Verbond van Dietse Nationaal-Solidaristen (VERDINASO) in Flanders (van der Wusten, 1987). Although drawing from a variety of social sources and two different nationalist traditions, however, they never succeeded in managing a large-scale take-off.

The Second World War, of course, damaged the legitimacy of the extreme right and for a while afterwards it was deemed tactically unwise to mobilize publicly. In Flanders there had been a well-known degree of pro-German sympathy, although this was far from unique to this part of the country. Active collaboration had been only a minority phenomenon. Even so, in the whole country after the war there had been as many as 346,283 cases of collaboration with the enemy, many dealt with *in absentia*. Among the 1,247 condemned to death, 699 were French-speaking and 548 Dutch-speaking. In view of the fact that collaborators from the country's two linguistic groups were fairly equally prosecuted, much of the extreme right within both traditions – and especially, of course, former collaborators – went into what became called the 'catacombs period' (Cappelle, 1984, p. 67).

A 1962 report of the Centre de Recherche et d'Information Socio-Politiques (CRISP) – inspired by a series of newspaper articles on the extreme right in Belgium arising from the supposed extensions of the activities of the French Organisation de l'Armée Secrète (OAS) and the neo-fascist Jeune Nation (JN) – remarked that 'public manifestations of extreme-right opinion (including notions of extreme nationalism and authoritarianism) were extremely rare in Belgium until 1960' (CRISP, 1962a, p. 2). Then, in July 1960 the Mouvement d'Action Civique (MAC) was founded, inspired by Belgium's lost colonial role and activated by some of those returning from the Congo. Also, a Parti National Belge (PNB), commemorating the thought of Charles Maurras, won 0.1 per cent of votes cast in the 1961 legislative elections (CRISP, 1962b, p. 2).

Between 1974 and 1976 CRISP published a further summary of the extreme right in both parts of the country, isolating types that it described in the French case as conservative, traditionalist, national, national-revolutionary and nostalgic (Verhoeyen, 1974). New groups had arisen since 1962 and in certain intellectual circles there was an interest in the French new right and its ideas (see Chapter 2), represented best by the Groupement de

Recherche et d'Études pour la Civilisation Européenne (GRECE) and writers such as Alain de Benoist. However, the more interesting and relevant development since 1962 was the rise of an extreme-right current within Flemish nationalism (Verhoeyen, 1975). There has long been a 'Flemish movement' in Belgium devoted to the general social and political emancipation and cultural self-determination of the Flemish population.[5] It has traditionally included groups as much from the political left as from the right, and during the twentieth century it has been an important current in the mainstream political parties. However, militant Flemish nationalism was more specific, being devoted to the aim of establishing a separate Flemish state. Given some of the twentieth-century resonances of this idea, it is unsurprising that this nationalism was the seedbed of extreme-right activity or that this latter was therefore accorded more tolerance than extreme-right phenomena elsewhere in Western Europe.

Among those untainted by suspicions of wartime collaboration, there had been an immediate and significant renewal of Flemish nationalism after the war. The smaller group of nationalists who had identified with the pre-war VNV was obliged to be more cautious before 'breaking cover'. The Flemish party of the post-war years, the Vlaamse Concentratie (VC), was an important vehicle of their nationalism. Founded officially in May 1949 for the parliamentary elections of that year, its general acceptance was assisted by the anti-communist mood of the time. It attracted suspicion of extreme-right sympathy by calling in its programme for a general amnesty for wartime collaborators (Gijsels and Vander Velpen, 1989, pp. 19–21). As it was an organization that included former members of the pre-war VNV (even if forming only a fraction of activists), the left regarded it as politically questionable and on occasion attacked it. The VC therefore felt the need to establish a protection squad for defending its meetings and for other duties. This was provided by the later-to-be-notorious VMO, created in 1949 or 1950 (there has been some dispute about the exact date) and subsequently to play such an important part in militant extreme-right Flemish nationalism. When the VC metamorphosed into the Volksunie (VU) in December 1954 and the latter became the inter-class-based respectable arm of Flemish nationalism, the VMO extended its protection service to the newly founded grouping. However, VMO activists came to feel resentful at their exclusion from VU deliberations and there was a formal parting of the ways in October 1963. The VMO went through several phases, including a slight change of name to Vlaamse Militantenorganisatie. Then, in June 1971 its founder and leader, Bob Maes, announced its dissolution. However, this was not accepted by a more radical wing of the membership and in July that year a group of militants in Antwerp reconstituted the VMO under its original name. The new VMO was open in seeking connections with extreme-right groups in other countries, in its calling for the destruction of the Belgian state and in its hostility to parliamentary democracy. In April 1974, under a new leadership, the VMO announced its intention of enlarging its activities to oppose leftist influence in Flemish life. It also produced various small spin-off organizations, mostly in the Antwerp area.[6]

Also active around Antwerp and important as the seedbed for some of the present leadership and activist membership of the VB was an organization founded in 1962 called Were Di Verbond van Nederlandse Werkgemeen- schappen (WD, VNW). It sought to maintain what it regarded as certain essential features of Flemish nationalism and reproached the VU for having allegedly compromised these. Neither a mass movement, nor very large in membership, it grew with the dissolution of the original VMO, being joined by Maes and other former VMO activists. In fact, WD, VNW is an import- ant link, in both ideology and even personnel, between the pre-war VNV inheritance and the present VB.

As indicated above, the late 1970s and early 1980s were particularly turbulent years in Belgian politics. For example, there were political prob- lems over the implementation of the 1977 so-called Egmont Pact – a scheme for the devolution of power into three political and economic regions, Flanders, Wallonia and Brussels – agreed to by the four parties of the 1977–9 coalition, including (to the disapproval of many Flemish nationalists) the VU. In fact, the scheme was not implemented, because the coalition govern- ment fell. Moreover, economic difficulties faced Belgium, perhaps greater than those which faced other industrialized countries in the wake of the 1973 oil crisis. Partly in consequence, the issue of immigration and the position of Belgium's not inconsiderable number of immigrants not only from black Africa but also especially from the North African littoral and Turkey, became an issue in domestic politics. The VMO, long tainted by racist ideological elements, as Verhoeyen (1975, p. 29) has explained, became aggressive in its activities against immigrants, organizing anti-immigrant marches that often led to violence from anti-fascist demonstrators and to counter-marches. For example, the VMO organized a public march through Antwerp in October 1980, bringing about a later counter-demonstration against racism and fascism by 50,000 people in Brussels in the same month. When the VMO was finally proscribed as a private militia in 1983, its membership – as is a frequent consequence of such proscriptions – metamor- phosed into various alternative groupings, including a Vlaamse Nieuwe Orde (VNO), with some finding its way into the VB. Furthermore, there have been doubts about the proper enforcement of this proscription.

In any case, the electoral success of anti-immigrant mobilization in France from 1983 gave the impetus to a different type of extreme-right politics in Belgium. The VB, as the next section describes, having existed formally since May 1979, increased its anti-immigrant profile from about 1982, perhaps pushed in this direction in part by the injection of former VMO activists. A number of extreme-right initiatives also emerged in Wallonia after 1983 or, having existed for some time previously, increased their public profile. However, they were not notably Walloon nationalist in their ideology, on which subject the situation remained as Dumont (1983, p. 41) had described it in 1983: 'although well-developed in Flanders, regionalist extreme-right movements are, on the other hand, mere splinter groups in the French- speaking part of the country'. He mentioned only the Mouvement Nationaliste Wallon (MNW). Mainstream Walloon nationalism has tended to be more left-wing.

Of course, there were and are in Wallonia other types of extreme-right groupings not especially dedicated to Walloon nationalism. The Union Démocratique pour le Respect du Travail (UDRT), founded in April 1978 and led by Robert Hendrickx, had a Poujadist flavour and was regarded by commentators as a part of the extreme right. There was also the so-called 'Nols phenomenon', named after Roger Nols, mayor of Schaerbeek (a suburb of Brussels) from 1970. His original notoriety was based on his illegal imposition of, as it were, a linguistic apartheid in his town, establishing separate municipal reception points for Dutch-only speakers. However, by the early 1980s, he had altered his appeal to being anti-immigrant. In the 1982 municipal elections, he was sweepingly re-elected in Schaerbeek after an exclusively anti-immigrant campaign, especially against North African immigrants. Subsequently, in 1984, Nols flirted with the idea of starting his own political party, inspired by the success in France of Jean-Marie Le Pen (see Chapter 2 for details), leader of the French Front national (FN). Following the latter's June Euro-poll success, he was invited to address a meeting in Schaerbeek in September, where he announced that he had come to launch 'the foundations of a wide national and popular front in Belgium'. Nols thereupon founded a number of so-called Nols Clubs as the basis for an independent political party. However, although (as described below) such a party was later established, it was not done through Nols' particular initiative, which was not successful. He resigned as a parliamentary deputy in February 1987 and further compromised himself with his former mainstream political allies by too ardent contact with explicitly extreme-right figures. His list lost support in Schaerbeek in the 1988 municipal elections and he retired from politics on health grounds. Even so, he is still an important figure because of his role in placing the issue of immigration so centrally on to the Belgian political agenda. Essentially, he had been doing this for a number of years before the publication of his book on the subject (Nols, 1987).

There are another two important groupings on the French-speaking extreme right, both now basing their principal appeal on the immigration issue.[7] The Parti des Forces Nouvelles (PFN) has been in existence in a number of forms since 1975, when it saw itself not as a political party but as a collection of activists, then calling itself merely Forces Nouvelles. In fact, in France there is a breakaway party from the FN having the same name, founded in 1974 by former Ordre Nouveau (ON) militants dissatisfied with Le Pen (see Chapter 2). Although anti-immigrant, the Belgian version has also identified with anti-Semitism, including revisionist perspectives on the Holocaust, and the anti-abortion campaign. Its progress has been hampered by internal divisions and its electoral forays have so far been undistinguished; thus, it won only 4,190 votes (1.1 per cent of those cast) in the French-speaking lists of the Brussels regional election on 18 June 1989.

The other important grouping is more recent – the Front National–Nationaal Front (FN–NF), which was founded in late 1984 and early 1985 and led by Daniel Féret and is effectively an organization of French-speakers, despite the concession to bilingualism in its title.[8] Describing itself as anti-immigrant, anti-communist, anti-socialist and against the 'cowardice of the liberals', it brought together individuals from a range of earlier groupings on the extreme right, including some with highly questionable international connections (Gijsels *et al.*, 1988, p. 41). Despite its newness, it has now clearly eclipsed the PFN in Brussels, largely because its title brings it some reflected glory from its French namesake. In the 1985 parliamentary elections it won only 3,738 votes (0.5 per cent) in the Brussels *arrondisse-ment*[9] while the PFN won 6,035 (0.7 per cent). In the corresponding elections two years later support for the FN–NF increased to 7,596 votes (0.9 per cent) and that for the PFN fell to 4,317 votes (0.5 per cent). In the October 1988 municipal elections the FN–NF won a surprise seat in Molenbeek, a Brussels suburb. Then the FN–NF's 14,392 votes in the June 1989 Brussels regional election gave it 3.9 per cent of those cast on that occasion within the French-speaking list. Anti-immigration politics have now shown some growth potential in the Belgian capital, although they are in general less entrenched in Wallonia. Riding on the general anti-immigrant wave, the council of Schaerbeek (where we recall Roger Nols was the former mayor) in 1989 passed a local ordinance permitting only French, Dutch or German to be used in shop-signs (*Le Monde*, 15 July 1989, p. 5). In the parliamentary elections in November 1991, the l N–NF won 1.7 per cent of French-speaking votes, thus giving it a seat for tl e first time in the House of Representatives.

A more detailed analysis of the extreme right in Belgium would have considered the Flemish and Walloon situations separately in view of the considerable degree of autonomy between them. The importance of specifi-cally Flemish nationalism for the mainstream Flemish movements, in addi-tion to Belgium's linguistic antagonisms, is a powerful factor enforcing separate development. On the other hand, anti-immigrant and anti-foreigner exclusionism is the powerful common theme that undoubtedly underlies much, though not all, of the popular support for the extreme right.

The Vlaams Blok

The rise to significance of the VB in Belgian politics may for many be one of the more worrying developments on the extreme-right scene in Western Europe during the 1980s, even though its roots can be traced back to before the Second World War, as Gijsels and Vander Velpen's (1989) recent book on the VB has demonstrated. Yet, perhaps because of the lower salience of Belgium on the international and European stage, there has been far less comment on this phenomenon in the English-speaking world than about what has happened in France, the Federal Republic of Germany, or even Austria. As suggested above, perhaps only in The Netherlands' press, more interested than other Europeans in the affairs of a fellow Benelux country, has there been much analysis of the rise of the VB, especially as the municipal elections in The Netherlands of March 1990 saw a revival of the country's own extreme-right parties (see Chapter 4).

Our analysis of the VB is organized under the following headings:

1. major developments since its founding;

2. the principal points of its programme, including its material prepared for recent local elections and for the 1989 European Parliament elections;
3. its organization and structure;
4. the extent and nature of its support, including some suggestions of the mix of motives that contribute to this support;
5. its links with extreme-right movements abroad; and
6. the impact of the country's linguistic division upon its character and success.

Developments since the Founding of the VB

The rise to prominence of the VB since the late 1970s is closely related to the idiosyncratic linguistic division in Belgium, which has continued to give to politics there a marked degree of tension and has on occasion threatened the stability of the polity. Having been subordinate throughout most of the history of Belgium since its independence in 1831, the Dutch-speaking Flemings have come to be the predominant linguistic group. The French-speaking Walloons were by tradition the more powerful. However, since the Second World War, Wallonia has become the region with the declining industries, whereas Flanders has unwontedly prospered. There has been an increasing demographic shift in favour of the Flemings, who dominate in numerical terms in a ratio of about six to four.

There has long been a tradition of Flemish nationalism, especially in the area around Antwerp, and, as already mentioned, there were some questionable accommodations with the German occupiers during the Second World War. During the 1970s the linguistic issue threatened the breakup of the polity, and in an attempt to meet this threat the major parties agreed various constitutional reforms in the aforementioned Egmont Pact in May 1977. The fact that as a member of the four-party coalition government of the time the VU was a party to this pact, was one impetus from which the VB was able to grow, since the Egmont Pact was far from universally popular, especially in Flanders, and indeed the issue split the VU, losing it both activists and votes to the benefit of the emerging VB.

After the pact there were preliminary but unsuccessful negotiations between two figures well known in Flemish nationalist circles, Karel Dillen and Lode Claes. Although the latter has no further role to play in this account, the former assumes particular significance. Now sixty-seven years old and an accountant by profession, Dillen had been active in the Flemish nationalist cause since shortly after the Second World War. In October 1977 he founded the Vlaams-Nationale Partij (VNP), and at the beginning of November of that year, Claes established the Vlaamse Volkspartij (VVP). In the autumn of 1978 new negotiations were held between the two groups with a view to putting forward a common list in the forthcoming parliamentary elections on 17 December 1978. The name chosen for this list was the Vlaams Blok. On that occasion the programme was not overtly xenophobic, instead making a conventional middle-class appeal against high taxes and political corruption. The party won over 75,000 votes for the House of Representatives (about 1.4 per cent) and over 80,000 in the Senate; Karel Dillen was elected to the House. In the spring of 1979 negotiations between the VNP and some from the VVP led to the conclusive metamorphosis of the VNP into the Vlaams Blok.

The new party avoided the 1979 Euro-elections and in the parliamentary elections of 8 November 1981 Dillen was re-elected to the House, though at 1.2 per cent of votes cast, support for the VB was slightly down in comparison with 1978. In local elections in October 1982 the VB made its first local breakthrough, with two councillors elected to the Antwerp City Council: the VB won 16,528 votes, 5.2 per cent of those cast. The parliamentary elections of October 1985 saw Dillen re-elected, although the party still received only 85,000 votes (1.4 per cent). However, two provincial councillors were simultaneously elected to the Antwerp provincial council. By 1987 the VB was clearly in the ascendant. In the December parliamentary elections it received 116,410 votes for the House (1.9 per cent which was enough to elect two representatives) and 122,925 for the Senate (sufficient for a seat there for the first time, which was occupied by Dillen). In the simultaneously held provincial elections the VB elected four members to the Antwerp provincial council. The VB's cause was undoubtedly also further assisted by the fact that the VU had again been a member of the national government since 1987. Then, in the municipal elections on 9 October 1988, came the breakthrough that for the first time attracted serious foreign interest to this aspect of extreme-right activity in Belgium. The VB elected twenty-three councillors in ten municipalities. The major success was in Antwerp, where ten councillors in a fifty-five member council were from the VB. In Antwerp alone the VB won 54,163 votes, 17.7 per cent of those cast. Its success was particularly at the expense of the VU, which lost nearly half its support received in the previous contest in 1982. The VB also won three seats in Mechelen (whose other reputation is based on its football team) and two in Gent, as well as individual seats in other smaller localities in the provinces of Antwerp and East Flanders. In the June 1989 Euro election the VB rather confounded the Belgian pollsters by winning 240,668 votes, enough to see Dillen into the European Parliament. It won 62,355 votes in the city of Antwerp itself, 20.8 per cent of those cast, better even than in October 1988. In a simultaneous contest for a new Brussels regional council the VB won 8,999 votes, only 2.1 per cent of all cast though 13.4 per cent of the Flemish lists (which received 15.3 per cent of all votes cast) (Blaise *et al.*, 1989, p. 7). This performance was enough to cause consternation because it put a VB member on to the seventy-five seat council holding one of the eleven seats for the Flemish lists.

Thus, it is fair to say in late 1991 – especially with the decline in mass support for the Federal Republic of Germany's Republicans since the 1989 Euro-elections, as that party has descended into internal vituperations – that Belgium contains one of the most successful (albeit localized) contemporary extreme-right examples in Western Europe, putting it into the company of France, Austria, and perhaps Italy and Norway. The headquarters of the local VB branch in Antwerp, located a short walk from the city centre, are comparatively modest, being an office converted from what was once a conventional terraced residence with its front door opening directly on to the pavement. Even so, it exudes a sense of presence and self-importance, for a flag with the Brabant lion rampant is often draped ostentatiously from the first-floor balcony.

The Programme of the VB

An article in the left-wing Antwerp newspaper, *De Morgen*, written in the light of the VB's successes in the Antwerp municipal elections in 1988, headlined the ideological progression of the VB between 1979 and 1988 as 'from Flemish nationalism to racism' (*De Morgen*, 11 October 1988).[10] The VB's early programmatic themes were constitutional reform and independence from Brussels. However, by 1982 there was a change of direction explicitly towards a 'foreign workers out' position. After some inconsequential election performances in the late 1970s and early 1980s, the party was desperate to find an issue that could galvanize its fortunes. The success of the Dutch Centrum Partij (CP) (see Chapter 4) and later the French FN in mobilizing against foreign workers and immigrants undoubtedly provided a model that the VB was keen to imitate. In 1982 the VB had issued a publication called *Dossier gastarbeid* (van de Wal, 1982), one chapter of which had posed as alternative scenarios integration, ghetto-formation and repatriation. A year later, the party had proposed a bill in favour of financial inducements to foreign workers to return to their countries of origin. In 1984 the party's election material for the Euro-election announced: '500,000 unemployed. Then why foreign workers? Vote Vlaams Blok'.

A list of the party's principal programme positions (VB, 1990) gives first place to the demand for an independent Flemish state. Brussels, as capital of Flanders and of Europe should as such receive a special constitution. The sixth point, headed 'A stop to immigration', demands the return of the great majority of foreign workers to their own country through the provision of work in their own area. It also mentions the re-orientation of development aid and no voting rights for foreigners.

Some of the more dramatic material produced for the 1988 municipal elections was more emphatic in its anti-foreigner appeal. Headed 'Own people first . . .',[11] one leaflet contained a cartoon-style drawing with numerous 'foreign' symbolisms (black faces, Sikh turbans, fezzes, chador-clad women, black Zapata-style moustaches and, significantly perhaps, an obvious financier figure with the ambiguously drawn features of an anti-Semitic stereotype). Standing behind these representations of various foreigners was the standard 'own people' family, with father, mother and baby – the man holding up his right hand implying simultaneously and ambiguously a gesture to demand attention and, more subtly, the last desperate wave of a man before disappearing below the surface of the 'sea' of foreigners pictured around him.[12] The inside centre column of the same leaflet announced:

The number of foreigners is increasing every day. The foreign-worker problem does not exist in the same degree everywhere. The Vlaams Blok wants the cities and municipalities that have not experienced it to be protected from it. The Vlaams Blok wants the cities that are plagued with it to be freed from it. . . . The Flemish cities and municipalities must remain cities and municipalities of towers and cathedrals and must not become north African ghettos with mosques.

During recent years the VB has established a profile based upon issues other than Flemish nationalism, xenophobia and racism. It has been strongly anti-homosexual (the leaflet quoted above also proclaimed that 'the Vlaams Blok chooses youth, not paedophiles and other deviants'). In October 1989 a VB member was sentenced to a fine and a suspended prison sentence for participating in an attack in March 1985 on a homosexual activist distributing leaflets on a college campus (*De Morgen*, 7 October 1989). The VB has also been vigorously anti-abortion and has organized campaigns on this specific theme. 'Because people are important . . . oppose the law for destroying babies!' [*géén baby-rot-op wet*] and 'This life is in danger' (accompanied by the picture of a foetus) claimed one leaflet. The party's newspaper (*Vlaams Blok*, October 1989, p. 8), under a title of 'Abortion: an ethical analysis', contained an extended consideration of the anti-abortion case, complete with an unflattering photograph of the woman Representative who had brought forward a pro-abortion bill in Parliament.

Organization and Structure of the VB

It would be a serious mistake to regard the VB as a one-person band; it has avoided the difficulties faced by some extreme-right parties that achieve sudden growth of having a dearth of suitably intelligent and qualified people to fill the elected offices won by its success, problems that have affected the German Republicans and the Geneva-based Vigilance (Husbands, forthcoming, ch. 6 and 7). It has instead been able to draw upon a depth of experience in the Flemish nationalist tradition. However, although several of its leading members show obvious competence, the figure of Karel Dillen as its leader and now its Member of the European Parliament stands supreme above his peers. His was the initiative that founded the party, as we saw. The anti-fascist publication *Verzet* (1989) gives some details about each of the VB's principal leaders. Dillen, born in Antwerp in 1925, was in 1949 a co-founder of the Jong-Nederlandse Gemeenschap (JNG), an initiative of a former leader of the Nationaal-Socialistisch Jeugdverbond (NSJV). During the 1950s Dillen was active in the VU and in 1962 founded WD, VNW (which was mentioned earlier) and led this until 1976. In 1973 he became leader of the Vlaams-Nationale Raad (VNR).

The VB, typical of extreme-right groups, has a fairly centralized organizational structure: even the important Antwerp branch refers written queries to the Brussels headquarters. The party's national administration consists of the leader, deputy leader (who chairs the national council), treasurer and a number of other officers, including the leader of the party's youth wing, Vlaams Blok Jongeren (VBJ). The party's national council consists of representatives of each *arrondissement* where there are local branches, as well as of each relevant provincial party administration. Each *arrondissement* administration has a collection of officers complementing most of those at the national level. There is an *arrondissement* council containing representatives of individual local branches. This lowest level has its complement of officers. Individual membership is at the branch level.

The Extent and Nature of VB Support

Enough has already been said to make clear certain aspects of the VB's popular support. It is still heavily concentrated in the city of Antwerp and its environs, with a levelling-off as one moves away from this epicentre. In parts of Antwerp itself the VB has won a third of the vote, as we shall see, and there are other areas of strength such as the town of Sint-Niklaas (before whose gate, 'in one of the traverses of the trench opposite to the salient angle of the demibastion of St Roch', Uncle Toby received his notorious war-wound in Laurence Sterne's *The Life and Opinions of Tristram Shandy*). The VB's strongholds, absolutely and relatively defined, are in the provinces of Antwerp and East Flanders, with noticeable distance-decay as one moves away from Antwerp. Whereas in Antwerp the VB vote in the June 1989 Euro-poll was the 20.8 per cent mentioned above, in Sint-Niklaas it was 7.9 per cent, in Aalst 4.7 per cent, and in Oudenaarde (otherwise famed for the battle there in 1708) 2.3 per cent. We shall return to the implications for analysing the extreme right in Belgium of this remarkable concentration around one epicentre of electoral support. It certainly stands out very clearly in the cartographic presentation of voting levels (e.g., Delruelle-Vosswinkel *et al.*, 1989), although the fact that Antwerp contains more than 10 per cent of Belgium's population should perhaps temper a too excessive emphasis on local concentration.

After its national-level 1.9 per cent in the December 1987 parliamentary elections, the VB was registering significantly in opinion polls, as revealed, for example, in the omnibus polling of the organization, DIMARSO, the Belgian affiliate of Gallup International, and reported regularly in *De Morgen*. Its national samples are self-weighting and are based on 1,500 cases, 600 in Flanders, 600 in Wallonia and 300 in Brussels. In late 1989 and the first part of 1990 the VB was averaging about 3 per cent nationally and 5 per cent in Flanders alone. Its support continued to maintain itself through 1990 and 1991. Even so, it was a considerable shock to mainstream politicians when, in the November 1991 parliamentary elections, the VB won 10.4 per cent of the Flemish vote, enabling it (at least to a certain extent) to break out from its traditional bastion around the immediate Antwerp area. The city of Antwerp remains its undoubted stronghold, of course; it won over 25 per cent of the votes there and became the individual party with the highest support. Its representation in the country's House of Representatives rose from two to twelve seats, as the VU's dropped from sixteen to ten. In the Senate the VB finished with five seats.

Small-case-base problems have clearly limited systematic analysis of the social background characteristics of VB supporters.[13] However, some conclusions may still be drawn on this matter from such individual-level data as do exist and from aggregate-data analyses. Unfortunately, the available individual-level studies do not offer unambiguous consistency. It is likely that the VB's activist support, in this respect like that of more or less all extreme-right movements, is disproportionately male, although Swyngedouw *et al.* (1990, p. 28) report that no party's support in the Flemish constituency in the June 1989 Euro-poll contained a significant gender differential. They also report an interaction effect on voting for the VB between educational attainment and age, support being disproportionately high among those aged 36 to 45 and among those aged 46 or more with *higher* educational attainment. There was no differential by religious belief, though they do report slightly higher support overall among those in low-status occupations (Swyngedouw *et al.*, 1990, pp. 29–37).

On the other hand, though not necessarily inconsistent, there is also evidence of the particular appeal of the VB in recent years to the young, again in agreement with similar findings about many (though not all) other such movements. A study of youth partisanship in Mechelen, reported in rather sparse detail by *De Morgen* (11 October 1988, p. 17), found that 16 per cent of pupils and students aged from 14 to 20 favoured the VB and among those aged 17 and 18 the figure was 24 per cent – much higher than the city-wide percentage.

Perhaps the most significant question to be asked about the support of a racist political movement is its predominant social class base, since this may offer important indications about the motive and type of racism being analysed (e.g., Husbands, 1988). The slightly lower status character of VB support overall in the June 1989 Euro-poll was mentioned above, and some further tentative suggestions may be made on this matter about the Antwerp case as well as elsewhere. It does seem likely that the VB in Antwerp, as its support has increased, has transcended its probable earlier working-class base to become a more genuinely inter-class movement now comprising considerable representations of Flemish activists disappointed with the VU, working-class racists, and right-wing extremists motivated by anti-communism and anti-Semitism. There has been a decline over the years, as its general support has grown, in the extent to which its vote on a subdistrict [*wijk*] basis correlates with the local concentration of foreigners, suggesting – as far as aggregate data permit such inference – a diffusion of support away from the working-class areas of the city where foreign workers are disproportionately located.

At the end of 1988, about 15 per cent of the city of Antwerp's population were foreigners, Moroccans being the most significant non-European group; in three subdistricts of the city the percentage of foreigners was between 20 and 25 per cent. In three selected elections between 1982 and 1989 – the 1982 municipal elections, the 1985 parliamentary elections and the 1989 European Parliament elections – VB support city-wide was 5.1, 7.0 and 20.8 per cent respectively.[14] The zero-order product-moment correlation coefficients, calculated across fourteen subdistricts of the city for which all the relevant data were available, between percentage-levels of VB support and the percentage of foreigners in the locally resident population at the end of 1987 were, correspondingly, 0.559, 0.440, and 0.241, showing a numerical decline that was especially apparent in the 1989 results.[15]

Although data were unavailable to permit more complex statistical analyses, even these simple relationships suggest that factors other than merely some contact-racism-based mechanism – as expounded in Husbands (1988) – are now at work in producing VB voting in the city. True, there are areas where high VB support and high foreigner-concentration coincide. One such is Stuivenberg near the docks to the north of the old city, where over 21 per cent of residents were foreigners in 1987. However, in the nearby Dam-Eilandje neighbourhood, where the VB won 34.1 per cent of the poll in the 1989 European elections, the percentage of foreigners is about that of the city average. In the 1989 Euro-poll the VB won a third of the vote in Oud-Borgerhout, to the immediate east of the city of Antwerp proper, although in Borgerhout as a whole only 16 per cent of residents were foreigners in 1988. On the other hand, it is a place of inter-ethnic tension, as evidenced by a reported incident in May 1990 when there was an unpleasant altercation between a group of young Moroccans and some young local basketball-players (*Het Nieuwsblad* (Antwerp), 22 May 1990, p. 11).

Clearly, the VB is by any conventional definition a xenophobic party, but the correlational data presented above suggest, as both VB activists have claimed and also other commentators have argued, that its support is now underpinned by a complex of motivations. Gijsels *et al.* (1988, p. 18) note that in Limburg province, where the foreign population is a more important factor (albeit also older) than in Antwerp, the VB has fared badly, its better performances there being in places with significant numbers of unemployed miners. Thus, there may well be some truth in the claim of Eric Deleu, who headed the VB list in the October 1988 municipal elections in Antwerp and said of the VB's success then that it was not merely 'due to our standpoint in connection with the immigrant problem but also to our fight against politicization, the selling-off of the docks, rising crime, the breakdown of law and order, and the impoverishment and brutalization of the city' (*Gazet van Antwerpen*, 10 October 1988, p. 2).

The VB's Links with Extreme-Right Movements Abroad

Flemish nationalism arises from a proud and self-conscious tradition. It has historically taken various forms and in a sense has been self-centred and insular. In other respects, however, it has been cosmopolitan and internationally oriented; this is certainly true of its extreme-right variant. The notorious international neo-Nazi gathering, long held annually at Diksmuide, is organised through the efforts of the VMO and its successor organizations. Such Flemish nationalists have always been happy to cultivate contacts abroad, especially in the Federal Republic of Germany and The Netherlands (though less keen on the 'Greater Netherlands' concept of some Dutch neo-fascists).[16] Most annual reports of the Bundesamt für Verfassungsschutz mention the VMO in connection with activities abroad of the German extreme right (e.g., BMI, 1989, p. 138). To a lesser extent Flemish nationalists have also developed contacts with the extreme right in Great Britain and France.

Le Pen had looked to the Flemish nationalists, even before the 1989 Euro-poll, as a possible contributor to the critical minimum number of deputies needed to compose an official grouping in the European Parliament, a status that carries a number of important privileges. Indeed, VB representatives had usually been guests at the FN's annual celebratory gathering. Until the spring of 1989 it seemed unlikely that there would be a significant German contribution to any extreme right grouping in the European Parliament; in any case, till then Dr Gerhard Frey's Deutsche Volksunion – Liste D (DVU – List D) was more likely to make an electoral breakthrough than were The Republicans. In late 1988 three VB leaders had been welcomed at a congress of Frey's organization in North Rhine – Westphalia and the VB was the object of much flattering attention from Le Pen's FN.

Certainly, the 1988 success of the VB in municipal elections was an inspiration to the European extreme right more generally, suggesting a possible revival in the 1989 Euro-poll. Even so, Dillen's success in becoming a member of the European Parliament was not predicted properly by pre-election polls. Of course, he joined the European Right group in the European Parliament, with the deputies of the French FN and the German Republicans. In the quarrel within this group, particularly between The Republicans and the Italian MSI representatives, Dillen sided strongly with the former. In fact, the quarrel – centred upon the status of South Tyrol (Alto Adige to the Italians), which the latter wanted to keep as Italian and which the Germans felt should be offered independence – led to the departure of the elected MSI deputies from the European Right group (*Le Monde*, 10 October 1989, p. 10). Dillen saw parallels between the status of the South Tyrol and that of Flanders. In an interview in the FN publication, *National-Hebdo*, he said that 'it [the quarrel] was a problem between Italians and Germans' though 'we others, as Flemings, are sensitive to the fact that this region has been made Italian by force.' He continued: 'We could compare this case to that of Brussels, which we want to have as the capital of our future Flemish state'.

The Linguistic Factor and the Character of the VB

As we saw in the previous section of this chapter, not all extreme-right phenomena in Belgium precisely mirror the linguistic cleavage that has become so important in the country's domestic politics. There are groups that purportedly attempt to cultivate a broad national appeal and sport bilingual titles. On the other hand, some of this is merely cosmetic and the groups concerned are effectively on one or other side of the dividing-line.

This is true of the FN–NF, for example, which is really French-speaking. Militant extreme-right Walloon nationalism has been largely inconsequential in Belgium's post-1945 politics, whereas Flemish nationalism, culminating in the contemporary VB, has been a major ingredient in the ideology and motivation of the extreme right there, especially in the Antwerp area. This aspect is paradoxical to the extent that Flemish nationalists have actively cultivated international contacts. On the other hand, it does make the extreme right in Belgium different from other major examples of the phenomenon in Western Europe, such as in France, the Federal Republic of Germany, Austria or The Netherlands. Instead, if one is seeking analogues of the VB, one has to look at some of the more recondite examples of the extreme right, such as Protestant militance in Northern Ireland or, as implied, the extreme-right German separatism of South Tyrol. Thus, although Flemish nationalism has now taken its place on the European stage, its equivalents are not the other major contemporary examples of extreme-right success.

It has undoubtedly been nurtured by the particularity of Belgian politics and society. It came from the extreme-right tradition of the pre-war and wartime period, was kept alive by a strand within cultural Flemish nationalism and the political nationalism of the VU. It received its decisive impetus from reactions within Flemish nationalism to the country's political crisis in the late 1970s, before assuming in the 1980s – under the influence of some of the younger members of its leadership – the exclusionist strategy and ideology of well-known extreme-right parties elsewhere in Europe. Even so, its Flemish nationalism remains incontrovertibly an idiosyncratic feature that still serves to differentiate it from the latter.

Prospects and Reactions

The extreme right in Belgium has undergone numerous changes since 1945, although there are also some remarkable continuities. During the immediate post-war years, the 'catacombs' period, it kept a low profile before, in the Flemish case, emerging in renewed forms of Flemish nationalism. During the late 1950s there was some reaction to Belgium's decolonization in the forms and expressions of extreme-right activity, though scarcely more so than in Great Britain. The early 1960s saw suggestions of influences from the French OAS; however this period passed without leaving a major long-term impact. A more persistent French influence, even if only really upon a minoritarian and self-consciously intellectual wing of the Belgian scene, was the new right, exemplified by GRECE, especially in the 1970s after the emergence of left-wing radicalism in 1968. Then, during the 1980s, Jean-Marie Le Pen's success was used as a model by both French and Flemish wings of Belgian extreme-right politics, when he (along with the Dutch) demonstrated the viability of anti-immigrant agitation. Thus, by the late 1980s anti-immigrant Flemish nationalism is clearly the major component. From the 1970s and especially during the early 1980s, there has been a parallel *Leitmotiv* of the participation of law enforcement agencies in extreme-right terrorism.

Perhaps two major questions are raised by the present state of the extreme right in Belgium. The first, of course, concerns its likely future development, a subject that may be addressed under two headings:

1.   the future stability of the Belgian polity in the light of suspicions about extreme-right sympathies within some of its major law enforcement agencies; and
2.   the electoral prospects of right-wing extremism in Belgium, especially the VB, and to a lesser extent, such groups as the FN–NF and the PFN.

The second major question is how the mainstream political groups and the government have responded to an extreme-right advance that, though locally concentrated, has placed on to the political agenda a number of items that mainstream politics prefer to eschew.

The Stability of the Belgian Polity.

The report of the recent parliamentary commission, *Les tueries du Brabant* (Mottard and Haquin, 1990), reviewed at length the events of the early 1980s. Although it is clear that some at least of the extreme-right criminals of that era are now behind bars, the questions about police and security service connivance live on. Those responsible for the Brabant massacres were never caught and the Commission's discussion of whether their activities amounted to politically motivated terrorism or mere banditry (pp. 309–11) is thoroughly inconclusive. The response of the current Minister of the Interior, Louis Tobback, to the publication of the report was to call for the disbandment of the security police, claiming that it was not performing suitably. Also, the former Belgian Prime Minister, Wilfried Martens, suspended the police counter-terrorist chief, who was implicated in the report (p. 68).

Electoral Prospects of Right-Wing Extremism

The rise in recent years of the electoral support for the extreme right in Belgium is, of course, analogous in one sense to the anti-immigrant politics to be seen in numerous other countries of Western Europe. However, as in other respects already mentioned, the Belgian case has its own ambiguities and specificities. Whilst the liberal outsider may stand aghast at support levels of 20 per cent in free elections and at a city council with nearly a fifth of its members from the extreme right, it remains true that VB strength is, even after the November 1991 parliamentary elections, still fairly locally concentrated – far more so when compared with similar movements in Western Europe, except perhaps the British National Front in the 1970s (Husbands, 1983, pp. 50–95) – and that its reliance on a type of Flemish nationalism confined to a small part of the country may perhaps militate against its wider success. This does to an extent contradict the judgement of the current mayor of Antwerp, who in an interview revealed how he had received burnt fingers from several of his pro-immigrant worker policies and in pointing to urban racism elsewhere (as in The Netherlands), concluded, 'we are dealing with a European phenomenon' (Eppink, 1990). On the other hand, levels of support for the FN–NF in French-speaking Belgium and on French-speaking electoral lists have not so far been genuinely significant, despite its recent small successes in the Brussels area.

Mainstream Political Responses to the Extreme Right

Of course, it is true that the emergence of the VB has noticeably increased tensions in Antwerp itself upon its foreign population, the local press and the mainstream political parties. A third of the readers of the largest regional daily, the traditional Catholic *Gazet van Antwerpen*, were purported VB voters and the correspondence to it has been full of anti-foreigner declarations. The rise of the VB in Antwerp has not occurred without anti-racist activities, as when 1,500 demonstrated while the new VB members of the City Council were installed in January 1989 (*De Morgen*, 4 January 1989, p. 2; *NRC Handelsblad* (Rotterdam), 4 January 1989, p. 5), though the role of anti-racist activism in stemming the tide of racist voting is perhaps as unclear here as in other situations where it has been attempted (e.g., the Anti-Nazi League against the British National Front in the late 1970s and SOS-Racisme against the FN in France more recently). Six months later the VB improved its percentage support in the Euro-poll and has continued to be publicly assertive in the streets of the city. In Antwerp, the mainstream parties have sometimes seen themselves forced to adopt VB policies. For example, in September 1988, shortly before the municipal elections, the Christelijke Volkspartij (CVP), while stressing that it would not work with the VB, accepted the latter's demand that there should be no more mosques built in Antwerp (*De Morgen*, 15 September 1988). Such absorption tactics, whose analogues on the national level are discussed below, have clearly not been conspicuously successful in Antwerp.

There have also been ramifications at the national level. Shortly before the 1989 Euro-poll five mainstream parties, the VU, the CVP, the Socialistische Partij (SP), the Partij voor Vrijheid en Vooruitgang (PVV) and Agalev (the radical ecologists), made an agreement to eschew all political contact with the VB. In the light of the VB's Euro-poll success, three of the five participants felt that it was not possible to isolate and stigmatize the VB in this way, claiming that it would merely increase VB support because of political martyrdom. Both CVP and PVV wanted to abandon the agreement, and the VU (a major loser of votes to the VB, of course) was similarly inclined, all none the less claiming that they still wanted no contact with the VB. Only the SP and Agalev seemed keen to maintain their earlier position (*De Morgen*, 27 June 1989, p. 7), although the former especially had also lost earlier votes to the VB in the 1989 Euro-poll (Swyngedouw *et al.*, 1990, p. 54).

In the light of the VB's 1988 electoral success, the Belgian government pledged itself to examine its policies on immigration. One result of this was a greater commitment to the full integration of immigrants already in the country. In November 1989 the commissioner for immigrants, Paula D'Hondt, published proposals that would give automatic Belgian citizenship to third-generation immigrant children, as well as a number of other measures intended to accelerate integration (*NRC Handelsblad*, 24 November 1989, p. 4). Unsurprisingly, the VB opposed these steps.

However, there has also been a more draconian side to the government's response. Perhaps more significant, and a story to be seen elsewhere in Europe, has been a hardening of the Belgian position on immigrants and asylum-seekers. Back in 1987 the government had already introduced a tightening of policy on asylum-seekers designed to discourage Iranians in particular from coming to Belgium. The change was carried out, despite some bad publicity from attempted suicides by some of those forcibly repatriated. In May 1990 the government introduced further restrictive measures because, said the Minister of Justice, 'Belgium can accept no more foreigners'. Certain cities already having large foreigner-populations are entitled to refuse non-EC nationals 'to prevent ghettos from forming'. At the same time the asylum-application process was accelerated – at present as many as 90 per cent of applications are in any case refused – and the principle of carrier liability on airlines was tightened (*NRC Handelsblad*, 11 May 1990, p. 4).

What one might call the 'Danegeld' approach to confronting the rise of the extreme right – attempting to convince the public of the stringency of existing or intended legislation on immigration and asylum matters – has a very mixed record of success. It scarcely worked for the 1974–9 Labour government in Britain, although, ruthlessly applied, it was successful for its Conservative successor. Neither governments of left nor right have been very successful with it in France, where the FN remains a major minority movement. One wonders, in the light of the fragmentation of the Belgian party system and the breakthrough by the VB revealed in the November 1991 parliamentary elections, whether Belgium's use of this time-honoured but questionable approach to the rise of electoral racism on the extreme right is likely to be any more successful, especially as several studies of the general population have revealed the extent of ethnic intolerance in Belgium.

Notes

1. In the preparation of this chapter I have benefited from being able to consult material made available to me by the Anne Frank Foundation in Amsterdam, the Central Public Library of Antwerp, the Election Office and the Statistical Office of the City of Antwerp, and the Vlaams Blok. I am grateful to have been given permission by Dr Luc Schulpen, Director of the polling agency DIMARSO in Brussels, to use polling data collected by his company. A research visit to

Belgium and The Netherlands to collect these materials was supported financially by the British Academy's Small Personal Research Grants scheme. My
thanks are extended to the British Academy.

2. Harris (1990, e.g., pp. 40–2) gives some incidental information on the extreme
   right in Belgium, not all of it completely accurate; there is a similar summary in
   European Parliament (1990, pp. 13–15).
3. To provide a suitably balanced perspective, it should be added that the left-wing
   assertions about extremist infiltrations of the apparatuses of state have been
   dismissed as exaggerated and alarmist by many in the political mainstream.
   Consequently, the literature upon which this section draws has all been written
   by self-defined left-wing journalists and writers. The mainstream, not accepting
   the purported seriousness of the threat, has consequently not written on it.
4. The non-specialist is perhaps unaware of the extent to which the linguistic issue
   dominates so many aspects of Belgium's life, very obviously its politics; for one
   study of this phenomenon, see Murphy (1988).
5. The origins of the 'Flemish movement' go back to the mid-nineteenth century as
   a search for self-determination in the light of the French-language domination of
   the newly autonomous Belgian state. It was common to compare the fight for
   self-determination by the Flemings with that by the various 'nationalities' of the
   Austro-Hungarian Empire. There is an extensive analytic and documentary
   literature on the Flemish movement. For nineteenth-century material, see, for
   example, Willemsen (1974), which is the first volume of a three-volume series.
   Zolberg (1974) gives a general account of the origins and consolidation of the
   Fleming–Walloon cleavage during the nineteenth century.
6. The city of Antwerp features prominently in the contemporary development of
   militant Flemish nationalism and its associated extreme-right aspects.
   Disproportionately severe urban decline has clearly exacerbated community
   tensions during recent years. The longer-term reasons for the city's status as the
   epicentre of such nationalism are more tentative, especially since the more
   general phenomenon of Flemish nationalism has been far from restricted to
   Antwerp. However, French–Dutch linguistic divisions were particularly tense
   there in the pre-war period. Dutch has convincingly 'won out': the JARDIN
   ZOOLOGIQUE engraved on one pillar (with DIERENTUIN on the other) of
   the rather shabby entrance to the city's zoo next to Antwerpen-Centraal railway
   station being one of the more whimsical reminders of the city's genuinely
   bilingual past.
7. It should be mentioned that certain other small extreme-right parties have
   operated during the 1980s. The Parti National Belge-Belgisch-Nationale Partij
   (PNP–BNP), around as we saw since the early 1960s, won tiny fractions of the
   vote in Brussels in the 1978 and 1981 parliamentary elections. The Union
   Nationale des Francophones (UNF) won 0.3 per cent of the vote in the 1981
   parliamentary elections. The Union Nationale et Démocratique (UND) won 0.6
   per cent in 1985 and the Parti Libéral Chrétien (PLC) (later the Parti de la
   Liberté du Citoyen [PLC]) won 0.5 per cent in 1985 and 0.6 per cent in 1987.
8. In fact, there is also a tiny militant ultra-nationalist Flemish non-electoral group
   called the Nationaal Front led by Werner Van Steen (a one-time leader of the
   VMO), which organized a European-wide 'Euroring' meeting of neo-Nazis at
   Kortrijk (near Lille) in August 1988. Van Steen apparently told Le Pen to stay
   away 'because he was a democrat' (*Le Monde*, 30 August 1988, p. 6).
9. A Belgian *arrondissement*, not to be confused with the French intra-city subdistrict, is a substantial administrative area within a province. Belgium as a whole
   contains nine provinces: four (Antwerp, Limburg, East Flanders and West

Flanders) are in Flanders and are predominantly Dutch-speaking, four (Hainaut, Liège, Luxembourg and Namur) are in Wallonia and are largely French-speaking. Brabant, in which Brussels is located, is considered bilingual.

10. Newspaper citations without page numbers have been taken from the unpaginated clippings of either the Anne Frank Foundation or the Central Public Library of Antwerp.

11. Incidentally, this phrase is also the title of a book by Filip Dewinter (1989), leader of the VB's youth wing, the VBJ, and at twenty-nine years old already one of the senior party's emerging leaders.

12. This particular drawing has been seen as significant by others. After completing a preliminary draft of this section of the chapter, I obtained a copy of Gijsels and Vander Velpen (1989). They concentrate on the same features (p. 149), although the 'own people' man's gesture is seen by them as an ambiguous approximation to the Hitler salute, an interpretation that they see as strengthened by the man's hair-style.

13. One obvious source for studying the electoral support of the VB – omnibus opinion-poll data – seems not to have been adequately exploited. Thus, none of these data has apparently been cumulated in order to produce a large enough sample for full social background analysis. In any case, there is a frequent flaw in such an approach, which is that only the most dedicated supporters of extreme-right racist movements may be ready actually to admit such support to opinion-pollsters. The quoted data from DIMARSO on recent VB strength are sufficiently high to suggest that this problem may be less acute in the example of support for the VB, although a poll in Antwerp in April 1988 did report a level of VB support of only 6 per cent, well below the October municipal election figure, as we have seen (*De Morgen*, 30 April 1988). For one of numerous examples of this approach to the analysis of extreme-right support whose data-set is likely to be affected by this problem, see Jaffré (1984).

14. It is instructive to note the decline in VU support across the same three elections – from 12.4 per cent in 1982, to 10.8 per cent in 1985 and to 4.5 per cent in 1989.

15. The Election Office of the City of Antwerp was unable to supply election results disaggregated by subdistrict (*wijk*) or district for Antwerp, and suggested that the political parties would be able to do this. These data were in fact supplied by the Vlaams Blok in Antwerp, albeit with some occasional gaps.

    Data on proportions of foreigners by subdistrict of Antwerp have been taken from Stad Antwerpen (1989, p. 18), Table 13, 'Stand van de werkelijke bevolking op 31 december 1988'.

16. Pan-Dutch sentiment does exist in parts of the Belgian extreme right, as in the organization, Voorpost. However, it is very much a minority current. The European Parliament's recently published report drawn up on behalf of the Committee of Inquiry into Racism and Xenophobia (European Parliament, 1990, p. 13) claims on the basis of a quotation from Filip Dewinter that the VB itself is a strong supporter of pan-Dutch sentiment. However, this is rather misleading for such claims do not figure prominently in the VB's policy statements.

    It is true that the VB does maintain a great interest in the activities of the extreme right in The Netherlands, and in 1989 – under the title 'The Dutch right-wing parties and the pan-Dutch idea' – its newspaper published two articles on the recent history of the Centrum Partij (CP)/Centrum Partij '86 (CP '86) and the Centrumdemocraten (CD) there (*Vlaams Blok*, July–August 1989, p. 8; September 1989, p. 8). It also reported the successes of the two Dutch parties in the country's municipal elections in March 1990 (*Vlaams Blok*, May

1990, p. 8). On 7 August 1990 sixteen members of the VB and CP '86, including Karel Dillen, were arrested in Dordrecht (about 20 kilometres south-east of Rotterdam), when they attempted to hold a forbidden press conference against an exhibition opposing the various extreme-right parties of several European countries (*NRC Handelsblad*, 7 August 1990, pp. 1, 3).

References

Blaise, P., Lentzen, E., Mabille, X., 1989. *L'élection régionale bruxelloise du 18 juin 1989*, Centre de Recherche et d'Information Socio-Politiques (CRISP), Courrier hebdomadaire no. 1243.

BMI (Bundesministerium des Innern), 1989. *Verfassungsschutzbericht, 1988*, Bonn.

Cappelle, J., 1984. 'L'ombre noire de la bourgeoisie flamande', in W. De Bock *et al.*, *L'extrême-droite et l'État*, EPO, Berchem, pp. 67–117.

CRISP (Centre de Recherche et d'Information Socio-Politiques), 1962a, *Nouvelles formes et tendances d'extrême-droite en Belgique – I*, Courrier hebdomadaire no. 140, 16 February.

——, 1962b. *Nouvelles formes et tendances d'extrême-droite en Belgique – II*, Courrier hebdomadaire no. 141, 22 February.

De Bock, W., 1984a. 'L'extrême-droite et la gendarmerie 25 octobre 1936: une tentative de coup d'État en Belgique', in W. De Bock *et al.*, *L'extrême-droite et l'État*, EPO, Berchem, pp. 11–57.

——, 1984b. 'La question royale: Léopold III, figure de proue de l'extrême-droite', in W. De Bock *et al.*, *L'extrême-droite et l'État*, EPO, Berchem, pp. 59–65.

——, 1984c. 'Le ministre, son baron et la Sûreté de l'État', in W. De Bock *et al.*, *L'extrême-droite et l'État*, EPO, Berchem, pp. 239–50.

Delruelle-Vosswinkel, N. *et al.*, 1989. 'De gemeenteraadsverkiezingen van 9 oktober 1988: evolutie van de politieke families en electorale geografie', *Driemaandelijke Tijdschrift van het Gemeentekrediet van België*, no. 169.

Dewinter, F., 1989. *Eigen volk eerst: antwoord op het vreemdelingenprobleem*, Vlaams Blok, Brussels.

Dumont, S., 1983. *Les brigades noires: l'extrême-droite en France et en Belgique francophone de 1944 à nos jours*, 2nd edn, EPO, Brussels.

Eppink, D-J, 1990. 'Racisme in maatkleding', *NRC Handelsblad* (Zaterdags Bijvoegsel), 12 May, p. 7.

European Parliament, 1990. *Report drawn up on behalf of the Committee of Inquiry into Racism and Xenophobia on the findings of the Committee of Inquiry*, European Parliament Document A3-195/90.

Gijsels, H., 1990. *De Bende & Co: 20 jaar destabilisering in België*, Uitgeverij Kritak, Leuven.

Gijsels, H. *et al.*, 1988. *Les barbares: les immigrés et le racisme dans la politique belge*, EPO/HALT/Celsius, Berchem.

Gijsels, H. and Vander Velpen, J., 1989. *Het Vlaams Blok, 1938–1988: het verdriet van Vlaanderen*, EPO/HALT, Berchem.

Haquin, R., 1984. *Operatie Staatsveiligheid: de staatsveiligheid en de WNP*, EPO, Antwerp.

——, 1985. *Des taupes dans l'extrême-droite: la sûreté de l'État et le WNP*, EPO, Brussels.

Harris, G., 1990. *The Dark side of Europe: The Extreme Right Today*, Edinburgh University Press, Edinburgh.

Husbands, C. T., 1983. *Racial Exclusionism and the City: The Urban Support of the*

National Front, Allen & Unwin, London.

——, 1988. 'The dynamics of racial exclusion and expulsion: racist politics in western Europe', *European Journal of Political Research*, Vol. 16, No. 6, 701–20.

——, forthcoming. *Racist Political Movements in Western Europe*, Routledge, London.

Jaffré, J., 1984. 'Qui vote Le Pen?', in E. Plenel and A. Rollat (eds), *L'effet Le Pen*, La Découverte/*Le Monde*, Paris, pp. 121–30.

Maesschalk, A., 1984. 'Front de la Jeunesse: une milice privée d'extrême-droite', in W. De Bock *et al.*, *L'extrême-droite et l'État*, EPO, Berchem, pp. 139–69.

Mottard, J. and Haquin, R. (eds), 1990. *Les tueries du Brabant: enquête parlementaire sur la manière dont la lutte contre le banditisme et le terrorisme est organisée*, Éditions Complexe, Brussels.

Murphy, A. B., 1988. The regional dynamics of language differentiation in Belgium: a study in cultural-political geography, University of Chicago, Geography Research Paper No. 227, Chicago.

Nols, R., 1987. *La Belgique en danger: la verité sur l'immigration*, Éditions Ligne Claire, Brussels.

Ó Maoláin, C. (comp.), 1987. *The Radical Right: A World Directory*, Longman, Harlow.

Stad Antwerpen, 1989. *Jaarverslag 1988*, 5e Directie, Antwerp.

Swyngedouw, M. *et al.*, 1990. *De verkiezingen voor het Europees Parlement 1989*, DIMARSO, Brussels.

van de Wal, D., 1982. *Dossier gastarbeid*, Vlaams Blok, Brussels.

van der Wusten, H., 1987. 'The Low Countries', in D. Mühlberger (ed.), *The Social Basis of European Fascist Movements*, Croom Helm, London, pp. 213–41.

VB (Vlaams Blok), 1990. *Voornaamste Programmapunten*, Vlaams Blok, Brussels.

Verhoeyen, E., 1974. L'extrême-droite en Belgique (I), Centre de Recherche et d'Information Socio-Politiques (CRISP), Courrier hebdomadaire no. 642–43, 26 April.

——, 1975. L'extrême-droite en Belgique (II), Centre de Recherche et d'Information Socio-Politiques (CRISP), Courrier hebdomadaire no. 675–76, 7 March.

Verzet, 1989. 'Wie is wie in het Vlaams Blok: de partijkaders van het Vlaams Blok', *Verzet*, January, pp. 8–11.

Willemsen, A. W., 1974. *De Vlaamse Beweging: I, van 1830 tot 1914*, Heideland-Orbis NV, Hasselt.

Zolberg, A. R., 1974. 'The making of Flemings and Walloons: Belgium, 1830–1914', *Journal of Interdisciplinary History*, Vol. 5, No. 2, 179–235.

6 The Extreme Right in Italy: Ideological Orphans and Countermobilization

Francesco Sidoti

Social Transformation and Anti-System Ideologies

At the centre of the Italian political system are those forces which fully identify with the Constitution. Extremists, as the term suggests, are furthest from the centre of the system. However, Italian political culture is rich and complex and the extreme right therein is situated along a continuum which stretches from the law-abiding right to the armed right. Historically, in fact, researchers have come across some unlikely figures wandering through this political landscape. For example, in 1924, Benedetto Croce, the most prestigious Italian intellectual of that age, still voted for Mussolini's government and, in 1927, Winston Churchill claimed that, had he been an Italian, he would have 'wholeheartedly' supported the Fascist leader's 'triumphant struggle against the bestial appetites and passions of Leninism'.

In post-war Italy, the political system is characterized by the co-existence of a formal constitution and also an unofficial *de facto* constitution. The former is decidedly anti-fascist and was approved in 1947 with the full support of the Italian Communist Party; the latter, partly unwritten and partly written in some of the international agreements of alliances of which Italy is a member, was formulated at the beginning of the Cold War and was decidedly anti-communist. NATO, for example, was set up on 4 April 1949 with the explicit aim of containing communism. This unofficial constitution is of fundamental importance for a country in the traditional sense of the term as used by classic scholars; for example, in Walter Bagehot's analysis of the 'English Constitution' or in Daniel Halévy's observations in relation to 'the two constitutions' of France's Fourth Republic, one official and inactive, the other unspoken but operative. In republican Italy this unwritten constitution is also of major importance to the political powers operating inside and outside a system which is voluntarily based on international alliances and agreements.

In the post-war period, those who identified themselves with the written constitution considered Italy's far right as being anti-system. On the contrary, those who identified themselves with the unofficial constitution saw the far right as a workable means of fighting communism (possibly as a means to be ashamed of, but one that could be used secretly).

The basic point in contemporary Italian politics is that the decline in the appeal of traditional ideologies, both left and right, has shattered old barriers and created an enormous diaspora of ideological orphans who wander without respite from one frontier to another. Italian culture has become, on the one hand, more pragmatic and, on the other hand, more iconoclastic.

One example that highlights the point the ideological diaspora has reached is the situation within the *Movimento Sociale Italiano* (MSI), the only parliamentary party which considers itself 'a right-wing organization'. This party has not only a right and a centre but also a sizeable (45 per cent) left which, on certain issues, is *more to the left than the Communist Party*. According to some observers, in fact, the *left of the MSI* is *the only left wing still existing in Italy*, because it supports issues such as the rejection of consumerism and the western capitalist model, withdrawal from NATO, the denunciation of American colonialism, 'Third World politics' – precisely those issues that the Italian Communist Party had partially abandoned.

As in the other political parties in Italy, the most important section of the MSI is the 'intermediate level' of activists, i.e. those who connect the party leadership with the electorate. Forty per cent of middle-level activists want to participate in day-to-day democratic routine, and even half of these see the Socialist Party (PSI) in a friendly light, hoping for the construction of some kind of 'patriotic socialism' in the future. According to some interpretations, at the top of the party there is a majority agreement over themes such as the condemnation of capitalism, pro-americanism, neo-colonialism and Atlanticism.

In the 1970s and in the 1980s terrorism constituted a major element of dispute and ideological self-questioning in leftist culture, posing basic questions about Marxism, democracy, violence, revolution, and legality. The debate involved the press, political parties, trade unions, academic circles, and militant pundits. Something similar happened within rightist culture through various intricate paths. One important angle was the experience of movements of the *non-conformist right* (critical towards the MSI) which covers such a wide political range as to encompass some ninety periodicals. Although many of these periodicals were short-lived and produced only on a local or irregular basis, they do give an indication of the intensity of the cultural debate.

Like the Marxist-Leninist left, the extreme right has difficulties in interpreting the new features of phenomena that are profoundly transforming European society, and which are very different from the ones existing when Leninism and fascism were originally formulated. Fascism and communism were distinct responses to the stresses and strains of industrialization, democratization, and modernization. Today certain features of the extreme right and of the extreme left are the outcome of a society characterized by different concerns from the redistributive problems that have been central issues since the Industrial Revolution. Traditional ideologies wax and wane but *leftism* and *rightism* survive, 'as a landscape survives those that travel through it' (Laponce, 1981, p. 52). We can still speak of the Italian political system as having a centre; and there are still anti-system forces that come within this spatial logic and which are ideologically self-defined. As in other western countries, in Italy also there has been a cultural development since the mid-1970s whose outcome is uncertain: we can neither speak of the 'end of the ideologies' nor of the predominance of a 'post-materialist mentality' (Inglehart, 1981). In Italy these changes have led to various types of cross-breeding and of ideological redefinition; for example, this situation has led to the creation of movements which assert their extraneousness with respect to traditional parties and declare that they are *neither right-wing or left-wing*.

Although the contemporary intellectual establishment has marginalized the authoritarian tendencies in Italian culture, they are still alive (notwithstanding the left's hegemony over public discourse). In spite of the many ideologues who, after having adhered to fascism opportunistically, switched with the tide, there is a persistence of authoritarian tendencies within Italian culture. However, such tendencies have no backing from those social groups which have historically constituted the institutional basis of authoritarianism: the monarchy, the aristocracy, the military, the business community, the big landowners, the church. These social groups nowadays are either much less influential than before or else have disappeared from the political scene or become much more pluralistic and segmented. From this point of view, the processes of modernization and democratization of Italy (and especially the replacement of the monarchy with the republic) have had as the major consequence the disappearance or the profound transformation of those social groups which once dominated Italian society. In contemporary Europe, Italy is one of those societies least marked by the weight of traditionalist elements, as opposed to Spain, France and Britain.

The sociological profile of the Italian extreme right is characterized by those minority groups which express the strongest resistance towards modernization and democracy – from opposition to abortion and divorce to demand for the death penalty and xenophobic measures. Whereas in other European countries, such as France, racism is a major political problem, the Italian extreme right to a large extent is not typified by racism. In a Europe in the throes of rediscovering its underclass, racism has advanced particularly where there are specific strains on the labour market: profit reductions, demand for cheap and unskilled work, loss of jobs, and competition between immigrants and native workers. Given the push of poverty and aspirations within the Third World, immigration is likely to continue. Italy borders upon overpopulated states on the southern edge of the Mediterranean: the emerging 'European dilemma' is not the prime issue in Italy today, but it is growing and will certainly be of greater importance in the future.

Linz's monumental study on the breakdown of democratic regimes has emphasized that several of the victories of the far right anti-system parties could have been avoided; but this does not invalidate the most accredited explanation (De Felice, 1970) among historians and sociologists which states that the affirmation of fascism cannot be understood without referring to *the rapid acceleration in social changes* in the period prior to the breakdown (Linz, 1978, p. 31). Obviously, not every social mobilization leads to a breakdown which is in fact the consequence of a complex combination of causal factors.

In his lucid comparative studies of European and Latin American fascism, Gino Germani has suggested that episodes of 'fascist counter-mobilization' may come about as a reaction to ethnic groups coming from other countries or to the mobilization of marginal groups within one's own country. In this sense fascism, as an attempt to react against sudden falls in social status, is a historical phenomenon that could even repeat itself (Germani, 1975, p. 34). *The importance of the cultural factors* consists in this: since ideology is an overall interpretation of reality and a guide to action (Putnam, 1971), counter-mobilization movements may take various forms according to how they are channelled into one ideology or another. It has been rightly claimed that conceptions of the world act in the same way as points on a railway line which may direct the force of a train in motion in one direction or another (Weber, 1922, p. 11).

In the early 1980s, Italy was the modern democratic country with not only the strongest far right party but also with the strongest communist party, a widespread and dangerous brand of terrorism and the most powerful form of organized crime. This situation was characterized by the marked development of movements that are 'ideological' in the worst sense of the term based on a distorted and a priori view of reality. The development of far right movements is part of this more general process of growth of ideological ways of perceiving reality.

Italy has generally been reputed to have a civic culture that is perceived (La Palombara, 1965; Almond and Verba, 1980) as moved by distrust, alienation, irrational beliefs or oriented towards objects which do not exist at present. A set of concepts well-established in psychology and in sociology (ideology, utopia, unconscious, relative deprivation, frustration, alienation, false consciousness) tells us that there are states of mind which are incongruous with the state of reality. Extremism – like fundamentalism, fanaticism and so on – is both a state of mind and a state of social transformation.

Neo-fascism and anti-communism were the two traditional features distinguishing the extreme right. During the 1970s and 1980s, however, there was a tortuous process of social, ideological and political destructuring of the extreme right. From this process (which is also intertwined with an analogous crisis of the extreme left) have evolved both an 'anti-authoritarian right' and a 'new right', while the parliamentary right has experienced factionalism and declined in importance. In the following pages we shall allocate a brief section to each of these phenomena of destructuring and recomposition of the extreme right in Italy.

The Traditional Anti-Communist Right

The ascent of European fascism was part of a complex reaction to the Russian Revolution; in Italy the core of the fascist identity is anti-communism. In Italy, unlike Spain after Franco and Portugal after Caetano, the self-transformation of the fascist regime and consensual post-fascism were impossible (Sani, 1980). The multiple connections between moderate and conservative ideologies in the history of fascism have led to the term 'right' being regarded as a taboo word in Italian politics. Many people who would otherwise undoubtedly have been thought of as right-wing prefer to camouflage themselves behind some other political label so as not to be confused with nostalgic fascists. 'In Italy the political struggle is so specific that a right-wing of a classic traditional type, that is a respectable, law-abiding right, is unthinkable because it would be soon labelled as fascist' (De Felice, 1975, p. 97). The possibility of creating a *non-fascist extreme right* was proved between 1976 and 1979, when more than half of the MSI's parliamentarians broke away to form a more *respectable* right-wing party (*Democrazia Nazionale*). However, the schism was a ruinous failure: in the 1979 elections, the 'moderates' could not re-elect a single one of their former deputies.

Although it is true that fascism was an anti-system movement; it is none the less debatable whether fascism was simply an extreme right movement. For some observers, fascism has nothing to do with the history of the Italian right: Mussolini was a revolutionary who, by founding fascism, went beyond the distinction between right and left (Accame, 1990). Just as some historians underline the difference between Mussolinism and Hitlerism, so others underline the difference between authoritarian systems *à la* Salazar and fascism (Ledeen, 1976).

Indeed, there are at least three types of fascism in Italy: the first, which ran from 1919 to the coup of 1925, was basically an anti-system movement; the second (from 1925 to 1943) was a totalitarian regime allied with the church and the monarchy; the third (from 1943 to 1945) was the fascist 'social republic', of anti-monarchist and socialist leanings. *All these three types of fascism were resolutely anti-communist.* None of the three had a great deal in common with the basic tenets of conservative thought: the market economy, hostility to state intervention in the economy, political liberty, moderation in civil reforms. Mussolini, on the contrary, was pro-interventionist and pro-state with regard to the economy and society as well as the social mobilization of the masses. This is of crucial importance in distinguishing between fascism and an authoritarian system of the Salazarian type. While the authoritarian right searches principally for order, fascism put pressures on every aspect of social life, ranging from the educational system to laissez-faire economics. Fascism was a mixture of incongruous ideologies: extremism, nationalism, anti-communism, conservatism, authoritarianism, populism, aristocracy, republicanism, monarchism, socialism, totalitarianism and Hegelianism.

Consequently, just as there are as many marxisms as there are marxists, so there are as many fascisms as there are fascists. Even the term extremism is vaguely defined by a tendency to take a political idea to its limits. If 'extremist' conservatism is for some almost like being oxymoronic, 'authoritarian' extremism is for others almost pleonastic. Of course, the meaning of political words is given by the dictionary but also depends upon the context. For instance, just as there are various types of fascism, so there are various kind of authoritarianism. Capitalist production relations being the Promethean solvent of social obligation based on custom and authority, certain types of authoritarianism are of an anti-capitalist nature, and intended to re-establish a political order that has been overthrown. Other types of authoritarianism, on the other hand, are of the modernizing kind: faced with resistance from traditional society, resort to authoritarianism is seen as the decisive means for cutting the Gordian knot which thwarts development. Certainly, a modernizing element was present in fascism (Gregor, 1979) and it is still present in Italian society today.

Some right-wing authors have affirmed that fascism is a movement that asserts itself in an exceptional situation, as *a sort of committee of public health* (Bardèche, 1980). Because the Italian Communist Party was the strongest non-ruling communist party in the world, the Italian context has been frequently interpreted as an *exceptional situation*. Since the communist bogey has disappeared (the Italian Communist Party has changed its name, and has lost substantial electoral support), a large part of extreme right identity has undergone a transformation. From this point of view, considerable importance should be given to the end of international politics dominated by the bipolar and conflictual relationship between East and West, in which a predominant section of rightist identity was characterized by its opposition to communism.

In the past, however, the anti-communist appeal was supported above all by the old middle-classes: the self-employed such as small farmers, craftsmen and so on, ideologically opposed to the communist movement but also to capitalist democracy. In spite of the declining importance of this section of Italian society, some social groups maintain stubborn anti-communist tendencies. For instance, in military circles, there are a large number of people who are receptive to authoritarian answers to communism and democracy. In fact, in Italian recent history, there have been major cases of top military officials explicitly adhering to extreme right movements. For example, in 1972, Admiral Birindelli was a candidate for the MSI as the expression of the non-fascist extreme right then preferred to join forces with the MSI. Previously commander-in-chief of NATO troops in Southern Europe, Birindelli later became president of the MSI. His stance within the extreme right was part of an attempt to transform the MSI from anti-American and anti-Atlanticist positions (the MSI has inherited the ideologies behind the wars fought in the fascist period) to pro-American and pro-Atlantic positions. Other important members of the army (especially from the secret services) have also been elected as MSI candidates: the monarchist General De Lorenzo, who previously was a hero of the anti-fascist resistance and later was accused of having planned an anti-leftist *coup d'état*; and General Miceli, who was accused of having assisted right-wing terrorists while head of secret services. But such support has occurred during the most dramatic moments of Italian history; in periods of political normality such cases are extremely rare (Prandstraller, 1985). At this point, it will be instructive to make a closer analysis of the MSI in view of the latter's key position on the Italian extreme right.

The MSI

The MSI is the only party which explicitly declares it is on the right in the Italian Parliament. For many years it was the strongest neo-fascist party among modern western democracies. At the beginning of the 1990s, however, there was a dramatic slump in support for the movement.

The MSI was founded in December 1946 with the stated purpose of preserving the fascist heritage. In the first post-war elections of 1948 (when the 'moderate' forces closed ranks against the communists), the MSI collected 525,408 votes (1.0 per cent), and the conservative block of nationalists and monarchists 1,860,525. The Christian Democrats (DC) scored 48.5 per cent of the vote. Until 1950, the radical part of the fascist heritage predominated within the MSI. During the 1950s and 1960s, the more moderate component of the fascist tradition prevailed. The MSI collaborated in various forms with the centrist coalitions that governed Italy, at local as well at national level, both openly and in more disguised way. In particular, it contributed in 1962 and in 1971 in helping to elect two Christian Democrats to the Presidency of the Republic. Moreover, on various occasions, it helped in keeping alive many coalition governments, which were based on small majorities and which were often exposed to political blackmail and defections. Important sectors of Italian society, in fact, had no prejudices against fascist, clerical and monarchical forces. All this changed though with the advent of the centre-left alliance.

After the wave of discontent due to the students' and workers' movements of 1968 and 1969, riots, street battles, terrorist attacks and prolonged strikes led to change on the extreme right. In elections from 1958 to 1968, the MSI always lost votes. In 1969, a new MSI leader, Giorgio Almirante, elaborated a new strategy, aimed at attracting the moderate and extremist components of the Italian right: he wanted to build a strong anti-communist alliance. According to many observers, this new group would compete against the DC which, fearing to lose power, would be even amenable to tactical and strategic agreements with the Italian Communist Party (PCI).

In 1972, early elections were held in an atmosphere of considerable political tension. In alliance with the remnants of the Monarchist Party, the MSI formed a coalition, called the Italian Social Movement-National Right (the name of the party has been MSI-DN ever since), which obtained fifty-six Members of Parliament and twenty-six Senators (in 1990 the party had thirty-five Members of Parliament and sixteen Senators). On that occasion, it received 2,894,788 votes (8.7 per cent) for the Chamber of Deputies and 2,763,719 for the Senate. The DC experienced a major loss of votes to the extreme right: a considerable number of political and social conflicts (particularly strikes both by workers and by sectors of the middle-class) drove part of the electorate towards far rightist positions.

After the defeat in the referendum of 1974 against divorce (in this campaign the Christian Democrats and MSI were allies), the DC chose the strategy of blocking the movement of DC voters to the right. While the MSI tried to rally the 'silent majority', the DC orchestrated a campaign to show that the turbulent situation of the country was the fault of the MSI. The Christian Democrats also denounced vigorously the danger from the far right and condemned 'the opposite extremes' of left and right. Moreover, many incidents nullified the MSI's attempt to court a respectable image in order to convince the nation that the new right-wing party was a party like all the others, without 'hotheads and outright Nazi-fascists' (Leonardi, 1977, p. 237).

In spite of allegations against the DC for having set up a new *de facto* alliance, few voices therein wanted to seem allies of 'the bloody fascists'. On 1 June 1976, for instance, even the leader of the MSI wrote in the official party newspaper:

> I am committed in all my conscience and will to preventing extremism of the right from facilitating the subversive manoeuvres of the left. It would be the greatest folly for supporters of the right in Italy – any of them – to maintain that only a violent right can stop the left.

Nevertheless, all the attempts to retain or increase the trust of the moderate electorate were in vain.

In the elections of 1976, the MSI fell to thirty-five Deputies, thus losing almost all gains in the 1972 election, during which it had reached the zenith of its parliamentary strength. Shortly afterwards, the party split in two: half the Senators and almost half the Deputies in the MSI parliamentary group left the party and founded a conservative group (*Democrazia Nazionale*), accusing the MSI of being involved in right-wing terrorism and of being incapable of building a parliamentary strategy that could bring them out of isolation. As already indicated, the following parliamentary elections in 1979 witnessed the electoral whitewash of *Democrazia Nazionale*.

By 1990, the MSI was a party divided into a multiplicity of groups: a new leader, Gianfranco Fini, was elected in 1987 by a majority which was split into six factions. His leadership aimed at continuing the strategy worked out by Giorgio Almirante, which was centred around the proposal of constitutional change, namely the transformation of the Italian political system into a presidential republic. This strategy aimed at making use of all the anti-system sentiments of the sub-proletarian classes of southern Italy and of all the anti-leftist trends in Italian society. The demands, for example, for the repeal of abortion legislation and for the restoration of the death penalty constituted the basic landmarks of this strategy. Some groups within the MSI proposed a new programme in order to counteract electoral losses. One of the largest opposition groups to Gianfranco Fini's strategy within the party was led by Pino Rauti, who proposed to revamp the party. According to him, the new party should have been a popular party whose aim should have been to remove Italy from the capitalist system. As regards foreign affairs, the new party should have adopted a new set of policies in which, for example, more attention should have been paid to the revival of the Islamic World and to the Palestinian question.

This party should have aimed at recruiting where communism had failed. Its political strategy should have been the constitution of a popular and modern fascism, rooted at various societal levels, capable of leading ecologist and anti-capitalist movements. The party goals should have been those of challenging the left parties on idealistic grounds and of picking up those million of floating voters released by the crisis of communism. Much importance is attached by Rauti to the replacement of the profit motive by the joint sharing of companies by management and workers, and to the fight 'against the pseudo-values imported by Americanism: agnosticism, materialism, hedonism, consumerism and selfishness'.

Another major grouping within the MSI was constituted by a faction led by Domenico Mennitti, who proposed to accept the Italian republic born out of the defeat of fascism. Seen in this perspective, the main political respondent should have been the Socialist Party. This faction has even gone so far as to criticize the split from the socialists undertaken by Mussolini in 1914. In terms of foreign policy, this group was against the anti-American stance but favoured a less subordinate role for Italy vis-à-vis the United States. Considerable importance was given to issues such as the willingness to discuss with other political forces: this thrust represented the party's modernist face which tried to go beyond the nostalgic appeal of fascism.

During the 1980s the MSI registered a long series of defeats in local and territorial elections. In 1991, after a further defeat, the MSI went through a serious crisis involving both its leadership and social basis (around half of its electorate abandoned the party). At the end of 1991 its electoral strength was estimated by many observers to be about 4 per cent, but the party still managed to poll 5.4 per cent in 1992 (see below).

The Anti-Authoritarian Right

According to one communist scholar, from 1969 to 1975 there were 4,384 acts of political violence in Italy, with 83 per cent of them committed by right-wing extremists (Pecchioli, 1981).

In 1974 there were two major anti-system right-wing groups harbouring terrorists: New Order and National Vanguard. After a series of trials, the government decided to dissolve both organizations, and the militants were tried and condemned for a crime explicitly included in the law: that of the attempt to reconstitute the fascist party. Judicial enquiries revealed the links between the right and certain apparatuses of the Italian state. Individuals within sectors of the secret services occupied positions in extreme right movements often in a managerial role over inexperienced extremists. Connections of this kind, however, were exceptions. The majority of secret service agents remained loyal to the laws of the country. In July 1978, moreover, the assassination of judge Vittorio Occorsio signified the end of the special relationship between state and extreme right. Old friends suddenly became enemies as rightist terrorists used the Red Brigades as their model – because 'red terrorists' were reputed to be the model of efficiency and invincibility. Extreme right terrorists attacked state representatives, politicians, judges, policemen. But within a few months this armed right movement was soon dismantled, not least since extreme right hideouts were well known to the security forces.

Another different wave of rightist extremism also followed after the 1977 leftist movement, which had an important impact on the right. 1977 marks the arrival on the extreme right of generations who were not linked to the historical memory of fascism and who were more sensitive to the issues of their peers on the left. This new generation of the extreme right (Weinberg, 1979) was similar to that of the extreme left from many points of view: disdain for the compromise of traditional politics, cultural preferences for a world of fantasy, a rejection of prosaic bourgeois values, a love of risk and adventure. The young extreme right in particular was characterized by one important feature: a hypercritical attitude towards authority whether represented by the Italian state or by the traditional right. Anti-authoritarian and seditious uprisings coincided in the so-called 'armed spontaneism'. The strategy of a privileged relationship with the state was completely abandoned. Still, this new movement failed, because of its inability to find enough young recruits. Even the attempt to build alliances with the left was a failure. Only official negligence by the state permitted this phenomenon to last a long time and an underestimation of the importance of extreme right terrorism – in comparison to red terrorism (which, however, in the same period was equally badly controlled) .

In June 1980, the judge Mario Amato was killed. He had been making a thorough investigation into right-wing terrorism. Mario Amato believed that terrorists had connections with key groups in the Italian state-machine. After his death people high up in the police and the judiciary were accused of covering up or ignoring right-wing extremism, and of having indirectly caused his death. The assassination of the judge Mario Amato and (the most serious episode in the history of Italian terrorism) the massacre of Bologna also in June 1980 provoked unequivocal reaction on the part of the state; from that moment, methods that had produced good results in the fight against extreme left terrorism were adopted. In particular, repentant terrorists played a crucial role, and specialized groups of judges were set up. The struggle against right-wing terrorists was now firmly on the agenda. Some critics accused the state of applying double standards of scrutiny to the different colours of terrorism and even making use of right-wing extremism in the so-called 'strategy of tension', intended to create in the country a political climate hostile to the entry of the communists into government. According to Borraccetti (1986, p. 17): 'There has not been one trial for a massacre in which we have not had to come up against at least the inertia of the state, but more often with attempts to sidetrack enquiries or even bring them to a halt'. Obviously, this interpretation is strongly rejected by those working in the secret services. They stress that delays and errors did take place, but claim that they were often due to factors outside their control and were not deliberate. At the end of the 1960s, in the early days of terrorism, the secret services were in the initial stages of developing countermeasures. As regards the existence of a national and international network of complicity, Vincenzo Parisi, Head of the Italian police, and an authority on these problems, asserted that there was no complicity with foreign states, even if certain connections existed with foreign terrorist groups. He does not completely absolve the Italian intelligence services, and he admits that it is possible that some judicial enquiries may have been influenced deliberately by individual members acting 'outside the administration as agents of illegal interests' (Parisi, 1988a, p. 100), and he also admits that 'in a phase characterized by the incapacity of the state machine, credibility has been given to certain individuals who do not have an official role' (Parisi, 1988b, p. 32).

The interpretation given by the security services contrasts with the interpetration given by some examining magistrates who, in the Italian legal system, have special and important powers. They have investigated the many massacres that mark the history of Italian terrorism and support the hypothesis of an international conspiracy connected with major personalities. On many issues, the Supreme Court of Cassation has rejected the conclusions given by examining magistrates or given by judges of the Court of Appeal. These controversies are symptomatic of the babel of tongues over terrorism (Sidoti, 1991): the judicial initiatives are often much-disputed and there have been cases of indictment of magistrates.

In Italy, there is a Parliamentary Committee 'to evaluate the results of the struggle against terrorism and to examine the causes which have prevented identification of the culprits of massacres'. The President of the Committee even stated (Gualtieri, 1988, p. 2):

> The impression of those who have attempted to penetrate these mysteries is that the judges and the police have constantly faced a barrier put up by institutional powers high enough to make for disobedience and strong enough to avoid any sanction.

His stance was indirect confirmation of the existence of a mastermind behind terrorism, and has been cited by sectors both of the right and of the left (Baldoni and Provvisionato, 1989), because this meant that much of the blame was attributed to enigmatic entities functioning outside Italy.

The truth about certain massacres has still not been ascertained in the courts: for the massacre of Piazza Fontana in 1969, there have been seven trials in twenty years. In addition, after diverse interventions by the Supreme Court of Cassation, all the alleged culprits have been absolved. For the massacre of Piazza della Loggia in 1974, there have been six trials in fifteen years, and again all the major alleged culprits have been absolved.

Even in the declaration of the judges who were critical and sceptical about the state's role we can find observations that strongly suggest that collective responsibilities are among the major casual factors of terrorism. In fact, in certain documents drawn up by judges we find that there have been people who, on certain occasions, deliberately plotted and made use of terrorism (at times conditioning it, at others ending up as a prisoner of it). Also, 'very serious events occurred essentially because there were both the means and the people available to commit such acts' (Borraccetti, 1986, p. 284). The phenomenon has been 'encouraged and influenced', but it has also 'matured naturally and grown spontaneously as a result of the general social and political situation' in which considerable importance was given to the wide-spread belief in terrorist impunity and 'in the absence of any real attempt at repression at any level' (Borraccetti, 1986, p. 222).

As to the attitude of extreme right terrorists towards other western countries, it has been claimed that they are not only 'hostile to the United States as a country, the US presence in Europe and US aims in the world', but are more dangerous than leftist terrorists, both because they are more willing to shed blood, and also because they may attract more support than left-wing terrorists. In conclusion, they 'may thus become a significant threat locally and therefore indirectly to NATO and the United States' (Hoffman, 1982, p. 26).

The 'Opposite Extremes'

According to De Felice, 'between fascism and neo-nazism, or the radical right, there is a deep difference, both of a cultural-ideological kind and of a psychological-moral kind; a difference that makes a very clear watershed' (De Felice, 1975, p. 101). The psychological-moral side of right-wing extremism has been studied from the point of view of the emotional stresses and strains which accompany the years between puberty and adulthood.

For Italian adolescents at the end of the 1960s and during the 1970s, we can repeat what has been affirmed in a well-established sociological theory concerning adolescence as a separate stage of life and an invention of modern societies. Prolonged childhood is responsible for the psychological peculiarities of youth culture: transformation of identity, uncertainty, bewilderment, self-expression, rebellion and militant idealism. Instead of becoming high school drop-outs, runaways from home, dangerous bandits and so on, right-wing adolescents temporarily over-identified with Nazi mythology and anti-democratic paranoia. Italian culture was distinguished by groups of young idealists on the right and on the left profoundly alienated from the values of democracy and from the contemporary world in general. The *weltanschauung* of those militant idealists was full of concepts such as the ethics of the warrior, the necessity of achieving a higher morality, the fight against bourgeois security and the mystical union of superior beings.

The psychopathological explanation of right-wing terrorism is derived from experiences like clinical examinations (particularly, psychiatric opinions requested during trials, or asked for in order to see the ability to withstand the prison regime, or solicited by parents of youths). This hypothesis focuses on the personality of the captured terrorists. From this point of view, at the root of the terrorist choice there are unsolved problems within the normal channels of socialization (a broken family, an unhappy adolescence, an incomplete schooling). Evidence suggests that many terrorists were moved by basic insecurity. According to Ferracuti, their personalities are distorted, aberrant, disturbed, borderline, or even psychotic, in some sense mentally ill even if an appropriate psychiatric label has still not been found. From this perspective, terrorists differ basically from *normal* criminals. Normal criminals can be best understood 'as prisoners of war, as foot soldiers captured in the course of activities designed to fortify combat positions in the struggle for the control of power' (Vold, 1979, p. 421). Terrorists are, on the contrary, like 'soldiers outside of time and space', living in a fantasy war which exists only in their mind (Ferracuti, 1982). In the reality of peacetime, this kind of fantasy becomes authentic with logical consequences: everyday values are subverted, men appear available to kill and be killed, the mastery of death over life is permitted and pervasive terror is plausible.

Even in the absence of a clear psychic disease, there is among right-wing terrorists a distinctive behaviour pattern: an authoritarian-extremist personality is defined by psychological traits such as ambivalence toward authority (submission-aggression, imbalance) and emotional detachment from the consequences of the action. These psychological traits would be typical of right-wing terrorism (Ferracuti and Bruno, 1981). Even if there are not specific psychopathological conditions, leftist and rightist terrorists are characterized by ideological fanaticism, destructiveness and unpredictability. They are prepared to surrender their own life for an issue considered as transcending ordinary reality. This self-destructive choice is not normal, because it is oriented against the biological instinct to survive, and that choice requires psychiatric and sociological explanations.

The deadly transition from participation in flick-knife bravado to becoming terrorists must be correlated also with the partial eclipse of the apparatuses of the Italian state during the height of Italian rightist and leftist terrorism (Solé, 1979, p. 136). Ideological fundamentalism, fanaticism and alienation become dangerous if they find little resistance within a large network of formal and informal social mechanisms. In spite of declarations against terrorism, both communist and neo-fascist parties have permitted the growth of a generation alienated from democratic values and have supported an interpretation which indicates external forces as ultimately responsible for terrorism (Pisano, 1984). However, political parties and law-enforcement authorities through their own behaviour may increase or decrease ideological hysteria.

The extreme right and the extreme left may be seen more as puppets than free actors on the Italian political scene. For instance, in 1990, the Italian judiciary examined the hypothesis that the long series of terrorist attacks, which at the beginning of the 1970s were carried out almost daily against the premises and the members of the MSI, could have been organized by secret service members. Terrorist attacks by the latter provoked retaliations against leftist groups, which in turn hunted out right-wingers. These activities of secret service members can be seen as part of a strategy intended to favour centrist parties: during the 1970s the electors were thus invited to vote 'against the opposite extremes of left and right'.

In 1989, official documentary analysis concerning the problems of security (presented in Parliament by the Prime Minister) emphasized that right wing terrorism like left wing terrorism was in a deep state of crisis. Mafia (Sidoti, 1987) and organized crime have surpassed terrorism in the scale of threats to public security. It is important to note that the official document claimed that the connection between leftist terrorism and organized crime appeared 'absolutely instrumental' and 'without common strategic ends' (Relazione, 1989, p. 48). On the contrary, the investigation of rightist terrorism confirmed 'profound and ever growing connections with illegal activities and, particularly and most dangerously, an intimate relationship with organized crime. . . . The demands of terrorists to obtain weapons, money, documents, refuge for fugitives and clandestines, favour such contacts'. The borderline between rightist subversion and organized crime becomes subtle, because the relationship with common criminals profoundly marks the mentality of terrorists. Many deviants who would normally flow into common delinquency have been absorbed by terrorism, and now they are returning to their origins. The report pointed to 'the effects of combining energies produced by the collaboration between extreme right and organized crime', and suggested that perhaps there is 'a common destabilizing project' and that 'it is in all likelihood a key for interpreting some episodes that are still unclear and for identifying a likely trend in the evolution of objectives'. The phenomena relative to young groups who use Nazi symbols are judged as 'forms of youth conduct analogous to experiences already realized in other western countries and characterized by a strong aggressivity, which breaks into unmotivated collective violence' (Relazione, 1989, p. 70).

The Italian New Right

The Italian new right is a phenomenon not identified by a single programme, but rather by a common origin within the extreme right and by an intolerance towards the issues typically raised by the traditional extreme right. In Italy the many groups that define themselves as belonging to the *nuova destra* (new right) generally have little in common with other new right groups operating in the Anglo-Saxon context, which are distinguished by a belief in opportunity and upward mobility, the creed in the unparalleled value of the individual against community, free market economics and, the connection between property and freedom.

The Italian extreme right and extreme left are both children of the same social and cultural transformation. Some of the specific issues nourished by the new rightists are: the proposal of an anti-system alliance between extreme right and extreme left; the fight against a *soft totalitarianism* represented by the *Americanization of the world*; and an openly declared anti-imperialism, completely extraneous to the dreams of the traditional extreme right which were nostalgic towards colonialism. Other issues include ecology, feminism, the Third World and fantasy literature, thus constituting a very, different type of politics with respect to the classic patterns of a moderate or authoritarian right.

Such a phenomenon has profoundly irritated the traditional right of the MSI which feared sleeping alongside strange bedfellows who were in actual fact the fascist right's most scathing critics: concerned environmentalists, angry feminists, humanitarian Third Worlders, diehard no-nukers and passionate civil rights activists. A section of the new rightists was thrown out of the party, another section lives on the fringe of the party, and another constitutes the party's left wing. Among the forerunners of the new right, together with a heretical and leftist fascism, there is the political thought of Julius Evola and the French *nouvelle droite*. The latter empathizes with sociobiology, genetical theories, paganism, opposition to the Hebrew-Christian roots of liberalism and Marxism, philosophical nominalism, and aversion to the United States and to the Soviet Union as the sources of egalitarianism and economic materialism. Some of these issues of the French new right were absorbed in their entirety by the Italian new right, while others were rejected.

The Italian new right developed to a large extent autonomously out of the left wing of the MSI – which, as suggested above, was and is both numerically and qualitatively a major component within the party. The new right has managed to involve a large number of young militants belonging to the MSI who are both committed and intent on playing a major political role within the party. Through the new right, a generation has found a social way of being rightist that radically differs from that of previous generations.

This new right, in Italy, is not an old right under a modern guise (Ferraresi, 1987). It is well worth noting that certain cultural elements of the extreme right have been profoundly reworked within the culture of the new right. For example, exasperated forms of intolerance are often replaced by an emphasis on parity between all men in terms of personal dignity and on the ensuing respect to which each individual is entitled. Some new right authors maintain that such values are beyond question and constitute a point of no return. The presence of differences and inequalities among men is recognized and underlined, but in a different cultural context compared to that of the past. In particular, the principle of tolerance is openly declared to be fundamental.

Another important new principle is the acceptance of modernity. Much traditional right-wing extremism is not at ease with modernity: in Nazism, for instance, technology was highly appreciated, but the past was the mythical realm for reconquering racial purity and original excellence. Many exponents of the new right are prepared to accept what is valuable in the achievements of modernity, and others are often involved in the search for a post-modern alternative which, in some respects, is similar to that of the Greens.

The new right (influenced by the thought of the Italian communist Gramsci) declares that it follows a 'metapolitical strategy' in the sense that engagement and cultural hegemony are indicated as necessary premises for political success. From this point of view, consent is not seen as the outcome but rather as the precondition of power. Other issues raised by the new right are the rejection of authoritarianism, racism and rabid anti-communism. These aspects – which mark a clear break with the past – are not present in all of the new right, but particularly in that part of the movement which has distanced itself most visibly from the MSI (Tarchi, 1989).

It has been underlined by many authors who believe in the lasting relevance of the anti-fascist struggle that the major issues raised by the new right were already present in the minority currents of fascism and Nazism. These authors maintain that the new right and the armed right *march divided in order to strike as one* (Ferraresi, 1988). Indeed, some issues do come from the extreme right tradition, whereas others are unused.

In many sections of the new right, the traditional features of extremist culture are missing: the intention to eliminate opposition; intolerance towards all views other than one's own; and the adoption of means for political ends which show disregard for the life, liberty and human rights of others. In part, the theory of Evola is rejected by the new right; this theory was light years from the possibility of accomplishment within the framework of modern parliamentary politics. His aristocratic elitism was the opposite of democratic means such as parties and electoral competition. Republicanism, *Fuehrerprinzip* and populism were aspects of Nazism and fascism not appreciated by Evola, who glorified integral imperialists, aristocrats, irreducible enemies of all democratic and plebeian politics and of every more or less disguised form of socialism. Basically, Evola was important for the Italian new right because he represented a cultural reference point, but his thought was criticized from various angles.

On the French new right, Hellenism and Paganism, as social and political ideals, are contrasted with Hebrew-Christian civilization. But this rediscovery and celebration of pre-Christian culture is not accepted by the Italian new rightists, whose majority is 'traditionalist'. For them, beyond the facts of ordinary human experience, there is the sacred: a force which human beings cannot understand rationally and which gives ultimate meaning to human lives. Sacredness has been transferred from the supernatural to the profane which, in contrast, is philistine: a world entirely conditioned by utilitarian, material and commonplace values. For many Italian new rightists, it is in religious duty that the obligation towards all human institutions must finally be based. This view of religion contrasts with the sceptical opinions which were common in extreme right thinkers such as Evola, who constantly attacked the Catholic Church and 'Semitic' Christianity. The Italian new right is, in part, religious and traditionalist; in part, atheist and anti-Semitic.

A component of the movement contesting traditional neo-fascism is principally concerned with rejecting the conclusions that other major currents within the new right have come to, i.e. the possibility of some kind of grouping *beyond the right and the left* (Veneziani, 1987). This part of the new right did not want to constitute an alternative to MSI, and continued to underline the importance of traditional rightist themes.

The search for an untrodden path and the desire to be dissimilar from an MSI accused of being an old and useless relic led many movements to define themselves through unlikely ideological labels such as the oxymoronic *conservative revolution*, *reactionary modernism*, *Bolshevik nationalism*, *Nazi-Maoism* or *red fascism*. Among the best-known heretics of the Italian new right, as in many writings of right-wing extremism, a frequent and striking feature is the presence of those esoteric controversies between theologians which seem quite meaningless to the uninitiated: controversies about the *true* meaning of fascism, of *authentic* rightism and the relationship between the sacred and the profane.

The Future of the Italian Extreme Right

During the 1960s and the 1970s an international network in Europe existed which facilitated the rebirth of right-wing extremism. From Algeria to Angola, from the Congo to Vietnam, the agony of colonialism had set in motion a series of transnational reactions conducive to an alliance of extreme right movements. During the height of Italian right-wing extremism, a network of right-wing extremist supporters existed in Europe, based in countries such as Greece (then under a military junta), Spain (then under Franco's autocracy) and Portugal (then under an authoritarian dictatorship). After 1975, the overthrow of these authoritarian regimes caused the loss of sanctuaries, logistic support, financial means and political strategy.

During the 1980s the extreme right movements lost these connections. An international network of protection and finance seemed to have disappeared into thin air and the extreme right in Italy suddenly found itself in a kind of quarantine: nobody wanted anything to do with it and it had no interlocutors. On the European electoral level the quarantine was confirmed as the Italian extreme right became increasingly isolated in Strasbourg. The links with Le Pen and French far right were highly tenuous. Moreover, in European elections, the conservatives or the left took the lion's share of the electoral arena, leaving little room for the extreme right.

In the Euro-elections of June 1989 the overall vote has been interpreted as a reversal for conservative philosophies that had flourished in Western Europe, and a success for extreme right parties and the Greens. Italy was an exception to this tendency of growth of extreme right growth as the Christian Democrats confirmed themselves as the biggest party, taking twenty-eight of the country's eighty-one seats (11,411,986 votes). The Communist Party attenuated its recent electoral losses and showed itself to be the second force in Italian politics, with twenty-two seats. The Socialists won fourteen seats. The MSI declined to four European Parliament seats from five, gathering only 1,915,596 votes. This was a personal blow for Gianfranco Fini as the party suffered the most serious defeat since he became the new leader in 1987. The MSI is no longer the fourth largest party in the country. The major winner was a heterogeneous grouping of environmentalists which won five seats; they entered the European Parliament for the first time, divided into two parties.

The opposition within the MSI has pointed to a transformation underway in the Italian political system, confirmed by the European election results themselves. In fact, in these elections the communists managed to slow-down their electoral decline but still lost 651,720 votes with respect to general elections held two years previously. In the European elections, while the extreme right and more moderate groups lost ground, other political groups which are either explicitly anti-system or are on the fringe of the Italian political system gained in strength e.g. *Democrazia proletaria* (440,476 votes and one seat), the 'anti-prohibitionists' (426,659 votes and one seat) and the autonomist movement *Lega Lombarda* (634,884 votes and two seats). Moreover the presence of a large number of disaffected voters was evident from the high percentage of abstentions, non-voters and annulled votes. In the Italian electoral system a non-vote is an offence, though the law has never been enforced. The average turnout among Italian voters was 84.4 per cent, the lowest turnout of the three direct elections that have so far been held for the Strasbourg-based European Parliament.

Critics of the traditional leadership of the MSI claim that the focus of the European elections was on ideological issues. From their point of view, in the European elections there is less incentive to vote in a 'clientelistic' way than in a national or local election. In the latter cases, the Italians choose a large number of representatives; in the European elections, on the contrary, the vote is more ideologically based. This electoral defeat is important for the MSI, therefore, because it signified the defeat of a strategy which attempts to combine continuity with the fascist heritage and moderate positions.

Many scholars have noted the weakness of post-war backlash rightist politics particularly when compared to the inter-war years. They speak of the structural changes which have reduced the social basis of traditional rightist movements. New left preferences seem based on a rapid growth in the numbers of people engaged in the expanding trends of post-industrial society, whereas the social base of right-wing extremism seems to be dimi-nishing, because it was drawn from pre-industrial strata of the population: artisans, small business people, farmers, residents in small towns, etc., who have declined greatly. Also, cultural changes (for instance, the decline of religion and nationalism) are associated with this trend.

For these reasons, it has been asserted that there seems little possibility that right-wing backlash movements will re-emerge as major threats to the democratic processes in developed countries (Lipset, 1981, p. 495). But, observers who support this interpretation also add that the failure of militant protest is connected to the widespread affluence of the post-World War Two years. Consequently, it could be hypothesized that a new and severe econ-omic recession could set off phenomena that may be compared to those of the inter-war years which were at the basis of European fascism (Bresciani-Turroni, 1953, pp. 315–20).

As regards the possibility of a rebirth of new forms of a mass right-wing and anti-system movement, crucial importance has been given to the poten-tial emergence of marginal sectors of society, uprooted as a result of the restructuring of industry, immigration and a breakdown in the traditional socio-economic balance. According to Pizzorno (1974, p. 334), an alliance of sectors of the middle-classes, the sub-proletariat and the industrial bourgeoi-sie was the 'nightmare' that obsessed the Christian Democrats from the

1950s to the 1970s because it represented a continuous threat to the constitutional pact and the political system and was capable of producing 'an alternative, of a more or less fascist nature, to the present regime'. A serious economic and social crisis characterized by massive unemployment, the blocking of upward social mobility, a decrease in per capita national income and so on, might have political consequences conclusive to a massive swing to the extreme right. For example, during the 1970s in Switzerland, a sizeable economic recession was enough for the growth of a large-scale indigenous reaction to the presence of foreign workers.

In the history of the decline of MSI there is one episode concerning its electoral fortune that may be considered as highly significant from this viewpoint. During the 1980s a succesful result was obtained by the MSI in Bolzano, a city on the borders of Italy, where the MSI tripled its vote and reached more than 25 per cent (Tempestini, 1990). The problem of Bolzano started in 1919 when Italy took over the South Tyrol, a German-speaking area enormously conscious of its own ethnic specificity. For a long time, Italian governments have tried unsuccessfully to assimilate this population. Over the years, the problem has given rise to conflicts and permanent tensions. Since the Second World War, there have been almost four hundred terrorist attempts therein, and some political organizations make strong claims for the creation of an independent South-Tyrolese state.

The great majority of South-Tyrolese are cautious about possible self-determination or unification with Austria. The fruit-growers, farmers, business people, tourist operators, hotel owners and politicians have benefited from a tremendous amount of Italian money in the form of public subsidies. It could even be said that the Italian government has tried to buy peace by paying the highest possible price in cash. In fact, the standard of living in the South Tyrol is one of the best in the world.

The reaction of the Italian community against public policies, which are seen as too favourable to the German community, has lead to widespread support for the nationalist extreme right, represented by the MSI, which in 1987 won first place with 25.7 per cent of the vote, followed by the Christian Democrats (15.2 per cent). Subsequently, in local elections, held in May 1989, the most significant results were obtained by the far right and the Greens. In particular, the MSI became the leading party in Bolzano with 27.1 per cent of the vote while the Greens confirmed their growth with 12.1 per cent. In the local council there are also representatives of pensioners and of another ethnic group: the Ladins. Communists, Christian Democrats, and exponents of the *Sudtiroler Volkspartei* are also well represented, and there is a scattering of members from minor parties.

This situation may be interpreted as one of mere protest: the Italians want to be represented by those who have a less conciliatory attitude towards the German-speaking ethnic group, which is why they vote for the MSI. However, this situation may also be interpreted as the consequence of long standing relative deprivation. Fluctuations in working-class grievances may be due either to absolute deprivation, such as a decrease in the per capita national income, or relative deprivation – the feeling of being threatened by other people.

The history of Bolzano teaches us several things at the same time: firstly it goes against the interpretation whereby the extreme right vote is closely correlated with two variables: subcultures and underdevelopment. It is true that there is a base of electoral support which is constant and enduring, connected with the fascist heritage; and it is true that the great reserves of the MSI are the South and the islands of Italy (Caciagli, 1988; Ignazi, 1989). Yet, it is also true that there are states of mind that may suddenly come into being and determine unexpected support for extreme right-wing movements. For instance, although the trend toward ethnically distinct immigration is likely to continue, future political relations will undoubtedly be affected by issues such as stereotypes, scapegoats and racial conflicts.

In a troubled situation, linked to ethnic deadlock, or to an economic recession, or to other sudden structural changes, the extremist appeal could be successful. As regards the future of Italian democracy, Norberto Bobbio, the most prestigious Italian democratic intellectual, has asserted: 'democracy has not become a deep-rooted part of our cultural heritage. I think that, even today, many would be willing to exchange liberty for perhaps more order, more discipline' (Bobbio, 1989, p. 24).

A good opportunity for the rebirth of right-wing extremism has been seen in the growing importance of two racist or pseudo-racist phenomena: the intolerance towards immigrants and the political gains of new local political groups, above all in the North, in the form of the Lombard League (*Lega lombarda*). The 'northern' groups constitute an agglomerate formed by voters deriving from different political experiences; this agglomerate is unified by an emphasis on the countless differences still existing between the South and the North of the country, and by the call for a new autonomist organization. The strengthening of 'northern', 'independentist' and 'disuniting' groups is associated with the enormous growth of protest against traditional national parties. In Europe, in general, satisfaction with democratic institutions is higher than in Italy: for instance, it is 75.7 per cent in Germany and 61.3 in Great Britain. In Italy, on the contrary, it is 28.4. Also, the confidence level in the capacity of representation of traditional parties is lower in Italy, than in the rest of Europe; in Italy this level is zero for 48.7 per cent of the population, in Germany for 16.2, in Great Britain for 25.1 (Mannheimer, 1991, p. 43).

The Lombard League obtained 18.9 per cent of the vote in the 1990 local elections and seems to be a substantial reflection of electoral mistrust. While other protest parties are less influential or are single-issue parties, i.e. expressions of a protest around a specific problem (for example, the party of the retired people, the Green Party, the party for the legalization of drugs), the Lombard League satisfies the need for more expansive political identification. In fact, surveys reveal that those who vote once for the Lombard League do not change their vote in following elections. Whereas single issue parties enhance 'participation', the Lombard League promotes 'counter-mobilization', and has an electorate which belongs not to the marginal strata, but to the middle classes and to the sector (in Italy a very dynamic sector) of the small industrial firm. In wealthy Northern urban areas this party achieves or surpasses 30 per cent of the votes (the national average is lower because in the South obviously this party has an insignificant number of votes). The MSI has attacked the autonomist parties vigorously because it sees its electoral decline as caused (at least partially) by a mass desertion towards the Lombard League, which has mobilized anti-system tendencies in the country.

The April 1992 general election, however, was significant in that the Northern League coalition and the MSI both performed well. The former won 8.7 per cent of the votes nation wide and fifty-five seats in the Chamber of Deputies. In Lombardy, the share of the vote was higher at 24 per cent and in the North of Italy as a whole the movement won 17.5 per cent. At the same time, the MSI vote held up well enough: with 5.4 per cent of the vote and thirty-four seats the MSI virtually repeated its previous general election performance. Northern League gains were predominantly as the expense of the Christian Democrats than the MSI. An interesting winner on the MSI list in Naples was Mussolini's granddaughter. Collectively, these two electoral performances revealed an important anti-system protest and undermined the already fragile stability of Italian politics.

The electoral returns of the Northern League and the MSI also indicated rising intolerance towards immigrants. The first national survey on immigration was carried out in 1987 and others followed in 1989 and 1991. By 1991 (Bollettino Doxa, 1991, p. 94), the percentage of people who considered that immigration was much too widespread had increased from 28.5 in 1987 to 45.9. In four years, the percentage of people who see in immigration 'only, or prevalently, trouble' jumped from 49 to 61; the percentage of people who think that Italy should not favour immigration increased from 51 to 75; the percentage of those who think that immigration should be authorized only in extraordinary circumstances was 37.8; this percentage was 24.2 in 1987, and even went down to 17.7 in 1989. Tables below sum up a clear trend: initially public opinion was not hostile to immigration but has changed especially since the end of the 1980s.

In conclusion, three Italians in four are hostile to any policy which favours immigration. Also, over two years there was a marked increase (from 17.7 to 37.8 per cent) of people prepared to consent to immigration 'only in exceptional circumstances'. At the last survey, public opinion appeared more and more afraid of immigration, and less and less inclined to demonstrate 'solidarity'. Xenophobic propensities can help to encourage extremists depending on circumstances notably the perception of the country's economic and social situation. On all these counts – rising

Table 6.1 Should Italy encourage immigration?

	1991	1989	1987
yes	13.0	31.8	24.9
no	75.0	50.7	57.1
don't know	12.0	17.5	18.0

Table 6.2   Specific question for interviewees who replied that Italy should not encourage immigration

So what should Italy do for immigration?			
	1991	1989	1987
prohibit it completely	10.9	7.2	7.8
allow it only in exceptional circumstances	37.8	17.7	24.2
leave it free, but with many controls	24.3	23.0	21.9
leave it free, but with a minimum of controls	0.9	1.6	1.8
don't know	1.1	1.2	1.4

Source: Doxa, 1991, p.121

xenophobia, hostility to immigration, growth of protest movements, economic problems and so on – the indicators in 1992 suggested fertile ground for the expansion of extreme right politics.

References

Accame, G., 1990. *Fascismo immenso e rosso*, Settimo Sigillo, Rome.
Almond, G. A., Verba, S., (eds), 1980. *The Civic Culture Revisited*, Little, Brown and Co., Boston.
Baldoni, A., Provvisionato S., 1989. *La notte più lunga della Repubblica*, Serarcangeli, Rome.
Bardèche, M., 1980. *Che cosa è il fascismo?*, Volpe, Rome.
Bobbio, N., 1989. L'etica delle convinzioni e l'etica della responsabilità contro il rischio della barbarie, *L'Opinione*, luglio 1989: 13–24.
Doxa, 1991. Gli stranieri in Italia. Risultati di tre sondaggi, *Bollettino della Doxa*, XLV, no. 9, 10, 11, 25 luglio 1991: 93–126.
Borraccetti, V., 1986. *Eversione di destra, terrorismo, stragi*, Angeli, Milan.
Bresciani-Turroni, C., 1953, *The Economics of Inflation. A Study of Currency Depreciation in Post-War Germany 1914–1933*, London.
Caciagli, M., 1988. The Movimento Sociale Italiano-Destra Nazionale and neo-fascism in Italy, *West European Politics*, Vol. 11 No. (2): 19–33.
De Felice, R., 1970. *Le interpretazioni del fascismo*, Laterza, Bari.
—— 1975. *Intervista sul fascismo*, Laterza, Bari.
Di Palma, G., 1980. Founding coalitions in southern Europe: Legitimacy and hegemony, *Government and Opposition*, 15: 162–89.
Ferracuti, F., 1982. A Sociopsychiatric interpretation of terrorism, *The Annals of the American Academy of Political and Social Science*, 463: 129–40.
Ferracuti, F., Bruno, F., 1981. *Psychiatric Aspects of terrorism in Italy*, in I. L. Barak-Glantz, I.L., Huff, C.R., eds., *The mad, the bad and the different: essays in honor of Simon Dinitz*, Lexington Books, Lexington: 199–13.

Ferraresi, F., 1987. Julius Evola: tradition, reaction, and the radical right, *European Journal of sociology*, No. 28,: 107–151.

—— 1988, The Radical right in postwar Italy, *Politics and Society*, Vol. 16, No. 1: 71–119.

Germani, G., 1975. *Autoritarismo, fascismo e classi sociali*, Il Mulino, Bologna.

Gregor, A. J., 1979. *Italian Fascism and Developmental Dictatorship*, Princeton University Press, Princeton.

Gualtieri, L., 1988. *Relazione alla Commissione parlamentare d'indagine*, unpublished Rome.

Hoffman, B., 1982. *Right-wing terrorism in Europe*, Rand Corp., Santa Monica, CA.

Ignazi, M., 1989. *Il polo escluso*, Il Mulino, Bologna.

Inglehart, R., 1981. Post-materialism in an environnement of insecurity, *American Political Science Review*, No. 75, n.4.

La Palombara, J., 1965. Italy: isolation, fragmentation and alienation in Pye L. W. and Verba S., eds., *Political culture and political development*, Princeton University Press, Princeton, NJ.

Laponce, J. A., 1981. *Left and Right. The Topography of Political Perceptions*, University of Toronto Press, Toronto.

Ledeen, M., 1976, Renzo De Felice and the controversy over Italian Fascism, *Journal of Contemporary History*, Vol. 11 No. 4 269–83.

Leonardi, R., 1977. The smaller parties in the 1976 Italian elections, in H. R. Penniman, *Italy at the polls. The parliamentary elections of 1976*, American Enterprise Institution, Washington DC.

Linz, J. J., Stepan, A., 1978. *The Breakdown of Democratic Regimes*, The Johns Hopkins University Press, Baltimore.

Lipset, S. M., 1960. *Political Man. The Social Basis of Politics*, Doubleday, New York.

—— 1981. The Revolt Against Modernity, in *Mobilization, Center-Periphery, structures, and nation-building: a volume in commemoration of Stein Rokkan*, Universitetsforlaget, Oslo.

Mannheimer, R., 1991. *La lega lombarda*, Feltrinelli, Milano.

Parisi, V., 1988a, *Commissione parlamentare d'inchiesta sul terrorismo in Italia e sulle cause della mancata individuazione dei responsabili delle stragi*, hearing of the Chief of Police, 6 December, Tipografia del Senato, Rome.

—— 1988b. *Commissione parlamentare d'inchiesta sul terrorismo in Italia e sulle cause della mancata individuazione dei responsabili delle stragi*, Chief of Police, 14 December 1988, Tipografia del Senato, Rome.

Pecchioli, 1981. Prefazione, in M. Galleni, *Rapporto sul terrorismo*, Rizzoli, Milan.

Pisano, V. S., 1984. *Report of the Subcommittee on Security and Terrorism of the Committee on the Judiciary, United States Senate*, US Government Printing Office, Washington DC.

Pizzorno, A., 1974. I ceti medi nel meccanismo del consenso, in Cavazza F. L Graubard S. R., *Il caso italiano*, Vol. II, Garzanti, Milan.

Solé, R., 1979. *Le défi terroriste. Lecons italiennes à l'usage de l'Europe*, Seuil, Paris.

Prandstraller, V., 1985. *La professione militare in Italia*, Angeli, Milan.

Putnam, R. D., 1971, Studying elite political culture: the case of ideology, *American Political Science Review*, No. 65 661–81.

Relazione sulla politica informativa e sulla sicurezza, Comunicata alla presidenza il 21 luglio 1989, Doc. xlvii n.5, Senato della Repubblica, Rome.

Sidoti, F., 1987. Mafia e Parlamento, *Queste Istituzioni*, Vol. 14 No. 71: 57–77.

—— 1990. Terrorism supporters in the West. The Italian case, in N. Gal-or, *Tolerating Terrorism in the West*, Routledge, London.

Sternhell, Z., 1983, *Ni droite ni gauche, L'idéologie fasciste en France*, Seuil, Paris.
Tarchi, M., 1989. Le tre vie del radicalismo di destra, *Trasgressioni*, Vol. 4 No. (1): 3–20.
Tempestini, A., 1990. *I partiti minori a Bolzano*, forthcoming.
Veneziani, M., 1987. Al di là della destra e della sinistra, in AA. VV., *La destra come categoria*, QuattroVenti, Urbino.
Vold, G. B., 1979. *Theoretical Criminology*, Oxford University Press, New York.
Weber, M.,1922. *Gesammelte Aufsatze zur Religionssoziologie*, Mohr, Tubingen.
Weinberg, L., 1979. *After Mussolini: Italian Neo-Fascism and the Nature of Fascism*, University Press of America, Washington DC.

7 Why Has the Extreme Right Failed in Britain?

Roger Eatwell

Britain: a Peripheral Concern?

During the inter-war years the extreme right in Britain failed dismally. Thus in post-war Britain there have been no significant continued pockets of extreme right support of the type which emerged especially in West Germany in the late 1940s and early 1950s. Nor has there been the major electoral breakthrough among new supporters of the sort achieved by the Front national in France during the 1980s. Indeed, the most 'sucessful' of the British post-war extreme right groups, the National Front (NF), has proved incapable of winning any form of election, and its peak membership was less than half of that achieved by Sir Oswald Mosley's British Union of Fascists (BUF) in the 1930s. During the 1970s the National Front held hopes of becoming England's third electoral force, but by the 1980s it had collapsed into miniscule rival factions.

These opening comments seem to point to the essential irrelevance of the British extreme right. However, closer study reveals at least two major questions relevant to both British and comparative politics. One concerns the very usage of the term 'extreme right', which is all too often taken as an unproblematic ascription, covering different types of fascist and non-fascist groups, in both the pre-and post-1945 periods. Yet Mosley's post-1945 philosophical-policy writings, and the little-studied debates within the NF during the 1980s, underline crucial problems about the placement of fascism on the left–right spectrum. Moreover, there is a complex mix of metamorphosis and continuity in relation to earlier extreme right groups. Similarities with the policies of some Conservatives raise the further question of whether a neat line can be drawn between the 'extreme' and 'moderate' rights. For example, it has been argued there is a pervasive 'new racism' which cuts across the right (Barker, 1980). This does not articulate the older type of racism, based on ideas of inferiority and superiority among racial groups. Rather, it stresses 'natural' group solidarity and exclusiveness.

However, questions of typology fall outside the remit of the national chapters in this book (for an attempt to develop a right-fascism typology see

Eatwell and O'Sullivan, 1989; Eatwell, 1992a). The main emphasis of what follows, therefore, is upon extreme right support rather than constructing typologies ('extreme right' is henceforth used as a generic term to encompass both fascist and non-fascist groups). In particular, the central theme is: Why has the British extreme right failed to make an electoral breakthrough at a time when there have been some propitious factors, notably periods of rising unemployment, inner-city deprivation, and brittle race relations?

An Overview of the Post-1945 Extreme Right

Mosley's extensive post-1945 writings undoubtedly represent one of the most sophisticated expositions of policy to come from a fascist leader (Skidelsky, 1975; Thurlow, 1987). In part, this was an attempt to defend his past. More originally, he sought to move away from nationalism to a defence of 'Europeanism', which was seen as providing a future 'third way' between capitalism and communism, though the linking of European development with the colonial development of Africa harked back to nineteenth-century themes. However, the goal was essentially modern: economic regeneration and 'progress'. In order to develop this 'third way', Mosley attempted to delineate a more refined analysis of the exact powers of the state *vis-à-vis* business and the individual, though he continued to place great emphasis on the role of the leader and 'will'. What he proposed was nothing less than an attempt to synthesize fascism and democracy! This was not just an economic or institutional question; it was also a quest for the rebirth of man, an attempt to create a new form of human nature, a man both dynamic and competitive, though ultimately not money-centred and individualistic (Mosley, 1947; Mosley, 1958, Mosley, 1961).

Mosley spent much of the post-war period in self-imposed exile, waiting for the economic crisis which he believed would bring him to power. The day-to-day running of the Union Movement, which he launched in 1948, was left in the hands of activist rather than intellectual lieutenants (corporals might be a better term, as Mosley's arrogance tended to alienate all but the most uncritical). The Union Movement's main activity, therefore, was a continuation of the old street politics of the BUF: small meetings, pub drinking, isolated harrassment of Jews, and clashes with 'anti-fascists', occasionally interspersed with a local election campaign.

The would-be activist 'movement' seemed to be dying of inaction in the mid-1950s; even anti-Semites would often have nothing to do with Mosley, a reflection of fascism's pariah status in the post-war world (Robb, 1954, p. 171). Dramatically, the movement was revived in the late 1950s by a growing awareness of a new issue: opposition to 'coloured' immigration. In the period after 1948 there was a rapid growth in the number of immigrants, initially mainly from the West Indies, later more from the Indian subcontinent. The amoral Mosley did nothing to counter racist tendencies within the Union Movement. Indeed, he came out of semi-retirement to stand in the 1959 general election for the North Kensington constituency, scene of the much-publicized 'race riots' the previous year. He gained 8.1

per cent of the vote, a bitter personal disappointment, though it was an ominous sign of the potential for racist politics.

Most other extreme right groups which emerged in the post-war era usually centred from the outset on nationalism or race, rather than regeneration, synthesis and the creation of a 'new man'. The majority of the League of Empire Loyalists, which was formed in 1954, tended to be Colonel Blimpish reactionary Conservatives rather than fascists, though it became increasingly extremist in the face of hostility from the Conservative leadership. Its membership also changed complexion as a result of the views of its leader, A. K. Chesterton. Although he had broken with Mosley in the late 1930s, mainly over the BUF's excessive support of fascism abroad, he retained an addiction to anti-Semitic conspiracy theory, thus helping to induct a new generation of anti-Semitic activists. Another key figure was Arnold Leese, an even more virulent anti-Semite, who had headed the inter-war Imperial Fascist League. His main post-war role was to help finance several small groups. These included the British National Party, formed in 1960 as an ideological mélange of pure Nazis and more conservative racists. In 1962 Colin Jordan, one of Leese's protégés, broke away to form his own National Socialist Movement, which sought to develop a paramilitary organization. A further split took place in 1964. It is difficult to separate personal from policy differences, but Jordan seems to have wanted to keep the overt Nazi line. A group of dissidents, led by John Tyndall and Martin Webster, believed that a covert approach, stressing British roots, would be more fruitful. Tyndall and Webster went on to found the Greater Britain Movement. In 1967 this amalgamated with the new National Front which had been formed mainly from the fusion of the British National Party and the League of Empire Loyalists.

The NF was formed at a time when a major change in extreme right tactics was taking place. Earlier groups had mainly sought to establish an active coterie based on racism, even violence. However, by the late 1960s, a considerable number had come to believe that the impact of immigration opened the possibility of actually winning elections. This was influenced especially by the arrival of expelled Kenyan 'Asians', and the popular reception of Conservative MP Enoch Powell's infamous 1968 'Rivers of Blood' speech, which had predicted the onset of racial violence in Britain (Schoen, 1977). Fighting elections offered the further advantage of appearing to offer democratic legitimacy. More specifically, it provided a bridge to Conservatives, especially those in the larger Monday Club, which had been set up in 1961 to press for more nationalistic and right-wing policies (on the Monday Club, see Seyd, 1972).

Two men were to dominate the NF's leadership for much of the 1970s: Tyndall and Webster (Billig, 1978; Taylor, 1982). In analysing the NF's ideology and politics at this time it is important to draw clear distinctions between its different fields of operation. In the inner core of the party, the message tended more to fascism, especially of the anti-Semitic Nazi kind. At the more public level, repatriation and the degeneration which had accompanied 'coloured' immigration were the target of its campaigns. By the early 1970s, there were growing signs that the NF was capable of performing much better than previous groups. In particular, the NF achieved several notable local and parliamentary results during 1972–3, for example in the 1973 West Bromwich parliamentary by-election where it won 16 per cent of the vote, its best ever performance in a parliamentary election. This period also corresponded with its peak membership of approximately 14,000. However, its fifty-four candidates in the February 1974 general election averaged only 3.3 per cent of the vote. In the October 1974 election it put up eighty-nine candidates, averaging an even more disappointing 3.1 per cent.

This set the scene for a power struggle which culminated in a major split in 1975. Some in the party, especially recent recruits from the Conservatives, blamed these disappointing performances on the neo-Nazi credentials of Tyndall, Webster and others (though the divisions also encompassed debates within fascism, especially support for a more working-class inclined 'Strasserism'). The resulting National Party was short-lived, though it succeeded in electing two councillors in Blackburn. This came at the time of a second peak in NF support, which occurred during 1976–7. Although the NF never succeeded in electing anyone, these elections produced, if anything, even more dramatic gains than in 1972–3. The NF averaged 8.9 per cent for the seats it contested in the 1976 local elections, including 16.6 per cent in Leicester. In the following year the NF won 119,00 votes in the Greater London Council elections, and almost quarter of a million nationally. This raised hopes that the party was on the verge of a national breakthrough, and for the 1979 general election the NF put forward 303 candidates. They averaged a dismal 1.4 per cent of the poll!

This result hastened further defections and schisms. There were some disagreements over the party's increasing use of major marches, a policy apparently adopted in the hope that these would attract publicity (rallies also appealed to the more violent side of the NF's membership, since they invited ethnic and 'anti-fascist' opposition). More fundamentally, the internal wrangles again centred on the desire to dump the more overt Nazi leaders. The first major split led to Tyndall's departure in 1980. He subsequently founded the British National Party (BNP). Its policies were similar to those of the early NF, though it was more openly anti-Semitic and leader-oriented (*Spearhead*, April 1989). In 1984 Martin Webster was pushed out, slipping into obscurity. In the meantime, many former Conservatives had drifted back into their former party, though some of this movement may have reflected a policy of deliberate infiltration of the Conservatives.

These splits also stemmed from the onset of a serious phase of political theorizing, especially among young radicals. This radical faction did not seek a mass membership to hold major street rallies, or to contest elections (at least in the short run). Rather, they turned to the remodelling of human nature (*Rising*, No. 1, 1982; *Nationalism Today*, No. 44, 1989). They sought 'political soldiers', willing to sacrifice all to create a new society. This new NF stressed an anti-modernist, ruralist form of society, based on community, and 'Distributist' principles of decentralization and wide property ownership. These views were presented as coming from a British rather than continental tradition (*Rising*, No. 3, 1983), though in fact this wing of the NF was heavily influenced by a group of Italian neo-fascists living in

London, and key continental theorists such as Julius Evola and Corneliu Codreanu. The radical wing of the NF accepted nationalism among other peoples, moving away from simple racial hierarchies. Amazingly, by 1988 it had even come to defend the ideas of the Ayatollah Khomeini and Colonel Gadaffi, seeing them as advocates of the 'third position' – 'Beyond Capitalism and Communism' (*National Front News*, No. 108, 1988).

In contrast, another wing retained similarities with the 1970s NF, though it too acquired some taste for theory and developed new issues, for example ecology (though this could be a 'surrogate' theme covering defence of the 'homeland': *Vanguard*, No. 34, 1991). However, this group's 'theory' has to be seen against the fact that it remained at the grass-roots level a street-activist organization. Thus, together with the BNP, it seems to have been at the centre of the continuation (or rather, the increase) in attacks on the ethnic community (Husbands, 1989), a tactic first systematically used by the British Movement, which Jordan had founded as the successor to the National Socialist Movement in 1968. It also remained active in attempting to influence youth culture through racist pop music and in promoting football hooliganism. On the other hand, this wing of the NF never lost sight of contesting elections and seeking to present a more respectable face. Indeed, in spite of the fact that the sole NF candidate in the 1987 general election and 1989 Euro-election had gained a meagre 0.6per cent of the *local* poll, in the early 1990s the NF seems to have taken a decision to contest more elections – a decision shared by the growing BNP.

Table 7.1 NF General Election Performances

	UK Seats	NF Candidates	Average NF Vote %	Highest NF Vote %
1970	630	10	3.6	5.6
1974 Feb.	635	54	3.3	7.8
1974 Oct.	635	90	3.1	9.4
1979	635	303	1.4	7.6
1983	650	60[1]	1.1	2.4
1987	650	1[2]	–	0.6
1992	651	14[3]	0.7	1.2

Notes:
1. Plus 53 BNP candidates: highest vote 1.3%
2. Plus 2 BNP candidates: highest vote 0.6%
3. Plus 13 BNP candidates: highest vote 3.6%

The anti-fascist magazine *Searchlight* has argued that behind the apparent split between these two wings, which became public in 1986–7, lay a co-ordinated strategy to develop different appeals (Gable, 1991, p. 255ff). Clearly there are connections, though the extreme right remains riven by

180   *Roger Eatwell*

personality splits. Moreover, some of the ideological debate reflects a genuine questioning about roots, especially the relationship to Hitler and Nazism. Moreover, in January 1990 the Third Position wing of the NF announced that it would cease to exist because many of the policies popularly associated with the organization did not reflect its current position (*National Front News*, No. 126, 1990, p. 1). The fact that its membership had dwindled to a handful was another factor, although there seems little doubt that many of its leaders had tried to develop an alternative ideology (albeit one which still had links with a broader extreme right tradition). The other wing of the NF soldiered on with approximately 3,000 members, convinced that its fortunes, like those of its French namesake a decade before, were about to be transformed. As one of its younger leaders wrote in 1987 (*Vanguard*, No. 6, p. 8): 'the public, by and large, are National Front supporters even if they don't know it yet' (for more detail on the ideology of the post-1945 extreme right see Eatwell, 1992b).

The Problem of Extreme Right Support

This apparently bizarre claim raises an important perspective when analysing the British extreme right. Has it failed because of a fundamental lack of support for its policies among the British people(s)? Or has the extreme right been blessed with a more fertile soil to till? If the latter is the case, why has it failed so dismally?

Surveys undertaken during the 1960s and 1970s revealed extensive support for extreme right principles, such as the desire for strong leadership, or nationalism. Major studies in the 1970s found that over a quarter of respondents agreed with the main policy-plank of the NF – namely the compulsory repatriation of non-white immigrants (Särlvik and Crewe, 1983, p. 243). Another study found that 21 per cent thought it would be 'good for Britain' if the NF was represented in the House of Commons; and a quarter of respondents thought that the NF expressed the views of 'ordinary working people' (Harrop et al., 1980, p. 281). The potential for extremism seems to be underlined by poll evidence from the European Community's journal *Eurobarometer*. The December 1985 issue revealed that 6.0 per cent of UK respondents self-located as polar 'extreme right' on a 10 point scale, the second highest number in the Community (p. 48). The December 1988 issue found 11 per cent who were completely, or to some extent, in favour of racist movements, the fifth highest in the Community (p. 65). The November 1989 issue divided national populations into five categories in terms of attitudes to democracy and race. The fourth category included those who rejected democracy as a good idea: 20 per cent of UK respondents came in this group, the fourth highest in the Community (pp. 91–5). (According to the European Commission, Britain's population at the end of the 1980s included approximately 3 per cent of non-EC origins, the fifth highest in the Community.)

It is important not to overstate the significance of this information. A yearning for strong leadership, or holding nationalist, even racist views, do not necessarily lead to conversion to the extreme right. The validity of some polls' findings too can be challenged, especially those done on small samples, or including potentially misleading categories. For example, the self-ascription 'extreme right' in the 1985 poll could encompass many positions, including *laissez-faire*/libertarian, or it could simply reflect a sense of alienation. The same point could be made about actually voting for the extreme right. Thus it has been argued that the key to NF voting was whether an alternative protest 'vehicle' was available, notably a Liberal candidate (Steed, 1974, p. 336). The same author has sought to show that there was a fairly constant 2–4 per cent of the vote 'available' to extreme right candidates in certain areas, with variations above this figure mainly reflecting factors such as differential turnout (see also Taylor, 1982, pp. 116ff).

On the other hand, there is evidence that people are less willing to admit to supporting extremist parties. People may also tend to explain their vote to pollsters in terms of everyday factors, such as economic prosperity, rather than more diffuse ones like nationalism, let alone admit 'illegitimate' influences such as racism. Moreover, the exact factors which influence voting may remain obscured by aggregate data analysis. This is not simply the statistical point that if enough correlations are run it would be surprising if some apparently significant relationships did not emerge (Sanders *et al.*, 1987, sought to demonstrate the importance of economics in voting after the 1982 Falklands War by using twenty-six factors, each lagged from one to twelve months, a total of 338 possible effects!). There is also more specific evidence. Correlating the NF vote with the presence of an alternative 'protest' candidate may produce an apparent relationship, but evidence from detailed local studies suggests that the simple protest explanation may be misleading. In particular, the Liberals at the local level, contrary to their national platform, were sometimes perceived as 'hard' on race (Deakin, 1984). Finally, the argument that NF voting is largely explained by factors such as differential turnout out confuses as much as it enlightens. For example, it does not fully explain the particularly high NF votes in some areas, notably parts of London's East End, or Leicester. And where did this constant reservoir go in the 1980s?

The potential for strong extreme right support can be illustrated by a hypothetical case. Enoch Powell gained considerable publicity and popularity after 1968 on account of his statements predicting racial violence, and trumpeting the 'voluntary' repatriation of the non-white community: a remarkable 74 per cent in 1968 agreed with his vivid prophecy of coming racial violence. In 1974 he broke with the Conservative Party over its acceptance of membership of the European Community and continued non-white immigration into Britain. What if he had joined the NF at this point? And what if elections to the European Parliament, held under proportional representation, had taken place during one of the NF's 1970s peaks?

It could be countered that this scenario glosses over important objections. There were notable ideological differences between Powell and the NF: in particular Powell was a great defender of parliamentary democracy and *laissez-faire* economics. Certainly, it is not being claimed here that Powell almost joined the NF, though many other Conservatives who were in no

182   *Roger Eatwell*

way fascist entered the NF in the 1970s. Taylor has also argued that the electoral system had little to do with the NF's failure, citing a single survey where only 5 per cent said that they would be likely to vote NF if they thought it could do well (Taylor, 1982, pp. 179–80). However, other polls cited above tend to indicate a greater NF potential, and polls tend to underestimate such support. Finally, it should be noted that the Front national in France seems to have been helped (and harmed) by changes in the electoral system.

Moreover, the Powell–proportional representation scenario is meant, not only to illustrate the potential for extreme right groups, but also to underline a point about the study of the extreme right. There has been a strong tendency to adopt what amounts to the classic Marxist distinction between 'base' and 'superstructure'. Factors such as the activities of individual politicians, or the operation of the party system, have been downplayed in favour of more sociological explanations, even a crude reductionism to the 'logic' of capitalism. The argument here is not that socio-economic factors are unimportant. The point is more to retrieve the relevance of a political dimension.

Who Voted for and Joined the NF in the 1970s?

This problem within Marxism has been compounded by a social science tendency to study NF support mainly through opinion polls, or by aggregate data analysis. This produces neatly quantified though remarkably inconsistent results: thus simple tables of the NF's socio-economic support tend to be misleading. The main area of agreement about 1970s NF support is based on the fact that it tended to be male, was negatively correlated with turnout, and was primarily English (NB: in Wales and Scotland moderate, catch-all nationalist parties grew dramatically after the mid-1960s; they emphasized national and socio-economic issues other than race). The two main areas of division concern the class and age base of the NF. Many have argued that the bulk of NF support came from an 'authoritarian' working class (Whiteley, 1979). However, when Husbands divided NF supporters into 'strong' and 'moderate', he found that although the former were heavily working class, overall there was no significant class factor. Husbands found that the main area of relative NF support was among the 'marginal' self-employed, that is, those without formal qualifications, who tended to employ no one outside the family (Husbands, 1983, p. 136ff). He explained this mainly by reference to the precarious economic position of many in this group. He also argued that when his two groups were combined, there was no strong age correlation, challenging the views of many others who have stressed the appeal of the NF to an alienated youth, which was experiencing growing unemployment.

The main emphasis of Husbands' work was on the locational side of NF support. He argued that there were two main types of environment where NF support was greatest. These were post-1945 boom areas, which were experiencing economic difficulties in the 1970s (e.g., Coventry and Slough), and declining traditional industrial areas (e.g., Bradford and Leicester). The

NF thus had little support in rural or suburban areas, being mainly a feature of parts of London, the Midlands and northern England. However, a problem with this approach is that there is no necessary connection: not all areas in these categories showed strong NF support, and it had pockets of 'deviant' support, such as seaside Blackpool. Alternative locational approaches have therefore centred on the correlation between NF voting and the immediate presence of ethnic communities, versus 'invasion' approaches which hold that racist voting is likely to be greater in areas on the periphery of ethnic settlement. In Britain, the former seems to offer the best explanation at the local level. Nevertheless, it is important to note that the NF's 1970s peaks came shortly after well-publicized new waves of immigration from the expelled Ugandan Asians in 1972–3, and Malawian Asians in 1976–7, which raised distinct invasion fears (Taylor, 1979).

A study of the NF's leadership and activists underlines the problems created in producing a model of support. Most of the leadership tended to be middle-class, though it was a mixed bag. There was a small number, especially in the early days, from relatively wealthy backgrounds, individuals who were often important financial props of the party. There was a larger group, typified by Tyndall and Webster, who can best be described as 'marginal' middle-class: they tended to be travelling salesmen, or to have some form of self-employed occupation. There was even a group with degree-level education; in the 1970s this included the author of the Holocaust denial pamphlet *Did Six Million Really Die?* (Harwood, 1974), and in the 1980s several of the young radical leadership were well-educated. The main linking strands at the top seems to have been a distinct lack of charismatic leadership potential, administrative incompetence, and a tendency to ideological schism. At the grass-roots level, studies have stressed the difficulites of generalizing about local activists (Billig, 1978; Scott, 1975). The main linking factor at this level seems to have been hostility to 'immigrants' rather than socio-economic background.

However, in spite of these problems, it must be stressed that the main centres of NF voting occurred within working-class communities. Husbands' division of NF supporters into 'strong' and 'moderate' is important to an understanding of the *potential* for the NF, though actual NF *voting* is better understood within the former category. The existence of a clearly demarcated, traditional working-class 'community' seems to have been particularly important in provoking anti-immigrant resentment, and in influencing non-working class groups within that community. It was especially a feature of areas with older extreme right traditions, or weak Labour traditions, for example London's East End (Husbands, 1982). Resentment was also the result of socio-economic fears: for example, possible falling house prices in areas of immigrant settlement; job competition as the labour market tightened; or the quality of schooling in areas of growing ethnic families. As such, a variety of motives influenced NF voting. There was unquestionably an element of racism, as well as an element of financial self-interest. There was even a defence of traditional working-class values such as 'respectability'. At the turn of the century the opprobrium was vented on those (whites) who left their houses dirty, or drank too much; now, the targets were more overcrowded (ethnic) homes, or the stereotypical view of immigrants as sexually immoral and prone to laziness. It might be added that some working-class areas, where the privatization of life was least developed (for example, the continued focal role of the pub in male life), may also have lent themselves to the activist aspects of extreme right politics. (This appeal to the working class was noted by many on the European Right).

The Extreme Right and the British Political System

This emphasis on factors such as community and particular traditions illustrates the importance of not assuming that all significant explanatory factors can be found contemporaneously. Lipset and Rokkan in their classic study of party systems argued that, with few exceptions, post-war divisions were based on the cleavages of the 1920s (Lipset and Rokkan, 1967, p. 50). Thus, a crucial question at any point is: Why had the extreme right failed to make a significant impact in the twentieth century?

The most common social science explanation of this lacuna is based on an analysis of political culture (Benewick, 1969). This analysis sees Britain as a 'civic culture', a country whose democratic institutions are held in high public esteem, possessing a unique blend of modernity and tradition. Pervasive consensual, deferential and non-violent traits, nourishing a deep-rooted civility, seemed to militate against radical and activist philosophies (Almond and Verba, 1963). This approach offers important insights, though it glosses over complex definitional and historical questions. Arguably, its major problem is that it sees Britain as having been an easy country to govern because of its civic culture. A more fruitful approach is to reverse the causality (though this still leaves unanswered causal and definitional questions). The argument thus becomes the claim that the civic culture, especially deference, has been a result of good government.

The problem about what constitutes 'good government' can be seen in a very specific context by considering a debate about the role of both extreme right and 'anti-fascist' street demonstrations. An important legacy of the inter-war extreme right has been the left-wing myth that fascism was stopped by street violence. Many have claimed that demonstrations, especially those by the Anti-Nazi League, furthered the decline of the NF (Messina, 1989, p. 121). It could be countered that the League began activity only after the beginning of the NF's demise, but the main point being made here is that the 'state' has on the whole handled such demonstrations well. Another legacy of the inter-war extreme right is the 1936 Public Order Act, which allows the banning of demonstrations. This has been invoked few times since 1945, and critics have argued that this reflects a certain complicity in extreme right politics. Certainly, there has been some worrying antipathy within the police to the ethnic population and hostility to left-wing demonstrators, a situation which has encouraged left-wing commentators especially to claim that racism is pervasive within the police (Scraton, 1985, esp. p. 104). However, the British forces of law and order have not shown the connivance or tendency to turn a blind eye towards the extreme right which was often a feature of its rise in other countries (see Chapters 5 and 6 particularly). Indeed, although difficult to prove (and thus hardly researched), it is possible that police (and anti-fascist) penetration of extremist groups has been an important factor in their failure (Hill and Bell, pp. 173–4; 1988, Porter, 1989). Permission to hold extreme right demonstrations seems to have been based mainly on the weighing of the interests of public order versus those of free association and speech – and probably ultimately on the belief that they diminished rather than increased extreme right support. Such a 'public interest' view helps explain the banning of some ethnic marches: it may have been felt that they would inflame racial tension. (Radical critics of the police see such bans as further proof of endemic racism, a view which further helps to undermine faith in the police; and trust is a vital element of successful policing).

More generally, the question of 'good government' raises debates about élites, and the party system. A party system has many facets. First, the British first past the post electoral system militates against new parties. Second, there is the very structure of parties. Britain's major parties have undoubtedly been well-organized, both locally and nationally, in comparison with their often cadre-based continental counterparts (and the small extreme right groups, which have been unable to mount serious campaigns outside a small number of areas unless they can bus activists in for single by-elections). Third, there is the relationship between the national and local political system. Britain's unitary state and developed communications helped 'nationalize' issues at an early stage. The extreme right on the continent was often helped by local structures, in which different messages could be disseminated by well-organized extremist parties. A fourth relevant aspect of party systems is the nature of the relationship between voters and parties. Are there close and stable ties of partisanship based on, say, class? Or do voters seem more influenced by specific issues and exhibit volatile behaviour?

The British party system from the 1920s to the 1960s exhibited strong alignment along predominantly class lines, though at the same time the Conservative and Labour parties were also archetypal programmatic parties. Purely sociological analyses have failed to see that class politics were intimately tied to a particular ideological form. The central ideological problem of British fascism in the inter-war period was its inability to delineate policies perceived as salient. This has also been true of the post-war period.

Labour ideology has included aspects such as the rejection of class analysis by its national leadership, and its espousal of a form of corporatism. A vital factor has been its sense of 'movement' which helped tide it through crises, such as after the major split of 1931, and which remained strong even after 1945 (contrast the decline of terms such as *Bewegung*, or *Movimiento* on the continent). Labour has also at times exhibited a form of nationalism, and although the Labour leadership in the post-war era could not be considered racist in the classic sense of legitimizing hierarchies, it could be considered racist in other senses. In particular, it has supported 'state racism' in areas such as immigration policy (see Reeves, 1983, for a discussion of racial party ideology), though this has been countered by a more positive support than from the Conservatives for protective race relations laws (including the Labour government, pioneering first Race Relations Act in 1965). The leadership's recent hostility to 'black sections' in a party which already has women's and other sections reflects a fear that growing ethnic political activity might damage the party, especially in working-class eyes. White votes come before positive discrimination, though the leadership has to balance this with a desire to maintain its predominant vote among the ethnic communities. Finally, it is important to distinguish between the local and national level: at the under researched local level, there was occasionally a more crude racism, especially in the unions.

Conservative ideology historically has served even more to defuse extreme right appeals. Important aspects of conservatism in this context include its organicism, linked to concepts such as its own form of corporatism and welfarism. It was also not anti-working class: indeed, British Conservatism has shown a remarkable understanding of and appeal to the working class. In the more specific context of post-1945 politics, it was the Conservatives who passed the first, restrictive, Commonwealth Immigrants Act of 1962, and it was the Conservatives who increasingly came to be viewed by electors as the party most opposed to 'immigration'. Whereas a 1964 poll gave the Conservatives a 21:19 per cent 'lead' over Labour on the issue of which party would be most likely to keep immigrants out, by 1970 the respective figures were 57:4 per cent (Layton Henry, 1978, p. 272). As government policy on race tended to be bi-partisan, much of the 'credit' for this dramatic change must go to the activities of Enoch Powell, the Monday Club, and local campaigning – it is interesting to note that Powell received more column inches in the national press during the 1970 general election campaign than was accorded to the entire Liberal party. After the two Conservative general election defeats in 1974, anti-immigrant themes resurfaced more visibly. For example, the 'moderate' William Whitelaw made a notable set of speeches on immigration during 1974–5, and during the late 1970s Margaret Thatcher sought to consolidate support among the racist constituency, most notably in her well-publicized 1978 reference to Britain being 'swamped' by alien cultures, a comment which was followed by notable Conservative gains in polls (see Chapter 1).

Party ideology also has to be understood within the context of media coverage, especially since the decline of street campaigning since 1945 has accorded the media an even greater role in political communication. The nature of the NF's coverage in the media is complex. Sections of the media, notably the tabloid market leader, *The Sun*, have undoubtedly exhibited forms of racism, or have concentrated somewhat chauvinistically on themes such as nationalism (Hartman and Husband, 1974; Murray, 1986; Troyna, 1981). There has also been some tendency to see the extreme right as a 'feature' (*Yorkshire Post*, 3 September 1970; *Observer* colour magazine 16 June 1991), or to play up the NF's electoral potential (*The Guardian*, 5 July 1977). However, the extreme right has received little in the way of direct media sympathy. In general it has simply been ignored, though in the late 1970s there was extensive coverage of the NF's links with Nazism, and its marches were often portrayed as provocative (*Daily Mirror*, 4 April and 19

July 1977). Even the under researched local press often took up the anti-fascist attack (*South East London and Kentish Mercury*, 5 May 1977; *Western Mail*, 27 April 1978). Such reporting has led to a common view on the extreme right that the mass media was its 'biggest single enemy' (*National Front News*, No. 95, September 1987, p. 2).

These points about mainstream ideology and the media are not meant to deny the importance of other factors in explaining the NF's decline. This had begun well before Thatcher's clear appeal to actual and potential NF supporters (see Chapter 1), though it could be argued that there has been a universal tendency among commentators to concentrate too much on Thatcher rather than other Conservatives who anticipated these themes, and campaigning at the local level also needs to be studied. A full discussion of the demise of the NF in the late 1970s would have to look too at factors such as its ideological and personality splits, the role of anti-fascist groups, and the salience of other electoral concerns, notably the general economic situation. Furthermore, it would have to look at the whole process of agenda-setting in political campaigning. Thus, how can the emphasis on economic issues in the campaign for the 1979 general election be squared with opinion poll evidence that race-related issues remained highly important to many voters (Studlar, 1985)? By what process did elites come to decide that it was unnecessary to pay serious attention to this primary fear other than through vague commitments to law and order, or to restricting further immigration?

During the 1980s the Conservatives continued to benefit from nationalist sentiment (though their ascendancy owed much to divisions and weaknesses within the opposition). This meant more than the fact that the Falklands War helped transform Mrs Thatcher from the most unpopular prime minister since Gallup polls began, to the landslide election victor of 1983 and 1987. Even before the Falklands, Thatcher's rhetoric had zoned in on the communist menace, and Labour's unilateral nuclear disarmament commitment. There was also a recurring nationalism in Conservative rhetoric on European unity, for example over the publicly conducted ritual demands for British Euro-budget rebates in the early 1980s. Anti-Europeanism was formulated more cogently in Thatcher's 1988 Bruges speech, which criticized the growing federalist approach (for a sympathetic view of this see A. Aughey, 'Mrs Thatcher and the European Community', *Salisbury Review*, No. 4, 1989), and expressed unguardedly in the interview with Nicholas Ridley, which led to his resignation as a Cabinet Minister in 1990 (*Spectator*, 14 July 1990).

Anti-immigration politics have also continued to emerge periodically, most notably with the passing of the 1981 Nationality Act, in 1986 with the tightening of regulations for visitors from some New Commonwealth countries, or in the references to asylum-seekers as defeat loomed in the 1992 general election. Law and order too has continued to be a concern, exhibiting a strong anti-ethnic aspect in the wake of inner-city riots in 1981, 1985 and 1991, and with growing problems such as the spread of addictive drugs (Fitzgerald, 1987). These developments are completely understandable in terms of past Conservative politics, though it is important to note that the continuing relevance of nationalism and even forms of 'new racism' have been eloquently pressed within the Conservative Party by some of its more intellectual supporters during the 1980s and 1990s. An important forum for such views is *The Salisbury Review*. In its early days it even published arguments in favour of repatriation (J. Casey, 'One Nation: the Politics of Race', No. 1, 1982). More recently, its aim has been a sustained attack on 'anti-racist' politics. These policies are criticized for often making matters worse for minorities, for discriminating against whites, and for encouraging yet another form of professional bureaucracy (A. Flew, 'The Monstrous Regiment of "Anti-Racism"', No. 4, 1989).

The fact that such criticism could come after a decade of Conservative government illustrates that 'Thatcherism' has not been a catalogue of sustained 'new' and 'state' racism, as some left critics have argued. It is true that 'anti-racist' policies often owe much to Labour local councils, or to professional pressures in fields such as social work and teaching, though they have also been supported by Conservative councils, notably in Bradford. Sometimes, Conservative 'anti-racist' policies included a pragmatic view of good government: how could a multicultural society be run without disorder? Sometimes, there was a party competition dimension in the sense that they were part of an attack on local Labour parties for practising municipal racism in council housing and employment, or they were an attempt to court ethnic votes. However, these points illustrate the dangers of making sweeping assertions about the (racial) ideological nature of Thatcherism. Indeed, part of Thatcherism's problem in the field of race relations has been its mixed ideological influences. Thus other, more free market-oriented, policies have tended to militate against community race relations. (It is interesting to note that libertarian free market principles are viewed with suspicion by *The Salisbury Review*). For example, the cuts in local expenditure have often hit subsidies to ethnic groups. The 1988 Education Act, with its emphasis on parental choice, also raises the spectre of school apartheid in some areas (though this is not necessarily opposed by all ethnic groups, especially Muslims). Last but by no means least, the emergence of what some see as a significant 'under-class', allegedly victims of free market policies, might also be seen as laying the seeds for future racism.

Can the Extreme Right Revive Electorally?

These tensions in Conservative policy point to the need for a brief, final consideration of whether the extreme right could revive electorally in the 1990s. The question can be usefully considered under four headings. First, are socio-economic conditions emerging which might provide the basis for a revival? Second, would such a 'trigger' operate spontaneously, or would it need a catalyst? Third, is there an extreme right capable of benefiting from such conditions? Finally, is the dominant party system able to marginalize a potential challenge?

The nature of socio-economic, change raises important problems about the emergence of an under-class, though in this context the dangers might not be too great. In particular, a sizeable part of this 'class' seems to be politically apathetic rather than radical. The main hope for the extreme right here is probably the continued evidence that racism remains a marked attitudinal feature. It is possible that racism will decline as the various communities adjust to each other. On the other hand, growing ethnic assertiveness, even extremism, might exacerbate relations. Surveys taken after the Ayatollah Khomeini imposed the death penalty on the British-resident novelist Salman Rushdie for his allegedly blasphemous *The Satanic Verses* (1989) indicated the continuing problems of race relations, especially, as many Muslims clearly supported the *fatwah*. Similarly, support for Iraq during the 1990–1 Gulf War indicated the presence of a growing radical group of British Muslims (including pirate radio stations in Bradford). Sustained inner-city rioting, perhaps provoked by police responses to the growing drugs problem, might also benefit the extreme right. The possible arrival of Hong Kong Chinese immigrants could provide a more immediate trigger, as could a major debate about the growing number of asylum-seekers. There is also evidence that attitudes towards Israel are becoming more critical, and this may help foster anti-Semitism, perhaps already manifested in growing attacks on synagogues and Jewish cemeteries. These situations could be enflamed by the media's coverage. Tabloids, notably *The Sun*, have shown a persistent tendency to report issues with a racial slant, for example in dealing with asylum-seekers in 1991–2. In terms of the third condition for extreme right progress, the NF no longer suffers from a debilitating split resulting from an esoteric ideological debate, though it still has problems here, and some of its leadership and membership seem attracted by the growing BNP. Finally, the extreme right might find it easier to delineate an ideological space in the 1990s. The choice of John Major as Conservative leader in 1990 seems especially important here: he lacks Thatcher's catchet of strong leadership, and ideologically his views seem less amenable to the exploitation of nationalism and racism. Moreover, he and others in the Conservative leadership seem keen to stamp on local party racism, as can be seen in the response to local opposition to the controversial choice of a black Conservative candidate in the Cheltenham constituency in 1991. At the same time, Labour is troubled by growing ethnic assertiveness within the party. Growing Europeanism within both the Conservative and Labour parties offers further opportunities. These follow not simply from the fact that the issue could split the parties. The point is more that the extreme right has often grown at moments of national self-doubt, which is likely to accompany any move in the EC towards federalism. A more truly united Europe also raises the spectre of whether Britain might have to standardize on a proportional representation (PR) electoral system – even if only for European elections, but this did not stop the Conservatives raising the formula PR= extremism when a hung Parliament seemed likely during the 1992 election campaign. Some forms of PR are unlikely to help extreme right parties unless they can grow considerably.

However, extensive attitudinal racism has in the past not led to notable political racism. New factors, such as the possible arrival of Hong Kong immigrants, may not be crucial. These new immigrants would tend to come from élite groups, which would not threaten communities or jobs in the same way as earlier immigration (polls on both Hong Kong and immigration in general show fewer fears than in the 1960s or 1970s). The media's coverage raises important questions, but much of the tabloid's coverage of these issues can be understood as anti-Labour politics. The desire is to help the Conservatives politically, not the extreme right. Although the NF may have reunited, its leadership on the whole is poor and there is certainly no charismatic figure like Jean-Marie Le Pen. Moreover, other extreme right groups remain active, including the BNP, and a reformed British Movement. Ample scope thus remains for infighting and schism, especially since there is still a major split between those who look for electoral success, and those who are more committed to street violence, including attacks on the ethnic communities, attacks which appear to be growing in the early 1990s (though a police decision to prioritize such attacks may simply mean more are being reported; thus an improvement in policing is seen by some as proof of a massive problem, which leads to further criticism of the police!). Finally, radical critics sometimes talk of the main British parties, especially the Conservatives, as if they had caused racism (Sivanandan, 1976). It has even been argued that 'Although the British state is still a long way from embracing fascism, it is the case that the development of state racism has helped prepare the ground for the emergence of neo-fascism as a political force in Britain' (Miles and Phizacklea, 1984, p. 118). Although it is true that there has been an unpleasant face to Conservatism, notably in groups such as the Monday Club, and even more so the secretive Tory Action, assertions such as this involve a serious misconception of what has happened at the party system level, and an inability to discern the complexities of Conservative policy. What the Conservatives, and to a lesser extent the Labour Party, have done is to *manage* racism. Thereby, they have legitimized forms of racism, although the general impact has been to defuse the issue as a potential extreme right clarion call.

This is likely to continue to be the case in the short run, though developments within both the Labour and Conservative parties pose problems for the future. Moreover, to revert to the original Almond and Verba causal paradigm, good government is most easy when social conditions are favourable. A full analysis of the future of the extreme right would therefore require more detail on socio-economic change and prospects than has been possible here. It would also require a more localized perspective to assess whether race relations really were deteriorating after a period of improvement since the 1960s, and whether ethnic faith in the police is collapsing. It would need more consideration of extreme right physical attacks on ethnic communities, especially in the context of whether this could produce a breakdown in general law and order. It also calls for more detailed analysis of the likely impact of not just extreme right propaganda (e.g., the Holocaust denial; see Eatwell, 1991), but also of trends in mainstream political rhetoric. The case of nationalism is especially interesting here for, paradoxically, British nationalist discourse may have harmed more than helped the extreme right. The Imperial myth, developed so powerfully in the late nineteenth century, had a strong sense of the existence of a harmonious family of nations (as well as a patriarchal sense of British supremacy). Moreover, the

United Kingdom is a multinational state: thus historically it has been difficult to develop a form of extreme British nationalism which did not threaten to divide, rather than unite (though in the earlier phases of the Union local cultures were suppressed by Anglicizing authorities). The Second World War provides excellent examples of powerful nationalist myths which did rally the United Kingdom ('The Dunkirk Spirit', 'Their Finest Hour'), though these are clearly anti-fascist myths too. The continuing salience of such myths can be seen in the rhetoric surrounding the Falkands War, which tended to make strong parallels with the Second World War, thus reviving the anti-fascist struggle. However, during the 1990–1 Gulf War, which revealed remarkable levels of British support for military action compared with other countries, the imagery tended to be different, though the demonization of Saddam Hussein as Hitler underlines the continuing pariah status of fascism. The war was partly legitimized by eulogies to the old Pax Britannica, and the civilizing mission of empire (P. Worsthorne, *The Sunday Telegraph*, 11 September 1990). The imagery is of a dangerous world where communism is collapsing in the face of East European national revival, where Islamic fundamentalism threatens civil and world disorder, and in which even Europe and the United States face growing ethnic problems. (The 'demonstration effect' of racial disharmony in other countries is a neglected topic. For example, serious, sustained inner-city rioting in, say, France could have a dramatic impact on British opinion.)

In the short run, the extreme right's electoral prospects look bleak, as the 1992 general election results show. In the longer run, there is more than a glimmer of a new dawn, as the major parties wrestle with the problems of managing such trends, not least the particularities of British nationalism.

Acknowledgements

The author would like to thank the British Academy for a grant to study the contemporary extreme right, and the editor and Arthur Aughey for comments on the first draft.

References

Almond, G. and Verba, S., 1963. *The Civic Culture*, Princeton University Press, Princeton, NJ.

Barker, M., 1980. *The New Racism*, Junction Books, London.

Benewick, R., 1969. *Political Violence and Public Order*, Allen Lane, London.

Billig, M., 1978. *Fascists*, Harcourt Jovanovich Brace, London.

Deakin, S., 1984. Immigration control: the Liberal Party and the West Midlands Liberals 1950–1970, *Immigrants and Minorities*, November.

Eatwell, R., 1991. The Holocaust denial: a study in propaganda technique, in L. Cheles *et al.* (eds), *Neo-Fascism in Europe*, Longman, London.

——1992a. Towards a new model of generic-fascism, *Journal of Theoretical Politics*, Vol. 4, No. 2.

—— 1992b. Metamorphosis and Continuity: Fascism in Britain, 1945–1989, in S. Larsen (ed.), *Modern Europe after Fascism*, University of Norway Press, Bergen.

Eatwell, R. and O'Sullivan, N. (eds), 1989. *The Nature of the Right*, Pinter, London.
Fitzgerald, M., 1987. *Black People and Party Politics in Britain*, Runnymede Trust, London.
Gable, G., 1991. The far right in contemporary Britain, in L. Cheles *et al.* (eds), *Neo-Fascism in Europe*, Longman, London.
Harrop. M. *et al.*, 1980. The bases of National Front support, *Political Studies*, Vol. 28, No. 2.
Hartman, P. and Husband, C., 1974. *Racism and the Mass Media*, Davis-Poynter, London.
Harwood, R., 1974. *Did Six Million Really Die?*, Historical Review Press, Southam.
Hill, R. and Bell, A., 1988. *The Other Face of Terror*, Grafton, London.
Husbands, C. T., 1982. East End racism, 1900–1980, *London Journal*, January.
—— 1983. *Racial Exclusionism and the City*, Allen and Unwin, London.
—— 1989. Racial attacks: the persistence of organised anti-Semitism in Britain during an anti-Nazi War, in T. Kushner and A. Lunn (eds), *Traditions of Intolerance*, Manchester University Press, Manchester.
Layton Henry, Z., 1978. Race, electoral strategy and the major parties, *Parliamentary Affairs*, Vol. 31, No. 3.
Lipset, S. M. and Rokkan, S., 1967. *Party Systems and Voter Alignments*, The Free Press, New York.
Messina, A., 1989. *Race and Party Competition in Britain*, Clarendon Press, Oxford.
Miles, R. and Phizacklea, A., 1984. *White Man's Country*, Pluto Press, London.
Mosley, Sir O., 1947. *The Alternative*, Mosley Publications, Ramsbury.
Mosley, Sir O., 1958. *Europe: Faith and Plan*, Euphorion Books, London.
Mosley, Sir O., 1961. *Mosley – Right or Wrong?*, Euphorion Books, London.
Murray, N., 1986. The press and ideology in Thatcher's Britain, *Race and Class*, Vol. 27, No. 3.
Porter, B., 1989. *Plots and Paranoia*, Unwin Hyman, London.
Reeves, F., 1983. *British Racial Discourse*, Cambridge University Press, Cambridge.
Robb, J. H., 1954. *Working-Class anti-Semite*, Tavistock, London.
Sanders, D. *et al.* 1987. Government popularity and the Falklands War: a reappraisal, *British Journal of Political Science*, Vol. 17, No. 3.
Särlvik, B. and Crewe, I. 1983. *Decade of Dealignment*, Cambridge University Press, Cambridge.
Schoen, D., 1977. *Enoch Powell and the Powellites*, Macmillan, London.
Scott, D., 1976. The National Front in local politics, in I. Crewe (ed.), *British Political Sociology Yearbook*, Croom Helm, London.
Scraton, P., 1985. *The State of the Police*, Pluto, London.
Seyd, P., 1972. Factionalism within the Conservative party: the Monday Club, *Government and Opposition*, Vol. 7, No. 4.
Sivanandan, A., 1976. *Race, Class and the State*, IRR, London.
Skidelsky, R., 1975. *Oswald Mosley*, Macmillan, London.
Steed, M., 1974. The results analysed, in D. E. Butler and D. Kavanagh, *The British General Election of February 1974*, Macmillan, London.
Studlar, D., 1985. Race in British politics, *Patterns of Prejudice*, Vol. 19, No. 2.
Taylor, S., 1979. The incidence of coloured populations and support for the National Front, *British Journal of Political Science*, Vol. 9, No. 2.
Taylor, S., 1982. *The National Front in English Politics*, Macmillan, Basingstoke.
Thurlow, R., 1987. *Fascism in Britain*, Blackwell, Oxford.
Troyna, B., 1981. *Public Awareness and the Media*, CRE, London.
Whiteley, P., 1979. The National Front vote in the 1977 GLC elections: an aggregate data analysis, *British Journal of Political Science*, Vol. 9, No. 3.

8 Denmark: the Progress Party – Populist Neo-Liberalism and Welfare State Chauvinism

Jørgen Goul Andersen

Introduction

When Mogens Glistrup launched his anti-tax Progress Party in 1972, he did not draw upon any Danish tradition of right-wing extremism, let alone populism or collective tax evasion. Like most other countries, Denmark had a small Nazi party in the 1930s. This was certainly an extremist organization, but was supported by only 2.1 per cent of the voters even during the German occupation (Djursaa, 1981). From 1953 to 1968, a small 'Independent Party' ran for elections, obtaining 2–3 per cent of the votes. Although far to the right, it could by no means be considered extremist; it was founded by a former Liberal Prime Minister, as a reaction against a constitutional change that abolished the two-chamber system, and the party simply advocated more orthodox liberal and bourgeois policies (Eriksen, 1978).[1] Glistrup himself was a successful tax lawyer without any previous political activity.

Despite the appearance of minor parties from time to time, Denmark had usually been described as a stable four or five-party system until 1973 (Damgaard, 1974). Thus it came as a great surprise when the Progress Party suddenly achieved 15.9 per cent of the votes in the Danish election of 1973. Furthermore, rather than being a 'flash party', the Progress Party had the most stable share of the vote among all Danish parties in the four general elections from 1973 to 1979. The party then recovered from severe electoral difficulties in the mid-1980s to win 9.0 per cent in the 1988 election.

Shortly before the election in December 1990, the Progress Party was split as Mogens Glistrup left the party along with three other MPs in order to launch yet another party; the 'Party of Well-Being'. Glistrup failed, however, to collect the sufficient number of signatures to have his party on the ballot; he then agreed with the populist 'Common Course' Party on the extreme left to put up candidates on its list. The 'Common Course' Party, however, did not pass the 2 per cent threshold of representation in

Parliament. Only a few supporters of the Progress Party appear to have followed Glistrup. The 'Common Course' Party gained fewer votes (1.8 per cent) than in previous elections, and despite extensive media coverage, Glistrup himself obtained only 2,700 votes. It thus seems that the 'Party of Well-Being' is unlikely to become more than a curiosity in Danish politics. The Progress Party, on the other hand, survived the election with 6.4 per cent of the votes cast (see Table 8.1).

Table 8.1 Support for the Progress Party in national elections, 1973–1990. Percentages of the votes cast

	1973:	15.9
	1975:	13.6
	1977:	14.6
	1979:	11.0
	1981:	8.9
	1984:	3.6
	1987:	4.8
	1988:	9.0
	1990:	6.4

Source: Statistical Yearbook, various volumes.

What kind of party is the Progress Party, and from which sources does it gain strength? From the analysis of the ideology, the main issues, and the electoral support below, it seems that the Progress Party represents a genuinely new type of party which is quite likely to survive in the future. The analysis below concentrates on the Progress Party and pays less attention to Glistrup's new party.

Ideology and Policy Style

Populism

The Progress Party can hardly be considered a genuinely 'extremist' party, either in its political ideology, or in its policy style. Nor is it a purely 'conventional' party, however. To a large degree, the unconventional style derives from Mogens Glistrup who, in his first appearance on television in 1971, compared tax evaders with railway saboteurs during the German occupation.

Almost from the beginning, the party has been plagued by conflicts between the adherents of Glistrup's provocative and uncompromising style on the one hand and the adherents of a somewhat more conventional bourgeois line on the other. Increasingly, the latter came to dominate the party. While Glistrup was imprisoned from 1983 to 1985 (sentenced for tax evasion) and consequently out of Parliament (until 1987), his substitute in Parliament, the (at least as far as style is concerned) much more conventional Pia Kjærsgaard, gradually became the *de facto* leader of the party. The conflict between her and Glistrup was aggravated in 1989–90, culminating in a divided party and Gilstrup's subsequent expulsion from it. Even the moderate wing of the Progress Party has always adhered to a somewhat populist style.

A case in point is the resignation of former Minister of Justice, Erik Ninn-Hansen, in 1988. He was accused by the Danish ombudsman of consciously delaying consideration of immigration applications from the relatives of asylum-seekers from Sri Lanka. He was finally forced to resign, despite support from most members of the bourgeois parties who argued that the minister's conduct did not clearly violate the law. The Progress Party, on the other hand, did not consider the legal argument at all but explicitly supported the Minister's course of action, arguing that it was in accordance with the attitudes of the majority of the population (which it was, according to opinion polls). This sort of explicit disregard for legal principles is unfamiliar in the Danish Parliament. But it corresponds perfectly with the classical definition of populism in Shils (1956, p. 98): 'Populism proclaims that the will of the people as such is supreme over every other standard . . . populism identifies the will of the people with justice and morality.'

Several other examples of a populist style could be mentioned, typically (individual) 'civil disobedience' by Progress Party MPs against what is considered excessive regulation by the state (e.g. speed limits or the obligatory use of seat-belts in cars). Such actions have been condemned by law-abiding MPs of other parties though they probably have some appeal to a tradition of individualism reflected in a folklore which speaks of Sweden as a 'state of prohibition' and which has sometimes been referred to in ethnological studies in explaining support for the Progress Party (e.g Højrup, 1983). Still, the Progress Party deviates in a number of respects from the ideal-typical picture of populism (Ionescu and Gellner, 1969; Canovan, 1981), let alone extremism. In the first place, the Progress Party has not participated in collective action or supported violent or illegal behaviour. Unlike Poujade (Hoffmann, 1957), it has not urged people to refuse to pay taxes, not even when Glistrup was at his zenith. Second, the party generally does not adhere to an aggressive or bitter rhetoric. Rather, it has skilfully employed a good sense of humour (Glistrup in the mid-1970s)[2] or the language of common sense (Kjærsgaard since the mid-1980s). Third, the party does not adhere to a conspiratorial view of society.[3] Fourth, under Kjærsgaard's leadership, the Progress Party has not been in simple opposition to all other parties; instead it has to a large degree sought co-operation and practical compromises with the bourgeois government.

By the same token, the organization of the party has increasingly become similar to other parties even though it still carries a populist legacy. The party has few members: some 15,000 by 1977, and just below 10,000 in the 1980s (Svensson and Togeby 1986, p. 296). In this respect the Progress Party resembles almost all new Danish parties established since the Second World War. In the beginning, Glistrup wanted the party to be a 'movement' rather than a party and strongly resisted the establishment of a formal party organization (Larsen, 1977). Although he eventually had to concede, he secured a position as 'life-long honourable member' of the executive committee which consisted of only seven members including Glistrup. Because of this and similar 'irregularities' compared with traditional parties (e.g. concerning the appointment of the representatives to the National Congress), the Norwegian Progress Party has refused to have any official contacts with the Danish party.

As far as the content of the ideology is concerned, the party exhibits relatively few of the traits frequently associated with 'populism': reaction against modernity, anti-capitalism, or nationalism. Nor is it a simple 'anti'-party: the policies and the ideology of the party may indeed be described as relatively coherent and consistent. This holds even for the period when Glistrup was dominant. Glistrup's new party, on the other hand, does seem to lack any sort of ideological coherence, for it has (so far) articulated only three demands: lower taxes, higher old-age pensions, and a stop on immigration.

No Reaction against Modernity

Lipset (1981) has frequently summarized 'populism', 'petty bourgeois protest' and 'fascism' under the heading 'revolt against modernity'. This is clearly inapplicable to the Progress Party. In the first place, the party does not express any 'nostalgia for the past', nor does it stress traditional values. Although the party may be intolerant of deviant groups, that is mainly when taxpayers' money is affected. In this respect, the party is clearly distinguished from e.g. the American 'New Right' movement which reacted against the 'permissive society' of the 1970s, stressing traditional moral or religious values. When measured by such yardsticks, the Progress Party is clearly a 'modern' party (Andersen and Bjørklund, 1990).

Second, whereas nationalism is a core principle in fascism (Linz 1978, p. 25) and frequently also in populism, the Progress Party originally appeared to be less nationalist than other parties. In one of his most quoted statements, Mogens Glistrup even proposed to abolish the Danish defence forces (in favour of an automatic telephone answering in Russian: 'We surrender'!), in order to save taxes. By the same token, he proposed to sell off Greenland and the Faeroe Islands to the highest bidder. On the defence issue, however, Glistrup was soon voted down in the party group in Parliament, and since then the party has largely been indistinguishable from the Conservatives and the Liberals regarding defence.

Third, there are no elements of petty bourgeois anti-capitalism in the political discourse of the Progress Party. On the contrary, the party has consistently demanded that all existing measures designed to protect small producers against 'big capital' should be abolished.

Neo-Liberalism of the Lower Strata

The demand for the abolition of such protective measures is consistent with the general conception of the state which has no resemblance to any sort of fascist or (traditional) populist ideology. The core principle which unites the image of society and the policies of the Progress Party is the neo-liberal belief in the forces of the market. This also means that even though the Progress Party until recently had no genuine party programme but only a small pamphlet (another populist legacy), its policies have always been less eclectic than they might appear at first glance.

However, the ideology of the Progress Party cannot be equated with mainstream neo-liberalism. Not only is the neo-liberal ideology expressed in a quite different (i.e., more 'populist') language, more importantly, the neo-liberalism of the Progress Party is not the neo-liberalism of the upper strata. This is evident from the concrete policies of the party. In the first place, the party has always demanded an increase in public expenditure for the health system and for public pensions (and it has supported the Danish pension system which is a unique flat-rate system, unrelated to previous work or earnings, apart from a small supplementary pension scheme related to work though not to earnings). Second, the party's proposals for lowering income taxes (around which the party originally emerged) are different from typical neo-liberal policies: the Progress Party has always demanded an increase in basic allowances, not a lowering of the marginal tax rates for higher incomes. Thus, apart from the lack of solidarity with the poorest strata, some of the redistributive aspects of the policies of the Progress Party bear more resemblance to Social Democratic policies than to mainstream neo-liberalism. Although this ideological position may be unusual, it can hardly be described as inconsistent.

Even though the Progress Party has in certain respects become a more 'conventional' bourgeois party than when it emerged, the difference between the Progress Party and other bourgeois parties on economic and distributive issues is evident from recent developments in Danish politics. The bourgeois minority government from 1988 to 1990 co-operated with the Progress Party on several occasions (although mainly when it was impossible to reach an agreement with the Social Democrats). For instance, the Progress Party ensured a majority for the government's budget in November 1989. It is instructive to see the party's demands in these negotiations. In 1989 its main demand was that all taxes on energy for the heating of dwellings should be abolished. These taxes, which are extremely high in Denmark, are in fact among the most regressive of all taxes. In 1990 the bourgeois government proposed a lowering of the income taxes for higher and middle-level incomes by 6 percentage points. However, the state has a large and increasing budget deficit (in 1990, interests on the debt of the state amounted to almost 10 per cent of the Gross National Income), and contrary to what one would expect from an anti-tax party, the Progress Party in the autumn of 1990 decided to give higher priority to balanced budgets than to lower taxes. Noteworthy also, the proposals for budget cuts were different from those of other parties. No traditional welfare areas were mentioned: the Progress

Party pointed critically at culture, refugees and foreigners, and aid to developing countries, i.e., at areas which are particularly unpopular among the lower strata. In the election campaign of 1990, the Progress Party demanded tax relief like most other bourgeois parties. However, unlike the governing parties it demanded an increase in basic allowances rather than a decline in marginal tax rates. Finally, unlike the conventional bourgeois parties and the Social Democrats, the Progress Party advocated a 'no' in the Danish referendum on the European Union held on 2 June 1992. On this point, the party is in accordance with a large majority of social democratic voters and of the lower strata in general in Denmark, who prefer to stay outside the Union.

Immigration: Racism or Welfare State Chauvinism?

In recent years, the immigration of refugees has become an important issue for the Progress Party. Originally, the party paid little attention to immigrants, and the party pamphlet does not even m :ntion such issues. Instead, in the early 1970s, the party criticized the abuse)f social security by people 'unwilling to work'. The immigration issue did not emerge in the party until 1979 when a local representative, A.Th.Riemann, was charged (and later fined) for writing that immigrants were 'multiplying like rats'.[4] Although Mogens Glistrup to a large degree supported the attack on immigrants, this apparently only accelerated the declining popularity of the party. From the late 1970s, the party lost many voters, and the loss of sympathy in the electorate was even larger, amounting to a virtual isolation of the party (Glans, 1986).

Then the issue almost died, and in the first half of the 1980s questions on immigration and immigrants were largely absent from the political agenda, including the statements of the Progress Party. Following a dramatic increase in the number of asylum-seeking refugees in 1985–6, however, the rise in the proportion number of foreigners again received public attention (Tonsgaard, 1989) and, in 1987 and 1988, it was one of the most important themes in the electoral campaigns of the Progress Party (Siune, 1989, pp. 118–19). First and foremost, it was Glistrup who saw the potential of the issue. Immediately when he was released from prison on 11 March 1985, he launched an aggressive attack on immigrants, phrased in much the same language as Riemann's, although he was not charged. At that time it certainly did not contribute to the popularity of the party (which continued to drop, reaching the lowest point of 1.7 per cent in the polls of February 1986 (Andersen, 1988)). Undoubtedly, however, a clear image of the party was cemented. Since then, Glistrup's statements have been radicalized, as reflected in the slogan: 'Make Denmark a Moslem Free Zone', which was also contained in a speech of MP Jane Oksen in the opening of the Parliament's 1990/1 session.

However, Jane Oksen is among the MPs who left the Progress Party along with Glistrup's party, and the slogan referred to was condemned by Pia Kjærsgaard and other MPs who remained in the Progress Party. Officially, the attacks on immigration have been justified mainly on economic grounds. The official arguments of the party may be better summarized as a sort of 'welfare state chauvinism', to some degree coupled with xenophobia, rather than as genuine racism. The concept of 'welfare state chauvinism' also fits nicely with the attacks on the expenses for aid to the developing countries (and Greenland) which has been a recurrent theme since the early 1970s. It must be added that until 1990, Pia Kjærsgaard was reluctant to repudiate even overt racist statements, and even in the electoral campaign of 1990 when the party was keen to dissociate itself from Glistrup's style, Pia Kjærsgaard spoke of the immigrants as 'multiplying like rabbits'.

Political Attitudes of Progress Party Voters

In the breakthrough election of 1973, anti-tax and anti-welfare state sentiments, as well as political distrust were clearly the key characteristics of Progress Party voters, compared with those of other non-socialist voters (Glans, 1986). In the 1980s, however, this changed. Although the Progress Party voters were still distinguished by a higher level of political distrust (Goul Andersen and Bjørklund, 1990) taxation has a considerably lower priority among the electorate than in the early 1970s. Even Progress Party voters, according to the 1988 Election Survey, attached little importance to taxation, and no more than other non-socialist voters: 17 per cent of the Progress Party voters mentioned taxes among the three most important issues, exactly the same proportion as in other non-socialist parties.

This is confirmed by a Gallup survey of the 1990 election, which revealed that around one-third of the voters who left the Progress Party in the 1990 election went to the Social Democrats, even though this party won the election by opposing tax relief.

The welfare state attitudes of the Progress Party supporters are equally surprising. In the 1987 and 1988 elections, Progress Party voters apparently held more positive attitudes towards the welfare state than the supporters of the four-party bourgeois government before the 1988 election (see Table 8.2). Thus in both elections, a majority of the Progress Party voters even agreed that 'social cuts have gone too far'. On conventional left-right issues, Progress Party voters have always been to the right, though not extremely to the right (Andersen, 1977; Nielsen, 1979). This is in part, due to a larger variation along the left–right continuum than in other parties (Nielsen, 1975). It also corresponds with the fact that the party has always attracted around one-third of its adherents from the socialist parties, in particular from the Social Democrats (Glans, 1986; Observa, 1988).

Today, the most significant characteristic of Progress Party voters is their attitude towards foreigners. On such issues the Radical Liberals and the left wing parties stand out as extremely liberal (or 'post-materialist', as Inglehart (Inglehart and Rabier, 1986) would probably prefer to call it). The adherents of most other parties are divided. However the supporters of the Progress Party agree almost unanimously that 'immigration constitutes a serious threat to our national character' and that 'refugees . . . must assimilate

Table 8.2 Attitudes towards the welfare state, by party, 1987 and 1988: balances of opinion (agree minus disagree) (percentage)

		Progr. Party	Governing Parties	Radical Liberals	Social Dem.	Left-wing p.
1. Maintain social	1987	+37	+39	+79	+81	+89
reforms	1988	+40	+16	+69	+79	+94
2. Social cuts have	1987	+15	−16	+29	+79	+83
gone too far	1988	+14	−33	−8	+65	+79
(N)	1987	74	622	108	499	400
	1988	48	243	36	187	113

Note: Governing parties: Conservatives, Liberals, Centre Democrats, Christian People's Party.
Radical Liberals: including a few 'Justice Party' voters in 1987.
Left-wing parties: including Greens.

Wording:
1. 'A says: Social reforms have gone too far. To a larger degree than now, people should manage without social security and contributions from society.
   B says: The social reforms in our country should be maintained at least at the present level.'
   (figures above indicate percentage agreeing with B minus percentage agreeing with A)
2. 'Social cuts have gone too far' (figures above indicate percentage agreeing minus percentage disagreeing)

Source: Danish Election Programme (including two surveys in 1987).

Table 8.3 Attitudes towards foreigners, by party, 1988: balances of opinion (agree minus disagree) (percentage)

	Progr. Party	Governing parties	Radical Liberals	Social Dem.	Left-wing p.
1. Threat to national character	+75	−10	−56	−6	−59
2. Refugees should assimilate	+65	+30	−11	+27	−43
(N)	48	243	36	187	113

Wording:
1. 'Immigration constitutes a serious threat to our national character' (figures indicate percentage agreeing minus percentage disagreeing).
2. 'A says: If refugees should live in this country, they must assimilate to Danish culture and Danish way of life.
   B says: Refugees should have the same rights as other people to maintain their own culture and way of life'
   (figures above indicate percentage agreeing with A minus percentage agreeing with B).

Source and Note: As for Table 8.1.

to Danish culture and the Danish way of life' (Table 8.3). Although the arguments of the Progress Party are officially justified in economic terms, and even though this may still be the basic motivating force of the Progress Party voters, it clearly carries with it also a more general antipathy towards foreigners.

Social Bases of Support

When the Progress Party emerged, interest was mainly focused on the overrepresentation of the party among the self-employed (e.g. Fryklund and Petersson 1981), though some observers also drew attention to its support among manual workers (Nielsen, 1975, 1979). Whilst the Progress Party was not overrepresented among manual workers in the 1970s, the social composition was unique, for no other bourgeois party recruited a comparably large share of workers. In 1973 this could be interpreted as evidence of the 'single-issue' nature of the party as it reflected opposition to increasing taxation, which was indeed a multi-class phenomenon. Better-educated middle-aged people also supported the party disproportionately, and despite a strong left-wing radicalism among well-educated young people the Progress Party in 1973 enjoyed the same support in all educational groups (see Table 8.4). However, in 1979 when Mogens Glistrup launched his first attack against foreigners, the better-educated left the party, and they have never returned. In general, the educational profile of Progress Party voters resembles that of the Social Democratic electorate. A further specification reveals that the Progress Party supporters are by far the poorest educated among young voters, whereas there is no difference in educational attainments between the Progress Party and other bourgeois parties among the oldest voters.

Table 8.4 Support for the Progress Party, by education (percentage)

Education	1973	1977	1979	1988
Low	16	16	13	11
Medium	16	14	9	9
High	16	11	3	3
(N)	2,172	2,524	1,023	1,279
	575	832	412	747
	307	326	194	421

Source: 1973 and 1977: Surveys carried out by Ingemar Glans, Institute of Political Science, University of Aarhus; 1979 and 1988: Surveys of the Danish Election Programme. All data collected by the Danish Gallup Institute.

To a large degree, this educational distribution also explains the unique class composition of the party. Some 50 per cent of the occupationally active Progress Party voters in the 1988 election could be classified as manual workers (see table 8.5). This is the same proportion as for Social Democrats

(52 per cent) and considerably higher than in all other parties. In other non-socialist parties, the proportion of workers has always been around 20 per cent or less (Andersen and Bjørklund, 1990). Despite substantial losses to the Social Democrats in the 1990 election, this class composition was maintained in 1990. The high figure is the result of a gradual increase in the proportion of workers since the 1973 election when the figure was 'only' 33 per cent. The same pattern can be observed in the Norwegian sister party (Andersen and Bjørklund, 1990) which is somewhat less populist and more genuinely neo-liberal than the Danish Progress Party, though it expresses a similar basic ideology and policies.

Table 8.5 Class composition of economically active voters, 1988 (percentage)

	Manual workers	Non-manual wage earners	Self-employed	Total	(N)
Progress Party	50	27	23	100	146
Other bourgeois P.	21	56	23	100	692
Social Democrats	52	43	5	100	464
Left-wing p.	40	58	2	100	322
Sample	36	50	14	100	1,623

Source: Danish Election Programme.

The working-class support for the Progress Party is an engaging theme. It may be interpreted as an effect of petty bourgeois cross-pressure: first-generation workers, workers in rural areas and small towns, workers in small enterprises, etc. are much more likely to vote for the Progress Party than workers in more traditional working-class milieux (Goul Andersen, 1980). However, it becomes increasingly relevant to ask which workers are 'deviant': the Progress Party has been significantly unable to gain support among workers in the traditional stronghold of working-class culture in the Copenhagen area, despite high taxes, a high density of immigrants, etc. It seems that this is one of the few enclaves of working-class prevalence which is able to resist the appeals of the Progress Party.

The Progress Party seems to derive much of its strength from the disintegration of working-class culture, i.e. declining class consciousness and political de-alignment. This disintegration seems to pave the way for more spontaneous forms of class consciousness, including the 'working-class authoritarianism' highlighted by Lipset (1981) as well as the 'dichotomous image of society' and the narrow materialist instrumentalism described in Goldthorpe and Lockwood (1968). To a large degree, such classic aspects of working-class culture, in the absence of the mediation and the 'political education' of the labour movement, appear to fit nicely with central aspects of the ideology of the Progress Party.

Of course, these considerations may run the risk of overstating the point, and it would certainly be wrong to describe the Progress Party simply as a party of the 'lower classes', let alone 'marginalized groups'. Up to a point, the class composition reflects a low support among public employees who are predominantly non-manual wage-earners. Still, even within the private sector, the party receives a much higher share of the vote (some 11 per cent) among manual workers than among non-manual employees (some 7 per cent). On the other hand, support for the Progress Party is higher among skilled than among unskilled workers, and higher among higher-level non-manuals than among lower-level non-manuals. To a lesser extent, this reflects the gender composition: in 1987 and 1988, 60 per cent of the voters were male; in 1981 and 1984, the figure was even higher with (over 70 per cent).

Conclusions

The Progress Party bears little resemblance to those protest movements of the past which are sometimes referred to as 'petty bourgeois' or a 'reaction against modernity'. Although the party exhibits some of the traits usually associated with the concept of 'populism', its social base of support is not 'petty bourgeois' and it bears no signs of 'traditionalism', 'moralism', or classical 'petty bourgeois' ideological elements such as anti-capitalism. Ideologically, the party expresses an unusual, and in part egalitarian, neo-liberalism. This difference from other neo-liberal parties is evident, not least on taxation and pension issues. As far as the public sector is concerned, the attacks of the party are not directed against the basic welfare services but rather against expenditure upon cultural purposes, foreigners, aid to developing countries, and for people unwilling to work. This is a sort of neo-liberalism which is largely compatible with the interests of the lower classes. In addition the targets for budget cuts as well as the hostility towards foreigners correspond even more closely with the values of the lower classes.

From an ideological point of view, the Progress Party may of course be regarded as right-wing, although it does not fit easily into the conventional left–right scheme. The same holds for the party's unique social base. Most of all, its significant appeal to the working-class indicates that we are faced with a genuinely new type of party, related to basic changes in the structural cleavages in post-industrial society. In particular, the Progress Party seems to express many of the interests and values of a disintegrating working-class culture, even though such an interpretation perhaps goes too far in ignoring the multi-class nature of support.

It does appear, though, that rather than being a renmant of the past, the Progress Party (in Denmark and Norway) derives its strength from social forces which are of enduring nature and which may also in other countries crystallize into new parties (see also Inglehart and Rabier, 1986). Although the Progress Party was invited to the meeting of the Euro-Right parties of the European Parliament in Denmark in 1990, it clearly refused to have any formal or informal contacts with these parties. However, even though the difference between the Progress Party and Le Pen's Front national, for example, is as considerable as the difference between Social Democrats and Communists, they may derive some of their strength from similar sources.

Notes

1. In the 1973 election, an election pact allowed the Independent Party to put up a few candidates on the list of the Progress Party. One of these candidates was elected and, according to the agreement, immediately declared herself as a representative of the Independent Party.
2. Glistrup's political style has changed significantly. It has always been provocative, but in the early and mid-1970s, it was always accompanied by humour (Mörch-Lassen, 1978). Since the late 1970s, Glistrup has become increasingly aggressive, most of all in his verbal attacks on foreigners.
3. Even though the party's attacks on the public sector, public employees and politicians have certainly been formulated in an unconventional language (in particular in the 1970s), it would push the meaning of 'conspiracy' (or even 'scapegoatism') too far to encompass such phenomena. Immigrants, on the other hand, do to some degree serve as scapegoats for the party.
4. On a later occasion Riemann was sentenced to prison (for 14 days), and his nomination as a candidate for the parliamentary election was withdrawn (Avisårbogen 18 November 1981).

References

Andersen, J.G., 1977. *Småborgerskabet og Fremskridtspartiet*. Institute of Political Science, University of Aarhus.
——, 1980. *Partipolitiske skillelinjer i arbejderklassen*. Working Paper, Institute of Political Science, University of Aarhus.
——, 1988. *Vælgermosaik*. Centre of Cultural Research, University of Aarhus. Working Paper Series No. 19.
Andersen, Jørgen Goul and Bjørklund, Tor, 1990 Structural changes and new cleavages: the Progress Parties in Denmark and Norway, *Acta Sociologica*, Vol. 33, No. 3.
Canovan, Margaret, 1981. *Populism*. Harcourt Brace Jovanovich, New York.
Damgaard, Erik, 1974 Stability and change of the Danish party system over half a century, *Scandinavian Political Studies* Vol. 9, 103–25.
Djursaa, Malene, 1981. *DNSAP. Danske Nazister*, 1–2, Glydendal, Copenhagen.
Eriksen, Hanne, 1978. *Partiet De Uafhængige 1953–1960*, Odense University Press Odense.
Fryklund, Bjøn and Petersson, Tomas, 1981. *Missnöjespartier i Norden*, Arkiv Avhandlingserie Lund.
Glans, Ingemar, 1986. Fremskridtspartiet – småborgerlig revolt, högerreaktion eller generell protest? ia J.Elklit and O. Tonsgaard (eds) *Valg og vælgeradfrd*, Politica, Aarhus, pp. 195–228.
Goldthorpe, John and Lockwood, David *et al.*, 1968–9. *The Affluent Worker*, Cambridge University Press, Cambridge.
Hoffmann, Stanley, 1957 *Le Mouvement Poujade*, Paris.
Hjørup, T., 1983. *Det glemte Folk*, Statens Byggeforskningsinstitut, Copenhagen.

Inglehart, Ronald D. and Rabier, Jean-Jacques, 1986. Political realignment in advanced industrial society: from class-based politics to quality of life-politics, *Government and Opposition* Vol. 21, 456–79.

Ionescu, Ghita and Gellner, Ernest (eds) 1969. *Populism. Its Meaning and National Characteristics*, Weidenfeld and Nicolson, London.

Larsen, B.V., 1977. *Fremskridtsparties Organisation*, MA thesis, Institute of Political Science, University of Aarhus.

Lipset, S.M., 1981. *Political Man*, expanded and updated edition, Johns Hopkins University Press, Baltimore.

Linz, Juan, 1978. Some notes toward a comparative study of fascism in historical perspective, in W. Laqueur (ed.), *Fascism: A Reader's Guide* Penguin, Harmondsworth.

Mörch Lassen, G., 1978. *Fremskridtspartiet og Poujadismen*, MA thesis, Institute of Political Science, University of Aarhus, Aarhus.

Nielsen, Hans Jørgen, 1975. *Fremskridtspartiet – et hre-orienteret protestparti for hvem?* Institute of Political Studies, Copenhagen.

——, 1979. *Politiske holdninger og Fremskridtsstemme*. Forlaget Politiske Studier, Copenhagen.

Observa 1988. 600.000 Vælgere skiftede parti, *Morgenavisen Jyllands-Posten*, 29 1988.

Shils, Edward, 1956. *The Torment of Secrecy*, Free Press, New York.

Siune, Karen, 1989. Valgkampene og vælgerne, in J. Elklit and O.Tonsgaard (eds.), *To Folketingsvalg*, Aarhus Politica pp. 107–34.

Svensson, P. and Togeby, L., 1986. *Politisk Opbrud*, Politica, Aarhus.

Tonsgaard, O., (1989) Flygtninge og indvandrere – et politisk spørgsmål, in J.Elklit and O. Tonsgaard (eds), *To Folketingsvalg*, Politica, Aarhus, pp. 255–270.

9 The Extreme Right in Spain: Blas Piñar and the Spirit of the Nationalist Uprising

John Gilmour

Historical Background

The Fall of the Bourbon Monarchy

Until the 1930s, Spain had been largely unaffected by the traumatic upheavals which were taking place elsewhere in Europe and providing such a breeding-ground for fascism. The country's political and social stability, however, had been seriously undermined by a succession of crises which culminated in the collapse of the constitutional monarchy of Alfonso XIII in April 1931. Although the Liberal governments of the nineteenth century had tried to bring about economic and cultural reform in a semi-feudal society, instead of unifying Spain they threatened more and more to break it apart (Payne, 1987, p. 9). An experiment to set up a democratic republic in the early 1870s in the wake of the 'Revolución Gloriosa' of 1868 against the monarchy of Isabel II had failed within a year, having provoked a second Carlist uprising in the north of Spain and various outbreaks of anarchist revolt. By the turn of the century, when Spain underwent the trauma of losing her remaining colonies in a disastrous war against the United States, local nationalist movements in Catalonia and the Basque Country were demanding a greater share of political power or pursuing separatist objectives, so that Spain's national unity was now even more fragile. General Miguel Primo de Rivera, who governed Spain with Alfonso's consent during the 1920s, undertook an ambitious programme of national regeneration. Seeking to establish a corporatist state modelled on Italian lines, he initiated a movement away from what he regarded as corrupt and pernicious liberalism by founding the Unión Patriótica, a Castilian organization bearing the motto 'Monarchy, Fatherland, Religion'. Although this movement did not survive the General after his ignominious departure from Spain in 1930, it can be regarded as a forerunner of Spanish extreme right groups which emerged under subsequent regimes.

Republicanism in Crisis

It was in the political cauldron of the Second Republic from 1931 to 1936 that parties of the extreme right took definitive shape, as a fierce reaction to the anti-clerical, regionalist and socially radical policies of the left-wing government, which had drawn up the democratic constitution of 1931 and held power until 1933. In their counter-revolutionary enthusiasm, the fascist Falange Española, the Alphonsine Renovación Española and the Carlist Comunión Tradicionalista were convinced that Spain had fallen prey to alien ideologies derived from a conspiracy of Jews and Masons (Pastor, 1975, p. 103). Each party, however, advocated its own way of national salvation – a symptom of the disunity and fragmentation which has constantly blighted Spanish politics of both right and left in recent times. Falange Española, formed in 1933 by José Antonio Primo de Rivera in honour of his dead father and united by him in 1934 with another Castilian extreme right group, the Juntas de Ofensiva Nacional Sindicalista, proposed a nationalist, corporatist state and a new pan-Hispanic empire. Renovación Española, led by José Calvo Sotelo, who had served under General Primo de Rivera, planned to revive the monarchy along authoritarian lines, untainted by liberal constitutionalism, while the Comunión Tradicionalista under Fal Conde pinned its hopes on the eventual creation of a theocratic state with the Carlist pretender installed as king. When the more moderate CEDA led by Gil Robles failed to secure an electoral victory for the right in February 1936, these hitherto small extremist parties quickly found favour with those Spaniards from the landowning and industrial oligarchies, the lower middle classes and peasantry who were highly traditionalist, devoutly Catholic, bitterly hostile to socialism and extremely fearful at the prospect of the revolutionary programme now being prepared by the left-wing, Popular Front government (Blinkhorn, 1988, p. 9). On a more sinister note, the extreme right was participating in preparations for a coup which was being planned by reactionary Army officers – a collaboration which has influenced the development of the Spanish extreme right ever since.

The Civil War and the Establishment of the Francoist State

The date 18 July 1936, the day of the Nationalist uprising against the legally constituted Republican government, occupies pride of place in the mythology of the Spanish extreme right. In the course of a savage, protracted conflict which the insurgents saw as a spiritual and ideological crusade to deliver Spain from a godless Republic and communist revolution, General Francisco Franco emerged not only as *Generalísimo* of the Nationalist forces, but also, more importantly on a political level, as Head of State of the Nationalist Zone and leader of a unified organization, Falange Española Tradicionalista y de las Juntas de Ofensiva Nacional Sindicalista, which was later known more simply as Movimiento Nacional. Formed by decree in April 1937, this organization was a forced amalgamation or synthesis of the extreme right-wing groups mentioned earlier. Franco's path to political unchallengeability had been facilitated by the murder of Calvo Sotelo by Republican security police on the eve of the 1936 uprising and by the execution of José Antonio in a Republican jail in Alicante in November 1936. The latter, however, quickly became a cult figure in Francoist circles (he was revered, for example as *el Ausente* and his name was inscribed on the walls of almost every church building in Spain); indeed he has remained so for the extreme right since the transition to democracy. By contrast, Calvo Sotelo has never been remembered in the same way despite being a 'proto-martyr' of the Nationalist cause – perhaps because he was not a victim of the war itself and did not possess the youthful charisma of José Antonio.

For almost forty years, Franco remained in total control of Spain, establishing out of the ravages of civil war a triumphalist, ultra-conservative and authoritarian regime, a disciplined political order which found no room for partisan, class or regional conflicts (Medhurst, 1982, p. 297). Although he adopted at first the kind of fascist rhetoric and ritual that characterized the German and Italian regimes of the day, he played down mass mobilization, for his major concerns were to maintain public order and restore strict Catholic morality. His brand of nationalism was a nostalgic revival of the spiritual values of Spain's glorious epoch of the *Reyes Católicos*, Ferdinand and Isabella, and Charles V and Philip II, when Spain was a leading European power, the model nation, and the *alma mater* of Western Christian civilization (Payne, 1987, p. 206). Having created his 'National Movement', Franco effectively deprived its constituent groups of political independence. The Falange, for example, had been conceived originally as an 'efficient and authoritarian instrument at the service of that irrevocable unity called the Fatherland' (Ellwood, 1987, p. 13), but Franco proceeded to neutralize its revolutionary identity in order for it to be transformed into *his* instrument of bureaucratic control. His policy of playing off one nationalist group against another in his cabinets while remaining in complete personal control meant that their own political advancement was minimized. They were unable to formulate any new ideology of their own and quickly fell into insignificance, ineffectuality and obscurity – a grim state of affairs which has persisted until the present time.

The Extreme Right Since 1945: Its Phases and Developments

The Fate of the Pre-War Extremist Groups

In response to the outcome of the Second World War, in which Franco had avoided becoming involved on the side of the Axis powers, he shifted the balance of his regime more towards Catholic conservatism, hoping to win international support, however limited. This traditionalist shift spread disillusionment among the Falangist *camisas viejas* (the party's original members) for it destroyed what lingering hopes still remained of a national-syndicalist social revolution. To make matters worse, the Falange was now unrecognizable from the mystical, idealistic group it had been in the mid-1930s. It was simply part of the machinery of the Francoist state, accommodating tens of thousands of new adherents from both right and left who were anxious to combine self-preservation with a semblance of socio-political radicalism (Blinkhorn, 1988, p. 44). As time went on and Franco finally abandoned in 1957 the old Falangist policy of economic autarky in favour of international capitalism, Falangism could neither adapt to the changes resulting from Spain's *desarrollismo* (growth strategy) of the 1960s nor attract the new generation of Spaniards who had little or no direct experience of the Republic and the Civil War. By the 1970s, the old party had broken up into a number of splinter groups, with at least four aspirants to the party's official title: Frente Nacional Español, Falange Española Auténtica, Junta Coordinadora Nacional Sindicalista and Guerrilleros de Cristo Rey. Indeed, at a Falangist council meeting held in the Don Hilarion Club in Madrid in January 1974, no fewer than eleven tendencies were represented, each presumably insisting on its own doctrinal purity (Oneto, 1975, p. 203). These Falangists greeted Franco's death in 1975 as a new opportunity to campaign for the revolution which had been denied to them for so long. The caption declaring 'Franco was a traitor' was featured on election posters put up in 1977 by Falange Española Auténtica, proving how cut off it felt from a regime which it had helped to create.

A similar fate befell the Alphonsine monarchists. After Don Juan de Borbón became heir and pretender to the throne after the death of Alfonso in 1941, he issued his own manifesto in Lausanne in 1945, calling for the restoration of the constitutional monarchy. Although he had offered Franco his services in the Civil War (which Franco politely refused), clearly he could not accept the totalitarian basis of the Franco regime and in 1947 vehemently criticized the Law of Succession according to which Franco was regent for life, ruling over a Catholic, social and traditional monarchy. After an overwhelming endorsement of this law in a national referendum which was held later that year, it was plain that there was precious little support within Spain for the Alphonsine cause. Consequently, apart from Don Juan's small entourage of advisers, including the former republican Gil Robles, no monarchist group of any significance re-emerged in Spain during the Franco period.

As for the Carlists, their movement underwent an ideological transformation which split it into rival factions and which, coming on top of Franco's decision to ignore the Carlist claims to the succession, rendered it totally powerless. Although a few Carlists remained loyal to Franco, the new pretender Carlos Hugo became a convert to the cause of 'self-governing socialism', triggering an angry response from the old guard who then transferred their allegiance to his younger brother, Don Sixto, a fanatical rightist. This bitter rivalry surfaced at a rally at Montejurra in Navarre in 1976 when two of Carlos Hugo's supporters were shot dead.

The Rise of a 'New' Extreme Right

On all fronts, the 1960s were a decade of change in Spain. Economically, it was a time of rapid development in which the growth rate was exceeded only by that of Japan. Spanish society became more affluent and far more open to Western influence. On the political stage preparations were in hand for a greater degree of liberalization, including a new Press law, a law of religious freedom, direct elections to part of the *Cortes* (the Spanish Parliament) and the nomination of Juan Carlos as Franco's successor. Inevitably, a fierce reaction came from the regime's hardliners who feared that these changes would make Spain succumb once again to the evils of liberalism against which the Civil War had been fought. The most vociferous protester was a Madrid notary, *procurador* (Member of Parliament) and Movement representative, Blas Piñar López. In May 1966 he set up a publishing house, Fuerza Nueva Editorial, and the following January, released the first edition of its journal which bore the defiant caption 'The 18th of July will not be broken' on its front cover. This attachment to the original principles of the 1936 uprising and condemnation of the changes which have occurred in Spain over the past thirty years have formed the basis of the ideology of Blas Piñar's organization ever since.

These unrepentant hardliners, or *Búnker* as journalists now called them, now intensified their attacks on the regime's policies of *apertura* (openness) in the early 1970s. Alarmed at the outbreak of revolution in neighbouring Portugal, the liberalization of the Spanish Roman Catholic Church and the escalation of Basque terrorism, they embarked on a relentless, if somewhat desperate and forlorn campaign to make the regime revert to its most dictatorial principles and bring the country once more under military rule. Six months after Admiral Carrero Blanco was assassinated by ETA terrorists in 1973, Blas Piñar publicly declared at a commemoration service that loyal Francoists stood for the 'spirit of 17 December, which was the true spirit of 18 July'. He was obviously harking back to 17 December 1970, when massive crowds thronged the Plaza de Oriente in Madrid to express their allegiance to Franco for his stand against those countries which were pressurizing him into commuting the death sentences served on ETA terrorists in the notorious Burgos court martials of that year. In September 1974, Blas Piñar inveighed against the government of Carlos Arias Navarro from the pages of his *Fuerza Nueva* journal, accusing the Prime Minister of gross deviation from Franco's fundamental laws and making it clear that his organization would dissociate itself from the government's policies and he would no longer collaborate in its legislative programme (Oneto, 1975, p. 146). Another dissenting voice came from an old Falangist and one of Franco's longest-serving ministers, José Antonio Girón de Velasco. Writing in the extreme right newspaper *El Alcázar*, which had first appeared during the Republican siege of the Alcázar in Toledo in 1936 and was now the mouthpiece of the Confederation of Civil War veterans, Girón unleashed a vitriolic attack on the regime's liberal reformers and singled out the Minister of Information, Pío Cabanillas, for particular criticism for allowing an offensive, anti-Franco foreign press to enjoy free circulation in Spain (Oneto, 1975, p. 87). During that summer, Girón had also been elected president of the recently formed veterans' confederation mentioned above. This organization, which quickly attracted a membership of over 300,000 former Nationalist militia and Blue Division volunteers, was now taking on a distinctly political character, declaring that its aim was to ensure that the regime remained committed to the national revolution, upheld the country's spiritual values in the face of Marxism and Western capitalism and bequeathed to future generations the solid principles of 18 July (Oneto, 1975, p. 167).

A concerted offensive finally led to the sacking of Pío Cabanillas. While the Falangist strong-arm squad Guerrilleros de Cristo Rey took to the streets and set fire to liberal newspaper offices and bookshops selling Marxist literature, the editors of the Falangist papers *Arriba* and *Pueblo* sent Franco a large dossier full of Cabanillas' liberal excesses, pinning on him the blame for the profusion of scantily clad females now appearing in magazines and public advertisements! Spain's leading government *aperturista* was thus summarily dismissed, putting paid to the faint chances of success of Arias Navarro's '12 February' reform programme. Leading churchmen too did not escape this extreme right onslaught. Cries of 'Tarancón for the firing squad' and 'Away with red priests' could be heard in street demonstrations as right-wingers protested at how soft the clergy had become towards Basque nationalists, trade unionists and students and rejected the conciliatory stance of the Primate, Cardinal Enrique y Tarancón. Their protests were understandable, given the church's remarkable conversion from being a staunch defender of the Franco regime to becoming a fearless opponent of it. The sense of betrayal was almost too painful for the extreme right to bear. The simple truth, however, was that the church had moved with the times whereas the extremists had not; indeed their attitude on religious matters had remained positively medieval. What their anger did provoke was an almost unprecedented occurrence in the annals of church-state relations in Spain: the rise of right-wing anti-clericalism.

Mass rallies were now commonplace, demanding an end to all permissiveness and a return to martial law. One such demonstration which was held in Madrid on the first anniversary of the murder of Carrero Blanco and timed to coincide with the promulgation of the mildly liberal Statute of Political Association, epitomized the attitude of the *Búnker* in the last months of the dictatorship. Their shouts of 'Down with traitors and weak governments' and 'Long live 18 July! Death to 12 February!' proved that they were not prepared to tolerate any democratic concessions and were hankering after another military take-over – a course of action which became their only desired objective in the early years of the transition to democracy.

The Extreme Right in Post-Franco Spain

Since the death of Franco in November 1975 Spain has undergone a remarkable political transformation. Democratic freedoms have been restored in accordance with the 1978 Constitution, and the PSOE (Socialist Party) has been in power since 1982: a far cry indeed from the previous forty years of illegality and suppression when Franco conditioned his people into believing that they were by nature unfit for liberal democracy and normal party politics.

Although in the initial stages of the transition the extreme right kept up their offensive both in and outside the *Cortes*, they were unable to force the government to step back from its reform programme. Their main parliamentary tactic was to try to muster sufficient opposition among *procuradores* and *consejeros nacionales* (national councillors) in order to block the passage of changes to Franco's *Leyes Fundamentales* which they regarded as immutable and sacrosanct. As most Members of Parliament and Movement councillors were government appointees and feared dismissal from their comfortable establishment posts if they opposed change, the extremists were unable to attract the necessary one-third support. As a result, the government's crucial *Ley de Reforma Política* bill was approved by an overwhelming majority in November 1976.

After this setback, the extreme right organized rallies on the anniversaries of the deaths of Franco and José Antonio (by coincidence 20 November) and the 1936 uprising. Although these events were well attended and demonstrated the extremists' capacity to stage impressive and colourful displays of nationalist fervour and defiance, there was nothing new about their ritual and rhetoric. While the political and social complexion of the country was dramatically changing, these Francoist diehards were only seeking to resurrect the past and had no different message from that put forward by the previous regime in its early years. Consequently, when the 1977 parliamentary elections were held and the Spanish voters made it clear that they wanted to bury extremisms of both left and right, support for undiluted Francoism was derisorily low. Indeed, if more liberally inclined ministers of the old regime such as Manuel Fraga Iribarne and Laureano López Rodó found votes hard to come by for their 'Conservative' Alianza Popular and were being rejected at the ballot box precisely because of their close links with the dictatorship, the extreme right's chances were even more remote. Their only option, therefore, was to goad sections of the Armed Forces into plotting a coup against the new democratic system which, in their eyes, had disunited the country and caused all manner of social ills: drugs, pornography, unemployment, street crime, etc. The *golpes* (military coups) of 1978, 1981 and 1982 were acts of a dwindling, desperate minority, convinced that Spain had once more become ungovernable and that military authority had to be reimposed 'to save the nation from chaos'. Although *ultra* generals were invariably the main protagonists of the coup attempts, civilian collaboration clearly existed. The 1982 plot to forestall a probable Socialist electoral victory implicated a close friend of Blas Piñar, Colonel Luis Muñoz Gutiérrez, whose wife was standing as an extreme right candidate for the Senate (Gilmour, 1985, p. 265; Preston, 1986, p. 224). Destabilizing tactics had already been employed in January 1977 when five pro-Communist labour lawyers were gunned down in their Madrid office, an outrage for which several members of Blas Piñar's organization subsequently received prison sentences. The intention on this occasion was to provoke the extreme left into some kind of retaliation, which in turn would have given the military the excuse to intervene. However, the whole affair backfired. Communist supporters did take to the streets, but in an admirably peaceful and restrained manner – the kind of responsible behaviour which helped to secure the legalization of the Partido Comunista three months later.

By January 1981, post-Franco democracy had lasted for the same length of time as the Second Republic had done in the 1930s prior to the Nationalist uprising. When a power vacuum occurred between the resignation of Prime Minister Adolfo Suárez and the appointment of his successor, the extreme right launched their spectacular coup of 23 February. Although this was carried out by the Civil Guard officer Antonio Tejero in Madrid and General Milans del Bosch in Valencia, civilian participation could not be ruled out. This failed attempt, however, proved as counterproductive for them as their previous efforts had been. It not only isolated them and destroyed their political respectability but also galvanized other right-wing parties like Manuel Fraga's Alianza Popular into throwing their weight behind the government's efforts to consolidate democracy. After the ringleaders were brought to trial and given long prison sentences, two new extreme right parties were formed, neither of which has made any real impact on the political scene. The first, Solidaridad Española, amounted to nothing more than Tejero's own fan club (he directed its activities from prison!), and it campaigned in the 1982 elections mainly for his release as a true patriot, eventually winning 20,000-odd votes. The second, Juntas Españolas, appeared in the late summer of 1984, with the specific purpose of unifying the extreme right as a civilian back-up in the event of any future coup attempt (*Cambio 16*, 29 Oct 1984).

Party Profiles[1]

Since the return of democracy to Spain, only a single extreme right candidate has been successful in a general election. This was Blas Piñar in 1979, representing Unión Nacional, a hastily formed alliance of extreme right groups including his own, Fuerza Nueva (which he had changed into a party in 1976). This one instance of electoral victory underlines just how insignificant the Spanish extreme right has become since 1975 and how emphatically the Spanish people have rejected the values and ideology of the dictatorship. Not that the original Falange had been any more successful during the Second Republic. Its 44,000 votes was probably the weakest showing of fascism in electoral competition anywhere in Europe (Payne, 1987, p. 65).

Results for Fuerza Nueva (relaunched as Frente Nacional in 1986) in elections since 1977 have been as follows:

1977–63,501 (Alianza Nacional del 18 de julio), 0.4%;
1979–382,463 (Unión Nacional), 2.1%, 1 seat in the *Congreso*;
1982–108,899 (Fuerza Nueva–Unidad Nacional), 0.5%;
1987 (Euro-election)–122,799 (Frente Nacional), 0.63%;
1989 (Euro-election)–59,964 (Frente Nacional), 0.38%.

The size of the vote in the last two elections referred to above was affected by the flamboyant candidature of the entrepreneur and fugitive from justice, José María Ruiz-Mateos, who had been conducting a personal vendetta against the PSOE government after its expropriation of his RUMASA business empire in 1983. Winning two Euro-seats in 1989, he attracted a definite protest vote, especially among supporters of the extreme right who saw him as a Francoist capable of posing awkward problems for the socialist majority. However, his refusal of an offer to join Blas Piñar on the same electoral platform prevented any real recovery of the extreme right from taking place.

The modest success of FN in 1979 merits closer examination. First, Blas Piñar was able to gain support from those right-wing Spaniards who had suffered an escalation of unemployment, inflation and terrorism under Suárez's Unión de Centro Democrático (UCD) government and had little confidence in the uncertain centre–right coalition consisting of the old monarchist José María de Areilza and Manuel Fraga, whose Alianza Popular, had been undergoing a crisis of its own since its 1977 election failure. Second, there were signs that the extreme right was becoming more effectively organized. FN now boasted an infrastructure which covered the whole of Spain, recruited a substantial number of activists, ran a thriving youth movement, Fuerza Joven, continued to publish its party journal, and could count on the charisma of Blas Piñar himself, whose unfailing oratorical ability to win over large crowds despite his advancing years gave the UCD government serious cause for concern about a possible reactionary backlash to their democratic reforms. Third, FN changed its political strategy, if not its basic message. Whereas it had previously existed to defend the original principles of Spanish nationalism against all moves to modify or liberalize them, now it put forward a 'national' alternative to rescue Spain from the ills of democracy. Last, Blas Piñar's presence in the *Congreso* (Lower Chamber) between 1979 and 1982 gave the extreme right the chance to make its opinions known in open parliamentary debate. The FN journal proudly described its single *diputado* (Member of Parliament) as the standard-bearer of unshakeable loyalty and living proof of 'that real Spain which assembles every year in the Plaza de Oriente to pay homage to Franco and José Antonio' (*Fuerza Nueva*, 7–21 June 1986 and 7–21 November 1987).

This marginal improvement in FN's fortunes could not be sustained. The 1981 coup attempt, which the party obviously regarded as an audacious act of patriotism against a government which had betrayed Franco and undone all his good works, proved to be a setback on two accounts. First, another extreme faction had stolen the limelight through direct military action, and second, Blas Piñar's own parliamentary position had by association become untenable. This turned out to be so in 1982 when he lost his seat and withdrew FN from the political arena soon after the general election had taken place. Had the 1981 coup not taken place – and there are rightists who have questioned whether it was really necessary (see *Fuerza Nueva*, 11–25 June 1988) – FN could conceivably have continued to develop as a potent source of extremist opposition within the *Cortes* against the centrist (UCD) government and, after 1982, that of the socialists (PSOE).

Membership of FN

By 1982 there were about 60,000 activists in the party (including its youth branch) – a membership figure which makes a mockery of its poor election performances. By 1990, according to FN sources, the total had fallen to 10,000. Its typical voter comes from rural Spain, from the lower middle class, and is mostly over 50 years of age or under 30 (this latter group having previously filled the ranks of Fuerza Joven at its height in the 1970s). Individual priests, soldiers, civil guards and policemen support the party: it fails to attract people from the banking, business and industry sectors. The middle class between the ages of 35 and 50 in urban and industrialized areas is the social group least likely to vote FN. The extreme right supporter of today has in fact changed from the one who voted that way in 1977. At that time there was a considerable number of people from different backgrounds who felt their existence threatened by the dismantling of Franco's system: members of the state syndicates and Movimiento bureaucrats, the Conservative military, older generations of middle and lower middle classes who were suspicious of any change and connected democracy with the traumatic experience of the Second Republic and Civil War, and industrialists whose incomes had increased through the economic autarky of the early Franco period (Kohler, 1982, pp. 14–15). Now people feel drawn towards FN because it offers, according to its general secretary, the kind of responsible leadership which will rescue Spain from the moral and political corruption which democracy has created. A graphic idea of the typical FN adherent of today is contained in the report of a talk given by Franco's physician, Dr Vicente Pozuelo, at the party's offices in Madrid: his audience was largely older people in their fifties, more women than men, the former dressed like Mrs Thatcher and the latter kitted out like ageing 1950s film stars, with silvery hair, moustache and dark glasses (*Cambio 16*, 26 November 1988). *La Vanguardia* a year earlier published a photograph of Blas Piñar standing beside Franco's daughter Carmen and José Antonio's sister Pilar and giving the raised arm salute at the rally to commemorate the twelfth anniversary of Franco's death (*La Vanguardia*, 23 November 1987). This scene seemed to be more in keeping with Spain of the early 1940s than the late 1980s.

Party Organization

FN has had one leader since its launch in 1966. Blas Piñar has the distinction of being one of the very few genuine politicians that the Franco regime has produced, the other two being Admiral Luis Carrero Blanco, the architect of the Francoist succession, and Manuel Fraga, the liberal reformist. During his time as leader, Piñar has been a prolific writer, speaker and political activist, expressing a wealth of ideas on moral and spiritual as well as social and political matters (see *Fuerza Nueva*, 20 April–10 May 1986 and 9–23 July 1988). In one of the editions of Spain's parliamentary 'Who's who' he is described as a respected and powerful orator who has gained a distinguished reputation for delivering patriotic speeches (*Quien es quien*, 1980, p. 572).

Election posters display him in a noble pose, emphasizing the great importance which FN attaches to him as a person of honour and dignity yet one
who prides himself on the direct contact which he has made with his grass-
roots supporters.

Below him in the party hierarchy come FN's national executive committee, made up of nine other elected members (two vice-presidents, a
general secretary, an assistant general secretary and five *vocales* whose role is
to represent the party's cultural, youth and trade union interests); then the
provincial councils throughout Spain and the party delegations in Latin
America and Europe (in Argentina, Chile, Paraguay, Brazil, Germany and
Belgium); and finally the town or village committees. The party's two
satellites are its youth front, Juventudes de Frente Nacional, and its affiliated
trade union, Frente Sindicalista Nacional. The latter organization was formerly known as Fuerza Nueva del Trabajo which existed alongside the party
until 1982 and sought to challenge the hegemony enjoyed in the Spanish
trade union system by the socialist Unión General de Trabajadores (UGT)
and the communist Comisiones Obreras (CC.OO). The union had three
representatives on Madrid City Council in 1989, out of a total of 36.
Juventudes de FN is made up of 20–30 year olds who are particularly active
in the Spanish university sector through such organizations as DISPAR and
Asociación Universitaria Española. It was set up on 20 November 1987
during the act of homage to Franco and José Antonio at their mausoleum in
the Valle de los Caídos. The youth front holds its own national and regional
congresses and has its own executive committee (president, general secretary, university association president and three national secretaries in charge
of organization, press, finance and international relations) and provincial
representatives, who are appointed by the party's provincial presidents. It is
a 'new look' youth movement which in no way resembles the Fuerza Joven
of old, having discarded the paramilitary uniform of blue (Falangist) shirts
and red (Carlist) berets and no longer parading like Nationalist militia
behind the old national flag to the extreme annoyance of the civic authorities. It claims to have renounced all forms of violence and to be more intent
on developing fraternal links with other right-wing youth groups in Europe.

Since 1986, when the party was reconstituted as the Frente Nacional, it
has not always taken part in the country's elections. It did not, for instance,
field any candidates in the 1989 General Election. This situation can be
explained by the simple fact that since it had no existing parliamentary
representation it did not receive any subsidy from the state to help meet its
electoral expenses, and therefore chose to concentrate its energies and
limited resources on the two Euro-campaigns of 1987 and 1989. Its principal
instrument of propaganda is still the party journal, *Fuerza Nueva*, which has
now published its thousandth edition. Described as a fine example of Spain's
'apocalyptic' press (Terrón Montero, 1981, p. 215), it contains reports of
meetings, commemorative events, demonstrations, conferences, *comidas de
hermandad* (party dinners) and other activities, together with extracts from
speeches by Blas Piñar and in-depth investigations into recent Spanish
history, above all the Civil War. The tone is strident and bellicose, particularly in attacks against the present system, government policy, and major

figures of the democratic establishment. A perusal of its contents creates the impression that the old hatreds of the Civil War are still very much alive.

In addition to the journal, there are other media outlets. The old FN *Editorial* is still operating, and the party has its own radio stations: Inter-Valencia Radio, for example, was recently set up by an FN offshoot, Unión Hispana, and was described by Blas Piñar at its opening ceremony as 'an effective instrument in the service of the ideological movement that unites us' (*Fuerza Nueva*, 27 September–1 Oct 1986). From 1966 to 1976, because of Franco's ban on all political parties of both left and right, FN functioned as a cultural association which disseminated right-wing literature. From 1982 to 1986 it again existed as such, through a network of 'ADES' ('Adelante España') agencies linked to CESPE (Centro de Estudios Sociales, Políticos y Económicos) in Madrid.

Party Ideology

Links with Francoism and Falangism

FN's calendar is full of dates which commemorate important events in recent Spanish history, such as the outbreak of the Civil War, the execution of José Antonio, the defence and relief of the Alcázar in Toledo, and the death of Franco. The whole *raison d'être* of the party seems to originate in its nostalgic veneration of those whom it regards as the twin figureheads of the Nationalist crusade and in an obsession with the key events of that dreadful conflict. As Blas Piñar told his followers in León in northern Spain in October 1981, his party did not have any new ideology to put forward; it simply had the great honour of continuing the work of two great men of history (*Fuerza Nueva*, 31 October–7 November 1981). FN is convinced that the condemnation which José Antonio made in the 1930s of Spain's deep political divisions, bitter class struggle and national disunity is just as relevant to the situation today – hence the urgent need to keep his memory alive and act as his legitimate heirs.

Religion

FN is primarily a confessional party. Roman Catholicism is another of its guiding principles, a fact which is demonstrated by the first word of its motto, *Dios*. Non-Catholics are not excluded from membership, although they would clearly feel ill at ease. FN has established links with the more extreme and reactionary elements in the Spanish church, such as the inquisit-orial and obscurantist Hermandad Sacerdotal Española and the schismatic movement of Palmar de Troya, led by the self-styled 'Pope' Clemente Domínguez. This particular cleric, a kind of Marcel Lefebvre in the making, is supposed to have interpreted a local apparition of the Virgin as a sign of God's wrath against the harm done to his church by the Second Vatican Council and by Pope Paul VI, whom he believed had been drugged by communists and Masons (*El País Semanal*, 3 October 1985). As far as his relationship with Blas Piñar is concerned, one of his political prophesies was the salvation of the world by Blas Piñar and General Augusto Pinochet! (*Radical Right*, 1987, p. 256).

Surprisingly, FN distances itself from the idea of a return to a confessional state. Ildefonso Rodríguez (1981, p. 56) reveals the party's position on this matter by declaring that church and state must remain separate:

> With regard to relations with the Church, we feel that we are, and have been throughout history, a people who are in the majority profoundly Catholic, and it is our duty to preserve and nurture that Catholic faith, witness to the Truth made flesh and honour the pledges made at our baptism. As regards relations between Church and State, these must be established and maintained on the basis of mutual independence and healthy cooperation. It is the responsibility of government to create and defend this climate of peaceful coexistence that enables the Church to perform its sacred mission and exercise its apostolate.

It is worth noting that this view corresponds closely with original Falangist ideology and is at odds with the Francoist principle of *nacionalcatolicismo* which bound church and state together almost indissolubly. Stanley Payne, discussing the Falange's 'mystical sense of nationalism', makes the point that the movement stressed the need to separate church and state, and although the Falange officially proclaimed its Catholicism, it did not propose to subject Spaniards to a religion-dominated state (Payne, 1987, p. 58). FN is prepared to defend religious freedom possibly because it wishes to practise and propagate its own ultramontane brand of Roman Catholicism without having to toe the more neutral and moderate line which the church hierarchy has adopted in Spain in recent years. Also, FN is alarmed at the prospect of church–state interdependence when the state is as godless as the present one. Blas Piñar was one of the first to denounce the 1978 Constitution as 'a document which makes God an outcast', and he openly criticized Spain's bishops for their refusal to speak out against a text which made no mention of God (*The Times*, 26 November 1978). He considered that the real villain was Cardinal Tarancón who had already incurred the wrath of the extreme right as a result of his liberal gestures in the early 1970s. Now Blas Piñar went so far as to accuse the Cardinal of sowing discord among Catholics in Spain by urging them to support socialism, condemning the church's blessing of the Nationalist cause in the Civil War as a mistake and burying his head in the sand over the question of divorce (*Fuerza Nueva*, 6–13 March 1982). Piñar just could not comprehend the Cardinal's desire for reconciliation and a more tolerant and pluralist church. He obviously believes in nothing but a crusading church, ready to do battle against immorality (drugs, prostitution, pornography, abortion and divorce) and the socio-economic ills of liberal democracy (unemployment, poor housing, hunger and bad working conditions).

Patriotism

In line with both Falangist and Francoist ideology, FN fervently upholds the concept of a unified Spain in which regional autonomy has no rightful place. No sooner did Blas Piñar take up his parliamentary seat in 1979 than he spoke out against the statutes of autonomy which were then being discussed for Catalonia and the Basque Country. As far as the Basques were concerned, he maintained that official mention of the term *Euskadi* immediately conferred national status on the region and that far-reaching powers in the political, cultural and economic spheres were being surrendered to those local authorities who were hell-bent on destroying the unity of Spain. In the case of Catalonia he argued that their degree of autonomy, if granted, would do away with the idea of solidarity among the people of Spain and allow the Catalans to transform their region into an integral state, separated from Spain (*Fuerza Nueva*, 18–25 September 1982). His emphatic 'No' at the final voting stage did not hinder the passage of the two bills but confirmed his party's complete opposition to autonomy (although this did not deter FN from fielding candidates in some of the subsequent regional elections). Invariably Blas Piñar, like Franco, José Antonio and other right-wingers before him, equates any degree of autonomy with separatism, even if it is just a question of recognizing the legitimate historical rights of the peripheral areas of Spain.

The Armed Forces

The Spanish military has in recent times readily assumed the role of guarantor of the country's unity, interpreter of the national will, and, to quote the Falange, 'the safeguard of what is permanent' (Ellwood, 1987, p. 30). Its role as an independent watchdog outside civilian authority is precisely the kind of function which FN wishes the military to perform. It rejects their present subordination to the Minister of Defence and proposes a chain of direct command from the Head of State via the Chiefs of Staff to the three military undersecretaries. In the past such independence meant that the military could directly challenge civilian authority if they felt that the nation's well-being was threatened. FN believes that it is in the national interest for this independent role to be restored. In the first phase of the transition to democracy, it was Suárez's Vice-President of Defence Affairs, Lt.-Gen. Gutiérrez Mellado, who initiated this idea of ministerial control with the aim of purging the Armed Forces of their strong Francoist loyalties and making them politically neutral. This policy predictably led to uproar on the extreme right who singled out Mellado for the kind of bitter criticism which they had previously levelled at Cardinal Tarancón. It was no coincidence that the person who was abused and manhandled the most during Tejero's seizure of the *Cortes* in 1981 should have been Mellado. The fact that he was by profession a military man made his critics brand him even more as a traitor who not only betrayed Franco, his former Commander-in-Chief, but also infiltrated the ranks with government agents in order to weed out those soldiers who remained loyal to their *Generalísimo*. More recently, the FN journal has published a series of long articles on Mellado's Civil War record which seek to incriminate him as a possible double agent.

Social Justice

This is the third main aspect of FN's ideology and brings to mind the national syndicalism which was first advocated by the Falange in the 1930s and then modified by Franco when he created his vertical *sindicatos* after the Civil War. Blas Piñar's rousing speech at a May Day demonstration organized by the FN trade union in 1982 indicates the kind of trade unionism which the extreme right wishes to promote in Spain. Piñar affirmed his implacable opposition to the current false system of worker representation 'which sows discord and hatred and turns the workplace into a battlefield' (*Fuerza Nueva*, 15–22 May 1982). He then proceeded to describe the cause in which he religiously believed, 'a cause which is national, Spanish and Christian, and which allows worker and boss to share the same bread in communion under God and the Fatherland'. Harking back to 1938 when Franco promulgated his Fuero de Trabajo and established the basis of the nationalist, social and Christian state of 18 July, he proudly declared that

> only within this type of legal framework will it be possible to achieve the goals of full employment, a just wage, a share in the profits and the running of a company, an adequate social security system, and proper representation in Parliament and in the agencies which control our economy.

Having reported Blas Piñar's speech, the FN journal then described the size and joyous spirit of this demonstration 'for work, dignity and progress' as a total vindication of the party's syndicalist policies and as proof of how many ordinary people had chosen to turn their backs on the UGT and CC.OO (*Fuerza Nueva*, 8–15 May 1982). Although FN believes that true social justice can be achieved only by repudiating the class struggle and creating a system of labour relations built on co-operation and not confrontation, it fails to admit that this is possible only if workers are kept in tight subjection and denied their basic human rights – an unjust situation such as that which prevailed during the Franco regime.

Traditionalism

FN proclaims that it offers an alternative not just to the present Socialist government but also to Spain's actual democratic system which it denounces as anti-religious, anti-Spanish and anti-social: such are the negative sentiments which are expressed in the party's official manifesto *La alternativa nacional (soluciones para España)*. Reiterating traditional reactionary thought, Blas Piñar rejects liberal politics and parliamentary democracy as concepts which, in the words of José Antonio, are alien to the eternal metaphysic of Spain; his party will participate in the 'false' parliamentary process for only as long as it takes to reintroduce the 'true' – and authentically Spanish – organic system of representation via the 'natural' channels of the family, syndicate and municipality. Just like Franco before him, he considers that political parties do not work in the national interest but in sterile and costly partisan confrontation, existing solely as artificial creations which are forced to rely on state subsidy for survival – a pointed remark concerning his own party's financial difficulties.

In short, *Piñarismo* is a modern version of the nineteenth-century political philosophy of Juan Donoso Cortés which inspired Primo de Rivera, José Antonio and Franco successively. Cortés' condemnation of liberalism and capitalist materialism in the early 1850s as pernicious and degenerative ideologies which lead irrevocably to mass alienation, the class struggle and atheistic socialism forms a cornerstone of FN thinking, together with his more positive conviction that the only salvation is to be found in a reformed Catholic system (Payne, 1984, p. 133).

Racism

Unlike extreme right movements elsewhere in Europe, Spanish nationalism has never been strongly imbued with racial prejudice and hatred. Franco was credited, for example, with having granted some Jews safe passage through Spain during the Second World War and given others Spanish passports to save them from Nazi concentration camps. Also the Jewish community in the Spanish enclave of Melilla in North Morocco reputedly gave their support to the 1936 uprising. Conversely, however, it goes without saying that Franco ruthlessly persecuted any Spaniard of Jewish origin who had been associated with the Republic and opposed the Nationalist uprising. After all he was obsessed with the idea that Spain had fallen prey to a Judaeo-Marxist conspiracy and that these were still the external enemies who would always be seeking to topple his regime. As for the FN, anti-Semitism is not mentioned anywhere in their literature. As regards other ethnic groups, notably gypsies, FN seems to treat those in Spain very sympathetically. Enrique Vargas, the so-called 'Gypsy Prince', stood as a FN candidate in 1982 because he felt that his fellow gypsies had grown tired of being deceived and hounded by the authorities and decided that only FN could help them put an end to their social discrimination (*Fuerza Nueva*, 27 February–6 March 1982).

Antagonism certainly exists between the extreme right and Catalan and Basque nationalists. Two FN activists, the president of the party in Navarre and the Mayor of Galdácano in the Basque Country, have been killed by ETA terrorists, and right-wing terror squads such as the Batallón Vasco Español have waged a counter-offensive in the past. Ironically, it was the original Basque Nationalist Party (founded in the 1890s) that was strikingly racist, preaching hatred for the Spanish invader or *maketo*.

The foreign country to be singled out for most criticism by FN is the

United Kingdom, on account of its refusal to return Gibraltar to Spain. The party's manifesto states that the relations between the two countries will be marred for as long as Spain's sovereignty over the Rock is not recognized by Britain, and that the persistence of this colonialist situation is an intolerable affront to Spain's dignity (*Frente Nacional*, p. 18). However, there is no sign of any hostility on the part of FN towards the conspicuous presence of many British ex-patriots who are currently resident in Spain.

Anti-Capitalism and Anti-Marxism

In line with certain traditional extreme right attitudes, FN directs its most vociferous attacks against what it claims to be a continuing conspiracy between capitalism and socialism on a world-wide scale. The party journal at the end of 1987 described the grim onslaught of these corrosive forces in uncompromising terms (*Fuerza Nueva*, 5–19 December 1987):

> Capitalism without a human face is today that financial empire which secretly acquires one monopoly after another, ably assisted by Fabian socialism which is actively promoting it on a Euro-American scale. What matters to these movements today is not the killing nor the defeat of their opponents but their confusion and their corruption.

Blas Piñar retains the old Francoist nightmare of an international Masonic conspiracy which he sees now at work in the Council of Europe (which he alleges is run by Masons) and closer to home in Spain's major political parties, many of whose members he claims belong to Masonic lodges.

Relations with Other Parties

Because Spain's right-wing parties grew out of Francoism, some overlap between them is inevitable. This was most apparent in the early stages of the democratic transition when Fraga's 'Conservative' alliance was unashamedly Francoist and when there was talk just before the 1979 election of a possible right-wing coalition against the UCD government, comprising Fraga and Blas Piñar. Also, there have been reported cases of individuals switching membership from AP to FN or actually holding dual membership of FN and FE de las JONS. Fraga, in his efforts to attract the tactical voter in 1982 and build a 'natural majority' to defeat the left, went to considerable lengths to woo the extreme right supporter. While he demanded the allegiance of former UCD voters in the centre, he took out full-page advertisements in *El Alcázar* and courted unreconstructed Francoists by declaring himself in favour of capital punishment and by remarking that he understood, although he did not excuse, the officers implicated in the 1981 coup attempt (Gilmour, 1985, pp. 266–7). FN deplored these tactics, bluntly accusing AP of spreading malicious propaganda which reported that Blas Piñar was seriously ill and about to sign a secret pact, pulling FN out of the election at the eleventh hour (*Fuerza Nueva*, 9–23 July 1988). Personal animosity between Blas Piñar and Fraga had made any *rapprochement* difficult in 1979. Attempts to form a coalition then had fallen through because AP felt that its chances of success would be hampered by FN's predisposition towards violence. Fraga also made it clear on that occasion that he wanted to have nothing to do with a group that wished to replace the new constitution with a system borrowed from the 1940s, took part in activities of a paramilitary nature and held integralist views of society (*Fuerza Nueva*, 23 July–6 August 1988). For its part, FN could never forgive Fraga for sharing the same political platform as its *bête noire*, Santiago Carrillo (the Communist leader), at the prestigious Club Siglo XXI in Madrid, and for marching arm-in-arm with the CC.OO president Marcelino Camacho in a pro-democracy street demonstration in Madrid after the 1981 coup attempt. More recently, it has attacked Fraga for his conversion to the cause of regional autonomy, accusing him of acting as the executioner, no less, of Spanish nationalism (*Fuerza Nueva*, 6–20 December 1986).

Relations between FN and other groups on the extreme right have been equally strained. A report in the party journal, 'Fuerza Nueva: 1976–1982, La alternativa nacional', describes all the uneasy alliances, petty rivalry, personal jealousy and recriminations which it claims resulted from the failure of other groups to match FN's organizational abilities and electoral impact (*Fuerza Nueva*, 23 July–6 August 1988). The various Falangist groups have also taken exception to the way in which FN has appropriated all the trappings and emblems of Spanish nationalism.

Official Reactions

Although FN maintains that it commands respect from the Socialist government for its coherent ideology and its status as a responsible political movement, its activities have often provoked a government clamp-down, particularly on mass demonstrations. For example, the annual rally to commemorate the deaths of Franco and José Antonio in the Plaza de Oriente in Madrid had been held there uninterruptedly until 1981. The location was especially dear to extreme right hearts since it was there that Franco had assembled huge crowds in support of his regime at times of international difficulty, and where in the late 1970s the diehards had staged fierce opposition to democratic change. However, in order to minimize the political embarrassment caused by this annual event, the government refused to allow it to take place there in subsequent years, transferring it in 1983 to Madrid's main thoroughfare, the Paseo de la Castellana, and then in 1987 to a small adjoining square where a statue of Franco was still standing (*Fuerza Nueva*, 7–21 November 1987). Although the authorities alleged that the reason for the change of venue was potential damage to public property and disruption to traffic, they were clearly seeking to depoliticize the event and reduce its public significance. The 1981 rally had ended in a punitive fine which the government levied against FN for having organized a paramilitary parade by its youth section and allowed some over-excited activists to drive recklessly through Madrid. As a result, the party complained bitterly of the various forms of victimization which it felt the government had inflicted on it: bans on political activities, fines, surveillance of party members, phone-tapping, infiltration of party offices, wrongful accusations and press misre-porting (*Fuerza Nueva*, 23–30 January 1982).

Additionally, FN's 18 July celebrations have been similarly frustrated. In 1982, the authorities refused FN's request to hold the event in the bull-rings of Madrid, Barcelona and Cuenca. The previous year they had been banned from using the ring in El Escorial for the same purpose, although the decision was subsequently challenged in court on the grounds that it was unconstitutional, and FN's appeal was upheld. The fact that the Catalans and the Basques have never been prevented since 1975 from celebrating their own national days and the Communist Party has gone ahead with its own public meetings sometimes on the very day when a FN event was banned does give credence to FN's sense of grievance that it has been singled out for unfair treatment (*Fuerza Nueva*, 10–17 July 1982).

FN's affiliated trade union has also landed the party in trouble. In June 1981 a meeting, organized by Fuerza Nueva del Trabajo (FNT) to protest at the UCD government paying out some 2, 500 million pesetas from the Trade Union Fund to the UGT and CC.OO, was broken up by the police. A number of arrests were made, including the FNT leader Jaime Alonso, who was slightly injured in the confrontation. The following year, during the election campaign for representation on Madrid City Council, the authori-ties ordered the removal of all FNT posters and propaganda, although this did not prevent the election of eleven FNT members on to the Council Workers' Committee. On a more sinister note, the city's police force were being asked to declare whether or not they belonged to FNT and state whether they knew of any colleagues who were also members of that union. Interestingly, of the 123 FNT candidates who stood in the above elections, well over half were from the *Policía Municipal*, which is perhaps a good indicator of the political sympathies of the force!

The Spanish media very rarely carries any coverage of the activities of the extreme right. Reports covering its major event of the year, the commemo-ration of the deaths of Franco and José Antonio have become briefer and briefer. When articles do appear, they either implicate the extreme right in criminal activities (see *El País*, 22 May 1989) or are intended to poke fun (see *Cambio 16*, 28 November 1988). As regards the two Euro-election cam-paigns, these were covered by the media without any reference to partici-pation by FN, so that voters were unaware that it was fielding candidates. As confirmation of this blanket of silence, the FN journal contrasted the absence of Spanish TV cameras from FN's closing rally in Madrid's Plaza Mayor with the full coverage given by Italian TV to FN's homage to the late Giorgio Almirante (*Fuerza Nueva*, 5–19 March 1988).

International Links

Latin America

The doctrine of *Hispanidad*, which was originally formulated by Ramiro de Maeztu, one of the members of Spain's intellectual generation of 1898, and subsequently taken up by the Franco regime as the basis of its Latin American 'policy', still characterizes extreme right-wing thinking. Paul Wilkinson (1981, p. 49) defines it as the export of Spanish-style fascism to interested Latin American regimes:

> After 1936 one sees the interesting influence of the *Hispanidad* movement. This pro-Spanish cultural movement became a vehicle for the advocacy of fascist-style dictatorship, militant suppression of communism, and a doctrine of total subservience to the state, with all democratic pretensions discarded. This new style ultra-nationalism was able to exploit the concepts of the essential unity of Spanish culture and institutions. The influence of these ideas on Argentinian leaders such as Ramírez and Perón was to prove considerable. Besides the latter, Peru, Venezuela, Paraguay and Bolivia were all responsive.

Over the years FN has maintained close links of this nature with dictatorships in Latin America. It has, as stated earlier, official delegations in Argentina, Chile, Paraguay and Brazil, although it is not clear to what extent these are tolerated by the more democratically inclined regimes. Blas Piñar has often attended formal ceremonies (such as General Stroessner's reassumption of the Paraguayan presidency). Commemorations of the Spanish Civil War are regularly held in some countries, mainly as a display of anti-communist solidarity. In Spain itself, the shadowy terrorist group Alianza Apostólica Anticomunista, which was active in the late 1970s and claimed responsibility for the 1977 Atocha massacre, was rumoured to have strong Argentinian connections.

Recent developments in Latin America have been particularly significant for the FN. It staunchly supported the Pinochet regime in Chile on account of its close similarity with the Franco regime. It argued that Pinochet was subjected to the kind of foreign harassment which Franco experienced at the hands of Spain's external enemies from 1939 to 1975. A visit by PSOE representatives in the International Socialist movement to Chile was criticized by FN as a conspiracy to use Spain as a launch-pad for subversive campaigns against right-wing regimes in Latin America (*Fuerza Nueva*, 9–23 July 1988). FN's admiration for the Pinochet regime was particularly strong because of the way in which it allegedly restored the nation's pride after 'the catastrophe' of Allende's Popular Unity government – just as Franco had done in Spain after 'the disasters' of the Frente Popular in 1936.

The Falklands War also provided FN with an opportunity to affirm its support for the military junta in Argentina and condemn the Spanish government's stance at the same time. As in the case of Chile, FN drew a parallel between Argentina and Spain, describing the Falklands as

Argentina's Gibraltar and the war as Argentina's 'Christian crusade of national reconquest'. FN deplored Spain's abstention at the United Nations (UN), at a time when 'our country is suffering the permanent humiliation of Gibraltar' and 'a UN resolution compels Britain to hand back her last colony in Europe to Spain' (*Fuerza Nueva*, 17–24 April 1982).

FN states that its current policy towards Latin America is two-fold. First, it pledges itself not to interfere in the internal politics of individual countries, although this does not imply the removal of moral support for particular regimes. Second, it recommends a new Marshall Plan to relieve poverty and the burden of foreign debt and looks forward to the possible creation of a Common Market for the area (*Frente Nacional*, p. 19).

Europe

In 1978, on the third anniversary of Franco's death, leaders of the French and Italian extreme right attended a mass rally in Madrid, organized by FN. Since then, Blas Piñar has attached great importance to his party's European connections, much more than he did during the Franco regime. This pro-European stance has become even more pronounced since Spain's accession to the EC and the holding of Euro-elections in Spain which, as already mentioned, FN seems to regard as being more vital than Spain's own. As *Europeísmo* has been an almost mythical aspiration for Spanish politicians of every hue in recent times (Share, 1986, p. 51), FN's interest in Europe is not surprising, although it contrasts with the intense xenophobia of the early years of the Franco regime when Spain was ostracized by almost the entire international community on account of Franco's Axis sympathies. FN's current position on Europe is detailed in its manifesto, which states that Spain has always been part of Europe, her destiny has been and is inextricably linked to Europe, and that Europe's future lies in the creation of an alliance of independent nations which should include those at present languishing under the tyranny of communism (*Frente Nacional*, p. 17).

European support for FN has been forthcoming mainly from Italy and in particular from Almirante's MSI (see Chapter 6). The Italian association of Civil War veterans regularly sends representatives to ceremonies commemorating the founding of the Falange, the siege of the Alcázar in Toledo and other incidents in the war. The Italian right-wing trade union organization CISNAL has taken part in FNT demonstrations under the banner of a united European syndicate of labour.

Fuerza Nueva's reappearance in 1986 as Frente Nacional came about as a direct result of the impact on French and European politics of Jean-Marie Le Pen (see Chapter 2). He paid a visit to Madrid in May 1986, to give his support to like-minded politicians and parties who were intending to participate in Spain's first Euro-elections (*La Vanguardia*, 6 May 1986). This visit happened to coincide with a meeting of delegates of Blas Piñar's CESPE association in the Valle de los Caídos near Madrid. At the end of this meeting, a decision was taken to reconstitute FN for the first since its dissolution in 1982. The new party's launch as Frente Nacional took place at a congress in Madrid on 26 October 1986, with Giorgio Almirante and Jean-Marc Brissaud (of Le Pen's FN) as invited guests.

Since that time, FN and its youth section have extended their European links to take in similar groups in Portugal and Greece; however, the cause of Jean-Marie Le Pen is still the one which they promote the most strongly. Blas Piñar attended Le Pen's French presidential campaign in 1988, and thirty-six members of Juventudes de FN were present at a European youth convention in Strasbourg, which was part of the same campaign. The FN journal published an editorial at the time of the election itself, and this reflected the party's wholehearted commitment to an extreme right political movement in Europe under the dynamic and constructive leadership of Le Pen. The following extract (*Fuerza Nueva*, 16–30 April 1988) expresses the fervently religious sentiment in FN's hopes of the ultimate success of Le Pen's candidature:

> From these pages an appeal goes out to all good Spaniards to pray for the victory of Le Pen. Europe needs a strong, anti-communist, anti-pornographic France which will defend the values of religion, the family, patriotism and tradition. Let us unite to support the candidate who came and collaborated with Blas Piñar in our elections to the European Parliament. If the right was crushed in France in 1945 but then re-formed itself a few years ago in that land of St Joan of Arc, may the Spanish right, which was smashed and betrayed in 1975, revive itself with the vigour which it has always been able to display in our history.

For his part, Blas Piñar looked forward to Le Pen's victory as one step further towards reinforcing European patriotism, breaking down Berlin's wall of shame and Yalta's infamous iron curtain, and transforming Europe into a 'community of destiny' (*Fuerza Nueva*, 23 January–6 February 1988).

The Extreme Right: Latest Developments

As to the destiny of the extreme right in Spain, the situation has now become more critical than ever. Despite the proud boast of Blas Piñar that millions of Spaniards still remain faithful to the high ideals of Spanish nationalism as represented by Franco's dictatorship and that Francoism will survive for the next thousand years, the reality is one of ever-quickening decline into obscurity and ineffectuality. In a lengthy article published by *Cambio 16* in November 1990 on the fifteenth anniversary of Franco's death, the extreme right is described as a dying breed and a relic of the past against which virtually all Spaniards have now turned their backs and from which previously faithful servants of the dictatorship have evidently dissociated themselves. Only a handful of *ultras melancólicos* now assemble to pay homage to Franco beside his tomb in the Valle de los Caídos or beneath his equestrian statue in Madrid – a far cry indeed from the earlier days of the democratic transition when Blas Piñar could call out thousands of demonstrators on to the streets of Madrid to protest at the treachery and immorality of the Suárez government and to demand the return of the military to power.

Two recent developments in particular indicate why the fortunes of the extreme right are at such a low ebb. First, the Spanish right under the dynamic leadership of José María Aznar has now organized itself into a serious political alternative to the PSOE and attracted substantial support from those arch-conservative sectors of Spanish society which in the past had responded to Franco's brand of authoritarian government. Second, the tendency for political mavericks to make their mark and capture the protest vote has been confirmed. After José-María Ruiz Mateos triumphed in the 1989 Euro-elections, another equally colourful and irrepressible personality has burst on to the political scene, this time at the local level, in the shape of the newly elected Mayor of Marbella, Jesús Gil. Although he can in no way be described as a representative of some newly emerging movement of the far right, he defines himself as a *dictador liberal* with a mission to rid Marbella of drugs, crime and prostitution and to turn it into a tourist paradise! His resounding success in the local elections on 26 May 1991 underlined the preparedness of many thousands of Spaniards to place their trust in an out-and-out entrepreneur seeking to drive a coach and horses through the Spanish political establishment.

There have also been recent signs of neo-Nazi activity. The drug problem has given rise to a number of attacks perpetrated on addicts by skinheads; in the case of gypsy victims, this violence has racist overtones. In October 1991, following a rally organized by Juntas Españolas to celebrate Empire Day [*Día de la Hispanidad*], skinheads belonging to the extreme right group Brigadas Blanquiazules, which has attached itself to the 'support' of the Barcelona football team Español, went on the rampage through the centre of Barcelona (*El País*, 13 October 1991). More ominously, CEDADE, the pro-Hitler group innocently calling itself 'The Spanish Circle of Friends of Europe', has had a serious brush with the Socialist government over its plans to pay homage to eight German airmen of the Condor Legion buried in Madrid's La Almudena cemetery and to organize a seminar in which three former Nazis, including an ex-SS officer, Leon Degrelle now resident in Spain, were due to deny the Jewish Holocaust. Although at present there is no ban in Spain on neo-Nazi parties, the government acted quickly to prohibit these events, alleging that the exercise of ideological freedom and freedom of expression could not be extended to demonstrations which were intended to insult particular ethnic or social groups. As CEDADE had issued invitations for representatives from over a hundred neo-Nazi groups world-wide to attend the Madrid gathering, the government was determined to avoid the embarrassment of Madrid becoming a temporary focal point of international fascist activity: Indeed, the Interior Minister, José Luís Corcuera, stated confidently that there was no danger of the far right being able to reorganize itself in Spain as it had done in other European countries (*El País*, 14 and 16 November 1991).

No such ban, however, was forthcoming on the rally to commemorate the deaths of Franco and José Antonio. The event took place for the first time since 1981 in the Plaza de Oriente in Madrid by courtesy of the recently formed Conservative council. Blas Piñar, addressing an estimated crowd of ten thousand including representatives of his party, Frente Nacional, Juntas Españolas and a new youth organization Nación Joven, reaffirmed his pride in Spain's noble crusade in 1936 and, capitalizing on recent developments in Eastern Europe, acclaimed Franco and José Antonio as originators of the fall of international communism (*El País*, 18 November 1991).

The political scene continues to be dominated by the continuing saga starring the controversial and irrepressible Mayor of Marbella, Jesús Gil. Now a television celebrity with his own highly popular show, he recently declared his intention to form his own political party and stand for the Presidencia del Gobierno in the next general election. The fact that he is unashamedly populist and a cult figure suggests that he is about to cause quite an impact on the Spanish political establishment. His recent statements that the government has sold out to multinationals, that the so-called *Padres de la Patria* (i.e., Spain's MPs and Senators) stand in the way of Spain becoming strong, and that his mission will be to revolutionize the country's political life, bear distinctly dictatorial overtones, despite his claim to be the world's most liberal figure (*Tiempo*, 23 September 1991).

Conclusion

Since the death of Franco in 1975, the political face of Spain has changed almost beyond recognition. The system which he developed in the course of nearly forty uninterrupted years in power and handed on 'well and truly tied up' to his chosen successor has been dismantled and virtually forgotten. Regional autonomy, which the Franco regime denounced as an unpardonable crime, is now a vigorous part of the democratic process, keenly promoted by all the major parties of both left and right. Freedom has permeated Spanish society to such an extent that it has now led the present Pope to denounce it as neo-pagan and hedonistic. Little wonder then that the extreme right, wallowing in nostalgia and traditionalism, is now nothing more than a marginalized movement which appears to be set on a downward course into oblivion. This trend began with the internal pressures for democratic change in the mid-1960s, continued with the constitutional changes of the 1970s and reached its climax with the thwarting of *golpismo* in the early 1980s. The consolidation of democracy and the increasingly moderate stances of the major political parties have consigned the fratricidal divisions of the Civil War and the cruel repression of the Franco dictatorship to the history books. Consensus and electoral stability have made it impossible for the extreme right, locked in a 1930s and 1940s time warp, to gain popular support for its beliefs. Indeed, as far back as 1967, the pro-Franco historian Brian Crozier observed that almost two-thirds of Spain's population were too young to have played any part in the Civil War and were bored by its liturgy, which to them belonged to history and had no bearing on their political views (*The Times*, 11 July 1967). Nowadays, more and more Spaniards are turning their backs on the moral values to which the extreme right adhere so rigidly. In November 1976, 72 per cent of Spaniards were prepared to accept abortion in certain circumstances; a couple of years later, 63 per cent favoured divorce; and by 1983, the number of civil marriages (32 per cent) had increased eightfold since 1975. Permissiveness has become the order of the day, particularly with the relaxation of legislation on soft drugs and pornography, and with an ever-increasing number of young people living together.

Democracy, however, has spawned *desencanto*, a phenomenon which first appeared in the late 1970s as a result of the UCD government's failure to grapple with the problems of terrorism, unemployment and inflation. By 1980, the slogan *'Con Franco vivíamos mejor'* (Life was better for us under Franco) had become commonplace among the middle-classes. This creeping disenchantment is now evident in the growth of abstentionism (the 1989 level showed a 10 per cent increase over that of 1982) and in the appeal of less orthodox parties to the electorate. The rise of José María Ruiz-Mateos was a good case in point. To quote one former socialist voter who was president of the Fuenlabrada association of rape-seed oil victims: 'we voted for Ruiz-Mateos because we do not have a government that represents us. What we need are strong fighters who belong neither to the left nor the right' (*Cambio 16*, 3 July 1989). If this crisis of confid·nce in the present political system becomes more widespread, if a Socialist government persists with the kind of Thatcherite policies which provoked a general strike in December 1988, and if the main right-wing opposition becomes torn again by internal discord, rivalry and vindictiveness, the polarization of political opinion may once again take hold, and in response to a renascent left, the extreme right may re-emerge as an attractive and desirable alternative.

Note

1. The remaining sections of this study of the extreme right in Spain are concentrated on the Fuerza Nueva/Frente Nacional movement which, unlike the Falange, has not yet been the subject of individual investigation. For a reasonably full, if not totally accurate list of the main extreme right groups, past and present, operating in Spain, see Ciarán Ó Maoláin *The Radical Right: a World Directory*, 1987, Longman, London, pp. 249–61. Also, I have chosen not to feature any of Spain's neo-Nazi groups such as CEDADE, because they do not really form part of Spain's own political traditions and are extremely marginalized.

References

Blinkhorn, M., 1988. *Democracy and Civil War in Spain 1931–1939*, Routledge, London.
Ellwood, S.M., 1987. *Spanish Fascism in the Franco Era: Falange Española de las JONS 1936–1976*, Macmillan, London.
Frente Nacional, 1987 *La alternativa nacional (soluciones para España)* Fuerza Nueva, Madrid.
Gilmour, D., 1985. *The Transformation of Spain*, Quartet Books, London.
Kohler, B., 1982. *Political Forces in Spain, Greece and Portugal*, Butterworth, London.

Medhurst K., 1982. Spanish conservative politics, in Z. Layton Henry (ed.), *Conservative Politics in Western Europe*, Macmillan, London.

Ó Maoláin, C., *The Radical Right: A World Directory*, 1987, Longman, London.

Oneto, J., 1975. *Arias entre dos crisis 1973–1975*, Información y Publicaciones, Madrid.

Pastor, M., 1975. *Los orígenes del fascismo en España*, Tucar, Madrid.

Payne, S., 1984. *El catolicismo español*, Planeta, Barcelona.

——, 1987. *The Franco Regime 1936–1975*, University of Wisconsin, Wisconsin.

Preston, P., 1986. *The Triumph of Democracy in Spain*, Methuen, London.

Quien es quien en las Cortes Generales 1979, 1980, DEC, Madrid.

Rodríguez Robles, I., 1981. *Nuestra razón: España*, Valladolid.

Share, D., 1986. *The Making of Spanish Democracy*, Praeger, New York.

Terrón Montero, J., 1981. *La prensa en España durante el régime de Franco*, CIS, Madrid.

Wilkinson, P., 1981. *The New Fascists*, Grant McIntyre, London.

Cambio 16,	29 October 1984
	28 November 1988
	3 July 1989
	26 November 1990
Fuerza Nueva,	31 October–7 November 1981
	23–30 January 1982
	27 February–6 March 1982
	6–13 March 1982
	17–24 April 1982
	8–15 May 1982
	15–22 May 1982
	10–17 July 1982
	18–25 September 1982
	26 April–10 May 1986
	7–21 June 1986
	27 September–1 October 1986
	6–20 December 1986
	7–21 November 1987
	5–19 December 1987
	23 January–6 February 1988
	5–19 March 1988
	16–30 April 1988
	11–25 June 1988
	9–23 July 1988
	23 July–6 August 1988
El País,	22 May 1989
	13 October 1991
	14 November 1991
	16 November 1991
	18 November 1991
El País Semanal,	3 October 1985
La Vanguardia,	6 May 1986
	23 November 1987
Tiempo,	23 September 1991
The Times,	11 July 1967
	26 November 1978

10 Portugal: The Marginalization of the Extreme Right

Tom Gallagher

First appearances suggest that the capacity of the ultra-right to mobilize in Portugal ought to be much higher than it actually is. In European terms the onset of democracy has been a very recent occurrence and pluralist politics are thus far from being a norm for most citizens. Not until 1987 was any single party in Portugal able to form a stable majority government, the preceding eleven years having witnessed five general elections and ten changes of government, proof for many that the democratic system was malfunctioning and facing an uncertain long-term future. By the mid-1980s living standards for large sections of the urban population had fallen to levels below those experienced during the closing stages of the preceding authoritarian era, a development hardly designed to engender much loyalty to the democratic system among ordinary Portuguese in whose name the cause of democracy was frequently invoked.

There were moments after 1976 when the shortcomings of the new democracy looked in danger of eclipsing baleful memories of the dictatorship in the eyes of many Portuguese who, in various opinion polls, expressed nostalgia for the rising living standards that characterized part of the premiership of Marcelo Caetano from 1968 to 1974. Dr António de Oliveira Salazar, Caetano's austere predecessor and the architect of the undemocratic New State, under which Portugal was to be ruled from 1933 till 1974, hardly inspired affection at least for those reasons. The fiscal rectitude which became the New State's chief symbol was achieved by imposing enormous privations on lower-income Portuguese while turning a blind eye to the dubious means whereby an oligarchy at the apex of the Portuguese social system was able to enrich itself over many decades.

However, at least Salazar's personal reputation stood the test of time better than Hitler's or Mussolini's. The ending of censorship in 1974, and the accompanying flood of publications about 'the dark night of fascism', did not reveal information that further tarnished his image. It remained a paradox that a regime distinguished by brutal policies in Africa, a super-efficient secret police at home, and a cold disregard for the fate of the illiterate, impoverished masses was controlled not by a cynical or fanatical adventurer, but by a learned civilian, contemptuous of personal wealth, whose quiet and respectable lifestyle as a patriotic Christian gentleman had won him the respect of many post-war European politicians. It was unusual for a Portuguese politician of any era to enjoy such a high standing abroad and certainly very few from the democratic era have achieved equivalent recognition. So, however dark his political and economic record, Salazar was a personal symbol which the ultra-right was able to press into service on its behalf.

Outwardly, neo-fascists stood to gain from the extent to which two generations of Portuguese were indoctrinated in the schoolroom, from the pulpit, and through the media by conservative propaganda which stressed the values of 'God, Nation and Authority'. Other more liberating influences could not be excluded, especially when the mass emigration of Portuguese workers to the EC countries got underway in the 1960s: thus the system fell a long way short of being one of full totalitarian control. Nevertheless, Portugal's geographical isolation, the existence of a neighbouring like-minded regime in Spain, and Salazar's ability to preserve Portuguese neutrality in the Second World War (upon which much of his surviving reputation rests), all helped to shield the country from modernizing trends that could have undermined Portugal's tenaciously backward-looking leader. At least during his own lifetime, the political system he created was very much in his own image – traditionalist, paternalistic, and conservative – the main aim being to minimize change and maximize stability by using the police-state methods of the twentieth century to keep alive an essentially nineteenth-century social order.

Salazar's longevity in power and his impact upon the Portuguese meant that, potentially, he was a powerful symbol available for co-option by neo-fascist bodies seeking to invoke, if not a heroic past, then certainly a more achieving past able to stand comparison with the shabby realities of Portuguese democracy.

However, one has to look hard for signs of neo-fascist strength in democratic Portugal, and Salazar is a curiously understated figure in current ultra-right propaganda. The reasons for neo-fascist weakness in Portugal (despite circumstances of objective promise), and the often equivocal role of Salazar in neo-fascist ideology are not unconnected. It is possible to argue that at the outset of his marathon premiership, Salazar took steps which fatally weakened the prospects of a vigorous movement emerging to defend the principles of the regime and to keep alive its appeal, either in the absence of its founder or following its own dissolution. Thus the gravedigger of the populist neo-fascism of the kind able to engineer electoral breakthroughs in France or West Germany was the architect of the authoritarian era no less, rather than the forces of democracy or of the revolution which had briefly triumphed in 1974–5.

The initial years of the dictatorship following the overthrow by a military coup of the parliamentary republic in 1926 were marked by confusion and deep uncertainty about what kind of political future lay in store for Portugal. It was only as the military regime became gradually consolidated under Dr Salazar at the end of the 1920s that the possibility of a return to open and semi-competitive politics disappeared. Salazar's goal, according to a 1934 speech, was to create 'a government without politics', a prospect that was as perhaps as uninviting to the radical right which had formed in reaction to the unstable republican regime and which had been reinforced by the triumph of Hitler in Germany, as it was to liberals, republicans and leftists being forced into clandestinity (Mónica, 1978, p. 88).

It is worth remembering that Salazar enjoyed no monopoly of affection or support on the ascendant right, and indeed was confonted with a number of rivals who felt that their claims to lead the 'national revolution' were much stronger than his. He had not commanded any movement or been at the forefront of any struggle during the chaotic republican days. Instead he had emerged from the shadows as an uncharismatic professor with a quavering public-speaking voice whose financial know-how had stabilized the military dictatorship and enabled the army to be coaxed to the political sidelines with its honour intact. Guile and statecraft of a high order, as well as technical competence, enabled Salazar to consolidate the 1926 revolution along his own authoritarian but conservative lines. Although outwardly the New State imported many of the other trappings of fascist states, essential characteristics such as the deification of the leader, the cult of violence, high levels of political mobilization and the predominant role of the party did not figure in Salazar's scheme of things. Some radical right-wingers, inspired by more exciting foreign models, had managed to swallow their disappointment and went on to exercise high political office, though others did not. In 1933–4 Salazar was confronted by a rival right-wing movement, the Blueshirts or National Syndicalists, and a more flamboyant alternative leader of the right in Dr Francisco Rolão Preto, who mobilized quite a large following in urban middle-class and student circles until a government crack-down occurred in 1934.

Many of Preto's younger supporters, with a living to make, took up posts in Salazar's busy propaganda machine or in such spheres as the government daily newspaper, *Diário de Manhã*, which enabled them to propagate their ideas, though in something of a vacuum. However, Preto remained irreconcilable and, along with other leading radicals of the right, Henrique Galvão and Humberto Delgado, he eventually crossed over to the opposition; the latter pair, both military officers, would actually provide the most daring challenges of any to the New State, when Delgado stormed the country in controlled presidential elections during 1958, which were the regime's principal concession to liberal democracy, and in 1961 when Galvão hijacked a Portuguese ocean-liner.

Thus Salazar was an object of distrust or disappointment for many of those Portuguese who derived their political inspiration from the triumph of fascism in inter-war Europe and for whom the New State was a pale substitute when compared with the excitement generated in Berlin or Rome by more purposeful dictators. The embargo on politics and the deliberately staid nature of the National Union (UN), the only political movement tolerated, meant that the post-1914 counter-revolutionary generation was not replenished in any meaningful way. Uniformed bodies like the Portuguese Legion and the Mocidade (a youth movement for which membership was theoretically compulsory for all adolescents), absorbed the energies of the diminishing numbers attracted by fascist paraphenalia. However, they did not exercise any power and steadily degenerated until in 1974 they were, along with the UN, swept away without trace.

Portugal's decision to resist the winds of change in Africa and to take up arms in 1961 to retain direct control of its colonial possessions was the Portuguese regime's equivalent of the 1941 Nazi invasion of the Soviet Union in terms of the disaster it was to bring upon the New State. For some years it gave the most reactionary and nationalist sectors of the regime a little more visibility than before. A high-risk strategy which placed Portugal at variance with its Western backers led to an outpouring of nationalist propaganda and gave rise to many ephemeral fascist groups with names like the National Revolutionary Front, Portuguese Youth, and the Vanguardist Movement. The political calm of the preceding decades, which had not been conducive to even ephemeral political mobilizations, gave way to a sense of uncertainty and impending crisis as the costly African wars dragged on and the ageing Salazar made no provision for a successor. In 1968, the extreme right had no convincing candidate of its own to thrust into the vacant chair, and under the professorial Marcelo Caetano the New State became rudderless as disagreements about the African wars turned even firm loyalists like General António de Spínola into advocates of disengagement.

The regime toppled like a house of cards when junior officers organized a coup on 25 April 1974. The far right proved unequal to the task of even mounting a rearguard defence. Perhaps only the prospect of communist-inspired insurgency or a perceived sell-out of the empire by Caetano could have mobilized the *ultras* and made the prospect of resistance to the 1974 coup likelier. However, Portugal was one of the few southern European countries to avoid significant outbreaks of terrorism both then and later, even though it was about to embark on a momentous nineteen months of revolution that would sweep away many, if not all, of the traces of the old order.

The ecstatic response that the coup-makers received from virtually the entire country, at least in the main populated areas was a dispiriting prospect for arch-conservatives contemplating the rebuilding of their shattered cause. Nevertheless, some of the first parties to be formed in the wake of the dictatorship's collapse were those of the ultra-right: the Liberal Party, the Progress Party, and the Portuguese Nationalist Party, the last dedicated to 'renewing the struggle interrupted by April 25' (*Sunday Times* Insight Team, 1975, p. 165). Many *ultras* were disorientated by the manner in which their political universe had collapsed and been replaced with a radical dystopia with communists in government, the civil and military apparatus being purged of anyone with right-wing loyalties, and decolonization just around the corner.

Blame was not easily apportioned for the New State's collapse and General Spínola, with his impeccable right-wing credentials was a contentious figure who divided the far right. The publication of his book, *Portugal and the Future*, calling for a negotiated African settlement, had brought to a head the pressures that had resulted in the collapse of the regime and Spínola was left with enough prestige to become provisional president and head of the ruling junta. However, his efforts to create a Gaullist-style presidential democracy and delay Portugal's African withdrawal left him increasingly isolated and his October 1974 appeal for help from 'the silent majority' evoked a much more lukewarm response for him than it would for others less than a year later. Spínola stepped down as president, and by March 1975 was on the run following the failure of a counter-coup which threw the political initiative firmly into the hands of the political left. By now, the ephemeral right-wing parties had been outlawed, many right-wing figures were in gaol or exile, and manifestly non-socialist parties like the Centre Social Democrats (CDS) only with difficulty preserved their legal status. Even more importantly, the authorities approved wholesale take-overs of Portuguese banks, insurance companies and most of the largest firms. Thus the revolution became a social as well as a political upheaval. Dissenting views were out of the question since with the banks owning or holding mortgages on most Portuguese newspapers, most of the print media passed into state hands.

Amid the revolutionary fervour, it was only with difficulty that elections for a constituent assembly were permitted to go ahead on 25 April 1975. The Socialist Party (PS) and the Popular Democratic Party (PPD), two pluralist parties then espousing radical and moderate brands of socialism respectively, obtained nearly two-thirds of the votes cast in a turnout which exceeded 90 per cent of the electorate. Those sections of the population, especially in the smallholding and Catholic north, who were alarmed by the drift towards what seemed to be a Marxist collective state, now discerned that their fears were widely shared, a discovery which encouraged the idea of resisting the new order in Lisbon.

Inhibitions in defying central government, which had been reinforced by nearly fifty years of strict political orthodoxy, vanished as thousands of small rural capitalists and clergymen became convinced of the imminence of a second Bolshevik revolution in their part of Europe likely to sweep them to their doom. In July and August 1975, serious rioting broke out in northern and central Portugal, directed against the homes, offices and cars of Communist Party (PCP) militants. Two underground movements, the Portuguese Liberation Army (ELP) founded by Spínola, and the Democratic Movement for the Liberation of Portugal (MDLP) were seen to be behind the wave of unrest (Paradela de Abreu, pp. 114–38). However, much of it may have been quite spontaneous, especially in prosperous areas with large properties where the threat of land seizures (which in the south would mean that a large area of Portugal's farm land would be converted into state co-operatives) seemed very real.

The owners of small and medium-sized properties who had shed their political inhibitions and taken to the streets in the summer of 1975 had proved to be more formidable opponents of the Lisbon radical left than the great industrialists and landowners. The emergency threw up a powerful rural lobby in the form of the Confederation of Portuguese Farmers (CAP) which, in November 1975, was threatening to cut Lisbon off from the rest of the country by blocking roads and discontinuing food, water and electricity supplies. A vigorous provincial reaction, whose origins lay in the emergency conditions of 1974–5, rather than the toppled authoritarian system, managed to unnerve the pro-communist authorities, and by the autumn of 1975 effective power had fallen into the hands of less doctrinaire leftist officers and their civilian backers. Although ultra-leftist feeling was still sweeping the lower strata of the army, by November 1975 the revolutionaries had been outmanœuvred and Portugal emerged dazed and shaken from its revolution.

A counter-revolution or right-wing backlash anticipated by many foreign observers did not subsequently materialize. The leadership of the anti-communist campaign had actually been assumed by Mário Soares, the PS leader who had played a more visible role in preventing democratic liberties from being extinguished than had anyone else in the more conservative parties allowed to function. Soares pursued a policy of national reconciliation in order to dampen down feelings, and during his first premiership he authorized the return from exile of General Spínola whose plotting was set aside and to whom state honours were granted. At the first parliamentary election in April 1976, the PS emerged as the largest party though without an overall majority. A particularly strong showing was made by the CDS, which had refused to endorse a new constitution that enshrined many of the gains of the revolution, and whose vote went up from 7.6 to 15.9 per cent. This party of Catholic squirearchy and high intellectuals had stuck to a moderate path during the revolution and had avoided being driven underground, a course which might have radicalized it. The ELP and MDLP, which had seemed so threatening as communist offices burned down in 1975, faded from the scene as a form of normality was restored, while the CAP lost its radical fervour and became simply another pressure group lobbying in the Lisbon ministries.

Although intensely bitter feelings were harboured by those who had lost liberty or property during the revolution, the sheer exhaustion felt by perhaps most who emerged from this chaotic, nerve-racking process prevented deep-seated polarization occurring. Extreme right-wingers whose lineage could be traced back to the former regime were scattered, lacking funds, or only just emerging from imprisonment. The northern crowds who had taken to the streets in 1975 were not sufficiently politicized to wish to be the vanguard of a far right movement and, for most, the sense of urgency that prompted them to act with such uncharacteristic boldness ended with the eclipse of the communists and their military and civilian allies. A measure of the uneasy peace which reigned in Portugal during 1976–7, as the revolutionary interlude gave way to the first constitutional government (a minority socialist administration under Dr Soares), was the failure of the far right Christian Democratic Party (PDC) to gain more than 0.5 per cent of the vote in the April 1976 elections.

However, opportunities for the far right to expand its credibility would emerge in the initial phase of the fledgling democracy's existence up to the next general election held at the end of 1979. During that period none of the democratic parties' behaviour inspired much public confidence at a time when the PCP, although on the sidelines, remained a force to be taken into account, with a power-base among the state co-operative farms in the south and considerable influence in several Lisbon ministries. The spirit of co-operation that had existed among the non-communist parties during the revolution evaporated as electoral competition got under way in 1976. Despite the grave economic problems resulting from decolonization, revolutionary upheaval and the long-term miscalculations of the Salazar–Caetano era, Dr Soares preferred to govern alone rather than in coalition with the PPD which, by the end of 1976, had changed its name to the Social Democratic Party (PSD) and had begun to define itself clearly as belonging to the centre-right. Suspicions that the PS decision was influenced by the desire to reward supporters with positions in the state administration were strengthened by a serious of corruption scandals. When the Minister of Industry had to resign in 1976, as a result of his son's involvement in a bank robbery, it drew attention to the rising crime rate which was one of the chief weapons that the ultra-right employed to condemn the new political order.

The first tangible sign of far right mobilization was the appearance in 1976 of two weekly newspapers which managed to attract enough readers to stay in business. *A Rua* [The Street], edited by Manuel Maria Múrias, whose father had edited the chief Salazarist daily, openly harked back to the old order and was linked with the Nationalist Movement (MN) which during the late 1970s, attracted attention by organizing provocative counter-commemorations on 10 June, Portugal's national day. Although *A Rua* carried advertisements for Portugal's leading travel agency, a better produced and less nostalgic weekly called *O Diabo* [The Devil], soon overshadowed it. *O Diabo*'s larger circulation attracted more advertising and has kept it afloat to the present day, unlike *A Rua* which folded in 1980. *O Diabo* is virulently anti-communist, written in an irreverent hard-hitting style, and has gathered a loyal following beyond the extreme right because of its disclosures about (and lampooning of) members of the political élite.

Vera Lagoa, *O Diabo*'s editor and proprietor, mobilized tens of thousands of people in December 1977 in a protest staged in the second city of Oporto against the decision of the authorities to commemorate the anniversary of the Russian Revolution. Much of the crowd was made up of former white colonials, an estimated 700,000 of whom had fled from Angola and Mozambique prior to the establishment of Marxist regimes in 1975–6. Their presence was viewed with apprehension by politicians in a traditionally francophile land who were well aware of the instability caused after 1962 by the *colons* fleeing from Algeria to France where the ratio of colonial refugees to members of the settled community was six times *less* than in the Portugal of the late 1970s. The Portuguese *retornados* appeared to some as a rootless, combustible force of the kind that had provided the footsoldiers for the radical fascism of inter-war Europe. *Time* magazine even profiled Vera Lagoa after she had led another well-attended demonstration on 1 December 1977, the day commemorating Portugal's independence from Spain (*Time*, 21 December 1977). It coincided with the defeat in parliament of the first constitutional government after Soares had approached the International Monetary Fund (IMF) for a loan to offset Portugal's economic difficulties. An unlikely coalition between the Socialists and the right-wing CDS then held office for six months until mounting uproar on the right about such apostasy led to its collapse. Portugal was then ruled by a series of non-party caretaker governments until fresh elections could be held in December 1979.

A tense, disgruntled atmosphere hung over Portugal as the democratic system failed to live up to its early promise and as the costs of the economic slump began to be borne by sections of the middle class as well as the working class. National commemorative events were marred by ugly violence in 1977 and 1978. In February 1978, Santa Comba Dão, Salazar's birthplace, was the scene of rioting in which shots were fired as attempts were made to replace a damaged head on a statue of the town's most famous son; and weeks later *retornados* roughed up the Deputy Prime Minister (*The Times*, 6 February and 16 April 1978).

During the preceding two years, dozens of bombs had exploded mainly in Lisbon, though none causing serious damage or injury. To some minds, this was part of a strategy of tension designed to engineer a right-wing intervention from the army on the pretext of restoring order. Contrasting figures such as Dr Soares and Otelo de Carvalho, the populist officer who masterminded the 1974 revolution, agreed that the possibility of a Chilean-style right-wing coup existed in 1977–8 (*El País*, 2 July 1989). Books critical of the manner in which Portugal quit Africa became bestsellers along with sympathetic portraits of Salazar or nostalgic accounts of his political era. Lampooning assaults on socialist functionaries led to their perpetrators being prosecuted and receiving prison sentences.

Perhaps most disconcerting of all was the sharp swing to the right among the nation's youth not merely in traditionally conservative areas or the comfortable suburbs of Portugal's major cities. The education system had been badly disrupted during the revolution and it was to be many years before normality could be restored. Against this background, a wave of pro-Salazar propaganda swept though a number of schools, especially in Oporto where one grammar school had to be closed for a week in 1978 after pupils staged a violent demonstration using the fascist salute (*The Times*, 6 February 1978; *Diário de Lisbõa*, 28 March 1977; *Expresso*, 22 December 1978). On occasions, an openly neo-Nazi list of candidates *were* able to perform well in elections to student councils (*Le Monde*, 28 April 1978). The report conveying this news mentioned that an alarmed Socialist Party had appointed its national secretary to mount a task-force against the 'veritable counter-revolution' sweeping the press, the schools and the church. The person concerned was a poet noted for his sense of the dramatic; nevertheless, legislation was introduced in the same year outlawing the promotion of fascism or violence against national institutions, with heavy prison sentences for those infringing the law.

A party of the far right with a distinct national profile took shape only in June 1977 when General Kaúlza de Arriaga launched the Independent Movement of National Reconstruction (MIRN). Its appearance coincided with a crisis for the parties of the constitutional right with the CDS shortly to be assailed for having kept the PS in office and the PSD locked in factional struggles. Kaúlza, a former Commander-in-Chief of the army in colonial

Mozambique, had won publicity when he and other members of the pre-1974 military élite published a book in 1976, which argued somewhat disingenuously that Portugal had been on course for victory in Africa before the 1974 coup by unpatriotic officers in league with foreign communist subversion (*The Guardian*, 4 September 1976). This charge had little impact since the thirteen-year war had been unpopular with most Portuguese, an unmilitary people who showed little interest in the war veterans' associations which are often to be found in countries which fight a war as long and as gruelling as that from which they had emerged. The declared aim of MIRN (renamed the Party of the Portuguese Right (PDP) in October 1978) was to 'bring about a convergence of all the non-marxist forces . . . and . . . to see the replacement of incompetent ministers with statesmen'. In addition the party called for a strong presidential democracy rather than outright dictatorship, Kaulza adding the proviso that 'it may well be that democracy will be abandoned . . . if statesmen do not emerge' (Pimlott, 1978).

However unimpressive party politicians were in the first years of the new democracy, the country was fortunate to possess a respected president in General Ramalho Eanes who, at that stage, did not identify with any specific party and earned considerable respect across the political spectrum for his dignified and ascetic manner. Since he had played a crucial role in ending the anarchy of the revolutionary times while still maintaining good lines of communication with mainstream leftist officers, calls for a 'Gaullist' type solution from Kaúlza did not carry much weight (although the latter managed to gain an audience with the French President Giscard d'Estaing, shortly before the launch of his party) (*The Guardian*, 4 September 1976).

If a window of opportunity had ever existed in electoral terms for the ultra-right, it effectively vanished when mainstream conservatives in the PSD and CDS decided to form an electoral pact in order to extract maximum advantage from the d'Hondt form of PR which favours multiple alliances rather than single parties. The formation, in 1979, of the Democratic Alliance ended a long bout of infighting for its largest component, the PSD, which had emerged as a coherent party under its founder, Dr Sá Carneiro, whose confrontational style of politics enabled him to appeal successfully to his party's conservative rank and file over the heads of less charismatic colleagues. Interestingly, there was never any question of the MIRN–PDP joining the AD even though the alliance needed every spare vote in its bid to defeat the left, as was shown by the inclusion of the small monarchist party (PPM). The 'right' still remained a discredited term in Portuguese politics even though that was the direction in which the country was gradually swinging. It is no coincidence that to those uninitiated in the ways of Portuguese politics, the names of the two leading parties in the AD suggest that they were parties which did not belong to the right at all (*Expresso*, 16 September 1983).

The AD proved a magnet for the alienated politically aware who might, in other circumstances, have provided a modest lift-off for the MIRN–PDP. It was able to appeal to the bulk of the *retornados* whom Kaúlza had courted with stirring assertions that the former colonies could be regained by Portugal and their white inhabitants allowed to return in order to resume their lives. However, the bulk of *retornados* had integrated surprisingly well into Portuguese life by the end of the 1970s, finding a niche in the black economy which flourished, thanks to constraints which the socialist constitution imposed on private business. Before when living in Africa, they had not possessed a tradition of political activism even though holding major grievances against Lisbon and, unlike the Algerian *colons*, they had not rebelled when the mother country announced its withdrawal from Africa.

Besides, many of the *retornados* were blacks or mulattos who had identified with the colonial rulers and this made it difficult for any extreme right-wing group to use racial animosity as a political weapon. Colonialist propaganda had always stressed Portugal as being a multiracial and pluricontinental entity, and it would have been straining credibility to offer hostility to the large black community in a country where violent racial prejudice has been notably absent.

In the 1980 general election which confirmed the AD in office, the MIRN–PDP received a derisory vote, having put forward candidates in most constituencies in conjunction with the PDC. This election revealed that the far right possessed no geographical power-base since the north rallied behind the AD and even the communists did far better – in what was clearly hostile territory – than Kaúlza's party. Although the presidential election held in December 1980 included two maverick right-wing generals, Pyres Veloso and Galvão de Melo, they cancelled each other out and made no impression on the result. Eanes, supported by the left, and the AD candidate received well over 90 per cent of the vote, victory going to Eanes as a stunned nation opted for safety first following the death in an aircrash of Premier Sá Carneiro (in circumstances still to be satisfactorily explained) two days before the contest.

Thereafter, politics became less confrontational as Sá Carneiro's successor stepped back from the showdown that the former had promised unless the socialist constitution was revised. The dropping of the political temperature proved frustrating for the far right as one event after another reduced its potential to intervene in the political arena during the 1980s. Gradually, the PS abandoned its remaining commitment to Marxism and was able to form a coalition with the PSD which lasted from 1983 to 1985. A successful revision of the constitution in 1982 removed the Marxist-sounding clauses against which *O Diabo* had railed for years. Ministers from the Salazar–Caetano era were able to engineer comebacks not on the political fringes but as respected figures in all of the non-communist parties, Caetano's Education Minister joining the PS and serving in the government, and a Minister of the Colonies under Salazar actually leading the CDS from 1984 to 1987. These developments were signs that notwithstanding a forty-eight year dictatorship and a revolution that had occurred within the lifetime of most Portuguese, ideological boundaries were becoming remarkably fluid and past political controversies raised passions only among restricted circles of people.

By the second decade of democracy, politics increasingly resembled a battle for state protection among different interest groups, a persistent feature of political life irrespective of the type of regime holding office. Privatization of the vast holdings acquired by the state in 1975 was finally made possible by a second revision of the constitution in 1989, although this was not owing to the rise of neo-liberal sentiments which remain weakly implanted in a country where the mainstream right (notwithstanding rhetoric about the centrality of the market) remains more comfortable operating in tandem with a powerful and protected state bureaucracy.

The overweening desire of most political forces to capture the state for their own ends, rather than to implement any national project or set of goals in a disinterested way holds out dangers for the political system if the accompanying tendency towards wholesale graft and corruption is not checked. In the army are to be found ultra-conservative senior officers who avoided being purged in 1974 because of their lowly rank and who are mindful of the tradition which caused the military to intervene in the past when the nation's finances had been mishandled by civilian politicians. However, after a decade of disappointment and uncertainty, the political system seemed to have stabilized in 1985 following the election of a minority PSD government which, benefiting from the austerity measures of its predecessor, gained an outright majority at the polls in 1987. Hitherto, the accepted wisdom had been that an overall majority for any one party was an impossibility, given the number of parties competing under a system of proportional representation. Nevertheless, a yearning for stability among Portuguese weary of short-term governments enabled PSD leader, Anibal Cavaco de Silva, to achieve just over 50 per cent of the vote. This austere technocrat from a humble background was particularly popular among young people from a wide variety of social classes, especially middle-class youth who in the late 1970s had identified with the extreme right.

Caetano's dream of a monolithic party of the civilized right, able to banish feverish politicking yet respecting certain basic liberties, seems to have been realized as the inflow of EC subsidies for the new member state and the virtual disappearance of unemployment created a sense of well-being in the Portugal of the late 1980s. That is a boon for any governing politician. It was cold comfort, however, for the extreme right to find opportunities for advancement so comprehensively blocked off by the constitutional right. In fact, little was heard after 1980 of the MIRN–PDP which surfaced only periodically at election time when it received a meagre handful of votes. For anybody wishing to chronicle the activities of the far right, the 1980s proved to be a difficult time for its constitutional part largely disappeared from view.

One new organization which briefly achieved publicity was 'New Order' (ON), a neo-Nazi 'pressure-group' founded in 1980. Its militants were mainly in the younger age-group and it attracted attention when, early on, it engaged in street battles and mounted an unsuccessful attack on the offices of the Freemasons as a new Grand Master was being elected. After the authorities had asked it to bring its statutes into line with the constitutional law prohibiting fascist organizations, New Order passed into clandestinity in 1982, a spokesman declaring: 'we have finished with folklorism, we want to be more selective and operational in times to come' (*Expresso*, 5 February 1983). Although ON is known to enjoy contacts with youth-orientated neo-Nazi associations elsewhere in Europe, its promise to be 'operational' has yet to be fulfilled, at least on home soil.

In the early 1980s ON sent sixty delegates to Madrid to take part in the commemoration of Franco's death. Albeit in better shape, the Spanish far right does not reinforce its Portuguese counterpart. In the past, the main threat to Portuguese national integrity has emanated from Spain which occupied the country for sixty years (1580–1640), and it is the right in Portugal which has tended to be most suspicious of Castilian expansionism. Blas Piñar, the leader of the National Front in Spain, has been a regular attender in Lisbon of an annual banquet to commemorate the revolution of 28 May 1926. However, the Portuguese are unable to lay on anything remotely comparable to the public mobilization which, in Spain, the far right organized on the fiftieth anniversary of the July 1936 military uprising. The relatively bland origins of the New State when compared with the life or death struggle from which Francoist Spain emerged triumphant, mean that there is none of the powerful symbolism upon which the Spanish ultra-right can still draw. In April 1989, the centenary of Salazar's birth was marked by some desultory commemorations among those who revered his memory. However, the media had shown no apprehension about the event being turned into a vehicle for far right propaganda, and the occasion was treated as an opportunity to reassess a figure who seemed as securely part of the vanished past as other commanding Portuguese figures like Henry the Navigator or Pombal.

Conclusion

In order to appreciate why the Portuguese far right is possibly in a weaker state than in any other southern European country, the specific nature of the marathon dictatorship that held Portugal in its grip from 1926 till 1974 needs to be clearly borne in mind. Salazar had rapidly decided that the long-term prospects of his traditional political order, one dedicated to 'government without politics', depended on muzzling a large part of the far right as well as Portugal's democratic forces. Radical right-wingers, keen to promote a populist version of authoritarianism which could put down roots in national life, were suppressed. At no time did they have a chance of playing a directing role in the life of the regime, so that the counter-revolutionary generation which had been on hand when democratic politics was extinguished in the 1920s, had virtually disappeared when conditions made possible the restoration of democracy after 1974.

It was not just the long embargo on politics which left the far right too enfeebled to compete in electoral contests. The autocratic and mean-spirited character of the Salazar regime had succeeded in alienating nearly all sectors of Portuguese opinion, including elements which otherwise might have been quite conservative in outlook. When the miscalculations of the radical officers in charge of Portugal in 1974–5 produced a backlash among small northern property-owners, it soon became clear that these protesting crowds were not sufficiently politicized to wish to be the vanguard of a renewed far right movement. With the eclipse of the communists and the restoration of democracy, the sense of urgency that had spurred them into action rapidly disappeared as did their counter-revolutionary potential.

Since the revolution resulted in remarkably little loss of life, the far right was unable to exploit martyrs who could have enabled it to build an emotive base among the discontented. The continuing importance of the family in Portuguese society enabled the shockwaves of the revolution to be absorbed quite easily. No backwash of terrorism or lawlessness occurred which political elements favouring the order and discipline of the toppled regime could exploit.

The electorate's preference for moderate political options that could guarantee a period of calm was shown by the strength of the constitutional right. Owing to factional infighting and opportunist tactics, its record, especially in the second half of the 1970s, was open to criticism, though at no point did it ever seem likely that the far right would forge ahead at its expense. In the aforementioned tense, disgruntled atmosphere of the late 1970s, as the democratic system failed to match its early promise, the far right enjoyed some low-level successes in high school elections and in the print media. However, the talented leaders, the organizing skills, and the infrastructure which could have enabled it to carve out even a modest power-base among discontented Portuguese in the revolutionary aftermath were lacking. Its incapacity was revealed by its failure to turn the 700,000 often destitute refugees from Africa into footsoldiers for *revanchiste* right-wing politics as has happened in France with the *colons*. They integrated surprisingly well into Portuguese life, and by the 1980s, the political temperature was dropping fast as the democratic right came to dominate political life.

The story of the far right in contemporary Portugal is not even one of missed opportunities or political 'what might have beens'. After 1974, those disorientated and backward-looking groups on the far right never looked in much danger of emerging from a shadowy political existence. The anti-immigration hysteria which has revived the far Right in France, Austria and elsewhere, has passed Portugal by, despite the presence of a large black or mixed race population. Five years of record economic growth rates have produced political calm, and introspection about the convulsions experienced by the country after years of dictatorship, has given way to a general desire to partake in material prosperity. These boom conditions may only prove to be shortlived because of the speculative nature of much of Portugal's recent growth and attendant corruption, but it is unlikely that the far Right will be a prime beneficiary even if Portugal returns to the days of unstable governments and frequent trips to the ballot box. If, in the future, the extreme right makes a comeback, it is more likely to be as a result of a change of mood in corporate interest groups like the army or the civilian bureaucracy than because of an upturn in the electoral fortunes of phantom parties and groups that even Portuguese of a conservative disposition now regard as irrelevant.

References

Owing to the absence of reliable monographs on the Portuguese far right since the 1974 revolution, much of the material for this chapter has been gathered from press sources, in particular the Lisbon political weeklies, *Expresso* and *O Jornal*, the daily press, mainly the *Diário de Lisbôa* and the *Diário de Notícias* as well as the right-wing weekly *O Diabo*. Foreign press sources ranging from *Time* magazine, to *El País* in Spain and *Le Monde* in France have also been utilized, along with *The Times* and *The Guardian* in Britain.

de Abreu, Paradela, n.d. *Do 25 De Abril Ao 25 de Novembro*, Intervenção, Lisbon.
de Arriaga, Kaúlza de, 1988. *Guerra e Política (Em Nome de Verdade – Os Anos Decisivos*, Edições Referendos, Lisbon.
Espada, João Carlos, 1983. 'Onde está e o que é a direita portuguesa', *Expresso*, 16 July.
Fafe, José Paulo, 1983. 'Do Jovem Portugal á Ordem Nova', *Expresso*, 5 February.
Fidalgo, Joaquim, 1988. *Expresso*, 10 June.
Gallagher, Tom, 1983. 'From hegemony to opposition: the ultra right before and after 1974', in L. S. Graham and D. Wheeler (eds) *In Search of Portugal*, University of Wisconsin Press, Madison.
Mónica, Maria Filomena, 1978. *Educação e sociedade no Portugal de Salazar*, GIS, Lisbon.
Pimlott, Ben, 1978. 'Right turn in Portugal', *Spectator*, 28 January.
Sunday Times Insight Team, 1975. *Portugal: The Year of the Captains*, André Deutsch, London.
Wallraff, Gunther, 1976, *A descoberta de una conspiração*, Livraria Bertrand, Lisbon.

11 Greece: The Virtual Absence of an Extreme Right

Panayote Elias Dimitras

The Extreme Right in Greek Political Culture

Extreme right-wing parties have existed in countries where the various themes and attitudes usually associated with such parties are rejected by the majority of the population and, at least formally and officially, by other parties, including those of the mainstream right-wing. When some of these themes (discussed below and throughout the book) become salient for small though mobilized sectors of public opinion, extreme right-wing political organizations emerge to channel the discontent of that public and put pressure on the mainstream parties to adapt their programmes to these attitudes and/or use various, often violent, means to impose these views on society in general. In Greece, in contrast, these themes have been shared by large sectors of public opinion and political parties for most of the post-war period, if not until today, for reasons related to the country's history and political culture. As a consequence, extreme right-wing parties *per se* did not exist in the first thirty years after the Second World War, and have played a minor role in more recent years, when a few extreme right-wing themes ceased to be part of the country's mainstream political culture, thus prompting the emergence of such parties.

Historically, most of these beliefs were the backbone of the country's two lasting dictatorial regimes: that of Metaxas (1936–41) and that of Papadopoulos-Ioannidis (1967–74). They had also characterized the ideological belief structure of the Greek military establishment between these regimes. A retired general, John Metaxas had been the leader of a small but militant right-wing party, the Free Opinion Party, in the inter-war period. When the January 1936 elections produced a 'hung' parliament with the communists (Communist Party of Greece – KKE) holding the balance and protracted negotiations to form a government were not fruitful, the king appointed Metaxas as a widely acceptable transitional prime minister, to whom Parliament, before recessing on 30 April, delegated legislative powers until 30 September. On 4 August, however, to prevent a nation-wide general strike that could have allegedly escalated into civil war, the king and Metaxas established a dictatorship, which banned all political parties, of the right, the centre and the left alike. As Keith Legg (1969, p. 189) has written:

> The Metaxas regime, which represented the older, more conservative, and highly professional military elements, attempted to eliminate all politics, Right, Center, and Left. The politicians of the Populist Party [the right-wing party] were formally royalist; this did not prevent their detention and exile. It would be a mistake to characterize the regime as merely super-royalist; rather it was antipolitical.

Metaxas, who enjoyed at least the 'resigned acquiescence' (Clogg, 1986, p. 134) of public opinion, admired the fascist regimes of Italy and Germany (Clogg, 1986, pp. 133–4):

> He shared to the full . . . their hostility towards liberalism, communism, and parliamentary government, and indeed their nationalism, although his nationalism was of the non-aggressive variety. Nor, moreover, was his ideology, such as it was, based on theories of superiority. . . . The most obvious difference between the Metaxas regime and the fascist regimes [was] the lack of any kind of mass party base for his power. . . . In conscious imitation of Hitler's Third Reich he evolved the concept of the Third Hellenic Civilization. The first was the pagan civilization of ancient Greece, the second the Christian civilization of Byzantium. The third, which would be fashioned under his aegis, would combine the virtues of both.

In 1940, however, when the choice had to be made about the country's strategy in the Second World War (1940–4), Metaxas never hesitated: Greece allied itself with its traditional Entente allies against the dictatorships of the Axis.

According to Legg (1969, pp. 191–2), after the Civil War (between the national government and communist guerilla forces) which followed the Second World War,

> The armed forces became a symbol of national unity; they had saved the nation from the barbarians. The new Greek army, created by the fight against the guerrillas, can be compared to armies formed by national liberation movements elsewhere. . . . The basic ideological position of the military, based on postwar experiences, was a hard-line anti-Communism. . . . The Greek military establishment view[ed] itself as a threatened group existing in a society mismanaged by corrupt politicians who [we]re bent only on personal power. From its perspective, the concerns of the parliamentary level seem[ed] trivial or dangerous.

So, after a prolonged political and constitutional crisis (1965–7) was leading the country towards an expected landslide electoral victory of a very radicalized (during the crisis) Centre Union (Clogg, 1986, p. 186),

A group of senior generals, in consultation with the king, had been secretly making contingency plans for the army to intervene if disorder were to follow the widely predicted Center Union victory at the polls. Moreover, unknown to their seniors, a group of relatively junior officers had been making their own plans. . . . On . . . 21 April 1967, they struck, catching the king, the politicians and the senior echelons of the armed forces alike off balance.

As regards the 1967 military coup Legg (1969, p. 233) explained:

It is necessary to repeat that political labels ha[d] little relevance in the Greek context. The coup can best be described as antipolitical. It was supposedly a right-wing government that was overthrown, and the military leaders ha[d] spoken and acted strongly against all the groups involved in parliamentary politics.

Moreover Clogg, (1986, p. 190) adds that:

The Colonels sought to give their regime an ideological base. Like the pre-war dictator General Metaxas, they placed much emphasis on the need to discipline the Greek character. . . . Much emphasis was laid in the regime's propaganda on the notion of 'Helleno–Christian Civilization', that attempts to reconcile the essentially contradictory values of ancient Greece and Christian Byzantium which had long been the ideological catchword of the far right.

In this endeavour, the school and the church were given central roles.

In a sense, military and dictatorship values were not unrepresentative of the mainstream Greek political world in the quarter-century between the two dictatorships. After the Greeks had fought heroically in 1940–1 first against the Italians and then against the Germans, under the leadership of the king and the first dictatorship, they embarrassed their Axis conquerors with a quite successful communist-led resistance (1941–4), only ultimately to involve themselves in the bloodier and longer Greek Civil War (1944–9), the only European battleground of the Cold War era. After the UK and then US-supported nationalist forces won, they continued to outlaw the communists and established a 'disciplined democracy', where many of the values usually associated with the extreme right reigned supreme. The obsessive fear of communist resurgence became the intensely nationalistic foundation of that system, where citizens were segregated even officially and formally through the 'certificates of social beliefs', into 'nationally minded' (εθνικο-΄φρονες) and 'anti-national elements' (αντεθνικά στοιχεία). As late as 1977, when this distinction had officially and practically become outdated, post-war Greece's most prominent politician, Constantine Karamanlis (Prime Minister from 1955 to 1963 and 1974 to 1980, and President of the Republic from 1980 to 1985 and again from 1990 onwards), gave the following very eloquent definition of a 'nationally-minded' citizen, when addressing New

Democracy (ND), now Greece's main right-wing party (*Eleftheros Kosmos*, 1 October 1977):

> Broadly speaking, the nationally-minded are all those who believe in the idea of the Nation – that is in the Fatherland; thus, all Greeks are Nationally-minded, except of course those who believe more in Moscow than in Greece. More narrowly, nationally-minded are all those who never, either indirectly or directly, cooperated with communism: they are indeed the people who make up today New Democracy.

In such a climate, various traditional values usually associated with the extreme right were components of the dominant ideology. The motto 'fatherland, religion, family' was the flag-bearer of conservatism; opposition to almost all social change, modernization and secularization was based on the suspicion that most demands in that direction were a covert communist operation to destabilize the status quo. To those who pointed out that a similar evolution was taking place in other West European societies that were equally anti-communist, Greece's millenary cultural anti-Westernism allowed the conservatives (who governed the country during most of the quarter-century between the Civil War and the collapse of the dictatorship in 1974) to argue that rock-n-roll, mini-skirts, long hair, sexual promiscuity, civil weddings, divorce by consent, and legal abortion were all signs of Western decadence. The Greek Orthodox Christian Church, the carrier of cultural anti-Westernism through the ages, has been both an official state religion and remained profoundly traditional. As such, it has not only avoided any fundamentalist or revivalist movements, but also lost touch with the younger generations. On the other hand, even the socialist and communist left has recently ventured into Orthodoxy's pre-capitalist, anti-Western tradition to seek a convergence with its own anti-capitalist and anti-Western ideology, on which a Greek way to socialism could be built. This 'neo-orthodox' intellectual zest, not devoid of Khomeinist tendencies, was a feature of Greek intellectual life in the early 1980s.

Traditionalist themes usually associated with right-wing extremism have therefore been part and parcel of the country's political culture, and so have most related political themes. Besides anti-communism, support for the monarchy had been widespread from the late 1940s until the early 1970s. Moreover, most modern Greek political parties and governments have been characterized by authoritarian and populist practices: in a country with hardly any effective checks and balances to defend citizens' rights though with a strong clientelistic tradition, politicians usually have been more responsive to their voters' demands, however irresponsible, than to the country's needs, when the two were in conflict. Furthermore, when major problems have emerged, the Mediterranean virus of blaming foreign-led anti-government or often anti-Hellenic conspiracies has almost always been adopted and scapegoats have often been sought. Broadly speaking, the communists before 1974, and the junta and/or American foreign policy/ NATO/the West after the restoration of democracy have been convenient targets. For example, in 1989 the Panhellenic Socialist Movement (PASOK) accused the CIA of having used an alleged swindler (George Koskotas) to destabilize its government; and in 1990 the ND government claimed that there was a 'foreign factor' (Libyan, according to some pro-ND newspapers) behind some anti-US bases violent demonstrations in Crete, thereby drawing criticism from even the most serious and highly respected pro-ND daily, *Kathimerini* (26 July 1990). As regards other political values generally associated with the extreme right, (neo)fascism has never had any appeal in Greece, although anti-parliamentarianism and hostility towards the existing political class in power have characterized the military establishment until 1974 and, to some extent, the extreme right after 1974.

As for the economic themes that have helped the extreme right elsewhere, the professional categories of the small and middle entrepreneurs and the farmers are not yet in decline in Greece and make up nearly half the country's work-force. Moreover, the prolonged economic crisis of the 1970s and the 1980s has not apparently hurt the Greeks so profoundly, as can be witnessed by the thriving taverns, the lack of poverty queues, the disappearance of beggars and the prospering black economy that many consider the life-jacket if not the backbone of Greece's economic activity.

Finally, turning to the most sensitive part of the international extreme right's agenda, racism in its various forms, it is widespread (albeit often latent) in the Greek population, even though the latter is one of the most homogeneous in the world. Some 98 per cent share the same religion – Orthodox Christianity, language – Greek, and race – white. The contrast with France, for example, is striking: therein, the courts immediately pursue and condemn people, like extreme right leader Jean-Marie Le Pen, who declared that 'the big internationals, like the Jewish international, play a not negligible role in the creation of an anti-national spirit' (*Libération*, 29 June 1990). On the other hand, in Greece, court decisions interpret as 'real facts' such assertions as the 'Zionist hopes of destruction of the Christian world' and the claim that the Jehovah's Witnesses are a 'Judaic-leaning organisation aiming at the creation of a world Zionist empire with Jerusalem as its centre' (Decision 272/1984 of the Court of First Instance of Iraklio, Crete). Moreover, high school students are taught that 'the dream of Zionism is the universal dominion of Judaism' (Massos *et al.*, 1985, p. 50). Finally, now that Greece receives its first Third World immigrants, racially-inspired incidents are in evidence, too. According to Diamandouros (1983, p. 55):

> The sensitivity surrounding the issue of minorities in Greece is further indication that the process of national integration initiated over a century ago remains incomplete. School texts at the primary and secondary levels are virtually silent on such groups as the Kutzovlachs, the Pomaks, the Sarakatsans, and the Albanian and Slav-speaking populations of Greece. The virtual identification of hellenicity with Orthodoxy, on the other hand, has made it very difficult for such religious minorities as the Roman Catholics, the Protestants, the Jews and the Muslims to become fully integrated into the dominant Greek culture. Even today, when the traumatic experiences associated with

the irredentist struggles of the turn of the century and of the civil war years are fading, these groups remain, for the vast majority of the ethnically homogeneous Greek population, at worst unknown and at best obscure and alien entities.

It is thus understandable that a November 1989 *Eurobarometer* survey found that among the twelve EC member-countries, Greece had the highest percentage of people (45 per cent of the population) who found disturbing the presence and/or favoured restricting the rights of minorities in their country. Turning to biological elitism, one can read in the editorial column of *Kathimerini* (16–17 June 1985) that PASOK 'did not receive the votes of two million five hundred and ninety thousand people [i.e. the ND voters], certainly the best, smarter, better educated, more patriotic Greeks', a statement that many ND politicians had been making after their 1985 electoral defeat, and which was considered symptomatic of a 'new racism' (*Vima*, 13 June 1985).

So, in Greece, the political culture is 'fragmented, isolative and xeno-phobic. . . . The conflict between modernisers and traditional indigenous elites . . . tended to subsume pre-existing cleavages, social, political or cultural' (Diamandouros, 1983, p. 47). The same author has described prophetically the emerging social strata of the late 1970s which were to govern the country in the 1980s, mainly through PASOK (Diamandouros, 1983, pp. 59–60):

If it is inappropriate to speak of an ideology in this case, it might perhaps be more correct to speak of a 'guild-type' mentality precisely in order to attempt to convey the defensive stance, the insecurity, the parochial attitudes, the crass materialism, the narrow concern with personal or professional issues, the self-centredness, the illiberal essence, and the profound xenophobia so deeply characteristic of this upwardly mobile stratum. The critical importance of this new mental-ity lies in the fact that its rise coincides with the slow but unmistakable decline of the upper bourgeois ideology of the Greeks of the diaspora which has been dominant in Greece since the late nineteenth century. Put somewhat differently, this new merger of the new with the old, so typical of all aspects of Greek life, seems to constitute an integral part of a process whereby the more sophisticated and cosmopolitan *Weltanschauung* of the Hellenic (diaspora) Greeks is slowly being superseded by the more narrow and parochial views of the Helladic (indigenous) element, a process in which the new petty bourgeois values are gradually becoming dominant on the ideological level.

One of PASOK's most successful slogans has been 'Greece belongs to the Greeks', a rallying cry not unlike Jean-Marie Le Pen's 'France for the French' (see Chapter 2). A *Eurodim* Greater Athens survey, indicated that public opinion preferred it over Karamanlis' 'Greece belongs to the West' by 79 per cent to 14 per cent (*Epikairotita*, 24 July 1989). Therefore, when one of PASOK's leading politicians, Constantine Simitis, criticized his party's

1990 draft of a new declaration of principles for its ethnocentrism and parochialism, his views were summarily dismissed by the party's leader, Andreas Papandreou, as 'naïve'. Against such a background, with the main political parties having used much of the extreme right's agenda, the absence or minor presence of the extreme right in Greece can easily be understood.

The Extreme Right since 1945

Nearly all authors who have written on post-war Greek politics agree that extreme right-wing parties are an electoral phenomenon of the post-1974 period. Mavrogordatos (1983, p. 75) states that, after 1974, 'the electoral appearance of a breakaway extreme right is an essentially new phenomenon'. Meynaud (1965, p. 140) argues that the right had avoided the creation of an extreme right, having absorbed all its elements. Elsewhere, Loulis (1981, p. 58) gives a figure for the evolution of the Greek right in which the only 'ancestors' of the post-1974 extreme right are the two dictatorships. Significantly, Legg (1969) and Clogg (1987) make no specific reference to an extreme right in the period 1944–74.

It is instructive to note that only Nikolakopoulos (1985, p. 152) called the Politically Independent Alignment (Politiki Anexartitos Parataxis – PAP) that ran in the 1950 elections (polling 8.2 per cent) extreme right-wing, because most of its *cadres* were office-holders in the Metaxas dictatorship. Using similar criteria, one could have called extreme right wing a number of other post-war formations: the Union of Nationally Minded (Enosis Ethnikofronon – EE) that contested the 1946 elections (polling 2.9 per cent); the National Alignment of the Working People (Ethniki Parataxis Ergazomenou Laou – EPEL) in the 1950 elections (1.6 per cent); the 'X' Party of National Resistance (Komma Hiton Ethnikis Antistaseos) with 0.2 per cent in 1946; the National Agrarian 'X' Party (Ethniko Agrotiko Komma Hiton) with 0.8 per cent in 1950; and the party of John Metaxas Principles (Komma Arhon Ioannou Metaxa) with 0.1 per cent in 1956. Similarly, various local electoral lists could be included in the above context: the Local List of National Royalists (Topikos Syndiasmos Ethnikovasilo-fronon) with 34.9 per cent in Cephalonia in 1946; the List of Independents (Syndiasmos Anexartiton) with 39 per cent in the Mantineia province of Arkadia in 1952; and the List of Independent Nationally Minded (Syndias-mos Anexartiton Ethnikofronon) with 12 per cent in Arkadia in 1956. (For a detailed compilation of the global Greek election results 1926–1989, see *Greek Opinion*, VI(6), June 1989.) In all these parties, four political leaders dominated: Aristidis Dimitratos, Constantine Maniadakis, Theodore Tourkovasilis and George Grivas. At the time they were hardly perceived as extreme rightists. It was thus possible for them, when they were not running separately, to co-operate or integrate with the mainstream right-wing or centre parties. In 1951 they were all in the People's Party (Laikon Komma – LK); in 1952 Tourkovasilis' independent list in Mantineia was supported by centrist parties; later, Grivas became the leader and the hero of the Greek Cypriot armed struggle against British rule and the short-lived leader of a centrist coalition in 1960–1, and the others eventually integrated with the National Radical Union of Karamanlis. We can therefore conclude that there was no distinct parliamentary extreme right in Greece before 1974.

After the collapse of the dictatorship in 1974, some of the traditional extreme right themes were rejected unsurprisingly by the majority of the people, which paved the way for the creation of distinct extreme right-wing parties (see Table 11.1). With one exception, they were nothing more than electoral coalitions of politicians which did not survive the respective election or, if successful, the term of the ensuing parliament.

Table 11.1 Election results of the extreme right

Year	Election	Name of party	Percentage	Seats
1974	Parliamentary	National Democratic Union (EDE)	1.1	–
1977	Parliamentary	National Alignment (EP)	6.8	5
1981	Parliamentary	Progressive Party (KP)	1.7	–
1981	European	Progressive Party (KP)	2.0	1
		Movement of Greek Reformers (KEME)	0.9	–
1984	European	National Political Union (EPEN)	2.3	1
		Progressive Party (KP)	0.2	–
		United Nationalist Movement (ENEK)	0.1	–
1985	Parliamentary	National Political Union (EPEN)	0.6	–
June 1989	Parliamentary	National Political Union (EPEN)	0.3	–
1989	European	National Political Union (EPEN)	1.2	–
		United Nationalist Movement (ENEK)	0.2	–
		New Politicians	0.2	–
		European Economic Movement (EOK)	0.1	–
		National Militants	0.1	–
November 1989	Parliamentary	–	–	–
1990	Parliamentary	National Party (EK)	0.1	–
		Nationalist Alignment	0.03	–

Note: There are 300 seats in the Greek Parliament and 24 Greek seats in the European Parliament.

Source: Ministry of the Interior's official results.

In October 1974, the National Democratic Union (Ethniki Demokratiki Enosis – EDE) was created. Its leader was Petros Garoufalias, ex-Minister of Defence in George Papandreou's centrist government (1964–5). He had refused to resign his post at the request of the Prime Minister, thus paving the way for the clash between Papandreou and King Constantine which led to the ousting of the former, to the split within his party and to political instability which ended in 1967 with the *coup-d'état*. The EDE polled 1.1 per cent in the November 1974 elections, failing to elect any deputies; it disintegrated soon after.

The 1974 elections were notable for a ND landslide (54.4 per cent of the vote and 220 out of 300 seats), which surprised many observers as well as the centrist and leftist parties. However, the referendum on the future of the monarchy on 8 December 1974 nearly cancelled out the psychological edge won by ND. Whereas the ND had to remain neutral, since its politicians were split on the issue, the centrist and leftist parties virtually coalesced in a republican front and not only claimed victory on the referendum night (when 69.2 per cent opted for a republic) but also helped establish a cleavage between it and the right which has played a crucial role in the country's evolution. On the other hand, ND's official attitude created profound discontent within the party and this led to the resignation on 13 December 1974 from both party and Parliament, of the royalist Corfu deputy, Spyros Theotokis.

Three years later, as Karamanlis prepared for what he expected to be an easy second victory at the polls in the early elections of 20 November 1977, many royalists (including Theotokis) and traditionalist politicians, frustrated by the modernist ND programme, combined on 6 October, just before the elections, to form the National Alignment (Ethniki Parataxis – EP) under the leadership of Stefanos Stefanopoulos. Widely respected, he had been a People's Party politician and a deputy Prime Minister to the rightist Marshal Papagos (1952–5) and the centrist George Papandreou (1964–5), though he led the walkout from the latter's party in 1965 to head a government for one year (1965–6) with the support of the right. Three deputies elected with ND in 1974 rallied to EP: its leader's nephew with the same name, Mr Stefanos Stefanopoulos, Mr Serepisios and, only for a brief period – as he was soon expelled – Mr Savouras.

The nascent National Alignment turned out to be the most successful Greek political party outside the mainstream – ND, PASOK, KKE and the centrist Centre Union-New Forces (in 1974)/Democratic Centre Union (in 1977) – since 1974. Although it was given little exposure by most of the media, it attracted 6.8 per cent and elected five deputies (including a Rodopi Muslim). Its presence spoiled Karamanlis' plans for a second victory with a near-50 per cent score and at least 180 deputies, required for his election to the presidency in May 1980, for ND received 41.8 per cent and 171 seats. According to a leading ND figure's comment to this author the successful electoral performance of the extreme right also backfired, as it negated the possibility of a release of the imprisoned junta leaders.

Although the parliamentary representation of EP guaranteed its formal existence for the next four years, there was hardly any party life outside the

parliamentary activities of the five deputies and some by EP's youth organization, the Greek Youth of the National Alignment (Elliniki Neolaia
Ethnikis Parataxeos – ENEP), created in October 1977. In the 1980 presidential vote, three of EP's deputies voted for Karamanlis, crucially helping
his election and thereby preparing their passage into ND. By 1981, in fact,
Theotokis remained the only EP deputy. Indeed, faced with the threat of a
PASOK victory, many extreme right politicians rallied to ND, or instead the
revival of Markezinis' KP (see below) attracted many others. Theotokis
refused to join Markezinis, though he was forced to declare EP a non-runner
in the elections of October 1981, only to appear a few days later in the safe
third position on ND's state list (a list of usually important candidates,
separate from those of the fifty-six districts).

In the 1981 election, the extreme right was represented by the Progressive
Party (Komma Proodeftikon – KP), which was revived in November 1979.
The KP was first created in February 1955 by Spyros Markezinis, after he
fell out with Marshal Papagos, in whose government he had been Minister of
Co-ordination until November 1954. It ran in subsequent elections either
separately (in 1956 and 1963) or in coalition with centrist parties (in 1958 and
1961) or with the right-wing National Radical Union (ERE) in 1964. In
1973, Markezinis became Prime Minister of the ill-fated 'opening' of the
dictatorship to the politicians, a move which did not outlive the Polytechnic
student unrest. In the polarized setting of the 1981 election, KP polled a
rather respectable 1.7 per cent in the parliamentary elections, making it the
fourth party in strength, and 2 per cent in the concurrent European election
which allowed it, because of the different electoral system, to have one of the
twenty-four seats in the European Parliament. It appears that the workings
of the Euro-election law had escaped Markezinis' attention; for he was not a
candidate on his Euro-list. Except for the Euro-deputy's presence in
Strasbourg, the party practically disintegrated and contested the 1984
European elections (when it polled 0.2 per cent) only to draw funds from the
European Parliament to pay off 1981 campaign debts.

With PASOK in power, most conservative politicians and voters felt they
should back the main conservative party, i.e. ND, leaving little room for an
extreme right party. In the event, the election to ND's leadership of the most
conservative of its main political figures, Evangelos Averoff, assisted this
process. Only one key issue was omitted by ND, the amnesty of the jailed
junta leaders. It was to be the rallying theme of the first, and as yet only, real
extreme right-wing party, the National Political Union (Ethniki Politiki
Enosis – EPEN). EPEN was created in January 1984, and headed by the first
junta leader himself, George Papadopoulos, from his gaol cell (where he was
serving a death sentence commuted to life). Papadopoulos had been Prime
Minister from 1967 to 1973 and President of the Republic for a few months
in 1973. EPEN ran in the June 1984 European elections polling 2.3 per cent
and electing one Euro-deputy; in the June 1985 national elections, receiving
0.6 per cent; and in the June 1989 double election, polling 0.3 per cent in the
national elections and 1.2 per cent in the European elections, without
electing any deputies. Throughout its existence of five and a half years,
EPEN's main concern was the release of the jailed junta leaders, a demand it

even brought before the European Parliament. Since its efforts had no results by late 1989 and with poor electoral performances in 1985 and in June 1989, the party was dissolved on 10 September 1989, a decision taken by the jailed leaders following alleged blackmailing in exchange for their future release: it was an official admission that EPEN had been an one-issue party.

In October 1989, most former EPEN politicians formed the National Party (Ethniko Komma) and the Nationalist Youth Front (Metopo Ethnikistikis Neolaias). The National Party aspired to be a new beginning for these politicians, now attempting to make the extreme right broader than the single-issue EPEN. They decided not to run in the November 1989 parliamentary elections for lack of adequate preparation, funds and support, though they did contest the April 1990 parliamentary election, receiving a mere 0.1 per cent.

Besides the above, five additional fringe extreme right parties ran in the Euro-elections of the 1980s: in 1981, the Movement of Greek Reformers (Kinima Ellinon Metarythmiston – KEME) polled 0.9 per cent; in 1984 and 1989, the United Nationalist Movement (Eniaio Ethnikistiko Kinima – ENEK) received 0.1 per cent and 0.2 per cent respectively; and in 1989, the New Politicians (Neoi Politikoi), the European Economic Movement (Evropaiko Ekonomiko Kinima) and the National Militants (Ethnikoi Agonistai) polled 0.2 per cent, 0.1 per cent and 0.1 per cent, respectively. In the 1990 parliamentary election, a second extreme right party was present, the Nationalist Alignment, which received 0.03 per cent. Overall, in the elections of 1974–90, the extreme right's strength oscillated between 0 per cent (in November 1989) and 2.8 per cent with the exception of the 1977 success of EP (6.8 per cent). However, in the municipal elections of 1975 and 1978, the extreme right did rather better, winning some town halls and polling more than 20 per cent on average in those cities where it ran separately from the right. The success was due to the candidacies of a number of mayors appointed during the dictatorship who were justifiably boasting good records in that period (Dimitras, 1982, p. 30).

The Electoral Profile of the Extreme Right

One result of the electoral weakness of the extreme right has been that there is little meaningful data on the nature of the movement's electorate. The only reliable data available refers to the 1977 and 1984 elections and comes from *Eurodim*'s Greater Athens surveys (3–10 October 1979, 11–18 March 1980, 3–14 November 1980 and 4–11 May 1980 for EP in 1977; and 29 June–5 July 1984 for EPEN, KP and ENEK in 1984). Quota sampling was used, with a sample size of 600 interviews. One-third of the total Greek population live in Greater Athens, and the election results in this metropolitan area differ only slightly from the national results, making the Greek capital very representative of the nation.

This data (see Table 11.2) indicates that the extreme right has been stronger among older voters (and consequently pensioners) and the non-salaried work-force (professionals and businessmen) as well as housewives. Moreover, in 1984 it was stronger among the less educated, whereas in its most successful election of 1977 it was stronger among the more educated.

Table 11.2 Vote for the extreme right and the right in 1977, 1984

| | 1977 | | 1984 | |
	EP %	ND %	EPEN, KP, ENEK %	ND %
TOTAL	5.5	39.5	1.5	33.5
Sex				
Men	6.5	30.5	1.5	32
Women	4.5	48.5	1.5	34.5
Age (at the time of survey)				
Under 24	na	na	1	6
25–34	2	29	*	20.5
35–49	3.5	40.5	1	38
50–64	8	43.5	2	46.5
Over 64	14.5	50	3	45.5
Education				
Some grade school	8	53.5	2.5	44
Grade school graduates	3.5	41.5		
Some secondary school	5.5	42	2	38
Secondary school graduates	4	39	1	33
Some college	11.5	22	0.5	23.5
College graduates	8.5	31		
Occupation				
Liberal professional & higher exe- cutives	7	27	2	38
Businessmen, tradesmen	5	31	2.5	40.5
Employees	4	37	*	24
Workers	1.5	21.5	*	26.5
Unemployed	7.5	7.5	*	9
Housewives	5	51	3	49
Pensioners	12.5	51.5	na	na

na: not applicable. *Less than 0.5%

Source: special analysis of *Eurodim* polls (see text).

With the exception of the latter, though, the extreme right's strengths were identical with those of the mainstream right wing ND, indicating that the extreme right has been a protest breakaway group of the global right.

As to the geographical distribution of the extreme right's vote, we consider as areas of strength the electoral districts where extreme right-wing parties have polled more than 50 per cent above the national average in at least half of the post-1974 elections. Fifteen of the fifty-six electoral districts fall into this category (see Table 11.3). Geographically, they form almost a continuous Γ line that includes most of the northern border districts; four central, mostly mountain districts; and five of the seven districts of the Peloponnese. Here again, the majority of the districts are also traditional

Table 11.3 Vote for the extreme right in its areas of strength, 1974–1990

Electoral districts	1974	1977	1981	1981E	1984E	1985	1989P	1989E	1990
Evros	1.3		6.0	5.2	4.4		0.5		0.2
Rodopi	6.7	27.3		5.6	5.4			3.4	
Xanthi	13.6		8.2	6.1	7.3	1.0		3.7	0.2
Kilkis	1.3	11.4	4.4	4.7		0.9	0.5	3.7	
Florina			3.8	4.1		0.9		2.5	0.2
Kastoria	1.2	13.5			7.1	1.5	0.6	2.7	
Grevena		10.3	3.7	4.2				2.9	
Trikala					4.9	1.1	0.5	2.8	
Karditsa[1]	5.5	14.3		3.9	5.1	0.9			
Phocida	2.7	10.6				1.0	0.5	3.0	0.3
Korinthia					5.0	0.9	0.6	2.5	0.2
Argolida	1.5	12.4			4.0	0.9			
Arkadia		11.2	3.3	4.0	4.0			2.5	
Lakonia		16.2	4.8	5.5	6.1	1.1	0.8	2.8	0.3
Messenia	2.1	14.1	2.8	4.2	5.3	0.9	0.6	2.8	0.2
Total Greece	1.1	6.8	1.7	2.9	2.6	0.6	0.3	1.8	0.1

Notes: 1. Including an independent. 1989P: June parliamentary elections, E: European.
Source: Ministry of the Interior's official results.

strongholds of the right and the centre (*Greek Opinion*, Vol. 2, No. 3, May–June 1985, pp. 4–5). Of the fourteen 'very strongly conservative' districts in the period 1960s–1980s, eleven are also strongholds of the extreme right. Two extreme right-wing areas of strength belong to the 'rather strongly conservative districts' (Grevena and Korinthia), whereas the last two (Karditsa and Trikala) are generally 'rather weak' conservative areas.

It is noteworthy that in nearly all elections, the extreme right's highest score was in either Xanthi or Rodopi, two districts where most of the Greek Muslim citizens live. However, contrary to what one might have expected from the experience of other countries, whenever the extreme right had high scores in these two Thrace districts, it was because of a Muslim vote in its favour. Thus, every time there was the possibility of a preferential vote, the Muslim candidate on the extreme right's lists received the large majority to near-unanimity of the votes. Voting behaviour in these two districts is very different from the rest of the country, for it is influenced by the Greek Muslims' repeated efforts to send to the Greek authorities a message of their discontent. After 1985, for the first time since the Second World War, independent Muslim candidates ran, quite successfully too, in parliamentary elections, thus depriving the extreme right of its potential Muslim electorate. However, the extreme right revived in the 1989 European elections, where there were no independent Muslim candidates.

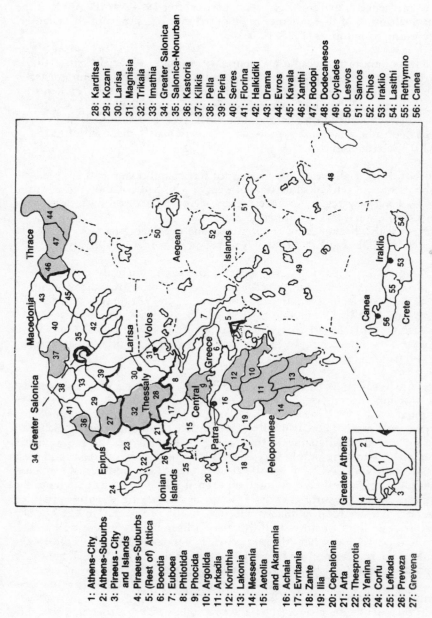

Figure 11.1 Map of Greece showing Parliamentary constituencies and areas of strong support for the extreme right.

260   *Panayote Elias Dimitras*

Ideological Belief Structures

The emergence of extreme right-wing parties after 1974 was the result of the
marginalization of three themes highlighted in the first part of this chapter.
According to Dimitras (1987, p. 66):

> anti-communism became a reactionary attitude, especially since the
> returning right-wing leader, Karamanlis, legalized the Communists;
> . . . traditional social values, an indispensable element of the 'Helleno-
> Christian civilization' were no longer unchallenged; . . . the
> Monarchy, without a reigning king since 1967 and abolished in 1973,
> ceased to be a national symbol and was summarily disposed of in the
> 1974 referendum

Moreover, the right-wing government of Karamanlis extensively purged the
public sector of tens of thousands of people who had collaborated with the
1967–74 military regime, whose leaders were sent to gaol with death sentences commuted to life imprisonment.

Against this background, the first extreme right-wing parties emerged in
the 1970s, EDE and EP. In the words of Mavrogordatos (1983, p. 75):

> Neither was a party in any sense of the term, but only an **ad hoc**
> assortment of converging reactionaries: royalist die-hards, dictatorship
> nostalgics, religious fanatics and fascists. . . . In 1974, the extreme right
> was essentially a negligible **protest** group. By 1977, however, it had
> become a **blackmail** party, exerting strong pressure on ND and its
> course by threatening to further erode its support among right-wing
> voters.

The qualification of the EDE and EP personnel as 'royalist die-hards,
dictatorship nostalgics, religious fanatics and fascists', unfortunately
adopted as an 'apt description' by Clogg (1987, p. 184), is too simplistic,
almost polemical. There is hardly any evidence of an important presence of
fascists or religious fanatics in these two parties, whereas there were many
politicians who were simply very conservative and/or traditionalist and were
dissatisfied with ND's near social-democratic and modernist policies.
Indeed, as we have already pointed out, when ND adapted its policies to the
extreme right's pressure after 1977, three of the five EP deputies provided
the crucial votes for Karamanlis' election to the presidency in 1980 (a fact
that most authors writing about that period have failed to mention), and all
of them, as well as other EP politicians, integrated with ND in the 1980s,
some even transferring as far as the centre-right Democratic Renewal, a
breakaway party from ND formed in 1985. For the same reasons,
Mavrogordatos' description would not apply either to the subsequent extreme right formations, EPEN or EK.

In the documents produced by extreme right parties or the main speeches
of their leaders, certain common themes emerged: promises of law and
order; appeal to the unity of the 'nationally-minded'; anti-communism; a

pro-Western political and economic orientation; economic (neo-)liberalism (which was rejected by ND until the mid-1980s); opposition to authoritarian rule; antipathy towards Karamanlis; and a call for the release of gaoled junta leaders. Support for the monarchy was never officially pronounced since it was a divisive issue for the extreme right's supporters, given the ex-king's opposition to the dictatorship and the latter's abolition of the monarchy in 1973. In the rest of this chapter, unless mentioned otherwise, all references will come from *Eleftheros Kosmos*, the pro-extreme right newspaper which supported the 1967–74 dictatorship. In 1982 it folded and reappeared as *Ellinikos Kosmos* in 1984. In such cases, only the publication date will follow the references.

The first extreme right party, the National Democratic Union (EDE), was created in October 1974 for three reasons, according to its leader, Petros Garoufalias (13 October 1974):

a. national dead-lock because of the unfortunate handling of the Cyprus problem; b. [the government's] opening to the left . . . that created feelings of fear and uneasiness in the Greeks; c. the 'dejuntization' [purging of the state from the junta elements], i.e. the indiscriminate persecution of a large number of nationally-minded citizens and the ruthless staining of reputations and the humiliation of the armed forces and the security forces, [facts] which have led to the division of the nationally-minded citizens.

In the same interview, Garoufalias said that 'systematic and persistent left-wing propaganda succeeded in characterizing the words "fatherland" and "nation" anachronistic and inconsistent with modern vocabulary', and explained that after the 'opening to the left', 'communist elements invaded the civil service'.

EDE's main principles were 'Work – National Power – Welfare' (23 October 1974). It opposed Karamanlis' August 1974 decision to withdraw the Greek armed forces from NATO's integrated command (13 October 1974), favoured Greece's integration into the EC, and economic recovery and expansion based on the private sector (23 October 1974). EDE opposed the electoral law of 'reinforced' proportional representation which favoured the large parties at the expense of the small ones (see *Greek Opinion*, Special Issue, April 1989, for a description of the Greek electoral systems). However, it did not take any stand on the referendum on the monarchy (26 October 1974), although wanting it to precede the parliamentary elections (13 October 1974), probably hoping to benefit from the rift in ND over the referendum. It was critical of 'dejuntization', nevertheless it favoured the prosecution of some junta ministers if found criminally responsible (26 October 1974). In an effort to put a distance between himself and the junta, Garoufalias revealed a plot against it which he had planned, though did not carry out, in 1969 (26 October 1974). In principle, EDE was 'against fascism both red or black; against any form of dictatorship, and against parties which, by their tactics, undermine democracy' (12 October 1974).

Moreover, EDE pledged itself to 'the systematic development of the

Greek-based national, social, political, economic and moral values on which Greek Christian civilization was founded'; and to 'the orientation towards Europe and the Atlantic Alliance as well as the reinforcement of relations with the non-aligned and the communist countries', in the spirit of both the global *détente* of the early 1970s and the regional Balkan *détente* initiated by the Greek dictatorship (29 October 1974). Promising that with 'order and democratic legitimacy, the guarantee of peace and quiet for our people and the honest management of public funds, it will lead the country out of the dead-lock and will safeguard democracy from the totalitarian threat', EDE called 'the nationally minded of all Greece to rally' around it (6 October 1974). On 17 November 1974 only a mere 1.1 per cent did so: it was such a shock for EDE that not even the traditional statement commenting on the results was issued, as the party faded away, and Garoufalias, except for a statement on the aftermath of the referendum (10 October 1974), was not heard of again.

The second extreme right party, EP, was created because, according to its leader, Stefanos Stefanopoulos (9 November 1977):

> the nationally minded people could not tolerate the contempt and the scorn from those they had elected as their representatives. Neither could they tolerate the distortion of their history and the defamation of their national symbol [the armed forces] . . . [The government] has abandoned youth to the corrosion of anarchist propaganda . . . and the anti-national proclamations of communism . . . *We are the alignment of nationally minded Greeks* . . . If the people, and especially the young generations alienate themselves from the masses of the nation, Greece is doomed to collapse.

Consequently, it will be instructive to quote at some length from EP's founding declaration to the Greek people (7 October 1977), which specified that:

> The destiny of EP is to face the chaos that one ruler [i.e. Karamanlis] has created because of his thirst for power. . . . EP is opposed to any overthrow of the democratic regime, as well as to all types of persecution and condemns any revolutionary action or upheaval . . .; it aspires to law and order but also to evolution. . . . EP will persistently avoid improvisations and dangerous socio-economic experiments that look like bad imitations of socialist and totalitarian regimes whose failure is well documented. . . . EP aims at *participatory democracy*. . . . EP's vision is a society of equality, freedom and justice that will be made up of Greeks and Greeks only united behind national and democratic principles. . . . EP believes that Greece belongs not only to the West but also to NATO and condemns the great mistake of withdrawal from the Atlantic Alliance [it is meant the military wing thereof]. It also believes that the national economy suffers dearly from sterile state interventionism and the improvised experiments that for the first time a Greek government has applied to this land. . . . EP will struggle for

Greece's entry into the EEC. . . . EP considers ideological confrontation necessary to face the danger of the corrosion of our youth by the
systematic propaganda of the communists, and to reduce the danger of
a new, violent confrontation in the future. . . . The result of national
reconciliation [through the legalization of the communist parties in
1974] is that the communists have become provocative, thus creating
among the victims of their crimes the conditions of a new national
schism. EP is determined to apply *the policy of forgetfulness* [authors's
emphasis] in all directions. It is equally determined to protect democracy from any conspiracy of whatever kind, be it communist or fascist.

On the controversial and divisive issue of the monarchy, Theotokis said
'during this campaign, we do not make the regime an issue. . . . Naturally,
we openly say to the Greek people that, later on, they will decide on the
nature of the regime. . . . If there was one person who resisted [the junta] in
Greece, it is the king.' Moreover, on the fate of the jailed junta leaders,
Theotokis pledged to use the July 1974 general amnesty to bring them out of
gaol (11 October 1977).

An excerpt of a Theotokis speech in Komotini, the capital of the Muslim-
populated district of Rodopi, indicates why the Greek extreme right was so
successful with that minority and why it was so different from the extreme
right elsewhere: 'ED makes no distinction whatever between the Greeks of
different religions. We want the Muslims – who live with us and are drafted
in the army with us – to be Greeks equal to the other Greeks and with the
same rights' (15 November 1977). In the Greek context, and given the
multiple official discriminations against that minority (Dimitras, 1990), this
was an unusual statement.

The Progressive Party (KP), the third extreme right party, was revived by
Mr Spyros Markezinis in November 1979, with a declaration (4 November
1979) which dealt essentially with the country's economic problems, offering (neo-)liberal solutions and appealing to the middle class:

KP is the only party that has proved it fully believes in the modern
liberal economy and does not confuse the implementation of social
policy with socialism as an economic system [a reference to ND]. . . .
KP believes in the predominant role of the private sector, aims at the
largest possible limitation of state intervention in the economy – as
opposed to the socialists or the socialist-leaning politicians [another
reference to ND]. . . . It aspires to appeal to the middle class. . . .
Classical education and the Church, which has recently also been
seriously and unjustifiably suffering, are our only weapons for the new
Great Idea [NB: Great Idea was the name given to the Greeks'
irredentist aspirations in the nineteenth and early twentieth centuries].
Otherwise, the good Greeks will disappear and those remaining could
not help but become second class citizens in a European international
community, whether we like it or not.

As for the mandatory reference to the junta-related Greeks, the KP declaration (4 November 1979) stated that:

> According even to the government's own claims, an unbelievable large number of people have been criminally or administratively persecuted retroactively, with the use of a legal procedure unprecedented for a European country; instead, the common interest required a swift application of forgetfulness. As a consequence [of the persecution], the unacceptable division of citizens in two categories continues.

Therefore, the KP (which also created a youth organization, the Progressive Youth – Neolaia Proodeftikon NEP) favoured the release of the gaoled junta leaders and the reinstatement of the allegedly persecuted citizens, rejecting an amnesty that would have meant recognition of crimes. During the 1981 campaign, Markezinis tried to reject the scare-mongering strategy of ND against PASOK by claiming that 'there is only one danger, the danger of the pavement [meaning street protests] because of the economic crisis' (10 October 1981), adding that he disagreed with ND, since 'I do not believe that PASOK is a national danger' (1 October 1981). This last statement cost him the support of many conservatives, voters and politicians alike, besides the extreme right newspapers *Eleftheros Kosmos* and *Estia*, and contributed to KP's low electoral performance, for it was then a widespread belief among the conservatives that PASOK was a danger for the country.

The fourth and most significant extreme right party, EPEN, had been created with a declaration by George Papadopoulos, in a cassette smuggled out of his prison. In it, the ex-dictator claimed to be 'breaking his silence for three reasons: first, because our country's affairs have never before reached such a critical point; second, to welcome the creation of EPEN; and, third, to present how I believe Greece's future can be safeguarded' (Papadopoulos, 1984). In the text of Papadopoulos' message, considered by EPEN as a declaration of principles, it was asserted that 'the [21 April 1967] Revolution was a historical necessity' and there was the following evaluation of the political situation at the time:

> [Since 1974], our country's affairs have been steadily deteriorating. . . . We are internationally isolated and prefer to embrace hysterically tendencies and nations that have nothing to offer us. Our national sovereignty has no reassuring guarantee. Anti-Americanism and anti-Westernism are officially fostered: the inevitable consequence is the Turks' growing impudence, because their special weight [within the Western Alliance] increases through our own foolishness: . . . Education at all three levels has been suffering from a chaotic devaluation. The Church is the object of fierce attacks from everywhere. Fundamental values like the family are in decay. Dignity and self-respect in social coexistence have disappeared. The youth, victim of criminal disorientation, lose their faith in vital ideals. Ideologically, Greece has rendered itself defenceless to the mercy of a marxist invasion. State media, schools, cultural and artistic life are dominated

and policed by uncouth communism, which, undeterred, distorts history, stupefies the souls of youth, attempts to substitute for patriotism servile devotion to the commands of foreigners and blackmails all cowardly and weak people.

In this text, ND is also criticized for 'pseudo-progressive measures' that paved the way for the 'reckless leftist invasion' since October 1981, and while a reference to 'the need to re-examine and revise even the fundamental constitutional provisions' was a clear appeal to the monarchists.

Besides these themes, in EPEN's programme, *Positions* (EPEN, no date), we find a 'belief in Freedom . . ., in constructive Parliamentarism and in private Initiative' and an opposition to 'enslaving Totalitarianism, to all forms of Socialism, and to parasitic Statism' as well as to 'reactionarism'. Its twelve-point programme consisted of:

1. Restoration and cleansing of Parliamentarism;
2. Return to the liberal economy;
3. Strengthening of individualized agrarian production;
4. Balanced social policy;
5. Restoration of independent Justice;
6. Giving a human dimension to the Civil Service;
7. Restitution to the Nation of its strength;
8. Protection of the Church from defamation;
9. Restoration of education;
10. Defence of historical truth;
11. Realistic foreign policy;
12. Information on the Cyprus problem [the capital letters are in the text].

The fifth extreme right party, the National Party (EK), tried to broaden the appeal of EPEN by dissociating itself from the single issue strategy of the latter. In January 1990 it presented a brief programme. In the economic sphere it was ultra-liberal, for it called for the abolition of income tax and its substitution with other indirect taxes; the limitation of the state sector; and the 'multiplication' of farmers' pensions. Moreover, it included the 'Hellenization' of education with the reintroduction of accents; the introduction of 'simple' proportional representation with the country as one electoral district; the 'abolition of the concept of political prisoners' with the freeing of the jailed junta leaders. Finally, it was much more nationalistic than the preceding parties' programmes, since it called for a 'nationalist orientation of Greece', pledged the party to a 'Europe of fatherlands', asked for the 'self-determination of the Cypriots and the North Epirus [Greeks of Albania]', and the representation in Parliament of 'emigrant and unredeemed Hellenism' i.e. the Greeks in Albania and Turkey] (28 January 1990). Finally, in a noted departure from the past practices of the extreme right, it showed hostility to the Muslim minority of Thrace, calling for the revision of the Treaty of Lausanne (which protects minorities in Greece and Turkey), and for 'the deportation of all those who claim they are Turks' (4 February

1990). As indicated above, EK failed at the polls in April 1990, receiving the lowest percentage ever for the main extreme right party (0.1 per cent).

Conclusion

In Greece, basically, the extreme right has spanned a sixteen-year period (1974–90), during which some of the traditional themes of the international extreme right (anti-communism, monarchism, and adherence to traditional social values) were devalued though they remained salient enough for a minority of voters. The purge of a large number of people associated with the junta also created a potential electorate. Except for the constant demand for the release of the junta leaders, which in the 1980s was virtually the only reason for the existence of the extreme right, the ideology of the extreme right parties was nearly identical with that of the traditional right wing (if not centrist) parties before 1967. It was no surprise, then, if the extreme right leaders before EPEN were older, respected politicians of the pre-1967 right (Markezinis, Theotokis) and centre (Stefanopoulos, Garoufalias), who apparently had not caught up with the rapid evolution of Greek society and politics after (and as a result of) the collapse of the junta in the 'national tragedy' of 1974.

With PASOK in power in the 1980s, the potential for the extreme right shrank, since most conservatives felt they had to join ranks behind ND, which in the meantime had picked up some of the extreme right's themes (economic liberalism, anti-marxism). Moreover, the international association of EPEN with the racist and provocative French extreme right of Le Pen probably tarnished its image, for although latent racism may be widespread in Greece according to opinion surveys, the semi-fascist Metaxas dictatorship or the post-war extreme right never openly espoused it.

Perhaps the best evidence that the extreme right's potential is nearly extinct, at least in parliamentary elections, was the inability of the National Party to find enough support even to contest the November 1989 election, and its negligible performance in the April 1990 election. Both elections were held under circumstances that could have been considered ideal for the extreme right in any other country or even in Greece, in the past. For four months (July–October 1989) before the first election, Greece had been governed by an odd alliance of the ND with the communist-led coalition (of the KKE with minor left-wing parties) which, among other things, introduced legislation that symbolically eliminated all negative references to the Civil War. Then, for another five months (November 1989–March 1990) before the second election, the country had a government with 'ecumenical' (conservative, socialist and communist) support. This coexistence of the conservatives with their erstwhile arch enemies, the communists – which, on the basis of the Karamanlis 1977 definition of the nationally-minded (see page 249 above), made ND lose that quality – and the conciliatory policies of these alliances, in other countries or at another time in Greece, would have created strong reactions among the most conservative voters, thus producing an important potential electorate for the extreme right. The absence of such an evolution indicates that those few themes of the international extreme right which had been supported by only the fringes of the right in Greece had by 1990, lost their salience even among the hard core of the conservative electorate.

Opinion polls in 1991 indicated that the Greeks were becoming disillusioned with mainstream political parties. Nevertheless, repugnance for the symbols of the dictatorship has remained very strong, especially among opinion leaders, as the conservative government discovered in late 1990. On 28 December, it announced its intention to pardon the 1967 coup leaders still serving prison sentences, with the agreement of the President of the Republic, Karamanlis. An uproar followed (opposition, intellectuals, media, even some ND deputies) leading the government to reverse its decision two days later. Moreover, the public reappearance abroad since 1990 of ex-king Constantine (press conferences, interviews – some with Greek media), has hardly had any impact on public opinion to encourage extreme right forces. At the same time, the November 1990 new electoral law included a 3 per cent national threshold to partake of the seat distribution, making representation of small parties impossible. Most observers therefore agree that in the near future, unless there are dramatic developments, no extreme right party will play a significant role on the Greek political scene.

Acknowledgement

1. The author is grateful to the editor and three anonymous referees for their useful suggestions and to Mr Aristidis Dimopoulos for providing him with valuable EPEN documents.

References

Clogg, Richard, 1986. *A Short History of Modern Greece*, 2nd edn, Cambridge University Press, Cambridge.
—— 1987. *Parties and Elections in Greece*, C. Hurst, London.
Commission of the European Communities, 1989. *Eurobarometer. Special: Racism and Xenophobia*, November.
Diamandouros, P. Nikiforos, 1983. Greek political culture in transition: Historical origins, evolution, current trends, in Richard Clogg (ed.), *Greece in the 1980s*, Macmillan, London, pp. 43–69.
Dimitras, Panayote Elias, 1982. O paragnorismenos thriamvos ton dyo akron [The neglected triumph of the two extremes], in *Economikos Tachydromos*, 7 October, 28–30.
—— 1987. Changes in public attitudes, in Kevin Featherstone and Dimitrios K. Katsoudas (eds), *Political Change in Greece: Before and After the Colonels*, Croom Helm, London, pp. 64–84.
—— 1990. The minorities in Western Thrace, in *Greek Opinion*, June, pp. 9–19.
EPEN (no date). *Theses* [Positions] (leaflet).
Legg, Keith R., 1969. *Politics in Modern Greece*, Stanford University Press, Stanford, California.

Loulis, J. C., 1981. New democracy: the new face of Conservatism, in Howard R. Penniman, *Greece at the Polls: The National Elections of 1974 and 1977*, American Enterprise Institute, Washington D. C., pp. 49–83.

Mavrogordatos, George Th., 1983. The emerging party system, in Richard Clogg (ed.), *Greece in the 1980s*, Macmillan, London, pp. 70–94.

Massos, I., Zagas, A. Kouvelas, G., 1985. *Christianismos kai Kosmos* [Christianity and the World], Organismos Ekdoseon Didaktikon Vivlion [Organization of Textbook Publication], Athens.

Meynaud, Jean, with the assistance of P. Merlopoulos and G. Notaras, 1965. *Les Forces Politiques en Grèce*, Etudes de Science Politique, Lausanne, Switzerland.

Nikolakopoulos, Elias, 1985. *Kommata kai Vouleftikes Ekloges stin Ellada 1946–1964* [Parties and Parliamentary Elections in Greece 1946–1964], EKKE, Athens.

Papadopoulos, George, 1984. *Minyma* [Message] (flyer published by EPEN).

12 After Stalinism: The Extreme Right in Russia, East Germany and Eastern Europe

Michael Cox

Introduction

Until the end of 1990 there was a genuine sense of optimism in the West about the changes taking place in the former communist countries of Europe. From the West's perspective at least there was much to be excited about. First, as a result of a major shift in Soviet foreign policy after 1985, the Cold War with its attendant fears and dangers came to an end, leaving East–West relations in better shape than at any time since the end of the Second World War. Second, faced with continuing economic stagnation at home, the former Soviet President Gorbachev was impelled to unleash an increasingly radical attack upon the whole Stalinist edifice which did little to improve the economic situation, though a great deal to destroy the global appeal of socialist planning. Finally, and most surprisingly of all to those who had grown used to the division of the European continent, when democratic forces pushed against sclerotic structures in Eastern Europe, the Soviet Union simply refused to intervene. As a result, the communist dominoes fell in rapid succession, beginning with Poland and Hungary in the summer, and ending with the collapse of the regimes in East Germany, Czechoslovakia, Bulgaria and Romania in November and December (Ash, 1990; Dahrendorf, 1990; Glenny, 1990; Selbourne, 1990).

The widespread euphoria which greeted the demise of Stalinism was perfectly understandable. Less understandable perhaps was the triumphalist assumption that the demise of communism would lead, almost inexorably, to a golden era of liberal humanism and prosperity. If nothing else, this sanguine prognosis both underestimated the obstacles standing in the way of economic reform, and the costs that would have to be borne by the people as reforms were implemented. There would be no easy road to capitalism in either Eastern Europe or the Soviet Union. The optimists also ignored the uncomfortable, though obvious, fact that Soviet rule had both constrained and accentuated reactionary ideologies that were bound to re-emerge once Stalinism imploded – especially in a region where persecution of minorities and rivalries between ethnic groups had been the historic rule rather than the exception. Once the Stalinist lid had been taken off the East European and Soviet pot, all manner of anti-democratic, intolerant forces were likely to resurface (Eyal, 1990; Dempsey 1990; Halliday, *Fortnight*, April 1991).

In this survey of what is, by definition, a rapidly changing situation, I shall try to provide a brief guide to the ideology and strength of these different forces. In the first two sections we shall examine the rise of the extreme right in Russia and East Germany respectively. The survey will then continue with an overview of developments in Eastern Europe as a whole. In the concluding section, the long-term prospects for right-wing extremism in the former Soviet empire will be assessed.

Russia

The Stalinist system in the Soviet Union was built upon three pillars: a web of tight controls which held the country together and prevented major political change; an inefficient command economy which provided the Soviet people with a minimal level of security; and an ideology which proclaimed that the Soviet Union after a glorious and heroic history – marred only by Stalin's excesses – was moving smoothly and irresistibly towards some higher communist goal. After 1985 each of these props was progressively weakened in an increasingly desperate attempt by the Soviet leadership to solve the country's economic problems. Far from improving the situation, however, the reforms unleashed by Gorbachev led to a measurable decline in living standards, a massive fall in Soviet industrial output and the erosion of the Soviet Union as a unified federal state. Gorbachev set out to restructure the Soviet Union in 1985, yet under his leadership the position of the country declined quite catastrophically (Ellman, 1991, pp. 23–8).

The successful attack upon Stalinist certainties, yet the failure of *perestroika* to resolve the contradictions of Soviet socialism, inevitably threw the Soviet Union into turmoil. Out of this emerged new political forces. Some proposed increasingly radical solutions to the Soviet crisis; others demanded an end to reform altogether. Not surprisingly, those most threatened by *perestroika* – in particular the party apparatus, the military, the industrial ministries and sections of the KGB – had the deepest reservations of all about reform. Increasingly critical of a leader who had brought the country to the point of economic and political collapse, they began to mobilize in the latter half of the 1980s in an attempt to stem the tide of change. Although this loose coalition comprised many diverse ideological strands, probably the one thing which united it was a conservative Russian nationalism which equated reform with economic decline, liberalism with the disintegration of the country, and the West with decadence and hostility to the integrity of the Soviet state (Brudny, 1989, pp. 162–200).

Standing on the fringes of this current was the organization Pamyat, possibly the best known of the right-wing groups in the Russian federation. Pamyat [Memory] was the most extreme, most vocal and, in some respects most interesting group on the new Russian right (*Radio Liberty Research Bulletin*, 19 December 1988; Pospielovsky, 1990, pp. 8–17). In its early stages a movement in defence of the Russian cultural heritage, after 1985 it began to assume a more openly political character (Laqueur, 1989, pp. 135–45; White, 1990, p. 40; Lane, 1990, p. 98). Branches started to appear in a number of Russian cities, and by 1988 there were at least thirty Pamyat groups in Russia, the largest and most active being in Leningrad and Moscow where the organization was reported to have several thousand members in each city (European Parliament, 1990, p. 38).

Like any political movement Pamyat consisted of numerous factions and strands. The most benign were not particularly chauvinist and aimed to protect and restore Russian monuments (Nove, 1989, p. 153). The more vocal wing had an altogether more sinister character. Strongly anti-Western and covertly anti-Gorbachev, it linked the defence of Russia with a crude attack on all those who had purposefully undermined the 'Motherland' by imposing upon it the false and unnatural doctrine of Marxism. Pamyat, however, rejected Marxism not because of its theoretical inconsistencies, but more precisely because it was (and remains) a 'Jewish' conspiracy perpetrated against the Russian people. It was the Jews, allegedly, who made and led the original Russian Revolution. It was the Jews who then sustained the regime and in the process liquidated all that was great in Russia including, amongst other things, the rural peasant economy. And it is the Jews, they argue, who are to blame for the massive problems facing the country today (*Soviet Jewish Affairs*, 1988, pp. 60–70).

The ideological world-view of Pamyat thus combined a crude mixture of anti-Semitism and anti-Marxism (*Soviet Jewish Affairs*, 1987, pp. 53–69; Woll, 1989, pp. 3–22; Wishnevsky, 1989b, pp. 7–9). However, although Pamyat appeared to reject socialism, it was never unambiguously pro-capitalist. Indeed, precisely because it equated capitalism with 'the Jews' and the West, in its statements it often appeared to be hostile to the market. Moreover, although it condemned Soviet communism, it appeared to be divided about the historic role of the country's most important non-Jewish leader, Joseph Stalin. Some members clearly regarded the Soviet dictator highly. Pamyat writer, Valery Yemelyanov, even extolled Stalin for having eliminated the Jews from the Communist Party leadership and having restored the spirit of Russia (Doder and Branson, 1990, p. 188). Others took a rather different view. Great man though he may have been, it was Stalin, according to his critics, who was responsible for the devastation of Russian peasant culture and its religious monuments (Nove, 1989, p. 153).

Many in Pamyat also subscribed to, indeed often approvingly quoted from, the forged anti-Semitic *Protocols of the Elders of Zion*. The organization and its various offshoots were indeed active in the peddling of virulently anti-Semitic material, including Vladimir Begun's *Creeping Counter Revolution* and Alexander Romanenko's *About the Class Essence of Zionism*. In addition, it became heavily involved in the broader Soviet political debate, often but not always on the side of conservative Russian forces opposed to pluralism and economic reform. In spring 1987 it demonstrated against prominent Gorbachev supporter, Yegor Yakovlev, editor of *Moscow News*. Some 1,500 Pamyat members gathered outside the newspaper's office in central Moscow, shouting abuse and accusing Yakovlev of 'harbouring Jews and Freemasons' on his staff. When the economist Abel Aganbegyan later spoke in favour of economic reform, Pamyat employed the same tactics, accusing Aganbegyan of actually being a Freemason, and claiming that he, like Yakovlev, also harboured 'too many Jews' on his staff (Doder and Branson, pp. 187–8). How seriously the organization's activities were taken is difficult to assess. However, Boris Yeltsin, then chief of the Moscow Communist Party, felt impelled to arrange a meeting with Pamyat in May in order to discuss a number of its grievances (Spier, 1989, p. 51).

True to the tradition of the extreme right, Pamyat underwent splits and experienced great internal dissension as it grew. In late 1987, for example, factions led by Igor Sytchev and Valery Emelyanov dissociated themselves from the larger tendency led by Dimitri Vasiliev (Laqueur, 1989, p. 143). However, this did not lead to any great reduction in Pamyat's activities. If anything, the organization now became more provocative. At its meetings members began to appear in classic fascist uniforms (black shirts), and from the platform its leaders called for a general 'cleansing' of Russian intellectual life, a ban on 'mixed' marriages, and the immediate deportation of 'Jews' and other 'minorities' to their 'original habitat' (Laqueur, 1989, p. 144). Physical attacks on Jews also escalated as Pamyat activists, or presumed sympathizers, resorted to fascist-style methods to intimidate and cow their chosen enemies. As a result, the list of anti-Semitic outrages steadily climbed, reaching a peak in late 1989 and early 1990. In January 1990, a Pamyat mob even attacked a meeting of the liberal Writers' Union (*Searchlight*, November 1990a, p. 13).

By the end of 1989 the situation had become extremely tense, so much so that at the historic Congress of Jewish Organizations held in Moscow in December, the most talked-about question was the 'real possibility of pogroms in the near future'. Severe economic dislocation and political instability, according to one delegate at the Congress, had aggravated tensions in the Soviet Union and 'allowed the Jews to be made scapegoat for the problems caused by *perestroika*' (Korey, 1990). In an interview published in the East German paper, *Junge Welt*, the chief rabbi of Moscow, Rabbi Adolf Shayevich, was equally pessimistic. He noted,

> Today anti-Semitism is a very real phenomenon, [previously] it existed passively; now those who profess it no longer make any bones about it. In this way, people of the same mind join together in organizations such as Pamyat which openly disseminates anti-Semitic propaganda and sometimes call directly for pogroms.

Significantly, Rabbi Shayevich complained bitterly that anti-Semitic propaganda and activities were rarely punished by those in authority. 'This impunity,' he commented, was 'an encouragement to all anti-Semites' (Kamm, 1990). Symptomatically, when the Lithuanian writer, Grigory

Kanovich, joined by two members of the Academy of Sciences, Vitaly Ginzburg and Oleg Gazenko, submitted to the presidium of the Congress of People's Deputies a petition calling for a condemnation of anti-Semitism and the creation of a special committee to investigate its growth, the petition was administratively buried (Korey, 1990).

If the attitude of many party officials towards Pamyat was less than vigilant (and frequently benevolent), then that of more respectable Russian nationalists was distinctly tolerant, implying that the organization had friends at the highest level who either shared its chauvinist views, or were prepared to use the organization to keep radicals and liberals at bay. Certainly, without such patronage and protection it would have been extremely difficult for Pamyat to have operated quite so freely. The organization could also count on support from influential individuals in the wider Russian intellectual community. A number of them spoke at Pamyat meetings, and writers such as Valentin Rasputin and Proskurin often made it clear that they welcomed Pamyat's championing of the patriotic cause. Mainstream conservative journals, such as *Nash Sovremennik*, also expressed a definite intellectual sympathy for Pamyat (Wishnevsky, 1989a, p. 4).

If the physical threat to Russian Jewry was possibly less than some feared, the fact remains that the position of Jews did become less secure under Gorbachev (Simes, 1989; McKenna, 1989; Steele, 1990; Prial, 1990). This caused the reticent Gorbachev some embarrassment not only abroad, particularly in the United States, but also at home among his more liberal supporters. No doubt under some pressure to do something, the authorities finally agreed in autumn 1990 to try Pamyat activist, Konstantin Smirnov-Ostashvili for his important part in the attack on the Writers' Union earlier in the year. Smirnov-Ostashvili, the leader of one of the Pamyat splinter groups, was finally convicted under Article 74 of the Russian Criminal Code which prohibits incitement to ethnic violence. Significantly, the trial was not only the first of its kind since the rise of Pamyat in the mid-1980s, but also one of the first in living memory against any Soviet citizen preaching racial hatred. For this reason it generated a great deal of press interest (Ivanov, 1990, pp. 14–15). Commentators, nevertheless, sounded a note of caution. The accused, after all, was sentenced to two years only and not the maximum of five years for his role in the attack. Moreover, as public prosecutor Andrei Makharov pointed out, 'the case came about not because of the state and the law enforcement bodies but in spite of them', suggesting that the trial may not have signified a major change in official policy towards anti-Semitic activities. The state also limited the scope of the case by bringing just one man to trial when sixty to seventy people had taken part in the original attack (Boulton, 1990). Even more worrying perhaps was the failure of Soviet authorities at the time to issue a strong statement against Pamyat. In fact, members of VAAD, the umbrella organization of Soviet Jewish cultural bodies, 'gained the impression during a meeting with top Soviet officials that a decision had been taken to hold the trial instead of issuing a high-level declaration on anti-Semitism' (Hirszowicz and Spier, 1991, p. 16).

Whatever purpose lay behind the trial, the one thing it clearly could not do was reassure Soviet Jewry. Long before the trial many had already concluded they no longer had a future in the Soviet Union (Garlizki, 1990, p. 350). The uncertain economic situation, plain fear and the inability (or refusal) of those in authority to challenge anti-Semitism seriously had led many to the conclusion that their place now lay outside of the country (Sheridan, 1990).

The election of Boris Yeltsin to President of the Russian Federation in early summer 1991 transformed the Soviet political situation – probably to the short-term detriment of organizations such as Pamyat. Yeltsin presented the chauvinists with a problem. On the one hand, he was an economic reformist and ostensibly in favour of the democratic changes most disliked by Pamyat. On the other hand, he was a 'good Russian' who was not beyond deploying the same nationalist and anti-communist rhetoric as his xenophobic opponents. Indeed, as observers like Boris Kagarlitsky then pointed out, Yeltsin often used the same language as the extreme nationalists.

Finally, the position of Pamyat was further complicated by the ignominious defeat of the coup in August, for this weakened the position of their protectors and sponsors in the state and party apparatuses. As a result of the failure of the coup, Pamyat was thrown into some disarray. No doubt if the coup had succeeded, Pamyat might have had a brighter future.

However, it would be naïve to think that organized chauvinism in Russia has finally been laid to rest. After all in the Russian presidential elections, nearly 7 per cent of the electorate voted for an openly chauvinist candidate. More generally virulent grass-roots anti-Semitism has shown no sign of abating – and will not do so while the economic situation continues to deteriorate. Furthermore, while Yeltsin may be no anti-Semite, he has been prepared to ally himself with the chauvinists and to exploit Russian nationalism to his own advantage. Also, if he fails to resolve the continuing economic crisis, one could easily envisage increased support for those who advocated a less democratic solution than his to Russia's immense problems.

The Extreme Right in East Germany

Memories of German war-time aggression, fears that a united German economy would dominate Europe, and the widely-held feeling that Germans were somehow more predisposed to authoritarian nationalism than most, together generated a great deal of anxiety amongst Germany's neighbours about the country's role in the new post-Cold War order. However, two unforeseen developments – the enormous burden imposed upon the West German economy by unification, and Germany's extraordinary passivity during the Gulf War – did much to allay these fears. Within a year of unification therefore earlier worries about a 'Fourth' Reich had given way to concerns about Germany not playing an international role commensurate with its new economic status (Usborne, 1991; Harper, 1991; Mauthner, 1991).

There was, however, a third reason why those originally concerned about the new Germany assumed a more relaxed stance: the immediate failure of the West German extreme right to capitalize on the movement towards unification. Indeed, far from working to the advantage of the Republikaner Partei (REP), unity actually seemed to weaken the organization's appeal (Atkinson, 1990, p. 10). The scale of its decline was really quite dramatic. In 1989 the Republicans had about 27,000 members. By the end of 1990 they had just over half that number. In the 1989 European elections, as Kolinsky (Chapter 3) points out, they captured 7.1 per cent of the popular vote in West Germany. In the first all-German elections in December 1990, their average support dropped to a mere 2.1 per cent of the votes cast. In West Berlin, where the Republicans had made major gains in January 1989, support fell by over two-thirds to 2.4 per cent. Only in their stronghold of Bavaria did the Republicans manage to poll over 5 per cent (*Searchlight*, January 1991, p. 20; Jeffrey, 1991, pp. 181–5).

Yet in spite of these blows to the now 'strife-torn' Republican cause (*Searchlight*, March 1991, p. 16), it would be extremely foolish to write off the extreme right in the new Germany. First, although it suffered setbacks, the Republican Party still managed to gain the support of a million voters in December 1990: 985,557 in West Germany and 17,118 in East Germany. When added to the total vote of 179,875 for the neo-Nazi NPD, this indicates a hard core of electoral support for the extreme right in Germany (a point driven home by the electoral success of the German People's Union (DVU) in various elections in Bremen (1991), Schleswig-Holstein (1992) and the REP in Baden-Würtenburg, also in 1992). Second, although unification may have dealt the Republicans a temporary electoral blow – primarily because Kohl played the German card and stole the extremists' thunder – in East Germany the extreme right in its various guises has begun to grow (*Searchlight*, December 1990a, p. 16; *Searchlight*, May 1991, pp. 2–6; European Parliament, 1990, p. 37).

Estimates of the extreme right's organizational strength and influence in East Germany vary. One calculation, by Bernd Wagner, head of the state security section of the Berlin CID, indicated that by spring 1991 about 30,000 young people in the East regarded themselves as supporters of the extreme right, and 1,500 could be defined as active members of groups such as National Resistance, German Alternative and the National People's Party. Maria Michalk, a Dresden Christian Democratic MP, calculated that in her home state of Saxony alone there was a hard core of 1,200 neo-Nazis with as many as 15,000 supporters (Gow, 1991). Compared with the western part of Germany where there was just over 60,000 activists on the extreme right, these figures may not look ominous (*Searchlight*, September 1990b, p. 14). However, if we recall that the population of the former East Germany is much smaller than that of the old Federal Republic, that the extreme right has been operating in the East for only a short period, and that since reunification it has tended to be highly active and very violent, then the situation looks a good deal more serious (*Searchlight*, December 1990b, p. 16).

The first target of the East German extreme right has been the country's numerous 'guest workers'. By 1990 there were 93,000 persons in this category: 60,000 from Vietnam, 16,000 from Mozambique, 9,000 from Cuba, 7,000 from Poland and 1,000 from Angola (*Radio Free Europe Report*, 6 July 1990, pp. 48–52; European Parliament, 1990, p. 74). Surplus to requirement since unity, and in the main unwilling to return home, they have become an easy scapegoat for unemployed East German youth. The list of incidents of abuse and beatings of guest workers has grown depressingly long. In many industrial cities the situation has become acute. For instance, in what has been described as 'an orgy of mayhem' in Dresden over the Easter weekend in 1991, Jorge Gomondai, a 28-year old Mozambican, was kicked to death after a group of fascist skinheads cornered him on a tram. In October, neo-fascists then launched a series of attacks on hostels for foreigners. Other more generalized assaults have been reported in East Berlin, Leipzig, Leisnig, Cottbus, Klötze, Hohe-Schönhausen and Eisenhüttenstadt. To talk of a 'reign of terror' is no exaggeration. As Heinz Galinski, leader of West Germany's Jewish community, has noted, the situation has clearly 'got out of hand', with the police apparently unable to do very much about it (Sherwell, 1991b).

Another group targeted by the extreme right have been Poles either in transit or visiting the country for short-term economic reasons. Some attacks have been straightforward robberies of travellers known, or assumed, to be carrying large sums of money (Field, 1991). Many incidents, however, have had a racial dimension, the most publicized being those which occurred in spring 1991 following the agreement between Bonn and Warsaw granting Polish citizens visa-free travel into Germany. More than 70,000 Poles streamed into the country, some en route to France, Italy, Belgium, Holland and Luxemburg. Unfortunately, at three border points – Frankfurt-on-Oder, Guben and Görlitz – they had to run the gauntlet of up to 400 neo-Nazi youths, who 'stoned a bus, overturned a car containing Poles, and fought with riot police' (*Searchlight*, June 1991, pp. 12–13). Skinheads, many of them drunk and masked, reportedly shouted 'Germany for the Germans' and 'foreigners out' (Leski and Gedye, 1991). A bus carrying members of the Lodz Symphony Orchestra returning from Amsterdam was also set upon. These and other incidents (and again the failure of the police to prevent them) so upset Polish authorities that the Polish border city of Gorzow cut off all ties with neighbouring Frankfurt-on-Oder (*Searchlight*, June 1991, pp. 12–13).

In addition to these more specific outrages, the extreme right has attempted to exploit the 'ethnic German' question. Several thousand Germans live in Polish territory east of the Oder–Neisse rivers, an area to which the West German state laid claim until Bonn formally recognized Polish control of the disputed region in 1990, much to the chagrin of many German nationalists, including some still living in Poland. While the 'eastern lands' question is not quite what it once was, it does present the extreme right with another exploitable issue. The Republicans indeed have already announced the establishment of a branch of their organization at Görlitz in East Germany, symbolically sited on the Neisse river, part of the border with Poland (Murray, 1990).

If attacks on foreigners (not to mention Soviet soldiers) have been the most obvious manifestation of right-wing extremism in East Germany, then football has provided it with a useful cover for its violent activities. There have been innumerable incidents since 1989. Ironically, one of the most publicized was the decision not to go ahead with the planned 'celebration final match' between the East and West German soccer teams in Leipzig in November 1990. Fearing that the extreme right would exploit the situation to their own advantage in a city of increasing incident, the authorities reluctantly decided to cancel the event (Tomforde, 1990). The decision seems to have been vindicated, for five months later a full-scale riot did break out, this time at the European Cup match between the home side Dynamo Dresden and visitors Red Star Belgrade. Trouble began before the match when buses carrying the 1,200 Yugoslav fans were wrecked in the city centre of Dresden. Over 1,000 police were then called up for duty at the ground, but the match· finally had to be abandoned after seventy-eight minutes because of crowd violence orchestrated by what one observer described as 'Nazi-inspired soccer louts'. A number of the visiting foreign fans were reported injured.

The extreme right has also been increasingly active against all manner of socialists and alternative lifestyle 'anarchists'. Blaming Marxism for the problems now facing East Germany, right-wing extremists see the left and its associated 'progressive' causes such as anti-racism and pacifism as being profoundly anti-German. Bitter clashes between rival forces have thus become a feature of East German political life. In one specific incident witnessed by Labour MEP Mike Hindley in the town of Bachstrasse, a 'howling mob of neo-Nazis attacked a café known to be frequented by local left-wingers and anti-fascists' (*Searchlight*, December 1990b, p. 16). In Dresden too, there have been regular right-wing sorties against left-wing squatters.

It would, of course, be easy to dismiss right-wing extremism in East Germany as a transitional phenomenon: a temporary outburst by alienated youth in a once repressed society now turned upside down by economic reform and the collapse of the traditional patterns of Stalinist authority. Thus, once life in East Germany returns to normal (or so the argument goes) extremism will fade and die. There is obviously some truth to the argument; an improvement in the economic situation and more positive life prospects would alleviate social tensions and weaken extremism on the right. Nevertheless, we should not be too optimistic. East Germany's 'morning after' is likely to last for a very long time (Evans, 1991, pp. 20–3).

First, in the short term at least, there is little chance of a marked improvement in the economic situation (Gow, 1991). For the foreseeable future East Germany will remain in a depressed economic state with a large and peripheral unemployed sector potentially susceptible to right-wing extremism. Second, although the Christian Democrats swept all before them in 1990, there is growing evidence to indicate that they are losing some of their original support. Significantly, Kohl's popularity has plummeted in the East since unification (Eisenhammer, 1991; Sherwell, 1991a). If this trend were to continue, then the extreme right might be a possible beneficiary.

Finally East Germans, we need to remind ourselves, have experienced a collective trauma since 1989, beginning with the fall of the communist state and continuing with the collapse of the planned economy. Although this need not necessarily translate itself into mass support for the extreme right, it is bound to make some people susceptible to their propaganda, especially in a country where anti-fascism had been central to the ideological identity of the old regime. When a way of life collapses, there is always a price to be paid. Perhaps right-wing extremism in the former East Germany is part of the cost that will have to be borne for the demise of an order that not only failed its own people, but also disintegrated with such speed once the Berlin Wall came tumbling down on that fateful day in November 1989.

Eastern Europe

The term Eastern Europe describes an area composed of quite distinct states whose primary common features were stamped upon them by the Soviet Union after the Second World War. Beyond that, the countries of Eastern Europe were, and remain, rather different entities. Czechoslovakia and Poland, for instance, were fairly industrialized when communism fell. Bulgaria and Albania on the other hand were basically rural in 1989. Most of the East European countries contain several different ethnic groups. However, Poland, the largest and arguably the most important country in Eastern Europe, is composed mainly of Poles. The majority of the East European states were closely allied to the Soviet Union for most of the post-war period. However, three – Yugoslavia, Albania and Romania – managed to break from Moscow and pursue more independent policies. Even the elections of 1990 did not produce uniform results. In Hungary and Czechoslovakia the communists were swept from power, but in Romania, Bulgaria and Albania reformed communist parties actually managed to cling to office (Central and East European Election Results, 1990).

Nevertheless, it is still possible to make some broad generalizations about the situation in Eastern Europe. The most obvious, perhaps, is that with the termination of Stalinism life has become freer although more uncertain for the people. Equally, with the collapse of Stalinism, a number of problems previously held in check by the heavy hand of the old state have risen to the surface. Some, like drug abuse and organized crime are quite new; others like anti-Semitism are a little less novel, although strange to report in a region where there are only 100,000 surviving Jews (European Parliament, 1990, p. 74).

The persistence of anti-Semitism should come as no surprise to those familiar with the history of Eastern Europe. Before the war anti-Semitism was prevalent, and after the introduction of communism continued to flourish for three reasons. Jews were prominent in the ruling communist parties. Hence hostility to the new regimes often took an anti-Semitic form. Anti-Semitism was also manipulated by sections of the communist élites themselves – partly as a means of preventing Jews gaining too much influence at the higher levels, and also as a way of deflecting criticism from the system in general towards one group in particular (Lendvai, 1971). Anti-Semitism lived on too in the popular culture with stereotypical images of the 'Jew' (mean, privileged and alien) often figuring prominently as an object of fun or abuse in everyday conversation and jokes.

With the demise of Stalinism many no doubt hoped that anti-Semitism would quickly fade away. Unfortunately, the opposite occurred, notably in Poland where 'anti-Semitism without Jews' (Jews constitute only 0.2 per cent of the population) took on a new lease of life following the disintegration of the old order. As one scholar observed (Brumberg, 1990, p. 6):

> In a country practically devoid of a Jewish minority, anti-Jewish paranoia is once more on the rise. The public imagination is obsessed with Jews in the government, in parliament, in the press, in television, and God knows where else. It's the subject of discussion in the barber shop, in the privacy of one's home, at the family table or, in a somewhat more guarded manner, publicly

The evidence supporting such a sweeping assertion is strong. In the Polish municipal council elections of May 1990 for instance, the right-wing of Solidarity attempted to weaken its opponents in the organization by characterizing them as 'Jewish'. In June, farmers occupying the Ministry of Agriculture to demand guaranteed prices attacked the government in Warsaw not only for its policies but also for being run for and by the 'Jews'. Two months later the far right National Party even stated that it was 'unfair for an ethnic minority to have dominance in the government'. Another organization, the Grunwald Society, asserted at the same time that 'German and Jewish chauvinists' now represented the most serious threat to 'Polish sovereignty' (Clough, 1990; *Searchlight*, September 1990a, p. 16; Atkinson, 1990, p. 16; *Searchlight*, November 1990a, p. 14).

The presidential campaign of 1990 illustrated only too well the resilience of anti-Semitism in Poland. Lech Walesa, no less, repeatedly invoked reliable anti-Jewish stereotypes in his public speeches. In one extraordinary statement he referred to those who talked about the 'gang of Jews who have got hold of the country's trough and is bent on destroying' it. This, he reassured his listeners, did not apply to the 'Jewish people as a whole; only those who are looking out for themselves while not giving a damn about anyone else'. Later, he advanced the somewhat disingenuous thesis that 'anti-Semitism was provoked by Jews who hid their nationality'. Walesa made it clear that he at least would not be hiding his origins for he was proud and happy to be 'a genuine Pole' (Engelberg, 1990; Boyes, 1990).

It is true that Walesa later went out of his way to repudiate his own behaviour during the presidential campaign. He even set up a high-level commission to improve Polish–Jewish relations. In speeches in both Israel and America in 1991, he also denounced anti-Semitism in Poland. Nor should we ignore the pastoral letter of the Polish bishops of 20 January 1991, in which the Catholic hierarchy unequivocally condemned anti-Semitism for the first time (Polonsky, 1991). However, all this came very late in the day, and after Walesa had already won power in part because he had been prepared to play the 'Jewish card'.

Although the situation looks bleak in Poland, in Hungary – the country with the largest Jewish minority in the whole of Eastern Europe – it appears somewhat less depressing. Even here, however, there is clear evidence of a rise in anti-Semitism. The most controversial (although by no means the only) incident was the radio speech in January 1990 by Istvan Csurka, the popular Hungarian writer. In this he not only blamed Jews for the problems that Hungary had suffered since the war, but also appealed to Hungarians to 'wake up' to the fact that a 'dwarf minority' was threatening to take control of the country. Such an outburst might have been considered the ravings of an illiterate and ignored but for two things: Czurka's own popularity, and the fact that he was closely and personally allied with the largest political party, Hungarian Democratic Forum, which since 1989 has often used anti-Semitism as a way of undermining its opponents, the Alliance of Free Democrats, an organization known to contain a number of Jewish intellectuals in its leadership (Bohlen, 1990).

In Romania, where there are very few Jews, there have also been signs of a resurgence in anti-Semitism. The chief Rabbi of Romania has already warned that fascist literature from the pre-war period, as well as copies of the *Protocols of the Elders of Zion*, are once again circulating freely in the country. Romanian nationalists of the right-wing Vatra Romanesca movement (which claims to have 400,000 supporters) have even called for a 'bloody war' against all non-Romanians who have 'soiled' the 'holy ground' of the Romanian nation. In addition, the government of Romania, the National Salvation Front, has been attacked by its enemies for containing too many Jews. Petre Roman, the Prime Minister in 1990, was even labelled 'a Spanish Yiddisher' by some of his more extreme opponents, and Romanian President Iliescu was branded 'a whore master presiding over a brothel of reds and yids' (*Searchlight*, March 1990, p. 9; *Searchlight*, August 1990, p. 17).

The apparent renaissance of anti-Semitism in Eastern Europe has not yet led to physical attacks against the Jewish minority. One group which has suffered such attacks, however, has been the gypsies. Since the revolution in Eastern Europe they have been subject to increased abuse, including murder, attacks on property and regular physical violence 'even in places where [they] have for a long time been settled' (McGregor, *The Times*, 1 July 1991).

Today, an estimated 4 million European gypsies inhabit Eastern Europe and the Balkans. Although a few are street traders, and in Romania members of the intelligentsia, the vast majority of gypsies are extremely poor. According to the most reliable estimates, 80 per cent of all gypsies in the East live below the officially designated poverty line. Of course, there has always been deeply ingrained hostility towards the gypsy community in Eastern Europe; hundreds of thousands were exterminated during the war. However, this now seems to be expressing itself more openly. As Rajko Djuric, head of the International Romany Union put it, as a result of the disintegration of the old order there are new 'social tensions, and these are turning against minorities just as before 1940'. In Czechoslovakia, for instance, there have been numerous reports of attacks on gypsies by emergent neo-fascist groups. In Romania too, they have been physically abused by both the police who regard them with racist disdain, as well as ordinary workers who see them as shiftless, parasitic marginals. Significantly, in the disturbances in Bucharest in June 1990, officials fuelled attacks on gypsies by blaming them for some of the nation's troubles. The Romanian sociologist, Nicolae Gheorghe, has in fact made the point that because there are so few Jews in Romania, 'the need to find scapegoats [has] focused on the Gypsies' (Simons, 1990).

Gypsies themselves have responded to this more threatening situation in two ways. First, taking advantage of laxer border controls, they have tended to move with more frequency from one country to another, a few even turning up in Vienna, Milan and Paris. Second, some have applied pressure on their own governments by appealing to the broader international community. In this way, gypsy organizations have tried to exploit the political space created by the end of the Cold War to draw attention to their plight. The best example of this has been the gypsies of Hungary whose representatives met their counterparts from the Conference on Security and Co-operation in Europe (CSCE) in March 1991 in an attempt to explain their situation (*CSCE Digest*, April 1991, p. 5).

The final manifestation of intolerant chauvinism in Eastern Europe has been ethnic nationalism. Potentially this menaces the whole area with Ulster, possibly Lebanon-like conflicts. The consequences of this have already been witnessed in Yugoslavia, and similar tragedies threaten elsewhere. In Transylvania for instance, Romanian nationalists set about and killed members of the Hungarian minority in March 1990, and the situation remained tense. In Bulgaria there is great antipathy between the native 'Bulgars' and the large Turkish minority. And in Hungary, the fate of the Hungarian minorities in neighbouring Romania, Slovakia and Yugoslavia is cynically exploited by the nationalist wing of the governing conservative Democratic Forum. Even in relatively enlightened Czechoslovakia, with its stronger democratic traditions, there are plenty of signs of defrosted xenophobia in the shape of resurgent Slovak nationalism. Slovak identity and Slovak nationalism have both proved to be powerful popular forces since 1989. Indeed, the extreme right, organized in the form of the Slovak National Party (SNP), has used this resurgent nationalism in an attempt to rehabilitate the wartime puppet regime led by Joseph Tiso. In the June elections of 1990 the SNP surprised its critics by gaining 15 per cent of the Slovak vote and since then has continued to agitate, pulling the rest of the country's political forces along in its wake.

An ominous cloud thus hangs over the new democracies in Eastern Europe. It is called the past. However, history alone cannot explain the present. Basically, with the Soviet Union gone, East Europeans have nobody left against whom to direct their animus except each other. This situation is rendered all the more explosive of course by the collapse of economic planning and the pain involved in reaching the market. Moreover, with the demise of official socialism, the newly emerging élites in the East have fallen back on traditional forms, including, most obviously, nationalism. The result, inevitably, has been increased antagonism between the East European states and its different peoples. Tension is thus now higher than at any time since the end of the Second World War. Although this may sound alarmist, five years ago, few would have predicted civil war in Yugoslavia. And, who in 1989 could have foreseen the collapse of the regime in Albania and thousands of its poverty-stricken citizens desperately clamouring to enter Italy? Yesterday's nightmares have become today's realities.

Conclusion

In this brief overview I have attempted to detail the occurrence and significance of racist and chauvinist activities in Russia, East Germany and Eastern Europe since the collapse of Stalinism in 1989. The picture is not a particularly edifying one. In Russia, organized anti-Semitic activities have contributed to a situation where there may be few Jews left in the country within a few years. In East Germany, extreme right organizations have publicly proclaimed their existence despite being in violation of the law. And in Eastern Europe as a whole, the collapse of the old order has brought forth tendencies that could possibly threaten the stability of the entire region.

The situation therefore looks ominous. However, are there no grounds for hope or optimism? The economic situation could improve. In a democracy problems can be addressed where before they were ignored. Also, the West can now use its not inconsiderable influence to ensure that the emerging democracies remain tolerant and stable. This all needs to be borne in mind when making a balanced assessment of the situation.

On the other hand, the weight of history, the immense contradictions thrown up by the collapse of Stalinism and the bleak economic situation make the future look anything but bright. Nor should we underestimate the serious political consequences of the disintegration of Stalinism in Eastern Europe upon its wealthier neighbours to the West. Already, the spectre of mass migration from Eastern Europe has helped force the issue of immigration back on to the political agenda in the capitals of the EC. In most countries of Western Europe, increased immigration from all parts of the world has produced a backlash in the shape of racist violence and greater electoral support for those organizations advocating tough measures against 'foreigners'. This in turn has put pressure on more mainstream politicians to adapt to the new mood of intolerance. How ironic it is that those who celebrated the collapse of the Iron Curtain and capitalism's triumph over communism in 1989 are now prepared to put up fresh barriers to deal with the results of their victory.

References

Ash, Timothy Garton, 1990. *We The People*, Granta Books, London.
Atkinson, Graeme, 1990. Germany united: democracy or danger?, *Searchlight*, No. 184, October.
Bohlen, Celestine, 1990. A survival of the past, anti-Semitism is back, *New York Times*, 20 February.
Boulton, Leyla, 1990. Extremist sent to labour camp for inciting race hate, *The Financial Times*, 13–14 October.

Boyes, Roger, 1990. Warsaw's racist ghosts on the loose, *The Times*, 15 November.

Brudny, Yitzhak M., 1989. The heralds of opposition to Perestroyka, *Soviet Economy*, Vol. 5, No. 2.

Brumberg, Abraham, 1990. Poland, the Polish intelligentsia and antisemitism, *Soviet Jewish Affairs*, Vol. 20, Nos 2–3.

Central And East European Election Results, 1990. Helsinki Commission on Security and Co-operation in Europe, Washington DC.

CSCE Digest, April 1991. Vol. 14, No. 3, Gypsies describe problems.

Clough, Patricia, 1990. Poland spews forth its anti-Semitism, *The Independent*, 24 May.

Dahrendorf, Ralf, 1990. *Reflections On The Revolution In Europe*, Chatto & Windus, London.

Dempsey, Judy, 1990. The past casts its long shadow, *The Financial Times* (London), 6 September.

Doder, Dusko and Louise Branson, 1990. *Gorbachev: Heretic In The Kremlin*, Futura, London.

Eisenhammer, John, 1991. Kohl squanders money and political credibility on the troubled east, *The Independent*, 18 March.

Ellman, Michael, 1991. The NATO economics colloquium on the Soviet economy. A general comment, *NATO Review*, Vol. 39, No. 2, April.

Engleberg, Stephen, 1990. Poland's Jewish uproar and with so few Jews, *New York Times*, 17 September.

European Parliament, 1990. *Report drawn up on behalf of the Committee of Inquiry into Racism and Xenophobia*, Session Documents, A3–195/90 23 July.

Evans, Richard, 1991. Germany's morning after, *Marxism Today*, June.

Eyal, Jonathan, 1990. On history's sharp edge, *The Guardian* (London), 18 January.

Field, Catherine, 1991. German gangs terrorise Poles, *Observer* (London), 28 March.

Glenny, Misha, 1990. *The Rebirth of History*, Penguin Books, London.

Gow, David, 1991. Bitter face of union, *The Guardian*, 8 March.

——, 1991. Extreme right makes headway with young East Germans, *The Guardian*, 12 June.

Guillebaud, Jean-Claude, 1990. L'antisémitisme dans les pays de l'Est, *Le Nouvel Observateur*, 29 March.

Harper, Keith, 1991. German economic miracle turns sour, *The Guardian*, 26 March.

Hirszowicz Lukasz and Spier Howard, 1991. In search of a scapegoat: antisemitism in the Soviet Union today, *Research Report*, No. 3, Institute Of Jewish Affairs.

Ionescu, Dan, 1990. The gypsies organize, *Radio Free Europe*, 29 June.

Ivanov, Konstantin, 1990. National patriotism a danger to Russia, *Searchlight*, No. 184, October.

Jeffrey, Charlie, 1991. United Germany goes to the polls, *Social Studies Review*, Vol. 6, No. 5, May.

Kamm, Henry, 1990. Soviet Rabbi tells of the new anti-Semitism, *New York Times*, 21 February.

Korey, William, 1990. A fear of pogroms haunts Soviet Jews, *New York Times*, 25 January.

Lane, David, 1990. *Soviet society under perestroika*, Unwin Hyman, Boston.

Laqueur, Walter, 1989. *The Long Road to Freedom: Russia and Glasnost*, Unwin Hyman, London.

Lendvai, Paul, 1971. *Anti-Semitism In Eastern Europe*, Macdonald, London.

Leski, Krzysztof and Gedye Robin, 'Nazi thugs fail to deter 70,000 visa-free Poles', *The Daily Telegraph*, 9 April 1991.

Mauthner, Robert, 1991. Germany finds it hard to strap on a helmet, *The Financial Times*, 20 March.

McKenna, Bruce, 1989. Don't underestimate anti-Semitic Soviet fringe, *New York Times*, 3 April.

Murray, Ian, 1990. German right moves East, *The Times*, 31 March.

Nove, Alec, 1989. *Glasnost In Action: Cultural Renaissance In Russia*, Unwin Hyman, Boston.

Polonsky, Antony, 1991. Loving and hating the dead, *The Financial Times*, 2 May.

Pospielovsky, Dimitry, 1990. Russian nationalism: an update, *Radio Liberty Research Bulletin*, Vol. 2, No. 6, 9 February.

Prial, Frank J., 1990. Survey in Moscow sees a high level of anti-Jewish feeling, *New York Times*, 30 March.

Radio Free Europe Report, 6 July 1990. Vol. 1, No. 27, Foreign workers in Eastern Europe.

Radio Liberty Research Bulletin, 19 December 1988. Special Edition, Russian nationalism today.

Searchlight, March 1990. Anti-Semitism rife, p. 9.

——, August 1990. Bucharest – the truth, p. 17.

——, September 1990a. Anti-Semitism on the rise.

——, September 1990b. No. 183, Neo-Nazis grow.

——, November 1990a. No. 185, The only good Jew is a dead Jew.

——, November 1990b. No. 185, Watching out for Soviet Jewry.

——, December 1990a. No. 186, Nazi numbers grow.

——, December 1990b. No. 186, Violence shocks MEP, p. 16.

——, January 1991. No. 187, Republican party waits in wings.

——, March 1991. No. 189, Dissent rocks REP after poll flop.

——, May 1991. No. 191, In the shadow of the Brownshirts.

——, June 1991. No. 192, Neo-Nazis in border battles.

Selbourne, David, 1990. *Death Of The Dark Hero: Eastern Europe, 1987–1990*, Cape, London.

Sheridan, Michael, 1990. Israel struggles to absorb Soviet influx, *The Independent* (London), 30 October.

Sherwell, Philip, 1991a. End of the honeymoon, *The Daily Telegraph*, 25 March.

——, 1991b. Neo-Nazi riots cause alarm in East Germany, *The Daily Telegraph* (London), 22 April.

Simes, Dimitri K., 1989. Even if Gorbachev falls, detente will last, *The New York Times*, 20 March.

Simons, Marlise, 1990. East Europe's gypsies: unwanted refugees, *New York Times*, 30 July.

Soviet Jewish Affairs, 1987. Vol. 17, No. 2, *Glasnost* and the new Russian antisemites.

——, 1988. Vol. 18, No. 1, Pamyat: an appeal to the Russian people.

Spier, Howard, 1989. Soviet anti-Semitism unchained: the rise of the 'Historical and Patriotic Association, Pamyat', in Robert O. Freedman, *The Politics of Anti-Semitism and Emigration*, Duke University Press.

Steele, Jonathan, 1990. Racism, not genocide under glasnost, *The Guardian* (London), 14 March.

Tomforde, Anna, 1990. Hooligans put paid to German unity soccer celebration, *The Guardian*, 14 November.

Usborne, David, 1991. German monetary union a disaster says Pohl, *The Independent*, 20 March.

White, Stephen, 1990. *Gorbachev In Power*, Cambridge University Press, Cambridge.

Wishnevsky, Julia, 1989a. Nash Sovremennik provides focus for 'Opposition Party', *Radio Liberty Research Bulletin*, Vol. 1, No. 3, 20 January.
——, 1989b. Soviet media sound alarm over anti-Semitism, *Radio Liberty Research Bulletin*, Vol. 1, No. 9, 3 March.
Woll, Josephine, 1989. Russians and Russophobes: antisemitism on the Russian literary scene, *Soviet Jewish Affairs*, Vol. 19, No. 3.

13 Beyond the Fringe: The Extreme Right in the United States of America

Michael Cox

Introduction

At least two expressions of right-wing extremism in the United States have excited the interest of scholars and political activists alike: the Ku Klux Klan with its roots in the history of the deep South, and what one writer has tellingly described as the 'paranoid style in American politics' (Hofstadter, 1967). In addition, there has over the past decade been a steady flow of studies analysing the role of individuals and groups on the extreme right (Coates, 1987; Jeansonne, 1988; Flynn and Gerhardt, 1989; Corcoran, 1991). Right-wing extremism has even caught the attention of Hollywood and at least three films dealing with the problem have been released recently: one on the rise and fall of the Ku Klux Klan in Indiana in the 1920s (Paul Wendkoss, 1989), another assessing the struggle for civil rights in Mississippi (Alan Parker, 1988), and a third detailing the activities of the extreme right in the Mid-West in the early 1980s (Costa-Gavras, 1988). However, in spite of this continuing fascination with the phenomenon, it is worth emphasizing that the extreme right in the United States is organizationally weaker today than at any time since the end of the Second World War. The Ku Klux Klan, to take the most obvious example, had about 4,000 members in 1989; only half of what it could muster at the beginning of the decade (*The Economist*, 1990, p. 46).

Nevertheless, there are good reasons for not shunting the extreme right into some intellectual siding and ignoring it. One is that there is an extraordinary variety of sects dotted around the contemporary American political landscape; although none is electorally significant, all are dangerous and certainly capable of inflicting harm on their intended victims. Moreover, even if small in number, right-wing extremists continue to have an impact at the local and even national levels. Highly active and frequently well organized, militants on the right (and here the example of David Duke stands out) can and do help shape public opinion, particularly on such crucial issues as affirmative action and inner city crime. There is also no guarantee they will remain minorities for ever. Historically, the extreme and racist right has exerted real influence on American political life, and it is unwise to assume they will never do so again. If there was a marked decline in American economic fortunes and an increase in racial tensions one could easily see the extremist right playing a bigger role in American politics.

Finally, although the extreme right remains politically weak by comparison with its West European counterparts, its world-view – combining a potent mix of religious fundamentalism, racist supremacism, muscular Americanism and a fetish for the 'gun' – is shared in varying degrees by many white Americans. Right-wing extremists are not exactly political fish swimming in friendly waters. On the other hand, there is no insurmountable ideological wall separating them from a large swathe of their fellow white citizens.

However, before looking at the present, it would perhaps be useful to plot the history of one of the most successful right-wing extremist organizations in the Western world: the Ku Klux Klan. After this we shall examine the activities of the more respectable, though equally influential 'radical right'. The ideology and organizational strength of the contemporary extreme right will then be looked at in some detail, to be followed by a discussion of the most potent right-wing force on the American political scene today: the David Duke phenomenon. Finally, an attempt will be made to assess what the future holds for right-wing extremism in the United States.

The Historical Origins of the Ku Klux Klan

One aspect of what has been termed American exceptionalism was the persistence of the institution of slavery, that peculiarly pre-capitalist social form adapted to capitalist purposes following the development of tobacco-growing in Virginia during the seventeenth century, and cotton in the states south of the Mason–Dixon line. Tragically, the abolition of slavery left the South economically shredded and morally bruised and its white inhabitants determined to reassert their dominance over the newly emancipated black population. The Ku Klux Klan was to be a key instrument in this process of reassertion (Trelease, 1972).

The original Klan was not some quaint, rather oddly-dressed group of nightriders standing on the edge of southern society, even less the romantic defenders of a misunderstood oppressed civilization portrayed in D.W. Griffith's 'rampantly racist' film *Birth of a Nation* (Wright, 1976, p. 28). Rather it was an organized conspiracy whose primary objective was to restore white supremacy after the Civil War (Horn, 1969). First established in 1865 when six ex-confederate soldiers met in their home town of Pulaski, Tennessee, the aims of the Klan were never in doubt: to force reforming northerners out of the Confederacy and to destroy every vestige of nascent black political power in the southern states. The ideology of the Klan was explicitly supremacist. The 'maintenance of the supremacy of the White Race in this Republic is the main and fundamental objective of the Ku Klux Klan' it was stated in 1867. Moreover, only those who opposed 'social and political equality for Negroes' and fought 'Congressional advocates of harsh Reconstruction measures' would be considered for membership of the organization.

In the pursuit of these goals the Klan instituted a relentless reign of terror throughout all the states of the former Confederacy between 1867 and 1871. In 1871 a joint Congressional Committee conducted an extensive investigation of Klan violence. It revealed that in the four-year period after 1867 the Klan had been responsible for hundreds, possibly thousands, of black deaths. One count showed that in a single county of northern Florida during a few months, more than 150 black men had been murdered by Klansmen. The commanding general of federal troops in Texas reported that 'murders of negroes' were so common 'as to render it impossible to keep accurate accounts of them'.

The results achieved by the Klan and other secret organizations such as the Knights of the White Camelia, Society of the White Rose and the '76 Association should not be underestimated (Carman and Syrett, 1952, p. 32; Brogan, 1986, p. 378). First, white terror slowed down, in some respects completely aborted the process of reform in the South. It also frightened a large number of blacks away from the polls and in this way guaranteed a white political monopoly. Finally, over the longer term, it created a violent pattern for regulating relations between the races in the United States which was to persist for nearly a century (Louks, 1936; Alexander, 1965; Lowe, 1967; Lester, 1971; Rice, 1962; Fisher, 1980; Wade, 1987).

The Rise and Fall of the 'Second' Klan: 1915–54

After lying dormant and inactive following its first bout of frenzied activity, the Klan was reborn in 1915 'under a blazing fiery torch' on top of Stone Mountain, near Atlanta. Colonel William Joseph Simmons, the founder of the new Klan, had for a long time given serious thought to the creation of an order standing for 'comprehensive Americanism' throughout the Republic. Fascinated from boyhood by the romantic story of the old Klan of Reconstruction days, he called his order the Knights of the Ku Klux Klan. The new Klan was as uncompromisingly racist as its predecessor. As one of its booklets, *Ideals Of the Knights Of The Klan*, made clear 'this is a White man's organization . . . teaching the doctrine of White supremacy'. The booklet even invoked Christ in the holy cause, insisting that 'all of Christian Civilization depends upon the preservation and up-building of the White race'.

The reactivated Klan was different from its predecessor, however, in at least two important ways. First, it extended its range of targets beyond American blacks. Jews, Catholics, non-aryan foreigners and socialists were all regarded as enemies by the Klan. Expressing and in turn attempting to fan the nativist reaction to mass Catholic and Jewish immigration into the country before 1914, the Klan thus became as anti-Semitic, anti-Catholic and anti-foreigner as it had always been anti-black. The Klan also attacked people considered immoral or traitors to the white race. Indeed, all those who deviated from a strict conservative norm were regarded as legitimate targets by Klansmen (Mecklin, 1963).

Second, the new Klan managed to extend its influence outside the South and by the mid-1920s had become a national organization, a reflection of the unsettled conditions in America following the First World War – a period in which a conservative, xenophobic reaction swept the country. At the peak of its power in 1925, Klan membership stood at between 4 and 5 million. In certain northern states such as Indiana and Ohio, Klan membership was actually larger than in any single state in the South (Jackson, 1967)

The Klan's impact upon American political life in the first half of the 1920s was considerable. Apart from pushing American politics to the right, many communities fell directly under Klan control. In 1922 Texas voters even sent Klansman Earl Mayfield to the US Senate. Klan campaigns also helped defeat two Jewish congressmen who had headed an inquiry into Klan activities in 1921. Klan efforts were credited too with helping to elect governors in Georgia, Alabama, California, Indiana and Oregon. In Colorado, Arkansas, Oklahoma and Ohio the Klan also acquired influence. During the 1924 Presidential campaign the Klan was particularly active, and its leader, Hiram Wesley Evans, later claimed it had helped secure the election of Calvin Coolidge. He even boasted that the Klan had been instrumental in forcing a tightening-up in US immigration laws when the quota allowing 'minorities' into the country was lowered to a mere 2 per cent (Miller, 1958, p. 355).

Still the new Klan, 'which in 1924 seemed to be sweeping all before it', quickly faded as a real force in the land (Brogan, 1986, p. 519). By 1926, membership had dropped by nearly 60 per cent to slightly more than 2 million. A year later, it had fallen again, this time quite catastrophically to 350,000. By 1930, the organization had little more than 35,000 members. Throughout the 1930s Klan numbers then fell annually, until in 1941 it stood at less than 10,000. By the early 1950s, membership was at its lowest level since its rebirth in 1915.

There were several reasons for this decline. One was the outbreak of schismatic divisions within the organization. These in turn led to damaging revelations about the Klan's violent activities. Friends in high (and low) office, fearful of being associated with the Klan, then began to desert their old ally, thus removing its respectable cover. Klan fortunes also failed to revive in the 1930s. If anything, the depression weakened the organization's appeal, partly because the average American was probably more concerned to find a job than to attack minorities, but also because the Klan's traditional message appeared irrelevant in a society gripped by mass unemployment and economic decay. The rise of dictatorship in Europe also created problems for the Klan for it associated the organization with Nazism and fascism. The War further weakened the Klan by furnishing those who favoured reform with an extremely potent argument against discrimination. After all, if black people were prepared to work, fight and die for their country, then the country in question (it was argued) should extend the same rights to them as it had already done to their white counterparts (Mullen, 1973, pp. 51–60; Moddell *et al.*, 1989, pp. 838–48).

Finally, the Klan declined for the simple, though important reason that there was no serious threat to white supremacy before the 1950s. Neither of the political parties was prepared to upset the racial apple-cart, and the Democrats, with their large southern wing, were positively afraid of challenging racism (Martin, 1979). The southern Democrats, moreover, were in possession of key places on pivotal congressional committees and could either snuff out civil rights measures in committee, dilute them before they reached the floor of Congress for debate, or filibuster them to death in the Senate. To make matters worse, the hysteria that accompanied the Cold War made it easier for conservatives to deploy the old, though effective, argument that those advocating civil rights were either communists or communist stooges. In this way 'anti-communism was wielded more effectively by those who wanted to preserve the status quo than by those who sought to change it' (Polenberg, 1980, p. 115; Fairclough, 1990, pp. 387–98).

The Klan and the Civil Rights Movement

Despairing of obtaining civil rights legislation from Congress, the National Association for the Advancement of Coloured People (NAACP) turned to the courts for redress and a key result was the US Supreme Court decision in May 1954, Brown *v.* Board of Education, in which the Court declared against separate, ostensibly equal, educational facilities. A year later, the Court then ruled that segregated school districts in seventeen states and the District of Columbia should implement desegregation programmes. From the point of view of the old South, these moves were tantamount to a revolution from above. What made the situation all the more threatening was the parallel rise of a mass civil rights campaign, a movement whose credibility was high abroad and which from the beginning held the moral high-ground because of the dignified, non-violent way in which it pursued its objectives (O'Neill, 1971, p. 158).

In this highly charged atmosphere, where southern whites felt squeezed between an establishment in Washington increasingly unsympathetic to their cause and demands for black equality, the Klan had no difficulty in attracting new members (Zanden, 1960, pp. 454–62). By the end of 1960, membership had grown four or fivefold to 40,000 to 50,000. It then remained steady for the next five years (in 1965 the Klan had 42,000 members), though during the 'long hot summer' of 1967 membership rose to 55,000, the highest since the late 1920s.

Accompanying the growth in membership was an inevitable escalation in Klan activities against the civil rights movement in particular and blacks in general. This assumed a particularly deadly form after 1960 when representatives of the different factions of the Klan met to co-ordinate their activities in Atlanta, Georgia. Significantly, whereas only six people had been murdered by racists before 1960 (four in Mississippi alone), thirty-four died during the next eight years, including Martin Luther King. In addition there were the 'normal' beatings, cross-burnings and floggings, all of which bore the hallmark of the Klan. Between 1956 and 1966 the organization and associated groups were responsible for more than 1,000 documented incidents, including the slaying of Cheney, Goodman and Schwerner in Mississippi in June 1964.

The third Klan renaissance, however, began to fade during the late 1960s, and by the mid-1970s it was clear the organization was facing a genuine crisis. The most obvious indication of this was a rapid decline in membership. By 1974 the various Klan groups could muster only about 4,500 members, a quite spectacular drop from the dizzy heights they had reached between 1965 and 1967.

The most obvious reason for the decline of the Klan was its failure to turn the tide of history. The civil rights movement was simply too strong for the forces of white reaction in the South. Many were no doubt alienated too by the increasing violence displayed by some of its more dangerous members. Moreover, in spite of its suspicion of and hostility towards black activists (Ungar, 1976, pp. 405–21; O'Reilly, 1989), the Federal Bureau of Investigation (FBI) was in the end forced to intervene against the Klan. Indeed, as a result of its efforts (of the estimated 10,000 active Klan members in 1967, some 2,000 were relaying information to the government), many key activists in the Klan were arrested and gaoled, including the leader of the biggest faction, Robert Shelton. The Johnson administration also contributed to the decline of the Klan by calling upon the House of Un-American Activities to investigate the organization. Its final report, *The Present Day Ku Klux Klan Movement*, released on 11 December 1967, did much to weaken the credibility of the Klan. The fact that the investigation was conducted by the House Committee on Un-American Activities made the attack all the more effective, for it clearly implied that the Klan was not only 'a hooded society of bigots' – to use Johnson's own words – but also disloyal to the American way of life.

Finally, as a result of post-war public spending and inflows of capital, the South was experiencing an economic transformation. This was now threatened by instability caused by white supremacist resistance to black demands. Herein perhaps was the biggest problem of all for the Klan. As an organization it may indeed have expressed what many whites felt about blacks. However, these attitudes were increasingly out of step with the new economic realities. In this respect, capitalism turned out to be every bit as subversive of organized racism in the deep South as it was later to be of apartheid in South Africa (Lipton, 1986).

The Decline of the Klan: 1982 and Beyond

For a brief period between 1975 and 1982 the Klan experienced a new lease of life, growing from just under seven to eleven thousand. Several reasons accounted for this, the most frequently cited being the organizational and presentational skills of one of its leaders former neo-Nazi David Duke (Applebome, 1991) white anxiety about black crime, antagonism towards measures of 'positive' discrimination, and a more general concern about the decline of the United States in world affairs. However, this new minor upsurge did not last, and by 1989 membership had virtually halved, bringing it to almost the lowest point in the organization's history. Possibly, one reason for this development was Ronald Reagan. With the conservative right in the White House shaping and defining the political agenda, many whites clearly felt more secure. Effective law enforcement against racially-motivated violence also played a part in keeping the Klan and like-minded organizations on the defensive. Thus, where once the hooded nightriders were able to get away with wholesale lawlessness, especially in rural southern areas, in the 1980s they generally confronted vigorous law enforcement by federal, state and local government agencies. In addition, the Klan was weakened by the fact that at least eighteen states passed legislation prohibiting all paramilitary or weapons training, if it could be demonstrated that either or both were to be used in the furtherance of civil disorder. Consequently, there was a measurable reduction in the paramilitary-type training that had been quite widespread in the early 1980s.

Finally, the one issue that did so much to harness support for the extreme right in Western Europe – immigration – had far less salience in the United States. It is true that there was hostility to poorer immigrants from Latin America and the Third World. However, the general attitude towards immigration in the United States was different (Barringer, 1990). The United States, after all, still perceived itself as a land composed of 'newcomers'. It even drew strength from the fact that it was able to attract the dispossessed and ambitious from other lands. Indeed, in the eyes of many conservatives, immigration was good for the American economy: it kept unions weak and helped replenish America's intellectual stock – crucial if the country was to remain competitive in world markets. One noted conservative commentator even argued that more immigration might solve the US deficit problem! (Simon, 1990).

The Klan Today

At present there is no single entity today called the Ku Klux Klan. Rather, there are several Klan factions. Most of these are based in the South with the one notable exception of the 'Invisible Empire' which in 1989 had between 1,500 and 2,000 members in twenty-one states, eleven outside the South. Two states can claim pride of place in the Klan: Alabama, which plays host to the United Klans of America, the Knights of the KKK and Don Black's similarly named Knights of the KKK; and North Carolina where the Klan has been reasonably active in recent years. In other southern states membership is patchy, and in three (Florida, Texas and Tennessee), there are only small remnants left of what once used to be active groups.

The Klan has not only declined in numbers but has also changed its nature in many ways. Traditionally, its main goal was the preservation of white privilege in the South, and the pursuit of this tended to draw support from all layers of white southern society. Now the Klan (or Klans) are nearly indistinguishable from other extremist organizations, often merging into and linking up with the different neo-fascist groups. Moreover, the middle class in the main seems to have abandoned the Klan. The Klan also seems to have lost its way ideologically, for in 1986 James W. Farrands, a Roman Catholic, was chosen as its 'Imperial Wizard', a move that apparently provoked outrage amongst southern traditionalists who insisted that the Klan was at heart a 'protestant' organization for a protestant white people. To make matters worse, it was subsequently revealed that Farrand's predecessor, Bill Wilkinson, a charismatic and articulate spokesman from Louisiana, had worked as an informant for the FBI. Then came the biggest blow of all, at least to the United Klans of America (UKA). In 1987, the mother of one of their murder victims (Michael Donald) was awarded $7m damages because of the participation of two of its members in his slaying. To add political insult to financial injury, the Southern Poverty Law Centre (an active opponent of the Klans and Mrs Donald's legal representative) was granted possession of the UKA's Alabama headquarters as part of the final settlement!

In spite of its travails the Klan remains as attached as ever to the doctrine of white supremacy. The reason for this was spelt out most clearly by James Farrands. 'All civilizations,' he noted, 'had grown to maturity because of 'the creativity of the White Race.' They had only decayed because of a 'decline in the racial purity of the culture-creating white race'. Hardly surprising to discover, therefore, that he, like the Klan, believes America to have been in decline for a very long time – beginning with the defeat of the South in the Civil War, and continuing in the twentieth century with the triumph of the general principle of equality and the attempt by successive American governments to put this quite 'unnatural' doctrine into practice.

The Klan's theoretical hostility to the idea of equality is reflected in a practical sense in its opposition to all forms of progressive legislation, especially if this aims to advance the position of different minorities. Such measures, they argue, are not only wrong in principle, but also disadvantage whites by giving preferment to their natural inferiors. Indeed, as a result of such laws, whites, they believe, have become second-class citizens in their own country. That many people do not seem to understand this fact is because of the propaganda churned out by a liberally-inclined, largely Jewish-controlled communications industry based in the main American metropolitan centres where Jews tend to live, notably New, or as the Klan sometimes calls it, 'Jew' York.

Anti-Semitism is central to the Klan's ideological world-view. From this perspective little has changed since the 1920s when the organization attacked Jews for their religious views and claimed they were not true Americans. If anything, the Klan's hostility to Jews has grown, reflecting its belief that the latter have become an extraordinarily powerful interest group in the United States. Because of their political influence, wealth and sheer numbers, Jews allegedly are possibly more of a threat to America than blacks. After all, they are the people who are actually 'running the country'. As one piece of fairly crude, though not untypical Klan propaganda expressed it:

We believe the old white American social structure has been irrepara-
bly damaged by the satanic Jewish one-world conspiracy. In fact we
know it because all control points of our nation are in Jewish hands
[which] have put the white American ship of state on the rocks.

The anti-Semitism of the Klan is paralleled by a fairly profound nativist
suspicion of most things foreign, especially non-white immigrants. Like its
counterparts in Europe, the Klan has tried to exploit this issue. With the
large influx of Hispanics and Asians into the country after the mid-1970s, it
hoped to tap white anxieties and turn these to its own advantage. Playing
upon white fears of job losses to newcomers, the Klan did its best to fan
resentment against non-white immigrants. In one notable case in 1981, Texas
Klansmen tried to exploit tensions between local fishermen and newly
Americanized Vietnamese boat-people. Earlier in 1979, the Klan even organized a border patrol to capture Mexican immigrants trying to cross illegally
into southern California.

Interestingly, in spite of its vague claims to speak for the American
working man (and occasional attempts to build a trade union base for itself),
the Klan has very little time for organized labour. This, in part, is due to its
belief that unions have traditionally been associated with such un-American
ideologies as socialism and communism. It is also an indication of the fact
that the Klan still draws what strength it has from the South, the one area in
America where unions have always been extremely weak and the Klan still
finds some limited support for its philosophy of white supremacy.
However, the Klan's suspicion of unions originates in an even deeper source.
At the heart of its philosophy are the twin doctrines of white supremacy and
race division. Labour organizations necessarily have to challenge these
assumptions if they are to be effective. As a former President of the United
Mine Workers noted in 1975, 'one cannot be a UMW member and a Klan
member too' (McLennan and Chalmers, 1985, p. 17).

While the Klan declined in numbers during the 1980s, it would be foolish
to conclude by underestimating its influence within the broader white power
movement. As a supremacist organization in the Western world it really has
no equal in terms of staying power and something vaguely defined as
tradition. Moreover, through its manipulation of symbol and ritual, the Klan
has been able to provide its members with something which many other
groups on the extreme right cannot: a sense of collective identity and
mystery. This may be one why reason why whites alienated from the
'system' will continue to be attracted – albeit in limited numbers – to
'Hooded Americanism' (Chalmers, 1981).

The Radical Right

Separate from, though perhaps more central to the American mainstream
than the Klan, stands the 'radical' right. Neither supremacist, violent nor
especially southern, this trend (for it has never really been a party or
organization) has nevertheless helped mould American political culture in

quite profound ways. The historical origins of this particular current can be traced back to traditions that have always existed in America anti-intellectualism, religious fundamentalism and suspicion of the outside world being perhaps the most significant elements of these (Lipset and Raab, 1978; Hoftstadter, 1979; Bruce, 1988). However, it was only with the rise of communism in the twentieth century that the modern radical right took shape: first in the wake of the Bolshevik Revolution when many Americans sought reassurance through attacks on all 'foreign ideologies', and then after the Second World War when the Soviet Union and communist China burst on to the stage of world history, creating a wave of fear that finally turned to hysteria following the North Korean invasion of South Korea in 1950 (Bell, 1955, 1964; Dudman, 1962; Sherwin, 1963; Janson and Eisman, 1963; Foster and Epstein, 1964; Newman, 1964; Thayer, 1967).

Politically, the most influential expression of right-wing radicalism in the Cold War was McCarthyism (Theoharis, 1971). McCarthyism was neither an economic protest movement; nor was it concerned to attack Jews or other minorities. Rather, it reflected a panic amongst many Americans that the United States had lost its way and was losing the Cold War not because of objective changes in the world, but because of treachery at the highest level of government. Of course, McCarthy's attack was a carefully calculated ploy by the Republicans designed to weaken popular support for the New Deal in the United States (Divine, 1974, pp. 3–85). However, by tapping into deeper traditions, including the ever-present one of the 'little guy's' suspicion of the liberal élite in Washington, McCarthy helped shape the US political agenda for nearly a decade. In addition, by successfully insinuating that there was a high-level conspiracy to subvert the nation, he fostered an atmosphere of paranoia and distrust that other less mainstream forces exploited to their advantage

One of these was the influential John Birch Society formed by Robert H. W. Welch in 1958 (Stone, 1974, pp. 184–97). By 1962 membership of the Society had reached over 60,000 with particular strength in traditional centres of religious fundamentalism such as Florida, Texas, Nashville, Wichita, Boston and southern California. The Society was both well-staffed and well financed. In 1962, for instance, it had over seventy-five full-time workers and an annual payroll of $625,000. It was also highly active, even at the national level, and was partly responsible in 1964 for defeating Rockefeller and ensuring Barry Goldwater's candidature for Republican President.

The message of the 'Birchers' was as simple as it was fantastic. Why, asked Welch in 1960, was communism gaining ground around the world? The answer was obvious: treason within the US government. Communists and their agents were everywhere. As Welch proclaimed in January 1961, 'communist influences were now in almost complete control of our Federal Government.' The same malevolent force was also behind demands for social and political reform. Indeed, according to the Society, the 'trouble in the South over integration' was communist contrived rather than the result of legitimate black demands. The Society was equally suspicious of those employed in the education of American children and students. These 'reducators' simply had to be purged, as should all those who had quietly and insiduously infiltrated themselves into the system in order to subvert it more effectively.

What made the John Birch Society noteworthy was not only that its paranoid message was readily accepted by large numbers of Americans, but also that it was one of hundreds of small radical right organizations spawned and sustained by the Cold War. According to one source there were well over 3,000 right-wing groups and publications in existence in the United States in 1965, all warning of the dangers of liberalism, communism in high places and social engineering of any kind (Thayer, 1967, p. 147). Suspicious of the outside world, intolerant of anyone who questioned or criticized the United States, and crudely though effectively using the Bible to sell its message to a wider public (one of its more successful leaders, Reverend Billy James Hargis of Christian Crusade, reached an extraordinarily wide audience in this way (Redekop, 1968)) the radical right had an enormous impact upon American public opinion in the 1950s and 1960s. Temporarily delegitimized by the trauma of Vietnam, and marginalized in the era of superpower *détente*, it made a partial though not altogether successful comeback in the Reagan years. Less aggressive than its predecessor (after 1980 there was little talk of treachery in high places or communist subversion at home), the 'new' right still managed to shape American attitudes in crucial ways. Like the radical right in the 1950s, it successfully forced liberalism on to the defensive and ensured once again that conservative values would dominate the American political agenda.

White Revolutionaries

The radical and later the 'new' right never strayed outside the law. Nor were they overtly supremacist. The same can hardly be said of the more peripheral white revolutionary groups. Few in number, they were nevertheless highly active in the 1980s. Indeed, while the Klan declined numerically, other factions on the extreme right seemed to experience a minor renaissance. Certainly by the middle of the decade, they probably constituted a majority within the broader 'white power' movement.

Basically, members of the movement often saw themselves as the vanguard of a white race in opposition to an oppressive system controlled by liberals and operated in the interests of Jews. One infamous faction, The Order, formed at the 1983 Aryan Nations Congress by a small faction of Klansmen and other extremists, even put their insurgent ideas into practice. Inspired in part by *The Turner Diaries*, a fantasy novel about a future fascist revolution in America, the group carried out bombings, murders and robberies before twenty-three of their number were convicted and finally sent to prison for terms ranging from forty to a hundred years. Two of its members were also found guilty in 1987 of murdering Alan Berg, a Jewish radio personality and outspoken critic of extremists on the right.

The Order was just one manifestation of right-wing militancy in the

United States in the 1980s. Some extremists, probably the majority, drew their inspiration from a distorted view of Christian fundamentalism. Others tapped an equally important source which believed America had to return to its frontier roots before it could find salvation. A few were anti-capitalist, although the majority were strongly in favour of private property. A minority were openly Nazi, though in the main the US extreme right drew upon native rather than imported traditions. None gained a mass base. All, however, shared a belief in the role of physical force and the need to create a white United States free from the degenerate influences of those who had polluted and destroyed what had once been a great country.

Identity Church

One of the most influential currents on the extreme right has been the *Identity Church*, a movement that traces its origins back to the Anglo-Israelites, a group in Britain in the mid-nineteenth century which preached that white Anglo-Saxons were the true descendants of the ten 'Lost Tribes' of Israel, and that they – not the Jews – were the biblical chosen people. The Jews were in fact the children of Satan according to the Anglo-Israelites, and the non-white races were mere 'mud people' on the same spiritual level as animals and therefore not in possession of a soul. The followers of the Identity churches also believe in the second coming of Christ. Unlike ordinary fundamentalists, however, they assume that before this takes place a cataclysm will have occurred, in which American cities will go up in flames as a result of a bloody conflict between the races. Fortunately they, the chosen ones, will survive and go on to build the new Israel in America.

The best-known advocate of the Identity doctrine in the United States was the late 'Reverend' Wesley Smith, a former KKK organizer. He died in 1970 after nearly forty years of preaching his anti-Semitic religious creed. His mantle was then claimed by the 'Reverend' Butler whose own Identity Church was based in Hayden Lake, Idaho, a regular meeting-place for the annual Aryan Nations World Congress. Mentioned in recent years as Butler's heir apparent has been Louis Beam, formerly a leader of one of the Klan factions and a close associate of David Duke in the late 1970s. All told there were approximately twenty-eight Identity churches and affiliated organizations by the 1980s, probably comprising between 3,000 and 4,000 members.

Posse Comitatus

Membership of the Identity churches does not necessarily preclude participation in other groups. Indeed, most of its leading figures at one time or another have been associated with the Klan and other supremacist, anti-Semitic factions. One of the more interesting and dangerous of these is *Posse Comitatus*, an organization which has been in existence since 1969 and is composed mainly of loosely affiliated bands of armed vigilantes and 'survivalists'.

The name *Posse Comitatus* is Latin for 'power of the county', and the Posse literally believes that all government power should be rooted at the county level. This not only reflects a hankering for a return to the days of the old frontier when there was no central or state authority, but also a suspicion that the government itself is controlled by enemies (usually Jewish) who cannot be trusted to preserve law and order or guarantee the security and purity of the white race. Not surprisingly, Posse followers are opposed to, and have often, taken part in attacks on government agencies and representatives. They also refuse to pay taxes to the US government and believe that the best form of justice is the vigilante kind that used to be meted out to wrongdoers by true Christian Americans in the nineteenth century.

Posse once claimed to have a national membership exceeding 2 million. However a realistic assessment indicates that in the early 1980s it had 2,000 to 3,000 in its ranks with groups at the county level in California, Colorado, Delaware, Idaho, Illinois, Kansas, Michigan, Nebraska, North Dakota, Oregon, Texas, Washington and Wisconsin. As an organization it attracted nation-wide attention when in 1983 Gordon Kahl, an active Posse member, murdered two federal marshalls in North Dakota. Kahl later died in a shoot-out with Arkansas law officers, in which a local sheriff was also killed. Kahl, however, went on to become a hero and martyr to the Posse Comitatus and other extremists.

Survivalists

Posse merges into, and in some ways is part of a broader tendency on the extreme right known as survivalism. The survivalists share with many on the white revolutionary right a belief in the collapse of the present social system into a racial civil war for which white Americans must now prepare. This vision of Armaggedon – partly religious in inspiration and partly derived from an almost Marxist-like reading of the contemporary contradictions of modern capitalism – is a particularly important component of the survivalist creed.

Two groups associated with survivalism have been The Covenant, The Sword and the Arm of the Lord (CSA) and The Christian Patriot's Defense League (CPDL). The CSA is (or at least was) a paramilitary survivalist organization operating a 'Christian' communal settlement called Zarepath-Horeb on 224 acres of secluded land near the Arkansas–Missouri border. Composed of about a hundred people, they believed American society to be approaching civil war and that it was essential to prepare for this by stockpiling arms, food and wilderness survival gear. The CSA ran a training-school offering courses in urban warfare and military tactics. Its leader, Jim Ellison, a former San Antonio fundamentalist, also conducted seminars throughout the South and Mid-West in which he not only demonstrated what weapons were available for 'self-protection', but also distributed the organization's propaganda which included such items as *Protocols Of The Elders Of Zion, The Negro And The World Crisis*, and *Who's Who In The Zionist Conspiracy*. Not surprisingly, the CSA soon found itself on the wrong side of the law, and in 1985, after a massive FBI raid on their encampment, four of its leaders were sentenced to lengthy federal prison terms for racketeering and possession of illegal weapons. Two years later, the group was effectively destroyed following further charges and convictions against some of its members.

The CPDL is very similar in philosophy and organization. Like the CSA, it preaches a conspiracy theory of history, uses Christianity as the basis of its bigotry and is heavily involved in paramilitarism. Formed in 1977 by John R. Harrell, an Illinois millionaire implicated in extremism since the 1950s, one of its chief activities has been the organization of a 'Freedom Festival' held bi-annually at his 55-acre estate in Louisville, Illinois. In 1980, over a thousand people attended the festival which included classes in weapons and combat, and discussion of the group's anti-Semitic and racist propaganda. No doubt encouraged by his early success, Harrell announced the opening of a 223-acre 'permanent base' in Missouri's Ozark region, and another survival base in West Virginia. Fears of law enforcement have, however, helped diminish the size of the 'Freedom Festivals', and since the passage in Missouri of laws governing paramilitarism the festival has been forced to drop weapons-training as part of its programme. Nevertheless, the group continues to operate, helped by Harrell's willingness to finance his own extremist proclivities.

American Nazis

One final tendency which deserves mention is the American neo-Nazi movement. Although the movement can trace its roots back to the 1930s, the modern phenomenon was formally established in 1958 by George Lincoln Rockwell, a publicity-seeking figure who was assassinated in the 1960s by one of his own followers. Even if Rockwell achieved national notoriety, he was never able to muster much of a following. After his death, the party was racked by deep splits and financial difficulties and went into steep decline. In an attempt to rebuild the organization it was relaunched in 1968 under a new name, the National Socialist White People's Party. This, however, made no difference, and during the 1970s the NSWPP split into diverse hostile fragments.

This splintering and steady decline has continued to the present and in 1985 there were probably no more than 450 people in the various neo-Nazi groups, including Matt Koehl's New Order faction totalling 100 dues-paying members, William Pierce's The National Alliance, and a number of other miniscule sectlets operating in about eight American states. The main purpose of these sects, it appears (apart from celebrating Hitler's birthday and giving meaning to its members' lives), is the distribution of openly anti-Semitic, pro-Nazi propaganda. Interestingly, at least from a legal viewpoint, whereas in the former West Germany it was a criminal offence to distribute this material, in the United States it is constitutionally impossible to impose such a ban. As a result, the largest source of neo-Nazi propaganda in the Federal Republic was probably the United States.

The largest publisher and distributor of pro-Nazi publications in America itself is Liberty Bell Publications of Reedy, West Virginia, operated by George Dietz, a farm broker. Dietz, a one-time member of the Hitler Youth, emigrated to the United States in 1957, presumably to exploit the less rigid controls existing across the Atlantic. In addition to publishing a wide variety of Nazi and anti-Jewish books and material, Dietz was the first extremist to establish a computerized bulletin board of neo-Nazi propaganda which can be accessed through use of a home computer and telephone hook-up.

Clearly, the neo-Nazis have had little impact in the United States. Unlike the Ku Klux Klan with its roots in native soil, groups like the NSWPP, the National Alliance and New Order look distinctly un-American. However, the neo-Nazis have not been without influence, and over the years a number of people have been attracted into extremist politics, including David Duke, who later went on to make their mark in other organizations. Although insignificant numerically, they have taken part in much violence, including the infamous incident in Greensboro, North Carolina in November 1979, when members of a local neo-Nazi group (and others) were implicated in the violent deaths of five revolutionary Marxists attending an anti-Klan rally (Wheaton, 1987).

Building a Base

The success of right-wing extremism ultimately depends on its message making sense to and winning support from alienated sections of white American society. Over the past few years extremists have specifically courted three distinct groups: skinheads, small farmers and white prisoners. These are discussed briefly below.

The US version of the right-wing skinhead phenomenon was inspired by the movement in Britain and has since maintained contact with its counterpart across the Atlantic. Like their British 'comrades', the American skinheads have been responsible for much vandalism (usually directed against Jewish property) and acts of violence, aimed at blacks, Hispanics, Vietnamese and homosexuals. Many of these attacks have been in southern California, although incidents have also been reported in a number of other states, including one in Wisconsin in 1988 when the Skinhead Army of Milwaukee (SHAM) set upon a group of non-racist skinheads.

Nearly all of the right-wing groups have made a concerted effort to recruit amongst the 'skins', although none has been as successful as Tom Metzger's White Aryan Resistance (WAR), an organization based in southern California. Metzger's association with racist skinheads stems from a number of sources. One is his belief that the 'skins' (whom he calls his 'frontline warriors') have already demonstrated a willingness to use violence. His enthusiasm for them is also a function of his own political strategy. Two decades of working within the system, he maintains, has finally convinced him that the only way forward is a white revolution leading to the overthrow of a 'totally corrupt capitalist system'. The skinheads, he believes, are the natural stormtroopers for such an uprising for they already stand outside of society.

Significantly, Metzger has attempted to reach out to his potential constituency through the medium of television. Exploiting the 'bourgeois' freedoms he appears to despise, Metzger has promoted his views through his cable TV show, *Race and Reason* which is broadcast in some twenty cable markets in various parts of the country, its visibility enhanced by frequent local debates about the suitability of exposing viewers to the militantly bigoted viewpoints expressed by Metzger and his guests. The influence of the programme is difficult to gauge, as is the exact size and extent of the racist skinhead movement. One estimate suggested there were approximately 3,000 individuals in 31 states in the various groups, some of whom were armed (*Law Enforcement Bulletin*, Fall 1989, p. 31). More recent figures from the North-West, however, indicate that this might be a gross underestimate.

The second group targeted by the extreme right have been small farmers in the West and mid-West struggling in the 1980s to survive, often unsuccessfully, in an increasingly harsh economic environment. At least five different groups have been active in attempting to exploit farmers' frustration, including the Posse Comitatus whose pamphlet, *The American Farmer: Twentieth Century Slave*, has apparently received wide distribution in the West. The most active group, however, has been the Populist Party, a political amalgam of the far right launched in 1984 to promote the political agenda of the Liberty Lobby, a coalition of former neo-Nazis, Klansmen and far right activists. A professional and sophisticated anti-Semitic group (one of whose specialities is the distribution and sale of Holocaust denial material), the party's original guru in the United States was Willis Carto.

The message of the extreme right to the farmers was, and remains, a simple one. The banks have foreclosed on many farms. Jews own the banks. Thus, the real enemy of the farmers are the Jews. Carto, the theoretician of the Populists, also links the specific problems facing the farmer with the wider menace of 'zionism', that 'conspiratorial scheme . . . which allied with the power of the supercapitalists effectively controls all aspects of western life'. Populism, he argues, is the only answer, and the only way of arresting the deleterious impact of 'monopoly finance capitalism' on the family and the white race.

The success of organizations such as the Populist Party in building a base among dispossessed or threatened farmers is difficult to gauge. It is generally agreed that a percentage of the 165,00 sales of the organization's newspaper, *The Spotlight*, does sell in rural America. According to a poll conducted in Iowa and Nebraska in 1986, anti-Semitism had not risen noticeably in the farm belt. However, this rather sanguine view has been disputed by some commentators who believe that the anti-Semitic message of the extreme right has left its mark.

The third area in which the extreme right has been working to win recruits is the prisons, in particular the white gangs that exist within the prison system. They have had varying degrees of success. The Aryan Nations, for example, has made connections with the Aryan Brotherhood prison gang that exists in prisons in seven states. A number of right-wing groups have also initiated an outreach programme to white prisoners, usually under the guise of one of the several 'churches' spawned and controlled by the right. The two most active of these are run by Robert Miles of the 'Mountain Church' in Michigan, and Robert Butler of the Aryan Nations organization. Miles, the former grand master of the United Klans Michigan chapter, spent six years in prison for conspiring to bomb school buses in Pontiac, Michigan, during an anti-bussing controversy. He has been particularly active over the past few years in developing contact with prisoners and claims correspondence with between 1,300 and 1,800 inmates, in spite of prison censorship and the right of the authorities to withhold any materials they believe might incite violence. Butler claims some success too, and it is reported that his Identity Church has been able to spread the 'gospel' among the several hundred inmates with whom the organization has established a link. However, prison authorities were alerted to the potential dangers presented by his church's particular brand of Christianity, and in 1984 restricted its availablity (a decision unsuccessfully challenged by some supremacist prisoners the following year).

Apart from Miles and Butler, there is good evidence to suggest that other extremist organizations have engaged in outreach to prisoners, including the Klan, the Euro-American alliance, several neo-Nazi and Identity groups, and George Dietz's Liberty Bell publishing organization. Of all these probably the Klan has had greatest success, especially in prisons located in the South. In a 1985 study, it was reported that there were Klan groups in prisons in Arkansas, Georgia and Texas.

The Duke Phenomenon

Although the various right-wing sects have actively attempted to gain adherents from the discontented and the peripheral within American white society, they have achieved only very limited success. The same cannot be said about David Duke. In a land where marketing the message seems nearly as important as the message itself, Duke has shown that the issue of race can still be successfully exploited (Zatarain, 1990).

David Duke began his political career with the neo-Nazis, then became a dominant figure in the Klan in the 1970s, left the organization after a bitter fight and then went on in 1980 to form his own organization, The National Association for the Advancement of White People (NAAWP). A past master at gaining publicity, Duke played a large role in the counter-demonstrations organized in January 1987 against those attempting to celebrate Martin Luther King's birthday in Forsyth County, Georgia. His real breakthrough came in the following year when he was elected to the Louisiana House of Representatives, thus making him a potent force in state politics. In late 1989, he then made an equally well-publicized bid to capture a seat in the US Senate by displacing a Democrat, J. Bennett Johnston (Applebome, 1989). To the surprise (and horror) of many, in the final vote in October 1990 he managed to capture 44 per cent of the total vote and over 60 per cent of the white vote (Maraniss, 1990a). His critics were stunned, and those who had previously given him little chance of doing well were forced to eat their words. News of the election result provoked comment internationally (Cohen, 1990).

Obviously the most important question is: why did Duke do so well in 1990? The superficial answer is that he cleaned up his act, changed his image and repeatedly apologized for past 'misdemeanours'. However, there was far more to it than that. Basically, Duke won votes because he identified a number of white fears and frustrations and directed them against a number of specific targets (Ferguson, 1990, pp. 16–18).

The first of these targets was the 'establishment' in Washington. According to Duke they had consistently ignored the interests of hardworking white Americans while lining their own pockets. Not surprisingly, this populist argument went down particularly well in Louisiana, a state where unemployment was higher than the national average and where living standards were either stagnant or in decline for the white majority. His second target was the outside world, or more specifically unfair foreign economic competition which was robbing honest Americans of their livelihoods. However, Duke's populist, economically nationalist message was only the icing on the cake. His real target was black America in general and poor black Americans in particular. In meeting after meeting around Louisiana he repeated the same, simple, alarming message: that all of America's problems from crime, education and drugs were the result of the welfare system and the burgeoning, predominantly black underclass. 'Working families' he declared at one rally in Baton Rouge, 'are paying for [their] illegitimate kids'. These people he went on 'are having children faster than they can raise your taxes to pay for them' (Barber, 1990). This oft-repeated message undoubtedly struck a chord with many whites, especially those who felt that social programmes such as affirmative action and welfare had given blacks an undeserved advantage. Duke, indeed, played the classic extremist card and declared that whites had actually become second-class citizens in their own country. 'We demand equal rights for whites ' Duke proclaimed at his meetings, skilfully manipulating the slogan traditionally associated with the civil rights movement in order to advance his own racist cause (Powell, 1990).

Having made real headway in the Senate race of 1990, Duke decided to run for governor in 1991 (Suro, 1991a). If anything his publicized campaign in October and November received even more media attention than his earlier bid for power. Again, he was extremely successful in mobilizing the white vote behind his banner. In the first ballot he received 32 per cent of the total vote and between 42 and 44 per cent of the white vote (Suro, 1991b). In the run-off he obtained over 700,000 of the 1.75 million votes: effectively 55 per cent of the white vote (Stothard, 1991b). Nor was his support drawn only from blue-collar groups. Many lower-middle and middle-class whites endorsed him too, partly because of his strong stand on race, but also because he promised to reduce their taxes, a large slice of which, according to Duke, was being used to support undeserving black welfare recipients.

Duke, in fact, lost to Democrat Edwin Edwards. However as he astutely pointed out after final returns showed a 61 to 39 per cent winning margin for his opponent, although white voters 'may have rejected' him they had not rejected his 'message'. The message was that white people wanted equal rights', rejected affirmative action programmes favouring minorities, and demanded that the government ensure economic prosperity while fighting drugs and crime effectively.

Duke's attempts to scapegoat the black 'welfare underclass' in 1990 and 1991 obviously struck a note in Louisiana, even if some doubted whether the message would have the same political appeal elsewhere – notably in the primaries leading up to the 1992 American presidential contest. Louisiana, after all, was in the South. Moreover, the state was highly depressed economically. Thus, it would be false (at least according to this line of argument) to extrapolate from the events in Louisiana to the broader American political scene. Perhaps so, although this somewhat sanguine reading of events ignores a number of crucial points.

The first is that Duke's denunciation of affirmative action programmes for blacks is only the more explicit version of the assault on the civil rights legacy which the Republicans have successfully exploited since 1972 to win five out of the last six presidential elections. Just as President Reagan in his 1984 campaign denounced the 'welfare queen' in New York – a woman who did inordinately well out of the benefits system – Duke used the example of the family in New Orleans whose single (black) mother and three teenage daughters were all pregnant by the same man. This, in a way, is why more mainstream Republicans were so embarrassed by Duke. Many of his themes were just inches away from the anti-government, anti-welfare, anti-quotas ideology of President Reagan's legacy. Indeed, when challenged to name one Duke policy that the Republicans did not also espouse, Mr Yeutter, the party chairman, lamely came up with his protectionist stance against a free-trade pact with Canada and Mexico! (Graham, 1991).

Second, even though he lost, Duke not only gained great publicity for his cause across the country, but also placed enormous pressure on both parties to address the taboo subjects of race, welfare and the 'underclass'. Although political leaders in Washington may despise and denounce the ex-Klansman, they can hardly ignore the point that his brand of racial populism struck a chord amongst whites of all classes in Louisiana, and could easily do so outside the state (Maraniss, 1990; Peter Applebome, 1991).

Finally, as one astute foreign observer noted, 'Duke's pitch and consti-tuency' stretched far beyond the issue of race. In fact, the question of race was in some ways 'incidental'. Although whites supported Duke for a variety of reasons, one of them, quite obviously, was economic fear and anxiety exacerbated by recession. This was the real message coming out of Louisiana. And, if more mainstream politicians did not understand that, there was a good chance that the 'message' (if not the tarnished David Duke) would win an increased following outside Louisiana (*The Guardian*, 19 November 1991).

Conclusion

The relative success of David Duke in Lousiana should not be exaggerated nourish exaggeration. Many things have changed in America which have reduced the strength of the organized extreme right. Most obviously, the South has undergone a political and economic metamorphosis since the Second World War. As a result, there is little chance of a serious revival of organizations like the Klan. Moreover, although they remain second-class economic citizens in the country of their birth, the position of many black Americans has improved since the 1950s, giving them greater self-confidence and power. It has also made them a force in the land which cannot be ignored by mainstream politicians. Nor should we underestimate the impact of current and future demographic shifts upon the United States. Prior to the Second World War, America was predominantly white in composition. Because of the large influx of Hispanics and Asians, this is no longer the case. White America is on the wane gradually forcing progressive changes in white attitudes. Finally, with the demise of international communism, it will be increasingly difficult for extremists and radicals on the right to mobilize support by using the traditional refrain that the 'Russians are coming'. Anxieties generated by the Cold War are withering away, and as they do so a less paranoid style in American politics is likely to emerge.

Even so, it would be absurd to be complacent. While David Duke may have eschewed violence, many on the extreme right have not; quite the contrary. Between October 1987 and April 1989, for instance, there were 169 convictions against 'racial and ethnic hate crimes', 31 implicating skinhead gangs. In August 1989, the offices of the NAACP in Atlanta were mailbombed. Two months earlier, a member of a 'White Pride' Skinhead gang in Portland, Oregon was jailed for life for beating an Ethiopian black man to death with a baseball bat. To this should be added attacks on Jewish property and more general racial violence in the area of housing. Significantly, a third of all racially-motivated attacks in the 1980s were housing-related, usually the intimidation of minorities who had recently moved into predominantly white neighbourhoods.

Further, as the Duke vote in Louisiana has revealed, although the South might have changed in many ways, southern white racial attitudes do not seem have not altered as much as many would have hoped – a point made some years ago in an important study on the South (Black and Black, 1987, p. 209). Moreover, the Republicans in office have often adapted to these attitudes rather than confront them. It is true that President Bush finally accepted a Civil Rights Bill designed to reinforce curbs on discrimination in the workplace in late 1991. However, this was only after a long, hard struggle stretching over two years of partisan wrangling. Indeed, in spite of his oft-repeated assertions that civil rights was a top priority, Bush consistently vetoed earlier versions of the Bill; many assumed this was because he was pandering to white majority antagonism to affirmative action programmes for blacks (Wicker, 1990; Tisdall, 1991a; 1991b; Fletcher, 1991).

Third, whereas the American economic situation in the 1980s was relatively buoyant, the same can hardly be said about the United States in the early 1990s. Certainly, if the present recession were to continue, or even worsen, this could easily increase the pool of whites from which right-wing extremists might recruit. And even if the organized right did not grow in strength, in a deteriorating economic situation there could easily be greater racial polarization, and thus greater support for the sort of ideas espoused by Duke (Bremner, 1989; Brimelow, 1989; Ellicott, 1990; Goleman, 1990).

Finally, it should be pointed out that right-wing extremists have been able to attract support in America by tapping into attitudes and beliefs present in the wider political culture. Again, one must not exaggerate the danger. The majority of white Americans are neither violently racist nor extreme in their views. Many whites, however, do regard blacks as being inferior, are fanatically Christian, believe it is their inalienable right to carry a gun, are easily mobilized behind the flag, and even without a Soviet threat, continue to regard the outside world with grave suspicion. So long as these values continue to persist – and there is no reason to assume that they will not – then the extremist right will continue to win recruits in the United States.

References

Alexander, C. C., 1965. *The Ku Klux Klan in the Southwest*, University of Kentucky Press, Lexington.

Anti-Defamation League, 1983. *The 'Identity Churches': A Theology of Hate*, Spring, New York.

——, 1985. *The Populist Party: The Politics of Right-Wing Extremism*, Autumn, New York.

——, 1986a. Extremism targets the prisons, Special Report, June, New York.

——, 1986b. Extremist group outreach to rural Americans, Special Edition, October.

——, 1987a. The liberty lobby network, Special Edition, October.

——, 1987b. *'Shaved for Battle': Skinheads Target America's Youth*, New York.

——, 1988a. The murder of Alan Berg, Special Edition, June.

——, 1988b. *Young and Violent: The Growing Menace of America's Neo-Nazi Skinheads*, New York.

——, 1988c. *Hate Groups in America: A Record of Bigotry and Violence*, New York.

——, 1990. *1989: Audit of Anti-Semitic Incidents*, New York.

Applebome, Peter, 1989. Ex-Klan leader facing first test in Senate bid, *New York Times*, 8 December.

——, 1991. Duke: the ex-Nazi who would be Governor, *New York Times*, 10 November.

Barber, Lionel, 1990. Former klansman puts a new face on racist past, *The Financial Times* (London), 5 October.

Barringer, Felicity, 1990. A land of immigrants gets uneasy about immigration, *New York Times*, 14 October.

Bell, Daniel (ed.), (1955;1964), *The Radical Right*, Anchor Books, New York.

Bennett, David H., 1988. *The Party of Fear: From Nativist Movements to the New Right in American History*, University of North Carolina Press, Chapel Hill.

Black, Earle and Merle Black, 1987. *Politics And Society In The South*, Harvard University Press.

Bremner, Charles, 1989. Race hatred renascent, *The Times* (London), September 9.

Brimelow, Peter, 1989. When the melting pot starts to boil over, *The Times* (London), September 16.

Brogan, Hugh, 1986. *The Pelican History of the United States of America*, Penguin, Harmondsworth.

Bruce, Steve, 1988. *The Rise and Fall of the New Christian Right: Conservative Protestant Politics in America, 1978–1988*, Clarendon Press, Oxford.

Carman, Harry J. and Syrett, Harold C., 1952. *A History of the American People since 1865: Volume II*, Columbia University Press, New York.

Center for Democratic Renewal, n.d. *It's not Populism – America's New Populist Party: A Fraud by Racist and Anti-Semites*, Atlanta.

——, 1981. *Violence, the Ku Klux Klan and the Struggle for Equality*, Atlanta.

——, 1985. *Racist Anti-Semitic Intervention in the Farm Protest Movement*, September, Atlanta.

Chalmers, David Mark, 1981. *Hooded Americanism*, Franklin Watts, New York.

Coates, James, 1987. *Armed and Dangerous: The Rise of the Survivalist Right*, Hill & Wang, New York.

Cohen, Richard, 1990. David Duke represents raw racism, *The Edmonton Journal*, 26 October.

Corcoran, James, 1991. *Bitter Harvest – Gordon Kahl and the Posse Comitatus: Murder in the Heartland*, Viking Penguin, New York.

Costa-Gavras, C. (Director), 1988. *Betrayed.*

Divine, Robert A., 1974. *Foreign Policy and US Presidential Elections: 1952–1960*, Franklin Watts, New York.

Dudman, Richard, 1962. *Men of the Far Right*, Pyramid Books, New York.

The Economist, 1990. The Ku Klux Klan in decline, 24 February.

Ellicott, Susan, 1990. Bush wins black support despite rise in US racism, *The Times* (London), 17 April.

Fairclough, Adam, 1990. Historians and the civil rights movement, *Journal of American Studies*, Vol. 24.

Ferguson, Andrew, 1990. The wizardry of David Duke, *The American Spectator*, October.

Fisher, William Harvey, 1980. *The Invisible Empire*, Scarecrow Press, New Jersey.

Fletcher, Martin, 1991. Bush lays plan to wield weapon of racial job quotas, *The Times*, 4 June.

Flynn, Kevin and Gerhardt, Gary, 1989. *The Silent Brotherhood: Inside America's Racist Underground*, Free Press, Macmillan New York.

Foster, Arnold and Benjamin Epstein, 1964. *Danger On The Right*, Random House, New York.

Goleman, Daniel, 1990. As bias crime seems to rise, scientists study roots of racism, *New York Times*, 29 May.

Graham, George, 1991. The greater of two evils, *The Financial Times*, 16 November.

The Guardian, 19 November 1991. The void that Bush must fill.

Hofstadter, Richard (ed.), 1967. *The Paranoid Style in American Politics and Other Essays*, Vintage Books, New York.

——, 1979. *Anti-Intellectualism in American Life*, Alfred A. Knopf, New York.

Horn, Stanley F., 1939; 1969. *Invisible Empire: The Story of the Ku Klux Klan, 1866–1871*, Patterson Smith, New Jersey.

Jackson, Kenneth T., 1967. *The Ku Klux Klan in the City, 1915–1930*, Oxford University Press, New York.

Janson, Donald and Eisman Bernard, 1963. *The Far Right*, McGraw Hill, New York.

Jeansonne, Glen, 1988. *Gerald L.K. Smith: a Minister of Hate*, Yale University Press, New York.

Katz, William Loren, n.d. *The Invisible Empire: The Ku Klux Klan's Impact on History*, Open Hand, Seattle.

Klanwatch, 1988. *The Ku Klux Klan: A History of Racism and Violence*, 3rd edn, Montgomery.

——, 1990. Terror in our neighbourhoods: A Klanwatch report on housing violence in America, April.

Law Enforcement Bulletin, 1989. No. 4, Autumn, Skinheads grow to 3,000, spread to 31 States.

Lester, John C., 1971. *Ku Klux Klan: Its Origin, Growth and Disbandment*, AMS Press, New York.

Lipset, S. M. and Raab, E., 1978. *The Politics of Unreason: Right-Wing Extremism in America, 1790–1977*, University of Chicago Press, Chicago.

Lipton, Merle, 1986. *Capitalism and Apartheid: South Africa, 1910–1986*, Widwood House, Aldershot.

Louks, E. H., 1936. *The Ku Klux Klan in Pennsylvania: a Study in Nativism*, Telegraph Press, Harrisburg.

Lowe, David, 1967. *The Ku Klux Klan: The Invisible Empire*, W. W. Norton, New York.

Lutz, Chris. *They Don't All Wear Sheets: A Chronolgy of Racist and Far Right Violence, 1980–1986*, Center for Democratic Renewal, Atlanta.

Maraniss, David, 1990a. Johnston Wins Vote In Lousiana, *The Washington Post*, 7 October.
—, 1990b. Duke emerges from loss stronger than ever, *The Washington Post*, 8 October.
Martin, John Frederick, 1979. *Civil Rights and the Crisis of Liberalism: The Democratic Party, 1945–1976*, Westview, Boulder.
McLennan, Paul and Trisha, with David Chalmers, 1985. *The True Story of the Ku Klux Klan vs Organized Labor*, Center for Democratic Renewal, Atlanta.
Mecklin, John Moffatt, 1924; 1963. *The Ku Klux Klan: a Study of the American Mind*, Russell and Russell, New York.
Miller, William, 1958. *A New History of the United States*, George Braziller, New York.
Moddell, John, with Marc Gouldner and Sigurdur Magnusson, 1989. World War II in the lives of black Americans: some findings and an interpretation, *Journal of American History*, Vol. 76, December.
Mullen, Robert W., 1973. *Blacks in America's Wars*, Monad Press, New York.
National Urban League, 1988. *The State of Black America: 1987*, New York.
Newman, Edwin S. (ed.), 1964. *The Hate Reader*, Oceana Publications, New York.
O'Neill, William L., 1971. *Coming Apart: An Informal History of America in the 1960's*, Times Books, New York.
O'Reilly, Kenneth, 1989. *'Racial Matters': The FBI's Secret File on Black America: 1960–1972*, Free Press, New York.
Parker, Alan (Director), 1988. *Mississippi Burning*.
Polenberg, Richard, 1980. *One Nation Divisible: Class, Race and Ethnicity in the United States since 1938*, Penguin Books, Harmondsworth.
Powell, Lawrence N., 1990. 'Read My Liposuction', *The New Republic*, 15 October.
Redekop, John H., 1968. *The American Far Right: A Case Study of Billy James Hargis and Christian Crusade*, William B. Eerdmans, Michigan.
Rice, Arnold S., 1962. *The Ku Klux Klan in American Politics*, Public Affairs Press, Washington.
Sherwin, Mark., 1963. *The Extremists*, St Martin's, New York.
Simon, Julian L., 1990. More immigration can cut deficit, *New York Times*, 10 May.
Stone, B. A., 1974. The John Birch Society: a profile, *Journal of Politics*, Vol. 36.
Stothard, Peter, 1991. Duke's big chance, *The Times*, 18 November.
Suro, Roberto, 1991a. Ex-Klan chief has even odds in Governor's race, *New York Times*, 19 October.
—, 1991b. Louisiana puts ex-Klan leader in runoff race, *New York Times*, 21 October.
Thayer, George, 1967. *The Farther Shore Of Politics: The American Political Fringe Today*, Simon & Schuster, New York, Chs 1–10.
Theoharis, Athan, 1971. *Seeds of Repression: Harry S. Truman and the Origins of McCarthyism*, Quadrangle Books, Chicago.
Tisdall, Simon, 1991a. US civil rights bill stirs race relations, *The Guardian*, 4 June.
—, 1991b. Defeated Duke may run against Bush next year, *The Guardian*, 18 November.
Trelease, Alan W., 1972. *White Terror: The Ku Klux Klan Conspiracy and Southern Reconstruction*, Secker & Warburg, London.
Ungar, Sanford J., 1976. *FBI: An Uncensored Look Behind the Walls*, Little, Brown, Boston.
Wade, Wyn Craig, 1987. *The Fiery Cross: The Ku Klux Klan in America*, Simon & Schuster, New York.
Wendkoss, Paul (Director), 1989. *Cross Of Fire*.

Wheaton, Elizabeth, 1987. *Codename GREENKIL: The 1979 Greensboro Killings*, University of Georgia Press, Athens, Ga.

Wicker, Tom, 1990. President dabbles in white backlash, *The Edmonton Journal*, 26 October.

Wilson, William Julius, 1987. *'The Truly Disadvantaged': The Inner City, the Underclass, and Public Policy*, University of Chicago Press.

Wright, Basil, 1976. *The Long View: An International History Of The Cinema*, Paladin, London.

Zanden, J. W. V., 1960. The Klan revival, *American Journal of Sociology*, Vol. 65.

Zatarain, Michael, 1990. *David Duke: Evolution of a Klansman*, Pelican, New York.

Zeskind, Leonard, 1986. *The 'Christian Identity Movement'*, Center for Democratic Renewal, Atlanta.

Index

DATE DUE

MAR 3 1 1997	